The Guide for Venture Investing Angels

Financing and Investing in Private Companies

The Guide for Venture Investing Angels

Financing and Investing in Private Companies

Arthur Lipper III

Missouri Innovation Center Publications
Columbia, Missouri

To order copies of this book, please contact:

Missouri Innovation Center, Inc.
5650A South Sinclair Road
Columbia, MO 65203
Tel (573) 446-3100; Fax (573) 443-3748

Cover design & page layout by *Kevin M. Magee, Magee Marketing & Design*, Columbia, MO

Library of Congress Catalog Card Number: 96-76265

ISBN 0-9652183-0-9

Printed in the United States of America

1 2 3 4 5 6 7 8 9 0

To
Anni Jensen Lipper,
with thanks for her love and strength,
both of which I need

&

To
Christopher Scott Lipper and
Gregory Jensen Lipper,
of whom I am so very proud

CONTENTS

PUBLISHER'S PREFACE

Our country relies on technology to create new jobs that pay a living wage. As long as our creativity and enterprising spirit keep generating new ideas and technology companies, the United States will be a formidable player in the world economy. But there is a serious weakness in the way we spawn new technology companies, and, unless we address it, our progress will be slowed.

The weakness? In general ... banks can't finance the creation of new technology companies, and venture capital funds don't finance the creation of new technology companies. Instead, individuals finance them.

In other words, in the United States, and certainly in Missouri, we are very dependent on individual investors, like you and me, to fuel the growth and development of technology companies.

This is illustrated by the case of Dr. Walter Lewis, senior biologist at Washington University in St. Louis. An ethnobotanist, he has spent his career searching for naturally occurring substances in plants that have medicinal value for humans. For decades, he and his wife, Dr. Memory Elvin-Lewis, have lived periodically with the Jivaro Indians of the Amazon river basin in Peru, learning their medical arts. One of the many important discoveries this relationship has yielded is a tree sap that appears to accelerate the healing of human wounds, including serious, hard-to-heal wounds like bed sores and diabetic ulcers.

The tree-sap compound was tested in recent experimental wounds on pigs, whose skin is more similar to human skin than that of any other animal. With application of the compound, the wounds sealed themselves with new skin in just over half the time it took for similar wounds with no treatment.

A plastic surgeon recently applied the substance to a hard-to-heal wound on a patient's hip and reported that, in the 33 years of his practice, he had never seen a wound heal so fast. Many people are excited about this drug's potential and wonder how they can obtain some. Unfortunately, getting from this point to commercial availability is less than assured.

In short, Woundfast Pharmaceuticals, Inc., was formed to develop the drug. The company, led by first-time entrepreneur Lewis, estimated that it would cost $500,000 to $1,000,000 to complete the basic research required to find an effective synthetic version of the drug and complete Phase 1 clinical studies in conjunction with the Food and Drug Administration. As with many new technology companies, little or no income is expected for many years, and few company assets exist other than the intellectual property reflected through patents. To return momentarily to the basic message: No bank could or would loan Woundfast money without collateral and an ability to make immediate payments ... and no venture capital fund would invest at this early, very risky stage.

Consequently, Dr. Lewis, like most entrepreneurs, has been raising the money, a few thousand at a time, from individuals. He never dreamed that he would have to "ask" for money from his friends, family, and associates; he reports that he is getting much better at it, although it is far more difficult and slower than he ever imagined. However, if he can keep the company alive long enough to better document the effectiveness of the drug, he may be able to reduce the perceived risk enough to interest a larger drug company in a joint venture or even attract investments from professional venture capitalists--a risky proposition, for sure.

For Missourians, and indeed for all Americans, this presents a perilous situation. If Dr. Lewis finds that he doesn't have the time, inclination, or skill to continue successfully "begging" for money, the benefits of the drug may never become available to the public, no jobs will be created, additional monies will not be invested in related research and no wealth will be created due to exporting products. The good news is that he doesn't seem inclined to give up and has already raised more than $400,000 from approximately 25 investors.

Surprisingly, in spite of the crucial role individuals play in new-venture formation, we are, as a culture, relatively ignorant about the art and science of investing in young, private companies. This kind of investing is not taught in business schools along with other forms of investing, nor can much be found on the subject in bookstores, libraries, or anywhere else. Additionally, without education to ease the anxiety associated with this kind of high-risk investing, we are unlikely to see an increased flow of capital into the entrepreneurial sector.

The individuals that Dr. Lewis approaches are, like himself, typically unfamiliar with making these kinds of investments and are, as a result, often reluctant to become involved. People willing to invest typically rely primarily on Dr. Lewis' reputation as a scientist in making their investment decision rather than their ability to analyze an investment of this type.

With these things in mind, the Missouri Innovation Center Network, in cooperation with the University of Missouri-Columbia College of Business and Public Administration, the Missouri Department of Economic Development and the Missouri Technology Corporation, is attempting to improve the odds of raising precious capital for Dr. Lewis--and thousands of other entrepreneurs. We have developed programs such as the Missouri SCOR Market Maker™, a new award-winning publication periodically inserted in Missouri business journals, to bring Dr. Lewis' company to the attention of the general public. This is possible as a result of the freedom to conduct inexpensive, quasi-public offerings permitted by the Small Corporate Offering Registration (SCOR) process that is sweeping the country.

The Missouri SCOR Market Maker™ also contains unique information for people who want to learn more about investing in young, private companies. With the publication of The Guide for Venture Investing Angels: Financing and Investing in Private Companies by Arthur Lipper III, our citizens will have access to quality, in-depth material that can help develop their interest and give them a solid basis for becoming involved in this type of high-risk investing.

The Missouri Innovation Center Network also provides assistance to help entrepreneurs learn more quickly the esoteric art and science of raising money from individuals. Unfortunately, the status quo typically requires first-time entrepreneurs to reinvent the wheel in understanding this complex process. They have far more productive uses for their time.

We have a long way to go in building our programs. But clearly with better informed citizen investors and entrepreneurs, our country is bound to see more technology companies formed in the years to come. It may not happen otherwise.

Banks can't finance the creation of new technology companies nor can professional venture capital firms. Only individuals can. If we want to see the creation of more technology companies and the good jobs they bring, we will have to get more of our citizens educated and involved in responsible early-stage investing. We hope that The Guide For Venture Investing Angels: Financing and Investing in Private Companies will make a major contribution to this process.

I would like to thank the Board of Directors of the Missouri Innovation Center, Inc. for their support of this project. Without them, it would not have been possible. They are:

Bo Fraser	President & CEO Boone County National Bank
Dr. Rick Finholt	Executive Director Missouri Research Park
Ernie Gaeth	Executive Vice President & General Manager Riback Supply Company, Inc.
Eugene Gerke	President Gerke & Associates, Inc.
Susan Stalcup Gray	President Isabelle's Country Mustard, Inc.
Kee W. Groshong	Vice Chancellor for Administrative Services University of Missouri - Columbia
Larry Grossmann	President The Add Sheet
Dr. Jake Halliday	President & CEO Analytical Bio-Chemistry Laboratories, Inc.
David Keller	President & CEO Union Planters Bank
Mariel Liggett, CPA	Partner Williams-Keepers
Jeff MacLellan	President & CEO First National Bank & Trust Company
Dr. John B. Miles	Professor of Mechanical and Aerospace Engineering University of Missouri - Columbia

Don Stamper	Presiding Commissioner Boone County Commission
Greg Steinhoff	President & CEO Option Care
John Thompson	Executive Vice President Toastmaster Inc.
Dr. Bruce J. Walker	Dean, College of Business & Public Administration University of Missouri - Columbia

Thanks is also due to Quinten Messbarger of the Missouri Innovation Center's staff for his meticulous management of this publishing project. Good work!

We thank Arthur Lipper III for his long-standing efforts to educate angel investors and champion entrepreneurship in general. Please enjoy this excellent book and get involved in backing your local entrepreneurs!!! If we don't do it ... who will?

Chip Cooper
Executive Director
Missouri Innovation Center, Inc.
May 1, 1996

Please contact us at:
Missouri Innovation Center, Inc.
5650A South Sinclair Road
Columbia, Missouri 65203
Phone: 573-446-3100
Fax: 573-443-3748

PREFACE

The unsung heroes of our American form of capitalism are the private individuals who provide financing for the more than 26,000 new startup companies formed every week in the United States. These informal investors, aptly known in the business world as Angels, venture where bankers fear to tread.

Entrepreneurs starting up a new business, without sufficient capital and credit of their own to get it under way, normally have four sources of possible funding: venture capitalists, the stock market, family and friends (who are usually in the position of being quasi-obliged Angels), and Angels. However, venture capitalists and other professional investors are involved in a maximum of only 2,000 of the more than 1.4 million companies started each year. Incidentally, the corporate failure rate in 1995, according to Dun and Bradstreet, ran about 65,000 a year, with another 5,000 businesses being discontinued. This isn't a high enough rate to justify the all too broadly accepted belief that most new businesses fail. This simply is not true. Nevertheless, the entrepreneur's chances of obtaining professional funding are not good, to put it mildly. Very few entrepreneurs can expect to be the beneficiary of a public offering. This leaves the huge majority of new companies to be funded by other than professional, or even experienced, investors.

Profit is not the sole motivation of many of these individual investors--they are often just "helping out" someone. Yet, the fact that most new companies fail to achieve the goals and objectives of the entrepreneur or investor is a reality that most of these Angels will have to face sooner or later. All too often, these business disappointments result in recrimination, broken friendships, and sometimes even financial disaster.

This book is intended to assist both the individual Angel investor who has readily available $50,000 to $250,000 for investment in one or more private companies and the entrepreneur seeking such an investment. From the Angel's standpoint, I hope to help in minimizing losses as well as in maximizing gains. I believe the entrepreneur will be assisted in learning more of the investor's fears and needs, as well as the techniques that best accommodate the needs and wishes of investors. The recommendations are based upon more than 42 years of involvement and observation of the investment process, with a particular focus on seed-capital and startup situations. If the Angel and entrepreneur structure a transaction based upon a realistic appraisal of the opportunity, they can accommodate almost any valuation if it is performance-based. My aim is to help both the Angel and entrepreneur do a better job of recognizing each other's needs and to offer some solutions for bridging the gap between hope and fear.

Some business observers detect a trend away from the highly managerial organizations of the 1960s and 1970s toward entrepreneurial enterprises. They see this change as part of a resurgence of America's tradition of self-reliance and personal independence. Certainly, the downsizing of corporate America is forcing upon many the need for personal reliance and the development of entrepreneurial skills. The social benefit that I hope will result from this book is that its readers, who make more money when right and lose less money when wrong, will be in a position to participate in the financing of an ever-increasing number of new ventures. Only through new company formation will our country be able to solve the problems of underutilization of its people and resources. It is also only through new company formation that many individuals will ever be able to utilize their talents to achieve true economic freedom through the accrual of wealth.

This book is *not* for those wealthy individuals who are naturally risk-averse and intent upon maintaining economic and social status quo. Nor is this a book for those who wish to gamble and see entrepreneurial investing as a means to fast and vast riches. The former should probably invest only in real estate, and the latter should learn the intricacies of futures and options.

Investing in entrepreneurs, for that is the real investment which is being made when one invests in new private companies, can be enormously rewarding, as well as highly frustrating and very expensive. The rewards can be much greater than financial gains, and the losses can result in much more pain and subsequent sacrifice than the investor expected.

Parenting a successful private company to the point of its going public or sale is an exhilarating experience. Of course, money accompanies this success. One can make, as I have made, 40, 50, or more times the amount originally invested. The great fortunes created in this country since World War II have been, for the most part, a result of either real estate speculation or entrepreneurial activity; the early investors, particularly those who invested at the outset with the founding entrepreneurs, have benefitted extraordinarily. Everyone has heard of the financial rewards of early and successful investment. All anyone needs in their lifetime is one such "hit."

The frustration, embarrassment, and pain of failure can be of such magnitude that marital and familial relationships become strained beyond repair. The loss of self-esteem in situations of significant financial loss can be serious for an investor. Whereas entrepreneurs in failure can feel they had no choice but to make the attempt, win or lose, investors are not provided with similar ego-protective devices. They did not *have* to make the investments and, therefore, must accept the responsibility, in their own eyes, of being stupid or greedy, or both. The failure of a private company is usually a great deal more traumatic than watching the price of a stock plummet on the stock exchange.

According to John Maynard Keynes, mere thrift is not by itself enough to build cities or improve mankind's possessions. He wrote in *Treatise on Money*: "If enterprise is afoot, wealth accumulates whatever may be happening to thrift; and if enterprise is asleep, wealth decays whatever thrift may be doing." Entrepreneurs represent America's spirit of enterprise, and they in turn must depend on individual investors to get their projects off the ground. Very often such investors make more than financial contributions to the new company, putting to the entrepreneur's use their experience, skills, and contacts.

I do not claim that I can be of assistance in finding the right entrepreneur for a particular Angel. But I do believe that as a result of reading this book, the prospective Angel will be in a better position to recognize the right entrepreneur for him (or, as is more likely, the *almost* right entrepreneur). Most importantly, this book should point out to both investor and entrepreneur what in all likelihood will occur in their business relationship, and how they can avoid, by prior agreement, common points of friction caused by the entrepreneur's nonachievement of projections. I do not claim to have all the answers to private company investing. I do not even claim to have as many investment answers as I have investment scars. I do understand the essence of the transaction that occurs between investor and entrepreneur, and I have been a player in the game a sufficient number of times to understand the rhythms and evolutions of both personal relationships and new company development. While deals are not all alike, entrepreneurs tend to have many characteristics in common.

This book could easily have been entitled *Do as I Say and Not as I Have Done*. Indeed, the Arthur Lipper Corporation, due to its financial experience with ownership of Venture magazine did change its name to DAIS-NAID, Inc. ("Do As I Say - Not As I Did") In the Venture experience, I made almost all the mistakes I warn others of making. The greatest mistake was that of permitting "the wish to become the parent of the thought" and believing sales projections made by salespeople.

This book could also have been entitled *I Wish I Had Always Done as I Now Know Enough to Say to Do*. As I guess is true with most books offering advice based upon experience, I am attempting to do the almost impossible--to pass on the benefits of experience. I must also admit that, even with the experience, I do not always follow the advice offered herein. However, when I do let myself get so overenthusiastic with an entrepreneur or project as to disregard the lessons learned previously, I do so with a knowing smile and some feeling that I am about to experience deja vu and relearn the same lessons. As Royal Little writes in his wonderfully instructive and entertaining book, *How to Lose $100,000,000 and Other Valuable Advice*, "Almost anyone can afford to make a single mistake, but when you make the same identical mistake twice, it is time to visit the head-shrinker!" I've lived long and actively enough to have run out of possible new mistakes, so I often just keep making the same ones over and over again. Hopefully, this book will spare readers the same masochistic exercise. All who are considering becoming Angels would do well to read Royal Little's book. There is a lot of wisdom dispensed with humor and humility. Private company Angels should also realize that increased humility is one of the probable results of private company investing, unless the Angel is very lucky, in which case arrogance will usually result.

Arthur Lipper III

ACKNOWLEDGMENTS

Many people helped me write this book, though many of them did-n't realize they were doing so. Many of them dislike me. Some of them I now dislike. Some are or have been in jail, and a number more should have served time. It is unfortunate for all of us involved in the new enterprise creation, sponsorship, and facilitation business that white collar crime is handled so differently by most courts than other forms of larceny. Most of those convicted of committing white collar criminal acts are apprehended through prosecution by the SEC. Unfortunately, there isn't a national agency focused on protecting Angels, and the interest of local law enforcement agencies in the plight of Angels is spotty, since physically violent crimes take precedence over crimes against Angel capital.

Is the making of earnings projections, stated or implied as promis-es, on which an Angel relies in the making of an investment, a crime if the entrepreneur or promoter making the projections knows or should have known the projections were not possible to achieve? The particular people to whom I now refer are those with whom, or through whom, I or those for whom I assumed a responsibility have lost money.

The mistakes made, for the most part, were all mine. They were usually mistakes of judgment regarding people and not situations. Sure, some products did not work and some markets were not there as hoped or projected, but the real problem was one of people-judgment error. A good manager can find or create a new product if the origi-nal one does not work as hoped. A good entrepreneur can find anoth-er way of marketing or maneuvering if the planned approach turns out to be wrong.

Being an Angel in private companies is not a popularity contest. Private company Angels just do not have the luxury of selling their stock, as does a stock market investor, if they become disenchanted with management. They either have to await destiny or try to do something about it. The latter seldom creates friends. I won't list those from whom I have learned the hard and disagreeable lessons, the essence of which has resulted in some of my approaches to investing and certain advice offered in this book. As they read the book, however, I hope that they will recognize themselves and, perhaps, with the passage of time, understand better the lessons that were there for both of us to benefit from in the future.

A lot of other people helped with this book in a more direct manner. Those people gave generously of their time and counsel. They put up with my interviews and questions. They offered me the use of materials they had prepared for their own use. They are all very busy people and were most gracious in the gifts of time and attention, and I thank them greatly. A list of these Angels of informational input follows.

George Ryan, author in his own right and book editor, assisted me in creating *Venture's Financing and Investing in Private Companies, Venture's Guide to Investing in Private Companies,* and *Thriving Up and Down the Free Market Food Chain: The Unrestrained Observations and Advice of a Business Darwinist,* and again in the editing of this book. He is one of the most dependable, pleasant, and competent people I have ever had the pleasure of working with. In some of the earlier works, George's name appeared on the dust jacket and cover page as "with George Ryan." A lot of the text of this book is based upon earlier writings, in which George played such a constructive role that the passage of time has only strengthened many of my beliefs based upon recurring experience. Although the role George filled was to organize and rewrite rather than write original text, he performed a vital function. Without his efforts, much of the submitted material would be much less readable. Any nonprofessional writer who ever considers writing a book would be well advised to contract with George. I wouldn't think of writing a new book without George's participation. He is a true professional writer and editor. When I first met George, he said, "What kind of book do you want to do? A western, romance, adventure?" He, at the time, knew almost nothing about business-related subjects and now, after much study, is almost an expert. Of course, if he tries to use his book-only knowledge, he is likely to end up paying some tuition in the form of a few losses--but then, that's how one learns.

Of course, my wonderful wife, Anni, has become used to putting up with almost total social withdrawal as I go "cold turkey," in terms of time spent with friends, during the period necessary to complete the book. As all who know her, and me, will agree, she is next in line for canonization anyway. Neither entrepreneurs nor entrepreneurial investors are easy to live with, and combining the two can be deadly for a relationship. Ours, due to her good judgment and firm guiding hand, has endured for more than 33 years, and we have both enjoyed a great return on our investment.

One cannot create a book such as this without the dedicated assistance of those with whom one works on a daily basis. Steven Marshall Cohen, previously *Venture's* special project manager, provided continuing assistance and guidance in the development and preparation of the earlier books from which I have drawn. Steve then went on to what is now Ernst and Young to work on the Entrepreneur of the Year award program, which was originally created as the *Venture*/Arthur Young Entrepreneur of the Year Award program and which has been very constructive and a good lead generator for Ernst and Young. Steve ran the *Venture*-affiliated Association of Venture Founders conference business. He managed my speaking engagements. He has written and edited two newsletters, *Venture's Capital Club Monthly and the Association of Venture Founders Newsletter*. He was responsible for coordinating and, at times, scripting our various radio and television projects. Steve edited and developed *The Venture Magazine Complete Guide to Venture Capital*, by Clint Richardson. All in all, Steve was a one-man strike force. He operated mostly alone, without the benefit of adequate administrative support or backup. Most importantly, he kept me organized and did it all with grace and charm. I miss his assistance.

The following knew they were helping me create *Venture's Guide to Investing in Private Companies*, and thus played a role in The development of this book. I thank each of them.

Burt Alimansky - *Alimansky Planning Group*
Howard Arvey - *Wildman, Harrold, Allen & Dixon*
Marshall L. Burman - *Wildman, Harrold, Allen & Dixon*
Scott Hodes - *Ross & Hardies*
Fred Shapiro - *Author*
Herbert S. Meeker - *Baer, Marks & Upham*

William R. Chandler - *Bay Venture Group*

W.R. Berkley - *W.R. Berkley Corporation*

Harold E. Bigler, Jr. - *Bigler Investment Company, Inc.*

David L. Epstein - *J.H. Chapman Group*

Frank J.A. Cilluffo - *Cilluffo Associates, L.P.*

John L. Hines - President, *Continental Illinois Equity Corporation*

James Bergman - *DSV Partners*

John A. Canning, Jr. - President, *The First Chicago Equity Group*

Martin L. Solomon - *Private Investor*

Joel Leff - *Forstmann-Leff Associates*

Stanley C. Golder - *Golder, Thoma, Cressey, Rauner, Inc.*

Evelyn Berezin - *The Greenhouse Investment Fund*

E.F. Heizer, Jr. - *Chairman, Heizer Corporation*

Howard Stevenson - *Harvard University*

Norman Mesirow - *Mesirow & Company*

Arthur D. Little - *Chief Executive Officer, Narragansett Capital Corporation*

Royal Little - *Narragansett Capital Corporation, Textron*

Steven D. Oppenheim - *Faust, Rabbach, Stranger & Oppenheim*

Seth H. Dubin - *Satterlee & Stephens*

Raymond J. Armstrong

Richard J. Testa - Testa, *Hurwitz & Thibeault*

Gerald Tsai, Jr.

William Wetzel, Jr. - *University of New Hampshire*

Karl H. Vesper - *University of Washington*

Dan W. Lufkin - *Venture Capitalist*

Jonathon B. Levine - *Business Week*

Carl Burgen - *Global Finance*

J. Patrick Welsh - *Welsh, Carson, Anderson & Stowe*

E.C. Whitehead - *Whitehead Associates*

There are a number of people who have helped me in gaining a greater understanding of the process of private company investing and who are also involved in the process of entrepreneurship education. In recent years, I have become committed to the proposition that we can and should help those having entrepreneurial tendencies develop their skills in such a manner as to avoid some problems they might otherwise have. Some of those listed hereunder have just plain helped me in my endeavors, and some have played a significant role in my gaining a range of insights and knowledge, much of which I have tried to present in this book.

Kathy Donohue
Professor Fran Jabara
Verne Harnish
Dr. George Solomon
Ken Sgro
Arnold M. Ganz
Don Binns
Nicholas Deak
Ruth Bishop
Don Boroian

I also wish to express my appreciation to Stanley E. Pratt and Norman Fast of Capital Publishing Corporation for so graciously allowing the use of certain articles appearing in various annual editions of the *Guide to Venture Capital Sources*. This valuable reference source and directory has become an industry standard. Readers of this book will note in the appendices several interesting and relevant articles which have appeared in *Guide to Venture Capital Sources* and are advised they will find many more in the original source.

In the development and publication of this book, Quinten Messbarger of the Missouri Innovation Center has played a constructive, critical and crucial coordinating role. Chip Cooper, the Executive Director of the Center has been directly responsible for doing that which was necessary in permitting me to share with a new and expanded constituency the experience I have accrued over the years. I have enjoyed my contact with both men and respect their motivation of assisting Missouri entrepreneurs.

A.L. III

Chapter 1

THE INVESTOR

When asked whether most individual investors should invest in private companies (as opposed to those that are publicly traded), almost without exception the advice of most of those burdened by conventional wisdom was that they should not.

However, this advice misses the question behind the question. The real issue is this: Are the potential benefits of investing in private companies sufficient to justify the increased risks of loss and, most importantly, the sacrifice of liquidity? Each year, several million Americans vote yes to this question by writing checks, signing subscription agreements, executing partnership forms and making bank loan and other credit substituting guarantees.

This book is intended to assist the individual angel investor in making better decisions as to whether or not to invest in private companies and how to do so more effectively.

The primary reason the vast majority of the professional investors I have interviewed advise against individuals investing in private companies is the inherent lack of liquidity associated with almost all private company investments. In reaching their conclusion, the professional investors were contrasting the making of private company against publicly traded company investments. They were contemplating direct equity investments rather than debt or indirect ones using the medium of guarantees, and they were primarily thinking of investments in companies that had the potential for super growth and either becoming public or being purchased by larger companies within the span of a few years. Not all private company owners want to or should go public or sell out. Many should not even consider doing so.

Yet some of these forever illiquid situations can be structured to be excellent investments.

Clearly we would all like to find, and have the necessary courage to invest in, future Apples, MCIs, Federal Expresses, Netscapes, and the many hundreds of other companies which have gone public and, thereby, made instant millionaires of the original investors as well as the founding entrepreneurs. However, for each of these winners there have been many more losers in which the investors have lost all of their original investment and, frequently, substantially more.

This last statement may confuse some as to how an investor can lose more than the amount originally invested. This is the subject of a later section and is perhaps one of the more important risks of private company investment to be understood.

The point under consideration in this chapter is whether you, as the investor, can afford financially, as well as psychologically, to be in the game at all.

It must be recognized that once a private company has received monies from investors, there are basically only two ways in which these investors can either make a profit or at least break even. One way is for the company to be profitable and, therefore, be able to pay their obligations or declare dividends. The other way is for something to be sold. That something can be either assets of the company or securities of the company owned by the investor. In either case, the company will probably have to enjoy some measure of success if the investor is to have a satisfactory experience. Yet it is not always so. The company can be sold, and/or the investor can sell something to someone before the company achieves success or its projected results. For example, most (in number, not necessarily aggregate value of their investment) initial shareholders in private companies frequently already have large unrealized, or more likely, unrealizable, "paper" profits based upon the capital valuation indicated by the offering price of an Initial Public Offering or IPO - before the earnings originally projected have been manifest.

The question of who should invest in a private company really cannot be addressed until the Angel's motivation for investing has been determined. Many people should make private company investments—if they can afford to do so. Angels gain a satisfaction from having a sense of participation in the growth and development of a company not generally available to those simply investing in publicly traded stocks. Investors in private companies also have an awareness of the important role they play in assisting in the creation of new jobs and economic opportunity in America. Intelligent private company investment is justified if the investor wishes to assist an entrepreneur or a community while having the opportunity for extraordinary profit.

No one should invest in a private company more than they can afford to lose. This trite-sounding statement is more profound than it may at first appear. In a private company investment, the investor is likely to have a total result—either his investment is likely to be totally lost or the result will be totally satisfactory. A satisfactory result will probably come at a time beyond the control of the investor and not close to the time originally predicted at the time of the original investment.

The investor would do well to prepare a personal business plan or personal financial projection to determine the exact amount of money he or, increasingly, she can afford to actually lose or lose access to. It is all well and good to say "I have $50,000 with which to speculate," but does that assume a similar level of disposable assets in future years? Can one foresee possible demands for investment funds for other projects? These and similar questions will assist investors in estimating how much of their capital they can truly put at high or simply incalculable risk. It is not nearly as simple a determination as is generally thought.

Since publicly traded securities have a liquidity (due to there being a cash bid at some level) that is totally absent in private company investments, it is very reasonable for Angels to expect a higher rate of return from the latter when similar risk levels are involved. In other words, if a net 15 percent annual average compound pretax return is anticipated by investors from the investors' publicly traded securities, then something higher, probably considerably higher, must be projected from their nonliquid investments. They must be compensated for the sacrifice of liquidity. Most professional investors suggest that, for companies of similar quality, the private company's projected investment return would have to be three to five times that of the publicly traded company before they would consider it worthwhile. Of course, these calculations presume a sale of the purchased securities and are not usually reflective of either a dividend or interest income assumption. Therefore, since a fifteen percent annual return compounded over five years doubles the amount of the principal, thereby producing a 100 percent gain, a cumulative gain of 300 to 500 percent is indicated by professional investors as being an appropriate five-year minimum objective for an illiquid investment.

One consideration of whether or not to invest in *anything* must be the level of the investor's own financial sophistication. In the case of private company investing, the investor's level of sophistication should be higher than that needed for publicly traded stocks because of two reasons. First, very few other people will review the company's investment offering proposal, so investors must rely more than usual on their own judgment. The standard investment services do not follow private companies, investment banking forms and securities analysts do not cover them, and the financial press does not typically comment on them or their prospects. Second, much less financial information is generated by the private company in the normal course of events than by its publicly traded counterpart. Also, the quality of the financial information provided by the private company will probably not be at as high a level as that of a similar publicly traded company, which has disclosure requirements and public-shareholder liabilities. Investors do not need a graduate degree in finance, but they do need, for private company investing, to truly understand cash flow analysis and that which goes into the making of projections of financial results.

Of course, if investors are lucky—very lucky—or are making the investment for purposes other than straightforward financial gain, they need not have a high degree of financial sophistication. Yet they will need the solace of having a sense of humor (or at least an acceptance of human inability to predict future events), since private company investment is an area in which Murphy's law—anything that can go wrong, will go wrong— can be seen in its most spectacular applications. Private company investors must maintain a sense of detachment and objectivity. This detachment can result from the size of the investment being relatively modest or from the investor's overall approach to high-risk investments.

In determining the appropriateness of a private company investment, the availability of the investor's time is a significant consideration,. A good deal of time is required to adequately monitor the progress of a private company, for the reason, as mentioned previously, that in all likelihood there will be no one to do it for the investor but himself. The investor must also expect to have to put questions to the managers of the private company, and expect the company to live up to its description as "private" in its reluctance to disclose information. Entrepreneurs are frequently "too busy" to be terribly communicative with investors, once they are in control of the investors' money.

Howard Stevenson, the Harvard Business School professor most concerned with entrepreneurship, recommends the following to the investor. "Every time you have a dumb question, ask it. Very often, these turn out to be the most probing questions an investor can put to an entrepreneur."

Stevenson says also,

The investor must not forget his skills and regard himself solely as a supplier of money. Money is not the most difficult thing in the world to come by. Usually, skills or other resources are more scarce than money. But, before investing his skills, the investor has to estimate how much time he can take off from his regular business. Thus, a dentist has special skills to be an investor in a dental supply company—if he can also spare the time.

The appropriate size of a private company investment relative to the Angel's own assets, or future income levels, is a matter which must take into consideration the age, health, financial resources, and socioeconomic and ethnic backgrounds of the Angel investor. Whether the Angel can *take* a loss is more than just a question of the money involved. Will the loss be embarrassing to the Angel? Has the Angel been brought up to believe that it is wrong to lose and only acceptable to be a "winner?" Are the Angel's friends all winners or very security conscious and, therefore, risk-averse to the point of being frightened by, or contemptuous of, those who sometimes lose or put themselves in a position of risk? If so, the Angel's position in private companies should be very minor and probably not of a size that can help or hurt him or her very much. All things considered, twenty percent of an investor's common-stock portfolio or a similar percentage of an individual's annual income seems like a reasonable figure to use once the Angel has passed the point of needing money to support present life-style necessities.

The issue of concentration or diversification of private company investment simply compounds the questions posed earlier that relate to the time and money availability of the investor. Diversification is one of the guiding principles of all portfolio management, especially when speculation as to predicted future events is a large factor. However, if the Angel is going to be active and participating, instead of passive, concentration is probably a more advantageous policy.

Being an active or passive investor is a basic decision the angel must make. This decision is very bottom line in that many of the other conclusions flow from it. If Angels wish to be passive, they are probably much better off turning in their wings and staying with a portfolio of publicly traded issues. The reality is that purely economic, risk/reward analyzed justification for private company investment by Angels is difficult to find. For the individual motivated by a desire to be actively involved in "growing" a business, some Angel-like private company investments are warranted and desirable.

Understanding the true intent and motivation of the investor is essential in weighing the merits of any investment. Many private company investments are made on a quasi-obligatory or favor basis because of a special relationship between the investor and entrepreneur/manager seeking the funds. Examples include an investment requested by a family member (cradle or pillow equity), good friend, customer, supplier (directly in cash or through providing goods and/or services on credit, known as vendor equity), or at the behest of business associate. In many cases, investments are made simply to assist someone. In other words, frequently the investor's exclusive concern is not profit. Recapture of capital may not even be a major concern when compared to the real reason for making the investment.

These quasi-obligatory investments are probably the most common type of private investment made and involve two primary concerns. One is the perception of fairness from the perspective of the recipient of the funds. The other is that the investment be structured in such a manner as to free investors from the obligation to make any follow-on investments, unless they wish to make them and then solely on the basis of increased profit expectation.

If the current return or future income, as opposed to appreciation, is the investor's primary objective, many private company investments can be structured attractively. Security of principal will probably be this type of investor's greatest concern.

Significant appreciation of capital is usually the private company investor's aim, ultimately achieved through the selling of the interests purchased to someone else, and such transactions must be structured very differently from either income-oriented or quasi-obligatory investor transactions.

In many instances, the development of an eventual adversarial relationship is almost inevitable between the investor and the entrepreneur/manager. This unpleasant fact of life can be a result of two factors or a combination of both: (1) the entrepreneur feels he has given the investor too good a deal on the project that he created; and (2) the investor blames the entrepreneur for his inability to achieve the results predicted in the time frame that the investor feels was used to induce him to invest. Both parties feel, and frequently so, that they have been taken. Often, the honeymoon period is short. On the other hand, as with some marriages, the relationship between investor and entrepreneur can evolve and mature from what was probably a set of unrealistic expectations in the first place. However, recognizing the fact that most new businesses cease to exist within five years of incorporation, investor disillusionment and unhappiness with entre- preneurs can be said to be natural, predictable, and widespread.

The Angel considering the risk and reward relationships of a pri- vate company investment should consider the possible personal aggravation involved in dealing with personalities who may be or become antipathetic to those having the ability to invest in private companies. In an extreme case, a desperate entrepreneur, who I had helped by arranging for all of the capital initially required, ultimately threatened "to slit my throat" when his company defaulted on its obligations to the investor group, which had provided the capital in a form that the entrepreneur perceived as being too protective of the Angels' capital. Many investors in private companies are unprepared for the intensity of personal involvements that result. These involve- ments can be the very best part of private company investing, but they can also be the most painful and disagreeable.

How much easier it is to sell a stock or a bond on the open market than it is to have to tell an entrepreneur, with whom you have been in constant contact for several years, that you have decided not to do something which would have permitted the company to continue along lines wished by the entrepreneur. How do you tell the entrepre- neur managing a business, who has become a friend, that your condi- tion for providing additional funds is his leaving the company? What about when the entrepreneur or manager is a relative or the son or daughter of a friend or a customer? How do you tell founders that their business has outgrown their abilities and that for the company to prosper, they will have to change (reduce the importance of) their position within it? On the other hand, there can be no more satisfying development than seeing a group of hardworking and capable young people "making it big" and feeling that you, as the investor, were at least partly responsible.

The sacrifice of liquidity required by private company investment is a matter for serious consideration. Alternative uses for the capital and the Angel's possible future need for the capital must be reviewed.

7

However, the most important aspect is understanding the motivation of the Angel and structuring transactions accordingly.

Investors should be aware that they often have more to offer a private company than simply hard cash. They may have successful business experience, judgment, technical know-how, or marketing knowledge to contribute. Their very involvement with the company may permit it to achieve better banking or customer relationships than would otherwise have been the case.

For a general overview of the informal venture capital market, see Appendixes A, B, and C.

It has been suggested to me that a simple, mechanical, how-to approach to private company investment would be more "positive" for entrepreneurs seeking capital or the use of capital than my investor-reward approach. I think the private company investing Angel could certainly benefit from a how-to book. However, my concern is with a more fundamental problem that most investors have— unrealistic expectations of wealth enhancement. These are the expectations that allow them to be persuaded by entrepreneurs into ventures of such impracticality and high risk that they are almost certain to incur losses The last thing such investors need is a how-to book. I, therefore, feel there is a more urgent need to *warn* investors of the pitfalls they will assuredly meet, and how these pitfalls may be circumvented or at least lessened.

A book advising entrepreneurs not to be entrepreneurs would be a total folly—they have little control over their destiny in this regard. Entrepreneurs are driven and compulsive. This book is certainly not written to advise private company investors not to invest. My intent is and has been solely to help Angels make better decision in their investments. Were I to be successful, the Angels would find themselves making more money and/or losing less. It is extremely important for Angels to at least lose less than is all too frequently the case. As long as they can recapture some of their capital, they can go on to another enterprise with the money they salvage from one which has been disappointing. Conversely, once they lose all of the money they wish to invest in private companies, they are out of the game. The loss of an Angel's participation, and of the other resources they provide to entrepreneurs, results in the loss of opportunity for many more of us than just the discouraged and withdrawing Angel. Angels are a national and natural resource and must be nurtured and protected.

Chapter 2

THE ENTREPRENEUR

What real knowledge have I, an investor and financial intermediary, about entrepreneurs? Being also an entrepreneur, having financed, studied, and liked entrepreneurs, having fought with them and litigated with and against them--in all humility, I claim a certain authority in describing them and dealing with them. My observations are also based on my prior functions as chairman and founder of the *Association of Venture Founders* and Chairman and CEO of *Venture* magazine, which was edited specifically for entrepreneurial business owners and investors. Incidentally, many of my observations and views are very similar to those of academics who have made formal studies of the character traits and common experiences of entrepreneurs.

The entrepreneur, as such, is not the subject of this book, not is the entrepreneur in general a social phenomenon about which I have particular insight or information. The person I refer to as an entrepreneur throughout this book is that rare breed, and sometimes endangered species, namely the *successful* entrepreneur. The distinction I am making here is similar to the one between people with artistic tendencies and desires and successful artists. People with artistic tendencies outnumber by far successful artists. In the same way, there are many more people with entrepreneurial tendencies than there are successful entrepreneurs. The reason is that tendencies have to be developed, through experience or education and training, into abilities and skills. Raw talent and desire alone are not enough.

One of the areas of great loss in natural wealth this country suffers is failing to identify young talent and to develop it fully for the benefit of the individual, as well as the community at large. In general, I

9

believe that gifted children are the world's largest wasted asset, since they hold the power, if developed fully, to solve the problems of humankind. Gifted children are the most highly leveraged of investments. Unfortunately, an early aptitude for athletics is the only classification of giftedness that gets special treatment in most societies and countries. A conviction that society suffers from a lack of willingness to identify and fully develop gifted children as a national natural resource, and that many achieving gifted children received special early nurturing, led to my founding the *Gifted Children Newsletter*, of which I was chairman. The newsletter, which ceased publication after ten years in 1989, served as a communication and networking medium for parents and teachers.

About thirty-five percent of the students in American university entrepreneurial classes are women, and a rapidly increasing number of women are starting businesses in the United States. The incidence of successful female entrepreneurs will undoubtedly grow rapidly. Female-owned businesses are presently being founded at a much greater rate than those owned by men. However, this growth will be temporarily held in check by the economic fact that it is much more difficult for a woman to gain the use of other people's money. Recognition programs and events such as the wonderfully effective Avon's Women of Enterprise award program, with which I have been pleased to be associated since its inception, are helpful in changing attitudes.

Successful entrepreneurs--and we can only study successful entrepreneurs as an identifiable group, since unsuccessful entrepreneurs are unemployed, employed, consultants, or even, as some would suggest in my case, self-proclaimed experts on entrepreneurs--have many characteristics in common. Successful entrepreneurs, in strange and wonderful ways, combine right-brain dominance, producing the necessary creativity, and left-brain needs for discipline and focus. Truly successful entrepreneurs combine the features of Pablo Picasso and General George Patton. They are often very persuasive and therefore good borrowers. One can spot such people easily, usually in airports. They are likely to be the ones who are walking quickly (unless they are on the phone), carrying their own bags, and standing tall. They know they are important and doing important things.

Greed is not usually a part of the makeup of entrepreneurs. They tend to be goal and achievement-motivated rather than money-motivated. Indeed, their focus on building wealth through the creation of a business separates them from the person with a small-business mind-set. Small-business-thinking persons typically relate their activities to the substitution, creation, or enhancement of personal income. For example, when small-business owners' concerns earn more money, they buy a more expensive car; when the entrepreneurs' companies earn more money, they are more likely to invest it in additional equipment, inventory, marketing, or research. It is perhaps a matter of tense that distinguishes the attitudes--the entrepreneur is future-focused, and the small-business person dwells primarily, if not only in the present. Of course, most large, publicly traded companies are firmly entrenched in the past.

The successful entrepreneur is first and foremost healthy. I know of no successful entrepreneurs who are sickly. The energy demands are just too great. A one of the early annual convention of the Association of Collegiate Entrepreneurs got these two words, among many others, of advise from T. Boone Pickens: "Don't smoke."

Luck plays a big role in the lives of successful entrepreneurs and those in their orbit. However, most entrepreneurs are people who feel the need to be in control of their lives and dislike the very idea of luck. They are seen by others as risk-takers. They do not themselves see the risks which others perceive them to be taking, because they know they are going to be successful in overcoming the difficulties. Typically, they do not think of themselves as risk-takers and are not gamblers. I suspect that a customer profile of the Atlantic City or Las Vegas casino patrons would show relatively few entrepreneurs as opposed to wage earners who feel the need for the unrestrictive randomness and the something-for-nothing excitement of gambling much more than the successful entrepreneur.

The luck which plays a role in the entrepreneur's life is that of location, of childhood years, of timing, of inspiration, and of associations. Location is important, since it determines the likely area of exposure and focus--there aren't too many high tech startups in Montana, though due to the evolution of the Internet and continuing dramatic improvement in communications, many entrepreneurs can now live wherever it suits them. Timing is perhaps the most important consideration, because the entrepreneur is more likely to be too early in an area of development than too late. Only major companies can usually afford the expense of being too early. Many of my own investments and entrepreneurial activities that failed to achieve success were years later successfully developed by others with less vision but better judgment and more money. On the other hand, entrepreneurs who have an "idea" feel a compulsion to go into business as soon as they can marshal the forces of development and production, because their need is for achievement and recognition more than financial, wealth-producing profit.

Chance associations are part of entrepreneurial luck; for example, the miliary service buddy, the college roommate, or childhood friend who in later years can provide special assistance. Successful entrepreneurs tend to be able to identify a single person who made a real difference in their lives. This extremely important mentor relationship seems to have been a random occurrence in most cases. Luck for the entrepreneur is a matter of synthesis. Due to their motivation, entrepreneurs make use of that which becomes available to them in ways which are very different from those of the nonentrepreneur. Many successful entrepreneurs are inveterate networkers and have a large Rolladex (or computer equivalent). Entrepreneurs, as opposed to inventors, are usually extroverts and do a good job of working the crowd when given the opportunity.

Among other traits, the entrepreneur is an achiever. The goal orientation of entrepreneurs may have something to do with the fact that most successful ones have had a particularly strong relationship with one of their parents, prior employers, or previous colleagues. Entrepreneurs seem to have an unusually strong need for recognition and approval. The relationship providing the stimuli can be based on either love or hate.

Another common characteristic is that the majority of successful entrepreneurs were either first-born or only children. Of course, those who are first born are always the only child for a period of time, and, therefore, for a while at least, can be the focus of their parents' attention. Most successful entrepreneurs grew up feeling loved and secure. However, many were raised in poor families and describe their childhood as "high on love, low on dollars." These people attribute their drive, work ethic, and present success to the fact that money was tight in their formative years.

The entrepreneur tends to be an early riser. In *Venture's* "Fast Track 100" survey, almost half these remarkably successful entrepreneurs said they rose between 6:00 and 6:30 AM, and one-quarter between 5:00 and 5:30 AM. For them, early to rise meant early to office--two-thirds of those surveyed arrived at their offices before 8:00 AM, and many started their work day as early as 7:30 AM. This is not surprising since most entrepreneurs are people with a high energy level, are achievement-oriented, and love what they are doing. They can't wait for the day to begin. They seem to require less sleep than others and tend to be in good health, perhaps as a result of their high energy.

Despite the fact that entrepreneurs have no special physical characteristics, many successful ones recollect that as children they felt that they were different--taller or shorter, thinner or fatter, and so on. The most commonly shared characteristic of entrepreneurs is that they had a job or jobs during childhood. The kinds of jobs are not significant, only that they worked for a tangible reward at an early age, and that the work was performed for others and not as a family duty. Obviously, there is a bias in this toward city and suburban children and away from rural children. But then most successful entrepreneurs are not farm-bred.

Entrepreneurs will probably have been successful, though unhappy and frustrated, employees before starting their own businesses. They may well have been fired from several jobs, because impatience and contempt for authority and established ways are common entrepreneurial characteristics.

Entrepreneurs are usually married. They have a lower than average divorce rate while their businesses are still growing. Truly married to their businesses, they are not likely to be interested in creating change in their home life. Problems arise when the spouse cannot sufficiently identify with the business to accept the sacrifice of attention. There are just so many waking hours in the day and product development seems to take precedence over child development and *nothing* is as important as generating cash flow. Further, many entrepreneurs building a business manifest a lower sex drive than their employed executives or professional counterparts and engage in extramarital liaisons less frequently than the opportunities presented would permit. Their "mistress/lover" tends to be the business they are building or struggling with. However, once entrepreneurs are successfully established--frequently reflected either by the sale of the business or by going public--their divorce and philandering rates seem to be much higher than average.

Entrepreneurs are often described by others as "compulsive" or "driven," yet do not see themselves in such a light, feeling that all they are doing is "getting the job done." Others may find entrepreneurs abrasive, since their need to please has been replaced by the sometimes conflicting need to achieve and prove something. Entrepreneurs--and this is vital to understanding and dealing with them--are controlling and power-wanting. The attraction of having their own business is one of being in more powerful and in control of their life than an employee can ever be.

Most entrepreneurs' lives are largely devoted to work and family, with little time for other personal interests. Those who make time for leisure activities lean toward adventurous, personally challenging activities such as motorcycling, car racing, flying, hot air ballooning, water skiing, scuba diving, and hunting. Entrepreneurs, questioned about the nature of their leisure activities, would be almost certain never to answer, "Relaxing." The majority of entrepreneurs also create some free time for community projects, charitable drives, youth sports, and so on. *Venture* magazine surveys indicated that fewer than one in three entrepreneurs were interested in politics, and most of these limit their involvement to making monetary donations.

The seemingly tireless pace of these successful men and women is frequently offset by regular vacations, usually two a year, but rarely for more than a week at a time. However, some feel their business can't do without them for more than a day at a time and limit their vacations to long weekends. As would be expected, the length of entrepreneurs' vacations is related to the developmental stage of their companies; the more mature the company, the greater the leisure time available.

This "composite portrait" of successful entrepreneurs has been put together for the purpose of aiding the investor in identifying them. Not everyone who has these characteristics will make a successful entrepreneur, but they will certainly not be held back by them. If it were solely the business that investors had to consider, the personality of the entrepreneur would have little interest for them. But the Angel investor invests in entrepreneurs. It is the entrepreneur who is the subject of the Angel's investment rather than the product or company. Products and companies can be created, altered, or replaced. Entrepreneurs have to be found and attracted to the right deal and dealt with thereafter.

For another general view of the entrepreneur, see Appendix D.

The following editorial appeared in *Venture* magazine.

Chairman's Comment

Entrepreneur is a word used with ever greater frequency. That's because there's more entrepreneurial activity going on and because the entrepreneur has a better image these days. The word is mow less likely to evoke an image of a Walter Mitty or of a fast-talking broker than previously. Nevertheless, the word is not satisfactorily defined. The Webster definition of one who "organizes and manages a business undertaking, *assuming the risk* for the sake of profit" is clearly restricted to those entrepreneurs who are entirely self-financed. As most successful entrepreneurs require out-side funding, there must be a better and broader definition.

In a speech describing entrepreneurs to an audience responsible for pension fund investing for major companies, I suggested the following definition of an entrepreneur who should be attractive to the venture capital investor. Readers having good ideas for definitions of an entrepreneur are asked to send them along to me.

The entrepreneur is someone who: makes something commercial happen.

The successful entrepreneur is someone who: makes something commercial happen which benefits others.

The commercially successful entrepreneur is someone who: makes something happen which benefits others and produces a profit.

The commercially successful business entrepreneur who is attractive to investors is someone who: makes something happen which benefits others, and which produces a profit of sufficient magnitude to justify the risks inherent in providing the funding for the entrepreneur.

Profit is the key word. The entrepreneur should not lose sight in seeking funding that the enterprise must produce a profit of sufficient magnitude to be an attractive alternative to competitive investment opportunities. To the investor, the art of investing is one of comparing ever-present alternatives. The professional investor must always be invested, but not in any one deal, or type of security. The entrepreneur is different. He is typically single-project focused and therefore may benefit in motivation but suffers in objectivity and realism.

Venture as a magazine is really all about profit. We are focused only on that   which was intended to ultimately produce a profit, or about those who have achieved profit. We also believe that loss avoidance or minimization is an integral part of profit making for both the investing angel and the entrepreneur, and for that reason, frequently publish articles on how entrepreneurs manage their companies to best effect.

I am always interested in learning from readers ways in which the magazine can be of more service. If you have thoughts, please share them with me. Profit is the name of our game and we know that profits are earned by benefiting others.

Arthur LipperIII,
Chairman

Since the fall of 1989, when *Venture* ceased publishing, after I sold control of the company, the general level of American business periodical journalism has improved. *Business Week*, *Fortune*, and the *Wall Street Journal* are each doing a better job of covering smaller enterprises. However, in my opinion, *Forbes* continues to consistently do the best job in terms of corporate reporting and editing. Unfortunately, no publication has filled the niche left by *Venture* in representing the interests and needs of the business owner as opposed to corporate executive. The reason is economic, because those making advertising placement decisions relate better to the concept of management than ownership in terms of their own experience and aspirations. If the media buyer doesn't relate to becoming a business owner, then a publication editorially representing such a strange breed will be viewed with some suspicion and, as a result, have a tougher time selling ads. One of the cruelest lessons I learned was that magazine publishing is a business of "buying subscribers and selling advertisers."

Chapter 3

FINDING PRIVATE COMPANY INVESTMENT OPPORTUNITIES

Objectives of the Angel Investor

We have all heard the golden rule of business: They who have the gold make the rules. There should also be an intelligent Angel's golden rule: They who have the gold should first understand their own true objectives and then make the rules.

Understanding what is in the Angel's own self-interest is very different from negotiating the hardest deal possible with an entrepreneur. If an Angel is going to have to depend on that entrepreneur to manage the enterprise, the hardest deal will most often not be the best deal for the Angel.

What return do you really expect on your investment? Why exactly are you investing in the enterprise? To show how smart or adventuresome you are? To be the Ted Turner or Bill Gates of your country club? To seek the highest possible current rate of return on your money? Ideally, you are accepting the challenge of private company investment with a balanced view of its risk and reward parameters, but you must also understand on a very personal level why you are investing. These personal reasons are the ones that cause the investor to ignore the well intended advice of others, for better or worse. There are many valid reasons for an individual to become an Angel and invest. The only ones you really need to understand are your own.

17

The Angel cannot use the entrepreneur as a sounding board, because, in most cases, entrepreneurs will agree to almost anything proposed by the funding source, certainly if they have been rejected often enough by others. The funding source has the responsibility to do the right and fair thing, and what turns out to be fair for the entrepreneur most often turns out right for the investor.

George Ablah's Twelve Commandments

George Ablah, a remarkable Wichita-based real-estate investing entrepreneur, is a meditative, sport-shirt-wearing man who has made hundreds of millions. He presented his twelve commandments to an Association of Collegiate Entrepreneurs and Young Entrepreneurs Organization conference in Chicago. To paraphrase his advice:

1. Use time efficiently.
2. Keep it simple.
3. Understand the basics.
4. Check supply and demand.
5. Sales come first.
6. Measure the upside and downside.
7. Crawl before walking.
8. Specialize.
9. Identify mutual benefit in all transactions.
10. Admit mistakes.
11. Manage egos.
12. Focus on timing.

How Many Opportunities Should Be Sought?

It is less a matter of the investor actively pursuing a certain number of opportunities than of his being exposed to a sufficient number of deals to be in position to judge the good from the bad. The average professional in the venture-capital field probably reviews 400-500 investment proposals and business plans in the course of a year. His success in part will depend upon having accurate and up-to-date information on what other opportunities are available. Individual Angels should not even try to cope with large numbers of proposals but certainly should see a number before feeling confident to tell whether they are being offered a fair deal in terms of the risk being assumed and the current competitive marketplace value for similar deals.

The chances are that if this is the Angel's first private company investment, the Angel will put the bulk of his money into the first proposal that comes along that looks attractive, regardless of what it is. Obviously, such a decision increases one's chances of losing the bulk of one's money. The advisability of holding back a part of one's investment capital for the purpose of refinancing the chosen enterprise is an issue which will be discussed elsewhere. Should investors concentrate on a single venture, or should they deliberately try to diversify their holdings? Investors with $50,000 to $250,000 to invest hardly expect to build a highly diversified portfolio, but they can put, say, $20,000 each into five new companies instead of $100,00 into one. Five companies will demand more of their time and energy than one; on the other hand, since so many new companies fail to be able to return a significant part of the Angel's funds, the Angel may feel they have a better statistical chance of success with five horses running in the race rather than one. Such reasonable diversification makes sense, so long as investors keep I mind that the limiting factor is more likely to be their own time--more than their money. Time spent working with entrepreneurs and reviewing financials can seem endless, and it is terribly important for the individual investor to understand the magnitude of the commitment one is making, in terms of time as well as money.

Building upon the strength of one's experience and skills is one aspect of being a successful Angel. Such knowledge gives the Angel strength, and that strength permits a concentration of effort and financial investment. When investors find a good opportunity in an area in which they are knowledgeable, they should concentrate on it, since it would be foolish for them under these circumstances to diversity simply for the sake of diversification. However, just because an investor knows something about the textile business does not mean he should invest in textiles, unless that particular segment of the textile industry is attractive in terms of future profit generation and therefore investment. By embracing only the familiar, one can turn a strength into a weakness.

The experience of the Angel may well be as important to the entrepreneur as the investor's money. However, the very experience of the investor that can be so helpful can also prompt what the entrepreneur comes to view as meddling.

Daniel Lufkin--one of the founding entrepreneurs of Donaldson, Lufkin and Jenrette, a director of many successful companies, and legend in the venture capital business--told me:

All sorts of Wall Street research reports describe the latest technology, the newest microprocessor, and so on. The advice I give is don't listen to other people when they tell you what you should invest your money in. Listen to yourself. By this I mean, pay attention to the products that you buy and use regularly. These products solve a need that you have. Obtain information from the companies that make them. In other words, think along familiar lines rather than looking for exotic things in which to invest.

James Bergman--a general partner in DSV Partners, the very successful Princeton-based venture capital organization--took this approach:

> The private company investor who has not the knowledge or contacts to get in on the leading edge of new high tech companies might very well concentrate on supplies of such companies. For example, he might avoid becoming involved in a genetic engineering company but invest in a company that produces instruments for genetic engineers.

Diversification of investment can be more rewarding in pre-startup companies, or seed-capital investments, than in those in the startup or development stages, because so many pre-startup companies never get off the ground. But diversification (particularly if it involves high-return, high-risk enterprises) can never be a substitute for knowledge gained through the commitment of time, energy, resources, contact, and study. The private company investor looking for significant risk reduction through diversification is recommended to get into a fund or play the stock market.

When You Are the One the Opportunity Finds

When offered the "chance-of-a-lifetime" opportunity, Angels-in-waiting have to ask themselves, with some degree of harshness, why they are the lucky ones to be selected. If you do not know the person making the offer and if they do not come to you with the endorsement of someone you know and respect, you should be wary. It is reasonable for the investor to ask such entrepreneurs to provide a list of the investors they have already approached. If such a list is forthcoming, the investor can then contact the people named in it to ask them why they did not invest in the venture. They may have made an excuse to the entrepreneur, wishing to spare his feelings or to avoid argument, saying they had no funds available or so forth. These declining Angels are frequently more likely to tell a fellow Angel the real reasons for their refusal to become involved. In many cases, investors can be sure that such a list of investors exists or could be made, and the reason the entrepreneur approached them was that their name was next on that list. Those previously having been offered the deal had most likely turned it down.

The entrepreneur is probably aware that many professional investment managers and venture capitalists are reluctant to invest the time to study a business plan unless it arrives with some sort of referral, which is frequently taken as an endorsement. Entrepreneurs should not be surprised, therefore, when the investor asks them for references, such as a letter of reference from a bank, an attorney, or an accountant. One professional often asks entrepreneurs for five references, telling them to make one of them someone who dislikes them, without saying which one of the references that person is.

Who Is Making the Offer and Why?

Not only must investors be wary of strangers offering them deals, they must also closely examine the credentials and motivation of *any* person offering or promoting a deal. My experience is that a financial intermediary, or "middleman," is more likely to misrepresent a deal than is an entrepreneur. Entrepreneurs know that they are going to have to justify, in an ongoing relationship with the investing Angel, all their initial representations and projections, whereas the financial intermediary may be interested only in making the sale, collecting his fee, and moving on to other deals. Having said that, it must be pointed out that the presence of a reputable financial intermediary or investment banker can add enormously to the credibility of a proposal. Such an investment banker's reputation is on the line, and he is probably assuming some legal liability in making the offer, notwithstanding claims to the contrary.

William R. Berkley, the strikingly successful entrepreneur and founder of the W.R. Berkley Corporation and a number of other highly successful businesses, is a firm believer in checking out references. He often goes one step further, sometimes with rewarding results, by checking on the validity of the reference. For example, when an entrepreneur tells Berkley, "Talk to John Smith at Citywide Bank, he'll vouch for me," Berkley does no such thing. Instead, he or his own banker calls someone else at Citywide and asks them about John Smith and the entrepreneur. Sometimes, the endorsement is warm and is all the more reassuring coming from a third party; sometimes, the warning is straightforward, acknowledging there are troubles with the account; and, at other times, the answering is evasive, which must be taken as a tipoff that all may not be well.

Some sophisticated investors expect that an entrepreneur or promoter will offer an investigatory background report on himself, such as those prepared by Bishop, Pinkerton, or Proudfoot. These reports note negative happenings in the career of the subject, such as litigation, poor credit ratings, divorce, prior directorships, and associations with a bankrupt company. The reports are not expensive, generally running from $150 to $700, depending on the amount of information required and the availability of data.

Investors should look for experienced entrepreneurs whose records cast no doubt as to their integrity. They should not accept previous wrongdoing on the part of the entrepreneur as an "early mistake." But neither should the investor always expect to find someone without a business mistake or failure in his career. The entrepreneur's integrity is the issue, not his perfection of business judgment. The investor should look for openness and candidness about prior business disappointments and, perhaps, failures on the part of the entrepreneur. There will frequently be an invention they were unable to finance or a situation they were unable to control. You won't have to ask them to tell you about their successes; they will do so without prompting.

When a financial intermediary is involved, the following are fair questions for the entrepreneurial investor to ask. How exactly are the middlemen involved in the deal? Do they have an ongoing interest in the company as part of their fee? Are they, in fact, investing in the company themselves? And if not, why not? If an investment is good enough for you, why isn't it good enough for them?

Deal Evaluation

It is vital for investors to understand that deal evaluation is a two-part decision-making process. The first part occurs to everybody--will the company be successful? Success or failure is 90 percent of the average Angel's decision-making focus, whereas it should really be no more than 60 percent. The second part, all too often insufficiently considered, concerns the *worth* of the deal investors get for their money. What will they have to pay for the projected success? What is their cost of admission? What is their sacrifice of liquidity? How much of their time will it take, and to what risk will they be exposed? Will they have to put in additional monies? What is the valuation? How much is this business *worth* today in terms of currently available alternatives?

Consider a startup business with a typical business plan, one that predicts losses in the first through third years, a small profit in the fourth year, and big profit in the fifth. Suppose the entrepreneur's projections are correct and that a profit of $500,000 after taxes is made in the fifth year. Using as a guideline the publicly traded stock of a comparable company selling in the market, for say, ten times its annual earnings after taxes, a public company with earnings of $500,000 would be worth $5 million. However, private companies are often valued at a fraction of the value of public companies. Suppose, therefore, that the private company is worth $2,500,000 or fifty percent of the public company's market valuation. Now investors are not being offered 100 percent of the company in exchange for their investment; if they are being offered 50 percent of the company's shares, the projected value of their share of the company in five years will be $1,250,000. They must then ask themselves if $1,250,000 in 60 month future dollars is worth the investment they are being asked to make in current dollars, considering also the risk, time, and effort that will be required on their part. Of course, if it is realistic to assume that the private company will go public within the three to five years, a higher valuation is warranted.

Well informed investors will be aware of stocks doubling or tripling their value in a single year in the stock market. They will consider their ability to sell downtrending publicly traded stock in order to cut their losses. They will also be painfully aware that there is no convenient way of admitting a mistake and bailing out of a private company investment. Perhaps they will consider investing their money in second mortgages, where they can get a high current return on their investment. Having considered these alternative investment opportunities, Angels will be justified in expecting a much higher rate of return from a private company investment, with its inherent ill-liquidity increased risk, than from a publicly traded transaction.

Too Good a Business Opportunity?

Have I got a deal for you. A $2 million equity investment will, I was pitched, allow this company to earn $2 million. I spent a day investigating this opportunity and decided to pass. Why? Wasn't the return good enough? No, the return was too good. How can that be?

23

It can be because the company was offering products--low-end furniture and branded electronics--on a no-down payment, credit basis to people who would not otherwise qualify for credit. The gross markup? A mere 350% to 450%. The sale signs in the store I visited quoted only the periodic payment price of $35.90 for a television set. That's $35.90 every two weeks for eighteen months, or $1,400 for a set which, for cash, would have sold for less than $500. Too good a business for me if I have to look into a mirror with any frequency. Surprise? The company was bankrupt. Moral: Sometimes it's so good, it's no good, and if it's not a good value for the consumer, it can't remain good business for the vendor. Fortunately, most entrepreneurs are not usually in business to take advantage of others. Making money by providing honest service and products is what quality entrepreneuring is all about.

Investors must also be "comfortable" with the business and should be able to look forward to being proud of their affiliation in the future. There's no way of being proud of ripping people off.

No Need for New Products or Exotic Businesses

For some entrepreneurs, developing a different, if not unique, business becomes an objective in itself. If this a result of entrepreneurship education's increasing emphasis on "creativity," I believe it is an unfortunate trend. The name of the game is to identify opportunities created by market demand and to develop businesses that fill those demands profitably. There's no need simply to be different or to base a company solely on new ideas or products.

A very smart friend, one who has been enormously successful and make hundreds of millions of dollars, once suggested the difference between him and me: I frequently become involved in projects requiring marketing effort, expense, and expertise, whereas he is only interested in finding or creating opportunities to make slightly more money than would otherwise be possible in accepting broadly recognized equivalent risks. With the mind of a mathematician, he simply studies and plays the odds. All my friend wants is 20 basis points more of return than an identical risk provides, so that he can arbitrage the spread--on a highly leveraged basis, since he is comfortable that he can't lose in the long run. As an approach, it's a sure winner. Entrepreneurs have a lot to learn from such an approach. Too often we focus on the process of entrepreneuring rather than creating profit through relative risk analysis.

24

Where the Grass Looks Greener

With the rise of industries overseas and with the incentives offered investors by some of these countries, American investors are often tempted by foreign opportunities. Also, there is a certain glamour to having investments in faraway places. One of the American investor's worries should be whether the party will be over by the time he gets in.

In the oil business, they say one should be wary of the drilling opportunity that has to come east of Houston for financing. Similarly, the American investor should wonder why the persuasive Australian entrepreneur sitting across the desk form him could not raise sufficient funds for his enterprise locally in Sydney or wherever. Why has this American investor been so lucky?

As a general rule, the greater the distance between the owners of the money and the management of the enterprise, the less likely the success of the investment. This can be put in a more positive way: the greater the distance between the investor and the company, the greater the need for a strong and directly involved local, cash-investing, partner in the investment.

Distance can be intellectual instead of geographical, with similar results. I believe that individuals from, or operating within, smaller, socially constricted communities, such as islands, tend to be relatively more stable and conscious of their reputation than those from large-land-mass areas representing psychological and geographical frontiers. These "pioneer-mentality" people tend frequently to be contemptuous of the status quo embracing the establishment and its financial institutions. So, to, on intellectual frontiers. Investors, being seen as a part of the establishment, are frequently viewed as fair game and may be divested of their investment without a great deal of entrepreneurial concern. This attitude, which amounts almost to contempt for people with money, is prevalent in elements of the scientific community and is only increased by the large amounts of money the investment community, including venture capitalists, so readily make available to academics unburdened by prior profit-making responsibilities or history. With investors (and their investment banker, Sherpa-like guides--being compensated to escort the investors to ever high levels of risk), there is all too often in inverse correlation between an understanding of the technology upon which a company in which an investment is being made is dependant and a willingness to speculate on future commercial success. Those doubting the valid-

25

ity of this observation are invited to review a sampling of initial public offering prospectuses of various bull market periods, with the appropriate inquiry, "Where are they now?"

Responding to Ads Seeking Money or "Partners"

The advertisement saying "Partner Wanted" is essentially a way of avoiding federal and state securities act restrictions and violations, since securities may not be sold directly through newspaper ads. Currently some entrepreneurs believe there is a freedom to offer securities through the Internet without adherence to securities regulations. I disagree and believe that in the case of most investments there should be a burden of full and complete disclosure. Nearly all ads for such partnerships are simply solicitations for money in exchange for that which is seen by the placer of the ad as an equity interest. The prospective "partner" is rarely requested to contribute anything more than his money.

Generally, I would not recommend answering such ads. Yet, if you decide to do so, do not send your name and address. If you do, chances are you will end up on a suckers list--to be pestered continually in the future. Informing strangers that you are in a position to invest $50,000 or more can have serious consequences. Should you be curious, you should respond through a post office box number or have your lawyers respond stating that they have a client who is interested and that all correspondence should be addressed to the law firm. In all cases, the offering must be made in writing. Do not ever respond to anything over the telephone. Ask for a business plan, get them to send references, and keep your distance early in the relationship.

The chances of coming across a scam or confidence game through such ads are clearly high, regardless of the publication's respectability. However, an ad in a restaurant trade publication stating "Partner Wanted for New Restaurant in Aurora, IL" may prove to be attractive and easily verifiable, while a blind ad in another publication with vague working about a "business opportunity" is obviously in a different category.

Placing Ads

Placing ads is an entrepreneurial act in that the investor takes the initiative. He can also more easily set up his own standards and conditions. If you wish to invest in a business in a particular geographic area, say a small town in New Hampshire, placing a "money available" ad in the local paper may be on the more effective ways of going about it. (Approaching a business broker in the area is another efficient way.) If you have knowledge of some field of technology, such as lasers, placing an ad in the appropriate trade journals indicating the availability of funding will no doubt elicit some interesting replies.

You have to be careful in the wording of the ad not to mislead the reader as to your capabilities or resources. You also must give enough information about what it is you seek in order for the reader to respond efficiently. If you want a business plan first time around, say so. If you want references, state that all responses must include references. The more specific you are, the more restricted will be the number of responses you receive, but you will probably have better quality responses.

The same precautions hold for placing ads as for responding to them: Do not give your name and address, and deal initially through a post office box number or your lawyer. Respondents to such ads may also elect to retain their anonymity at first, and this indicates a desirable level of sophistication. Clearly state that all submissions will be treated in confidence. Also state that, unless accompanied by a stamped and addressed envelope, submissions will not be returned. Without such notice, the investors are likely to find themselves with either a large postage bill or a flock of unhappy entrepreneurs.

Contacting Investment Bankers

Investment bankers are an excellent source of investment opportunities. However, they are not, as a rule, experiences in investments of less than $250,000, except when such an amount represents part of a much larger investment. Indeed, the relative smallness of the amount involved may be the primary reason why investment bankers are not interested and are willing to pass the opportunity on, or it may be that the deal does not fit their particular interests at the moment. Investment bankers also have available to them a wide range of opportunities for secondary financing companies beyond the startup stage and, at times, of companies in trouble, which may be of great interest to the investor. The investor's own commercial banker, attorney, or accountant can often recommend a reputable investment banker.

Investment bankers having interest in smaller companies tend to flourish with an active new issue market. When the stock market

27

declines and interest in new issues contracts, the number of smaller investment bankers tends to diminish. The size and quality of investment bankers range from very small and unscrupulous to large and prestigious. Size, however, is not indicative of quality. The roles of the investment banker and venture capitalist are not to be confused. Typically, the venture capitalist is not involved in the act of transferring ownership of securities to others. The investment banker, in marrying other people's money to management, takes some form of commission, as opposed to the investors or venture capitalists, who put in their own funds or those for which they are responsible.

Independent financial planners or individual financiers also may have investment opportunities available. The general role of financiers is to provide funding for projects, without it being significant whether the funds are their own or those of others.

The investment banker who has an office in the community in which the investor lives has a greater motivation to deliver a good deal than has another investment banker, finder, or intermediary with a base of operations elsewhere. This issue of reputation within a community is vitally important. When a local investment banker, who sees a range of investment opportunities, offers a deal to a local investor, it normally means that the banker thinks highly enough of the proposal to risk his reputation locally by recommending it. The banker may or may not know the entrepreneur will but presumably has checked him out; the investor should certainly enquire about this.

In the crudest sense, an investment banker can serve as a protective device for the investor in that the investor can sue him if the banker made any misrepresentations that induced the investor into a bad investment. The most important aspect of the presence of an investment banker in a private company is in terms of future exit. Whether the company is successful or unsuccessful, the investment banker is going to be helpful to the investor who wants out of the deal. Because of the banker's contact with other investors, he can be of great assistance when a company needs additional funds.

Investment bankers can act both as general and limited partners in venture partnerships. As well as participating in the high anticipated returns some private company investments promise to offer, the investment bankers may regard the young companies as future underwriting clients for initial public offerings. The banking firm involved may also have a general interest in the field in which the new company will operate. Because of fees and/or free or bargain priced stock, or other forms of carried interests, the investment banker's involvement can be quite costly to a private company.

The most advantageous situation for investors is when the investment banker tells them, "The company needs $100,000. I am going to invest $10,000 of my own money, will you invest the other $90,000?" Although the banker will probably be collecting a 10 percent fee and, therefore, will not be at the same risk level as the investor, the fact that the banker is investing his own money in the enterprise indicates his level of confidence to the investor.

Commercial Banks, Insurance Companies, and Other Institutional Referrals

Although regulations prevent many commercial banks from directly investing in private companies, they often become involved when young companies cannot pay back bank loans. The bank's loan officers are usually glad to hear from an investor willing to assist in their salvage operations. When a bank wants badly to extricate itself form a situation, the investor can often pick up a real bargain especially because, in some cases, the investor himself may not be able to turn the company around. The commercial lending officers at the bank will no doubt have turned down some loans for lack of collateral, and they are often willing to put the investor in touch with these deals. They can certainly provide introductions to local businessmen and provide other valuable contacts. For a viewpoint on commercial bankers' relationships with entrepreneurs, see Appendix E.

Insurance companies have long been involved in venture capital investing to various degrees and are normally attracted only by very large deals. As with commercial bank officers, their staff members can provide the investor with important personal introductions in the local business community.

Anywhere business people tend to congregate will prove fertile ground for those seeking private company investments. Business clubs and organizations, such as the Rotary Clubs, the CEO Clubs, the Young Presidents Organization and the Chamber of Commerce, are recommended; so too are state and municipal development authorities. High-potential opportunities are not typical of businessmen's clubs, and high-tech deals are even rarer. The professors at the nearest business school will have a greater exposure to such deals. They often sit on private company boards of directors and frequently possess an interestingly different perspective on investment opportunities. Trade shows and conventions, particularly those in which exposition booth can be visited provide opportunities for investor research regarding the business of the exhibitors. Such trade shows are in themselves highly educational for private company investors.

The Internet has a number of home page sites where investment opportunities are described and promoted. I am developing a home page, to be known as VenVest, for use by an association (that I may form) of venture investing Angels. The professional venture capital industry members have an enormous advantage in that they exchange information freely regarding individuals and technology, since the venture capital industry is a very collegial and not too competitive environment. An association (irrespective of whether such a group is formalized) of Angels could be highly productive for the members.

I am also considering a resurrection of the Association of Venture Founders, which Anni Lipper, my wife and partner since 1962, managed on behalf of Venture magazine. It was a very constructive experience for all concerned. With the Internet and e-mail, many networking activities are much easier and more cost-effective today than they were only a few years ago.

The prospective Angels should make an attempt to become a part of what William E. Wetzel, Jr., calls the network of informal investors. These informal investors are known to entrepreneurs as Angels, not because they are necessarily "nice" but because they are "heaven sent" for the entrepreneurs. For more discussion of Angels, see Appendix F.

From what is written, it seems that many believe that most Angels fly in flocks; however, most of my advice is intended for the solo and therefore unassisted Angel.

This difference prompts some thoughts on the flocking of Angels. My principal concern would be, who's the boss Angel? There has to be a "leader of the money," because in most cases there is going to be some postinvestment interaction with the entrepreneur and the cohesiveness of the investor group will permit a better investor result than if the group is fractionated. Entrepreneurs probably are going to fall short of their projections and, therefore, require greater financial assistance than had originally been expected. There is always a feeling, partly true in most cases, that entrepreneurs have worked very hard, and it is not their fault that "things did not work out as planned." That is, of course, the first time. The reaction of Angels to such disappointments is likely to harden and be less "understanding" with repeat performances. But what about the first time when there is a group of equals? Are all of the Angels on the board of directors? Do they all agree as to their best course of action? Are they investing as a group either legally or in practice? What should be done with the one dissenter who favors holding the entrepreneur, in some manner, to his original projections? Does not the situation of flocked Angels create a "we" the money and "they" the management? Does not this situation, by its very description, increase the chances of the parties' attitudes becoming adversarial? Is the result the operation of two boards of directors--those responding to the needs of money or management?

Of course, it depends on the size of the Angel flock and the relationship between the Angels, but, in most cases, I would have the Angels invest through an entity rather than directly in bits and pieces in the company. The reason for this view--and remember that in this book I serve, or at least attempt to, the interests of venture investing Angels over those of capital consuming entrepreneurs--is the ability to gain control of the enterprise. Structured properly from the Angel's perspective, early stage financings should permit the Angel to assume a position of protecting his interests as they become increasingly threatened. The manner of accomplishing this is, in one word, *control*. This is not to say that investors have to exercise the control they have as soon as the acquire it--or ever, for that matter. It is to say that the Angels will have an advantage by being able to control the remnants of their capital.

The investing group through which the Angels made their investment can always merge itself into the investee company on terms suitable to the Angels. Also, the investing entity might develop a separate life of its own if the Angels interact well together. After all, investors in private companies usually expect to invest their talents as well as their money, and if a group of talented people got together to facilitate their common interest in one project, why not consider additional projects?

Investors in private companies should always meet and get to know their partner Angels before the deal jells. Meeting for the first time at a creditors' meeting would be silly. Do not let the entrepreneur simply put together a "private placement" of investor slices of the same pie. There is strength for the Angel in getting the circle together.

One point must be understood by both investors and entrepreneurs. The point is that the winning investments must result in large enough gains for the investor to provide an acceptable overall result *after* deducting the losses from other investments. If the investor is going to lose half his investment in four out of five deals (which would be a better than average result), how much does he have to make in the fifth to give him a net 30 percent annual average compound result. Don't bother doing the calculation for a five year period . . . it's a lot. The point is simple and it is the essence of this book. The less you lose in private company investing, the less dramatic need by the winning (and, therefore, more likely to achieve) investment result to yield an overall satisfactory investment experience. The better the Angel population's overall experience, the greater the number of entrepreneurs likely to be assisted. That is my personal goal--helping more entrepreneurs to gain access to ever greater amounts of Angel capital.

The number of informal investors is staggering, and their investment resources exceed the funds available to professional investors. Assume that there are as many as 750 professional (acting as fiduciaries) venture capital providing entities in the United States and that each of these is responsible for totally funding as few as two startups a year (probably a very high estimate). This, of more than 700,000 businesses started each year, in the United States, then only amounts to 1,500 new companies having the benefit of assistance of professional venture capitalists. In 1987, subscribers to *Venture* magazine alone were involved in more than 200,000 business startups. I am certain the number of companies in which there is a financial involvement by the readers of *Inc.* and *Forbes* currently exceeds a third of all startups. Unfortunately, the degree of involvement is unknown and there may be some duplication of survey results from individual businesses in this astounding display of socially constructive activity. From these figures, Angels can readily see their potential value to entrepreneurs relative to that of professional investors. Entrepreneurs have good reason to refer to the informal investor as an Angel. The perception of the investor as an Angel is likely, however, to change 180 degrees when sophisticated Angels find they must protect their interests versus those of the entrepreneur.

How Entrepreneurs Can Deal Successfully with Finders and Financial Intermediaries

When investors learn of an entrepreneurial opportunity through a person acting as a financial intermediary or finder, they should discover what relationship exists between the finder and the entrepreneur. An arrangement between the finder and entrepreneur that the entrepreneur later finds burdensome may adversely affect the business and cause a loss to the investor. This section, written for the entrepreneur, gives the investor an idea of what kind of relationship the entrepreneur *ought* to have with the finder.

One of the most common experiences of entrepreneurs is encountering an individual or firm that offers to perform introductory services for a fee. The services we are addressing are those relating to the raising of money. However, similar use of intermediaries arises in regard to obtaining contracts for other than the investment of money, and many of the same principles apply.

The finder, financial intermediary, or investment banker frequently offers a valuable service, one which ultimately leads to a financing. Those performing a finding or introductory function may also have the ability to make valuable advisory and other contributions to the entrepreneur. The compensation for these other contributions can be, but is not necessarily, included in the original payment for service. There is a tendency on the part of many inexperienced entrepreneurs, those who ultimately become successful, to part with too much of the stock of their company too early in the development process as a result of becoming overly impressed with the contribution which can or will be forthcoming from an early associate or advisor. Of course, if the entrepreneur fails to succeed, the amount of stock retained is irrelevant.

The negotiation of fee arrangements with a finder requires some experience. The finder will seek terms, which may be reasonable. However, frequently commitments to finders become impediments, not only to the original transaction, but also to other possible relationships. The finder will seek compensation, and the entrepreneur is advised to have a clear understanding of the expectation of the finder in advance of accepting the offer of introductory assistance. A written agreement is usually advisable for both the intermediary and the entrepreneur. In certain states, New York being one, finder fee agreements are only enforceable if they are written.

Entrepreneurs should understand that they are the client and will be paying the fees. The finder is the agent, or financial servant, of the client. It is vital that both parties understand the roles being played and anticipated.

As compensation the finder will usually seek:

- A retainer, or advance fee, which can be, but is not always, credited against an additional, and usually larger, "success" fee, which is only earned upon the consummation of a transaction. The size of the fee is always subject to negotiation. There is no standard finder's fee arrangement. However one commonly used schedule is the so-called Lehman formula of 5-4-3-2-1%. This translates into 5% of the first one million ($50,000), 4% of the second million ($40,000), etc. Therefore, on a transaction of $5.0 million, the total fee, using a 5-4-3-2-1 arrangement, would be $150,000 ($50,000 + $40,000 + $30,000 + 20,000 + 10,000), or 3%. Similarly, for a $10.0 million transaction, the fee, using the same formula, would be $200,000 or 2%; and at $20.0 million, $300,000 or 1.5%. (See the section on "Fees" in Chapter 10.) The finder will also frequently seek an equity interest in the business. This interest can take the form of stock in the company or a right to acquire stock in the company on an agreed upon basis.

- Full reimbursement of expenses: It should be understood whether the expenses are to be (1) subject to a maximum, as previously approved by the client; (2) directly related to the specific transaction (rather than being related to the overhead of the finder; (3) as incurred or with a permitted markup, as is the tradition in advertising agencies; (4) reimbursable regardless of the success of the finder; and (5) payable by the client on a fixed schedule.

- Exclusivity of relationship: This is one of the more onerous aspects of a representation agreement from the perspective of the entrepreneur. The critical issue is the period of relationship. The longer the entrepreneur has a commitment to pay fees or to be represented by an intermediary, the more valuable the right to the intermediary and restricting to the entrepreneur. Also, the entrepreneur should be aware that exclusivity can be restricted to previously nominated entities, and then for specific periods of time, as well as for specific geographic or industrial sectors.

The following rules for contracting with finders are not intended to be all-inclusive or to indicate an inflexibility on the part of the entrepreneur. They are intended to be points for consideration and discussion. There should be a written agreement reflecting the understanding of the entrepreneur and the finder, or finders, if there are more than one, as is frequently the case.

Rule 1. The role actually being played by the finder, the fully disclosed identities of all associated finders (if any), and the proposed compensation basis must be fully understood and agreed upon by the entrepreneur before accepting the offered service. From the entrepreneur's perspective, the finder should indemnify the entrepreneur against all claims for compensation by others with whom the finder has operated.

Rule 2. The true quality of the finder's relationship with the parties to whom introduction is offered must be disclosed and understood by the entrepreneur. The entrepreneur being offered service by the finder or wishing to sell something should obtain hard evidence of the agent's relationship with the potential buyer or resource provider. There should be a different level or basis of compensation depending upon the ability of the agent to influence an outcome, once an idea has been proposed or an introduction created. Does the finder really know the parties to which he is offering an introduction? Has the finder had a prior relationship and/or participated in transactions with the same parties? Does the party to be introduced by the finder know the basis of the finder's retention by the entrepreneur? I believe the finder's relationship with the entrepreneur should be disclosed to the buyer or resource provider.

Rule 3. The entrepreneur selling property or expecting to receive money should insist on receiving copies, or full written reports, of all communications with the prospective investor or purchaser. The failure of the appointed agent to provide such communication can be, if included in the agency agreement, grounds for not paying any introductory fee.

Rule 4. There should be a relatively short time limit placed upon the period during which the entrepreneur has any obligation to the agent for providing an introduction, or even simply the presentation of an idea. If the negotiations reach the point of the principals exchanging draft agreements, then the period should be extended.

Rule 5. The intermediaries or agents should fully disclose to all the principals their anticipated or proposed compensation from the parties to the transaction, and the distribution between the intermediaries or agents. The fee schedule or basis proposed should be within the bounds of that which is currently considered normal and customary, because otherwise the principal effectively paying the fees, frequently the Angel, is likely to feel unfairly treated upon an ultimate revelation. I believe the discourse should be made early in the process, because if there is to be disagreement, the sooner it surfaces, the easier it will be to satisfy.

Rule 6. The principals should have direct contact very early in the negotiation process to ascertain their real objectives. Agents can sometimes help in the process of negotiation, but the principals must agree directly as to their ultimately desired conclusion.

The use of intermediaries is an accepted part of business. Successful entrepreneurs have almost always used intermediaries successfully.

Franchises

Whereas a very high percentage of all new businesses fail in the early years, the reverse is true of franchised operations. The reason that only a very small percentage of franchises fail is that the franchisor, in most cases, has had to have had sufficient success to prove the fundamentals of the business, and that he also imposes discipline and provides systems which otherwise might not have been available to the individual entrepreneur. The franchisor tells entrepreneurs how to purchase, how to hire, what hours to run his establishment, and so forth, thereby saving them a great many mistakes. The investor recognizing this knows that, with the benefit of the franchisor's supervision, entrepreneurs are less likely to fail than would be the case were they to be on their own.

One hears the somewhat vague and overstated estimates that 90 percent of all new businesses fail within the first five years. Interestingly, according to the U.S. Department of Commerce publication Franchising in the Economy, less than 5 percent of franchisees fail. One proviso that must be mentioned in regard to the low failure rate of franchises is that it is possible for the franchise to "succeed"-- from the franchisor's point of view--when the original failing franchise-investor team is replaced without delay by another such team or indeed a series of them. Franchise resales, even at losses to the original franchisee, are not counted as failures, even though the original franchisee may have lost a large portion of his original investment.

Franchises need not necessarily be thought of in terms of roadside pizza stands. A seat on the New York Stock Exchange is a form of franchise, entitling its holder to solicit and transact business on the Exchange but also binding him to its rules and requiring him to pay fees. The local dry cleaner may be a franchisee, with the equipment manufacturer or process owner the franchisor. Holiday Inn and Coca-Cola bottling franchises have had highly publicized success stories.

An investor with 10 McDonald's franchises would today be a very rich man. Franchises are rare in manufacturing businesses, and the investor will not find one in computer chips. Service businesses where the product is an intangible constitute the most successful area for franchises, and this area is not nearly as well understood by private company investors as it might be, though increasing numbers of service companies are making initial public offerings. Of course, the subject of the IPOs are more likely to be franchisors than franchisees.

When investing in a well-known franchise with a good bottom-line income, the investor can borrow more money and leverage himself more highly because of the franchisor's name recognition factor. Any investor who has confidence in a young entrepreneur or manager could do a lot worse than to set him up as a franchisee in a well chosen franchise. He'd earn both profit and experience.

Entrepreneurial investors sometimes have a general contempt for franchises. They have heard horror stories of how the franchisee has been taken advantage of by the franchisor, of how franchisees can be squeezed out of their franchises, if successful, by the franchisor raising the prices of supplies they must purchase from him, and of the huge merchandise turnover needed to produce even low profits. As in any area of business, in franchises there are bad deals, good deals, and very good deals. Before going into an investment, investors should enquire from other holders of the same franchise how it has worked out for them . They should try to spot the success factor or factors common to all their franchises and judge whether their prospective franchise also has this factor. For example, in a business that sells low-priced items to a population with low mobility, the site of the franchise will probably be its overwhelming factor of success.

Some Angels say that while a franchise can make an attractive investment with lowered risk, it does not deliver the high potential they seek from investments. Obviously, "high potential" in the fast-food business must be defined differently, or least viewed differently, from what it is in the semiconductor business. Holders of Mexican fast-food franchises have been pleasantly surprised by the high potential of their businesses. The holder of a McDonald's franchise a block away from a new junior college is in a high-potential situation.

Those considering investing in franchisors or franchisees may also find interesting the following *Venture* "Chairman's Comment" column.

37

Chairman's Comment

I once attended a seminar on Franchisee/Franchisor Relationships (known in the franchising industry as "zees" and "zors"), created and conducted by Robert E. Kushell, founder of Dunhill Personnel Systems and sponsored by the International Franchise Association, Washington. [As of 1996, the more than 3100 members of the IFA have more than 30,500 zees.] This particular meeting was attended by representatives of 35 zors. The average annual growth in zee units predicted by the attending zors for the next three years was more than 180 percent. Predictions of tenfold growth were not unusual. Of course, it is easy to be misled by the use of percentages when the base is small. Accepting such projections is not easy. But it's a big country, and many of the newer zors have enormous energy motivation, and momentum going for them. Some of the zors had familiar names; many were new to me. [For those interested, the IFA will be pleased to provide a list of IFA members, as well as other educational material (International Franchise Association, 1350 New York Avenue, Washington, D.C. 20005-4709; (202) 628-8000). According to a recent Business Week article, there are more than 500,000 zees and 3,000 to 5,000 zors operating in the U.S. alone.]

There are some interesting trends emerging. The franchising industry is broadening, and food operations, though still a large part of the zor population, are being challenged for zee fees by a diverse range of retail and service businesses. The zor's claim is much the same: a zee, with average intelligence, hard work, the necessary amount of capital, and, most importantly, a willingness to follow the zor's formula, will succeed. Strangely enough, it does seem to work out that way. Whereas the average life expectancy of a newly formed business is tenuous at best, less than 10 percent of zees fail in the first five years. The zor's requirement that the zee unswervingly follow instructions raises questions regarding the inherent entrepreneurial tendencies of the zee.

Predictably, rapid growth and zee success have given rise to communication problems, and the Garden of Zor is on the verge of becoming more of a Zoo of Zees and Zors. The zees, with success, are becoming restless. The zors must continually stroke and assist existing zees while, at the same time, pursuing the primary business of most zors, the creation, through relentless marketing, of new zees. The care and feeding of zees is becoming increasingly important as now, on the horizon, are two unions of zees. [The following are two sources of information. The American Franchisee Association, 53 West Jackson Blvd., Suite 205, Chicago, IL 60604; (800) 334-4232. American Association of Franchisees & Dealers, P.O. Box 81887, San Diego, CA 92138-1887; (800) 733-9858.] Many zees of a particular zor have already formed, frequently with the cooperation and sponsorship of the zor, an advisory board or council to better communicate with their zor and to define and assert their demands. The zor is naturally concerned by the prospect of zee defections, and the zee, as he becomes more sophisticated, demands more assistance for the royalty flow he is providing the zor. There comes a time in the development cycle of most zees when they feel they know as much or more than the zor. Zees then may question whether they need to use the zor's name on new units. The zor may be in a situation of a zee's very success breeding discontent. Of course, not all zees are successful.

[With annual zee sales in 1993 of more than $970 billion, representing over 40 percent of all retail sales, franchising is an important, rapidly growing aspect of America's economy. Presently, a number of business-related periodicals have greatly increased their coverage of franchising, but none with the objectivity and expertise of the departed *Venture* magazine.]

Arthur Lipper III,
Chairman

Francorp® Test

Francorp of Olympia Fields, IL, (708) 481-2900, the largest of the consulting firms specializing in franchise development, assisted the author in the preparation of material for this book relating to franchising.

Francorp® 10-Point Franchisability Test

1. Do you have a profitable operating prototype?

    No   1 pt.
    Yes   10 pts.

2. How many units do you have in operation? Assign 1 point per unit up to 10.

3. How long has your business been in operation?

    Not in operation yet.   0 pts.
    Less than 6 months   2 pts.

One year	4 pts.
Two years	6 pts.
Three years	8 pts.
Four years or more	10 pts.

4. Has anyone inquired about the possibility of buying a franchise of your business in the last year? Assign 1 point up to a total of 10 points for each inquiry by someone who is financially capable and seriously interested.

5. How long would it take you to teach someone how to operate your business?

Too difficult	0 pts.
More than 6 months	5 pts.
Two to six months	7 pts.
One week to two months	10 pts.

6. How much capital do you have available to invest in the development of a franchise program?

Under $50,000	0 pts.
$50,000 to $100,000	4 pts.
$100,000 to $150,000	6 pts.
$150,000 to $200,000	8 pts.
Over $200,000	10 pts.

7. How many years of management experience do you have? Assign 1 point for every year of management experience up t o 10.

8. How much *actual* cash would a franchisee need to open one of your units, not including financeable portion?

$400,00 or more	2 pts.
$200,000 to $399,000	4 pts.
$100,000 to $199,000	6 pts.
$50,000 to $99,000	8 pts.
Less than $50,000	10 pts.

9. The market for your business or service is:

Local	2 pts.
Regional	6 pts.
National	8 pts.
International	10 pts.

10. Your industry is:

Highly competitive	1 pt.
Moderately competitive	5 pts.
Minimally competitive	10 pts.

Ratings

0-39: NOT READY FOR PRIME TIME. While you may have a potentially sound business concept, you have not yet conclusively demonstrated its readiness for franchising. You should concentrate upon refining the business, perhaps with the aid of professionals and experts in your industry. You may perceive that an enormous market awaits your business, but a hasty decision to franchise now could be unwise.

40-59: CLOSE, BUT QUESTIONABLE. Your business is on the borderline. It may need refinement prior to franchising. Several components are already in place, yet your likelihood for success is in doubt - probably due to your inadequate capitalization or high investment requirements on the part of a franchisee.

60-79: A RISING STAR. Your chances of success in franchising appear quite good. It looks a as though you have a franchisable business.

80-100: LOOK OUT, McDONALD'S! Your business has outstanding potential for rapid expansion through franchising. You appear to have a sound concept, a broad market, and sufficient capital to make it happen. Go for it!

Copyright © 1987 by Francorp, Inc. All rights reserved.

Acquisition of Distressed Assets

Some private company investors have been extremely successful in buying assets from creditors or through various bankruptcy proceedings. It is not my style to do so, because I think of myself as a creator of assets rather than an acquiror. Yet, I am fully aware that such transactions may be the single most profitable area of private company or asset investment. Fortunes have been earned through the acquisition of assets from the Resolution Trust Corporation and now the Federal Deposit Insurance Corporation. Indeed, some of us find it disgraceful that the RTC and FDIC, as agents of the taxpayers, permitted sales to occur at levels generating such quick and easy profits for the buyers. If there was ever a need for there to have been an entrepreneur in government, it was in the management of the RTC.

Even operating in the asset creation end of things, I am forced to be involved with enough pain and anguish on the part of entrepreneurs and Angels so as not to want involvement in situations which have their roots in the financial loss and possible destruction of others.

41

Those reading this may be surprised at this idealistic, unrealistic, or perhaps quixotic sentiment expressed by one who no doubt they have come to think of as hard-bitten, tough, callous, money-grubbing, and so forth. I am tough. One has to be to survive in commerce, which is an environment that is often hostile. But it is one thing to be a tough survivor in competitive situations, as I am, and quite another to deliberately search for benefits from the greed, stupidity, or just plain misfortune of others.

Newsletters, Magazines, and Other Publications

Every industry has at least one newsletter or periodical. One or more of these publications are often essential reading for anyone who wishes to stay abreast of developments in the particular industry. Most of these publications are not angled toward the investor. However, their editors and writers are normally responsive to queries on the part of investors. Needless to say, they may not be wiling or in a position to actually recommend specific investments, but often they will steer the private company investor to individuals who can provide them with the information they seek. If the Angel has identified an industry in which profit margins can be expected to be both satisfactory and maintainable, all the Angel needs is to be directed to companies enjoying or anticipating expanding revenues.

Bill Berkley told me how he felt about the importance of reading in the following way.

> Imagine a man who goes into a pet shop and buys a tank and hundred dollars' worth of ornamental fish, but won't bother to buy a booklet on how to take care of them. This is how most individual investors invest in private companies. They don't know what they are doing. Unfortunately, it is not the same as investing on the stock market. Essentially all that is needed [in stock market investing] apart from funds are common sense and a certain amount of knowledge that can be gained from reading. The private company investor needs a broad overview of what is happening, what is going on in the business, what deals are being made, what they look like. This in an investment in itself, of knowledge and time, and may take place over years. I do not mean 10 hours a day, but reading on a regular basis over a period of time to learn what is going on. Most investors like the excitement of private deals, but do not understand the commitment of time and learning required in order to participate in a success-oriented way.

Or as the placque on my wall reads: CAPITAL PUNISHMENT IS THE RESULT OF INADEQUATE INVESTMENT RESEARCH.

Getting to Know Entrepreneurs

Entrepreneurs are not hard to meet, and they are perhaps too easy for Angels to meet. Almost by definition, entrepreneurs are open people. Both entrepreneurs and Angel investors in entrepreneurs generally have no reluctance whatsoever to share experiences with others. The experienced Angel knows the dangers of the game and welcomes the association of others with money and intelligence. It is for this reason that I am developing an Internet web home page and an association for Angels, as I mentioned previously. Membership in the association, with the possible title of Venture Investing Angels (VIA), will be restricted to those qualified by experience and resources. As with successful entrepreneurs, successful Angels have no choice but to keep themselves open to experience and listen carefully to what new information providers have to say.

Also being created--or, more properly, resurrected in a new electronic media--is the *Association of Venture Founders* (AVF). AVF, too, will have an Internet home page; its membership will be restricted to those having played a significant role in the creation of one or more successful businesses.

Essentially, private company investing is a people business. Go to people who can introduce you to people. Invest in people you can rely on in a personal sense. When Angels have selected an industry they feel comfortable in and decide has extraordinary growth potential, being. I hope, ever mindful of profit margin maintenance, they can ask the suppliers to that industry to recommend entrepreneurs and investments to them. After all, few people know an industry better than those who sell to it. Thus, wholesale meat or vegetable suppliers can be an investor's best guide to a promising new restaurant opportunity, or certainly to the experience and character of a restaurant's proprietor.

The Importance of Contacts

Almost without exception, professional venture capitalists and others who invest, rather than lend, will confirm that very few deals are done, let alone seriously looked at, without an introduction or endorsement being involved. Members of the "venture clan" tend to cooperate and co-invest with one another, with one of the members of the group effectively syndicating the opportunity to the others. One of the motivations for operating as a group is that of risk sharing and lightening a little of the career concerning burden of individual decision-making. Professional venture capitalists tend to have herd instincts. similar to those of other professional investment managers. Reliance on their own decision-making and judgment is essential to Angels because only future events will demonstrate the wisdom of their investments. Unlike the Angel, the lender normally has collateral to provide security and justify the risk assumed relative to the anticipated return. Lenders seek only the difference between their cost of money and the interest or rent received for it. This limited-return possibility is the primary reason that lenders are so reluctant to provide capital to entrepreneurs, other than to those dealing in asset-related transactions. The approach of entrepreneurs who deal in real property and the redeployment of assets is very different from that of entrepreneurs who develop concepts and build companies. Almost by necessity, those dealing in current assets are more financially and legally sophisticated than those dealing in the creation of future assets. Entrepreneurs who deal in assets, like lawyers, tend to look backward to precedent rather an forward to future events to gain confidence as to value.

Dealing in hard assets is frequently a matter of deriving benefits from the mistakes of others, such as in the case of both borrowers and lenders in the RTC and FDIC fiascos. Sellers are either making a mistake in selling if the property subsequently increases significantly in value (institutional sellers typically do not have the buyer's motivation, energy, vision, sophistication, or economic power to cause change) or are simply recognizing loss incurred at the time of acquiring the property. In the case of dealing with assets, the gain or loss is typically a function of the buy decision, and not subsequent occurrences. Of course, the seller may be the smarter party to the trade. My grandfather, a very successful stockbroker circa 1898-1928, advised me to always assume that the seller of a stock is at least as equally well informed as the buyer as to the future prospects for the company.

The entrepreneur building a company from scratch must depend on financing from those who have been convinced that the entrepreneur's view of the future will evolve. A large part of this conviction comes from "knowing" that the entrepreneur is not going to do something that will embarrass or harm the provider of funds. Thus, the investor relies on the integrity of the entrepreneur, and this integrity is the matter implicit in all introductions and endorsements. An intro-duction or endorsement is in part a warranty. Entrepreneurs are well advised, therefore, to obtain as many introductions and endorsements as possible, particularly from people themselves in positions of trust, such as Angels, bankers, and attorneys. Providers of capital, howev-er, need to inform themselves on the depth of knowledge of the per-son who provided the introduction. Of course, Angels should never lightly give an entrepreneur an introduction to fellow Angels. They will eventually not be thanked by them if their fellow investors subse-quently lose money on this entrepreneur's project.

Contacts are vital to the Angel. The great advantage professional investors have over Angels is that they can check out deals and peo-ple more quickly and effectively--thus the formation of the associa-tion of Venture Investing Angels. After all, knowing people is the professional's stock in trade. Angels find it easier to make contacts than do entrepreneurs, because Angels have something to give those from whom they are seeking information, whereas the entrepreneurs are frequently viewed as people who only want something from everyone with whom they come into contact.

Community Guarantee Corporation

While preparing to address the College Executive Forum in Utica, New York, I had an idea how communities might reflect their atti-tudes and at the same time make themselves more attractive to entre-preneurs (or others) considering establishing a business within the community. The idea is for 1,000 or more residents to each pledge or invest $1,000 in a community guarantee corporation (CGC). The CGC, which could be managed by residents successful in founding and managing their own businesses, would guarantee loans for incoming businesses in return for a revenue or profit-based fee. The fees would be ongoing after the loans were repaid, thus adding to the capability of the CGC to guarantee more loans for new businesses. No single exposure would be more than 10 percent of the CGC's capi-tal. Perhaps the CGC could further bolster its lending ability by bor-rowing. The lending institutions funding the guarantees should be wiling to accept less than a total guarantee to demonstrate their own willingness to assist in the business establishment process so vital to an increasing number of communities suffering from a decaying, debilitating deindustrialization caused by factors seemingly beyond their control.

It was also in Utica that I first became aware of the needs and potentials of the American Indian nations. Reservation-based gaming activity is a natural exploitation of the "sovereignty" of reservations. My thought was, why not establish private banks on reservations? Why should Cayman have all the fun and profit? Also, it might be possible to create businesses on reservations offering non-FDA-approved drugs and medical treatment.

Chapter 4

EVALUATING THE INVESTMENT OPPORTUNITY

"Big" and "Small" Concepts

Professional venture capitalists, usually acting in the capacity of being a fiduciary (responsible for the capital of others), frequently take the position that they wish to invest only in companies that have the potential of $100 million in sales. This position is taken because they are usually considering investing solely in companies they hope will go public, possibly even becoming major companies. Professional venture capitalists must achieve a significant return on the money they invest and, like any investor, must keep the number of their investments within a manageable number. The postinvestment monitoring of private company investments is critical to investor loss prevention or minimization. The average venture capitalist's pool certainly exceeds $10 million, and investments are often limited to a $250,000 minimum to keep the number of investments within bounds. Venture capital pool managers also recognize that they will have to invest significant time in companies they have funded.

For information on the kinds of investments sought by a general partner of a major international venture fund, see Appendix G.

Angels with $50,000 to $250,000 to invest in private companies should realize the "bigness" of the prospective investee company's concept to the capital they have available. Clearly, there is no sense in investing a large amount of money in an enterprise that will generate for the Angel, assuming everything goes well, $20,000 a year in profit. There is nothing wrong with $20,000 a year worth of extra income, but there is no reason to invest more than a few thousand dollars in something which has the potential of generating only $20,000. The company's concept has to be big enough to make the investment worthwhile. It's obvious that a correlation must exist between the size of the investment and the size of potential of the prospective business.

As a general criterion and Angel objective, I would require a company to have the realistic potential for a tenfold return on investment to the investor in a five-year period. An investment appreciating ten times in five years produces a 58 percent internal rate of return (IRR) or compound annual average return, and is usually only achievable through the assumption of significant risk. Yet, there is nothing sacrosanct about this rule. Exceptions are made for companies where the potential is less but so is the risk. Angels consistently hitting singles are likely to have a better overall result than Angels consistently going only for home runs. At the other end of the spectrum, non-leveraged equity deals made with an expectation of a five-year hundredfold return on the investor's money are most often silly. The greater the expectation, the greater the probability of disappointment.

Small ideas are worthy of investment if they require a small amount of money, time, or risk.

The Not-for-Profit-Only Investor

Angels whose investment decision is premised on something other than achieving a maximum return on their investment are the major source of funding for new companies. Of the more than 700,000 new companies started in the United States annually (probably only half of these are able to hire even a single employee), less than two percent have any professional investor input or participation. In other words, the professional investment and venture capital community is involved in only a presumed maximum of 4,500 new companies each year. Actually, the major venture capita organizations are involved in fewer than 500 startups annually. It is worth remembering also that of the 30,000-plus public companies, there are regularly quoted markets for fewer than 10,000. We are a country of independently owned businesses. It's all part of the American dream and tradition.

Who finances all these new companies other than professionals? Relatives, friends, business associates, and Angel-like informal investors are and have always been the primary source of funds. However, relatives and friends form by far the largest category. Apart from cases in which entrepreneurs use their own or personally borrowed funds, my guess would be that relatives and friends finance over 80 percent of new businesses. If a knowledgeable source suggested a 95 percent figure, I would not be surprised. I also would not be surprised if family funds, cradle equity, greatly surpassed the amount of friend-generated funds.

Relatives or friends are really not-for-profit-only or perhaps even obliged investors. The investment is not one which they would normally seek out or choose to participate in were it not for the relationship.

Since the majority of new business ventures fail to achieve success, relatives and friends must assume that the opportunity they are being asked to consider will also probably fail to achieve the projected and desired results within anything like the business-plan-projected time frame. This assumes, which I doubt in most cases, the existence of business plan. In addition, because most business failures are due to insufficient planning and, as a consequence, inadequate funding, the relatives and friends must expect that the goals of the new company will not be accomplished with the amount of money originally estimated or provided.

It does not take much imagination for the relative or friend to see how such an ongoing demand for more money to sustain a faltering enterprise could put a strain on the personal relationship as well as, if acceded to, place the provider of the money in financial jeopardy. In order to preserve friendships and familial relationships as well as one's capital, it is better to *donate* the funds requested, with the specific statement and understanding that no subsequent investment will be made to protect the money already "invested." Although this may amount to effectively giving the money as a gift, it is better, for the nonobliged, and certainly for the obliged, Angel to psychologically write off the amount as a loss and go on to other deals than to become embroiled in a continuing financial disaster. Of course, if the enterprise is successful, the recipient of the funds always has the option of repaying or re-transferring, the money and/or sharing appropriately the rewards of the investment.

Not-for-profit-only investors, who should really be described as being "sponsors" or "patrons," should first, however, insist that the entrepreneur prepare a business plan. In so doing they will be doing the entrepreneur a great favor. The sponsor can then base the amount of money they provide upon the apparent viability and requirements of this plan. In the case of sponsor-based financings, family and friend investors will not want to negotiate with the entrepreneurs for their own maximum advantage or, as normally would be the case, shift the reward balance in their favor. They would not wish to penalize the entrepreneur for risk, charge high money rent, or put in place the same sort of penalty clauses for nonachievement that they would with an entrepreneur to whom they were not related. Here, investors genuinely want to help and are not seeking a maximum or even normal return on their investment. I suggest a contract which simply states that the entrepreneur will, at some point in the future, either return the funds or provide the investor with an appropriate interest in the business, leaving the amount of interest and equity up to the entrepreneur. If the deal works out, the parties can easily be satisfied; and if it does not the loss has already been emotionally recognized by the investor.

Some sponsors treat such a request for funds not as an investment but as they would a personal loan. They provide the money but do not tally it as an asset on their personal balance sheets. To look upon the transaction as a loan to a friend without high expectations of getting any of the money back is generally a much more realistic approach than to expect to secure, enhance, or recoup the investment through further cash infusions.

To whatever extent possible, tax considerations should determine the deal structure, since losses will probably develop and may be more useful to the investor than the entrepreneur recipient of the funds.

Almost inevitably, more money will be required. Further investment based upon that often used rational of "hostage ransom" for the initial investment is the worst basis for investing in anything. Investors or obliged Angels who find themselves compelled, for whatever reason, to make the initial investment must themselves ensure that they will not feel equally compelled when the second, third, fifth, or tenth calls for money are made. It is vital for the Angel that the recipients of the funds know that the Angel is making the full commitment at that point in time. The capital-consuming entrepreneur should be made to understand that, even at the risk that the money which has been "invested" will be lost or jeopardized should the Angel fail to reinvest, the Angel has no intention of reinvesting. Should the new business prove to be a success, investors, of course, can always change their minds.

Investing in Development-Stage Technology Companies

In addressing the broad topic of investing in technology, one should first consider the primary reasons *why* informed and rational investors should take an action that could result in significantly increasing the investor's risk of loss. Few investors focus on the specific justification for investing in opportunities which have little or no current earnings. The simplistic answer of achieving a greater gain potential in technology-based investments must be understood.

Is it a matter of the investor wishing to be associated with the excitement and glamour of something new and different? Is it an attempt to profit from the madness of crowds? Is it a bet on the greater fool theory, which presupposes that there always are other less informed and less sophisticated investors than ourselves who will only later discover that which we already know? Or can it be the even more Machiavellian ploy of enticing other less sophisticated investors to invest in situations because, at least, in part, depending on our own perceived status, of our own investor presence? It is certainly true that the presence of highly visible, and presumed to be sophisticated investors prompts investment by others, many of whom presume themselves to be less informed than the investors upon whose judgment they are relying. No, these are not the rational and responsible reasons for investing in technology, though in each there are elements of truth.

The professional manager's primary reason to invest in technology is, or should be, the existence of a reasonable basis for projecting extraordinary profits; these profits would be made possible by the demand for the ultimately developed product. Most importantly, the predicted technological advance must be sufficiently unique so that the company will be able to enjoy the benefits of noncompetitive pricing.

The principal reason to invest in something new should be the opportunity it offers to escape, or at least postpone, the burden of competitive pricing. This is what patents and the lure of investing in intellectual property driven companies is all about. If one holds a patent, or exclusive knowledge of how to make something, and if there is a substantial demand for the product, one can price that produce without regard to the cost of production. The owner of the developed technology does not have the burden of having to be an efficient manager or producer. How many pharmaceutical companies can be described as efficient? For the most part, their profit margins

51

are a function of not having to compete in price to sell their patent-protected products. This situation is fortunate, since very few technology-oriented entrepreneurs excel in management skills.

Earlier technological innovations, such as those commercialized at the time of the Industrial Revolution, enjoyed a similar advantage. If one created a truly superior tool, vehicle, or means of communication that was protected by law or circumstance from the perils of competition, could not much-superior-to-market rates of return be earned? These superior rates of return were possible not necessarily through efficiency of production, but rather by virtue of an ability to charge whatever the market would bear. The market usually bears any price which still results in an improvement in user productivity, convenience, or pleasure.

Investing in technology is simply another means of attempting to find, or create, a means of benefitting from a monopoly on intellectual property. If this is the case, then perhaps it is worthwhile to observe some of the usually longer term results of investing in monopolies.

Monopolies are wonderful for their owners during their early and successful stages. It seems to make little difference if the monopoly is the result of a grant or award, the acquisition or concentration of competing factors, the exclusive ownership of production or supply source, so long as there is market demand. Such demand can already be present, or be created or stimulated through marketing or natural factors. As time passes, monopolies tend to deteriorate, atrophy, and become bureaucratic and thus inefficient. Then they become subject to dismemberment or various asset-rationalization programs.

Due to pricing elasticity and the lessened need for efficiency, the investor naturally wishes to he the owner of a monopolistic company, given an attractive acquisition price. However, the investor must recognize that free competition causes the continuation of both social and corporate progress. Without such competition, we would all be forced to suffer many more businesses managed with the same efficiency as artificially competition-insulated or typically subsidized railroads, utilities, and government departments.

If successful in both technological development and marketing, high tech equals high profit margins--and that is the attraction for the professional investor. I am not always clear on the distinction between investor and speculator. I do, however, define professionals as people who spend all their time in pursuit of a goal associated with a process, and who derive continuous income from this pursuit. Professional investment managers are typically dealing, as fiduciary agents, utilizing assets other than their own. They are, therefore, burdened by career security and advancement concerns that can, and frequently do, interfere with the balancing decision of investment risk acceptance versus gain prospect.

I believe that there is insufficient professional or institutional investment and speculation in technology. A clear indication of this situation is when the investment portfolio contains only winners or only the best-known technology-oriented companies. The presence of a number of losing positions indicates a willingness to explore. This is not to say that losses should not be taken and positions not cleared out. Positions certainly should be reviewed constantly. But playing safe on everything is not as constructive as taking a broader view Of course, over time, in the aggregate, substantially more money will be made than lost if the investor is to be successful.

Investing in technology is, to some extent, a numbers game in that it is almost impossible to predict most future events. This is particularly true when the prediction relates to new and evolving combinations of technology and human resources. The obvious conclusion therefore is that the investor's best policy is one of diversification. Because most human endeavors fail--and certainly fail to meet the hopes and expectations of the initiating forces--the spreading of risk has to be appropriate in the pursuit of capital preservation and appreciation. Thus there is an implied obligation to spread risk, and thereby also increase the investor's exposure to success. This is particularly true if one believes that inflation will reappear in the near future. The specter of inflation requires fiduciaries to adopt more aggressive investment policies than those with which they would usually be comfortable. The prospect of inflation requires performance as a means of capital preservation.

To some investors, diversification represents speculation, because it forces investment in other than save harbors of well-known names. On the other hand, this often results in one of the least predictable investments producing the greatest return on investment. Therefore, a portfolio of intelligently selected and diversified speculations seems to be appropriate for investors wishing to profit from future events rather than being subject to them. Of course, managing such a portfolio is labor-intensive, but I believe the effort justified. I feel that the greater risk is in not investing in technology.

There is probably an obligation to society for fiduciaries of major institutions to invest in technology and thereby influence the future. If banks are required by law to invest through making loans within their community then other fiduciaries should be required to invest in companies engaged in activities which, if successful, will benefit the larger community. Such support will be well-rewarded if the investment manager is wise and lucky. One cannot discount serendipity, nor does one have to be lucky to profit from being a prophet--although it certainly helps.

During periods of war and national crisis, governments sponsor creativity and development. In periods of peace, when normal economic pressures force governments to focus on balancing the political demands of haves and have nots, the private sector must assume leadership in financing the future.

Technological development is happening so fast, so much more quickly than before, that keeping one's mind in tune with current events is increasingly difficult. Everything that has to do with technology seems to be moving so quickly that only those directly involved can be truly aware of the nuances of announced developments. Even more difficult is the economic assessment of those developments that are believed present but that have not been announced officially or authoritatively. What, then, are investors to do? Can they participate in the future without having to become technologists? This problem can be dealt with in the same way as when a business needs the advice of a specialist in something; the business identifies its needs and sources of talent, surveys and selects, and hires or retains the talent needed. In the end, it all comes down to people. People selection is even more critical in technology investing than it is in other management exercises.

Investors should make valuation judgments about their present or prospective holdings as if they either held all the shares in the company or had the ability to do so. Investors should continually compare total market capitalization valuations. Private company investments and public company investments can be compared easily, and the premium for that which is quoted can be measured precisely. I strongly believe there should be a significant market capitalization premium for technology investment opportunities that have the advantage of liquidity associated with being quoted.

The privately owned technology company has one significant advantage over companies that have gone public--being free from the pressures of uninformed investors and brokers to produce positive financial results more quickly than orderly technological development dictates. Technological progress should be management-scheduled, and remedial action by the board of directors should be taken in the case of consistent management non-achievement of projected results. However, there should not be investor pressure for premature product announcement, revenues, or profits. It is very difficult for the directors and managers of technology-driven companies to withstand pressure from investors. The investors are forever seeking reassurance regarding levels of revenue and profit to be achieved within a time frame shorter than is realistic.

There seems to be an inverse relationship between the level of technological understanding of investors (and many stock brokers) and the market valuation they are willing to pay. Of course, investors would happily settle for a profit on their shares and usually prefer that to having any real concern for the profitability of the company. In the absence of continuing share price increases, public shareholders demand immediate earnings and asset realization results from the company. No doubt, in some cases, certain members of the management of the company have been guilty of provoking the natural greed of the investors to persuade them to become investors in the first place, and thereafter will justly have to put up with responding to inquiries and prods.

The use of so-called loyalty shares in some initial public offerings addresses this issue. In this exercise in financial creativity, investors who agree to continue to hold their shares for a stipulated period automatically receive "bonus" shares or warrants from the company at the end of the period. Although clever, this is not altogether meaningful, since the bonus shares cause dilution. But it sounds good to investors and helps them to be more patient.

Entrepreneur Enthusiasm Is Catching . . .
Investors Beware

To be even a fledgling entrepreneur, an individual must possess powers of persuasion. Typically, entrepreneurs can also persuade themselves of almost anything. The investor catches the enthusiasm and is swept along in the project, frequently forgetting the risks and the probability that projected results will not be achieved. The enthusiasm of the entrepreneur is to be guarded against. I used to keep a sign on the wall in my Singapore office: ALL LOANS APPEAR

SOUND AT THE TIME OF THE GRANT. I only wish my manager there had fully understood its meaning.

Good advice for Angels, even those who like to get things done immediately, is to wait one week after negotiating the final terms of a deal before executing any document. During that week, the Angel should compile two lists. The first should enumerate the good things that can occur to the company being financed and the effect of those good things on the earnings, . The second should be a list of the bad things which may possibly thwart the efforts of all concerned. Inevitably, the list of bad possibilities will be longer than the list of good ones, but that in itself should not dissuade the investor, since it is the probability of occurrence that counts more than the raw possibility.

The making of lists jointly by the investor and entrepreneur as to that which can go right and wrong is a good idea, both prior to the investment decision and afterward, perhaps even on a monthly basis, in order to anticipate problems and to update the business plan.

The business plan should be viewed as a working document, not simply a means of raising capital. In many cases, the primary function of the business plan is unfortunately only to obtain an audience with a prospective capital provider. The plan should be updated monthly, and, from this, the investor can learn the entrepreneur/manager's areas of strength and weakness in projecting various aspects of the different elements of the business. Values indicating the probability of achievement should be assigned to projections. Clearly, those projections of events occurring further in the future will be assigned lesser probability weightings than those occurring sooner. However, certain business areas can be projected more easily than others. Among the more difficult are those under the control of others, such as sales to customers and the development of anything new or different.

Investors should beware the entrepreneur who pretends an ability to foretell the future with perfect clarity. Professional venture capital providers are amused by business-plan projections carried out to the last dollar and cent. Reid Dennis, the managing partner of Institutional Venture Partners, tells of being put off by an entrepreneur who have the clear impression of never having made a mistake. A man who sees himself to be free of failures may just have chosen not to recognize them--and if he cannot recognize failures, he cannot deal with them or learn from them. One cannot stress the need for entrepreneurial integrity too much, and part of integrity is being honest with oneself.

"Blunder Forth"

Some of us who should have "Blunder Forth" as our company mottos are really not-so-closet excitement junkies who enjoy courting danger. This must be the case, because more thorough investigation and planning could remove a large element of the risk of involvement in new ventures. This omission raises the question of whether or not a significant number of entrepreneurs are self-destructive. I suspect many are. Of course, being action-oriented rather than contemplative is part of the entrepreneur's macho image, and maintaining such a derring-do image can itself be destructive.

Frequently, the entrepreneur substitutes his intuition for study and personal conviction for research. This display of ego is responsible for many unnecessary mistakes. New ideas are fun to conjure up and satisfying to put into play, but old ideas, improved upon or applied in different areas, usually are better business. The successful entrepreneur normally is able to define and articulate his "edge" or particular niche advantage.

The losses an entrepreneur can avoid by planning can be thought of as profits earned. Being price competitive is not as constructive as being product or service superior. Promotional flair, so necessary in the marketing of most new products, can be studied for technique but seldom practiced effectively by those not inherently promotional by nature. To be successful, the entrepreneur and the Angel must understand profit margin analysis and cash flow projection. Without knowing the ingredients of profit, timing, and magnitude or revenues, an entrepreneur's success becomes an exercise in serendipity. Adequate funding permits options, and options are normally a requirement of success and, frequently, of survival. And misplaced pride, reflected by an unwillingness to admit and correct a business error or predictable failure, often results in increased self-inflicted "capital" punishment. Failure analysis is a vital part of failure reduction. If one doesn't know what went wrong initially, how can one fix it the next time?

Investor Expectations Versus Entrepreneur Expectations

One can have an excellent business idea, the quality of which may soon outgrow the individual with the idea. This is the classic case of the Angel who has the concept but not the ability to create the business. Investors must never forget that they are investing in the business and not in the product of the business--that is, investors must never fall in love with the product concept. They are really investing in the entrepreneur as a person, betting that the entrepreneur can transform the concept into a profitable ongoing business. If you are not a good judge of people, you will probably not make a good investor in private companies.

One hears that excuses must be made for geniuses. Geniuses probably cost investors much more money than they made for them. Angels have to recognize what they are investing in. They hope to find an individual who has the ability to manufacture a product or create a service and sell that product or service at a profit. The world does not beat a path to the door of the manufacturer of a superior mousetrap. Geniuses are terrific, but businesspeople are relieved that most of them are in academic life, because they clutter up the commercial landscape. Typically, a lot of debris follows the genius-turned-entrepreneur/promotor.

A neat and thoroughly prepared business plan is a favorable sign that the entrepreneur is competent, at least as a planer and possibly as a marketer. I like to meet entrepreneurs in their homes and have some sort of feel for their family lives and relationships before making an investment. If they cannot maintain some sort of order and discipline in their personal lives, they are unlikely to be able to do so in their professional lives.

The investor should be able to like the entrepreneur/manager as a person; although I believe it is a mistake for them to become social friends, certainly in the early stages of the relationship. The adversarial relationship between money and management is inherent in business. Some of the hard decisions investors are going to have to make can very quickly become clouded by friendships developed with the entrepreneur/managers. It is very hard to reach a decision under the best of conditions that managers must be replaced or that their role must change as a condition for investing needed new money and it is that much harder when an investor has become a friend and confidant of the manager and manager's family. Good decisions are hard enough to make on an impersonal basis, and they are almost impossible to make when there is a heavy level of personal relationship.

The argument that the relationship between investor and entrepreneur is similar to that of a marriage is answered by the fact that nearly two-thirds of all marriages fail and that investors can reasonably expect strain in their relationships with entrepreneurs. Investors want to like entrepreneurs, want them to succeed, and want their relationship to be amicable. However, their relationships are complicated not only by failure but often also by success. Entrepreneurs may grow to feel they have given Angels too good a deal and become resentful of the profits earned by them, conveniently forgetting, or possibly never having understood or recognized, the risks investors originally assumed. Joining a country club is a wiser way to make friends than investing in private companies.

Investors must look for a certain toughness in the entrepreneur, entrepreneurs must be realistic and have backbone. For example, managers or prospective managers with a present business position might be asked how many people they have fired in the past year. If they have not fired anybody, is it because they are not sufficiently demanding? People are a commodity in the business world, and excellence within an organization is dependent upon continually improving through training, motivating, and upgrading the staff. Such decisions are never pleasant to make, but if one is not willing to assume responsibility for continually upgrading the human resources of a company, one is not ready to assume responsibility for running a company.

While the relationship between investor and entrepreneur may be naturally adversarial, it need not necessarily be unpleasant. Investors should make it clear from the outset they are businesspersons. They should be direct, precise, and never vague. Investors must listen carefully and remember everything they are told, and, for this purpose, it is a very good idea for them to keep a notebook for each of their private company investments. After a while, an interesting library will evolve.

A loose-leaf or flimsy notebook is much less effective for Angels to use than a well-bound substantial notebook, which is suggestive of permanence. By visibly taking notes during meetings and conversations, investors are proclaiming their expectations that there will be a large amount of accountability required. Obviously, a certain amount of intimidation is involved. Everything of importance that the entrepreneur/manager tells the investor should be logged in, both before and after the investment is made. If these points are not logged in, investors have no really effective means of knowing what they believed prior to making the investment and during the early stages of the business. Angels will, in all likelihood, be called upon to make an additional investment, and, at that point, they need to be able to judge both the predictive and operational ability of the entrepreneur. If entrepreneurs prove to be consistently overly optimistic, according to the entries in the notebook, investors probably should discount any projections that they are making and, perhaps, walk away from the deal. Records kept of a successful business startup can be a useful future reference source for both investor and entrepreneur. Conversely, the log of a failed business venture can provide equally valuable information and may even represent evidence of what the investor was told when induced to make the investment.

A notebook is a way for investors to let the entrepreneur know that they are taking seriously what they are being told, and that they will hold entrepreneurs accountable for what they undertake to accomplish. Investors are not trying to entrap the entrepreneurs, to get them to say something they did not intend to say, or to make glibber projections than they wish to make. They are simply forcing them to be precise, and thereby establishing the good communications that are an absolute necessity between the owner and user of the investors' money.

The first conflict between investor and entrepreneur is likely to occur in negotiation for interest in the company. After startup, frustration, concern, and conflict may be expected if the first level of projections are not achieved. These may not necessarily be earnings projections--they may be projections of when equipment will be installed, when a secretary will be hired, when certain studies will be delivered, when auditors will deliver their report, or when lawyers will finish a contract. Since the entrepreneur most often has made in good faith, the projection that has failed to materialize, Angels, before reacting, must make sure they understand what exactly the original projection was and who or what was responsible for its nonachievement. Just as important, Angels must understand the significance of the failure. They should certainly not permit themselves to become the "heavy" over a minor item. Yet, it is perfectly appropriate for the Angel to say to the entrepreneur, "John, in our meeting six weeks ago, I indicated in my notes your statement that the lawyers would finish the contract by this time, and now you tell me that they say they need another two weeks. Don't you think we should try another law firm for future contracts?"

Investors can come up with constructive suggestions in cases where delay is costing the company money. They are a captive partner in the business. Although the investment the Angel holds may be a debt instrument, an unsecured creditor in a private company should be treated as a partner in the business. Even while Angels are contributing constructive suggestions, they must remain aware that their most important role may be the one of holding entrepreneurs accountable for their projections, When the call comes for more money, the investor has to be able to develop a judgment of the entrepreneur's ability based upon his track record.

Some of the unachieved projections may be beyond the control of everybody involved. However, such explanations merit close examination. For example, if equipment was not delivered on time through no apparent fault of the entrepreneur, had he checked with the shipper two weeks before scheduled delivery to make sure the equipment would arrive on time? It is one thing for equipment to be late and quite another to discover a few days beforehand that the equipment will not arrive on time and find it is now too late to make alternative plans. One of the chief roles of any manager is to ensure freedom from surprise.

A common area of contention is the involvement of the entrepreneur's family in the business. One aspect of this is putting members of the family on the payroll. I see nothing wrong with this, so long as they are paid a fair, not exorbitant, wage and so long as they pull their own weight. Some investors take the view that family members on the payroll are detrimental to the company because of the attitude of other people within the company toward nepotism. Because of the dedication and effort required from a manager to make a new company successful, I think it is beneficial for the spouse to be involved and have a sense of participation.

As long as the business is going well, an investor can only benefit from an entrepreneur's identification with the company, and that identification is obviously heightened when it is a family affair. The problem arises when the business starts going badly and investors, by virtue of their having to invest additional money, find themselves in a position of increased influence and control in the company and decide that part of the problem is the entrepreneur himself. The greater the sense of personal identification, the more difficult it is to dislodge the entrepreneur/manger.

Members of the entrepreneur's family are frequently at odds with the investors, because they see the effort, anxiety, and involvement of the entrepreneur and do not see with the same level of appreciation the fear, concern, and risk assumption of the investors.

A situation that frequently evolves is where the entrepreneur's spouse poisons the entrepreneur against the once loved Angel. The spouse and the entrepreneur often feel, and sometimes express, that they should not have given so much of the company to a person who simply wants to make a profit--to the investor it's "just an investment," to them it's "their lives." The entrepreneur often feels that the Angels are undeservedly getting a higher rate of interest on their money than a bank or others would charge. All too frequently, the entrepreneur, now that the business is successful or its prospects more attractive, would like to replace Angels with new ones and, of course, on terms more favorable to the entrepreneur.

Differences often arise when the investor requires the entrepreneur to issue personal guarantees, which in some cases is neither an unreasonable request nor an unusual one. From the investor's standpoint, it remains an open question whether the entrepreneur should be financially at risk in the venture. Some professional investors think that too much pressure on an entrepreneur is a bad thing, whereas others will invest only in situations where the entrepreneur has something significant to the entrepreneur to lose as well as gain. I have found that entrepreneurs are primarily ego-driven and that they work neither more nor less hard when they are at financial risk.

One disadvantage of putting the entrepreneurs at financial risk is that this can give them the status of being a creditor of the company. Such an entrepreneur-creditor with the right to attend and participate in creditors' meetings could use his minor holdings to become a major nuisance in winding up a company's affairs or in selling it.

One straightforward way for the investor to seek guarantees is to require the entrepreneur to become a personal guarantor of company obligations if a particular ratio falls below a stipulated level (for example, if sales as predicted by the entrepreneur, of a certain amount are not achieved by a certain date). In other words, entrepreneurs who are in a position to do so, undertake an obligation that is contingent upon the passing of a certain event which they claim is within their control and which then becomes a factor in the investor's decision to invest.

There should be a contract or shareholder's agreement that provides investors with the right to change management and the functions of management at such time as their investments are placed in jeopardy. The investor should have increased control or influence in a business in inverse proportion to the achievement of projections.

How the Entrepreneur Should Care for the Investor--After the Check Is Cashed

Is it necessary that the personal relationship between the investor and the entrepreneur deteriorate as the investor is exposed to reality? I do not believe such need be the case. Animosity, frustration, and embarrassment result frequently from an Angel's feelings of betrayal and cause a fracture in the personal relationships; therefore the entrepreneur loses a valuable asset. That valuable asset is the goodwill of the investor and associated willingness to invest additional funds in the entrepreneur's project. In this section, I suggest ways in which the investor can be more intelligently treated by the entrepreneur than is usually the case.

To better understand how to treat the entrepreneurial investor for the mutual benefit of both the entrepreneur and the Angel, one must try to understand the probable mind-set of the investor in a private company. First, it must be understood that the initial investment has probably been made for at least two different and divergent, if not conflicting reasons. One reason is the desire to earn a greater return than can reasonably be believed to be available from liquid investment opportunities. The second reason is to help the entrepreneur. It is my experience and observation that the investor is more likely to be successful in the second objective than the first. This is not the appropriate time to inventory the list of things which can go wrong and which will result in the projections on which the investor ventured not being achieved. We all know many of the problems. What we want to do is to explore ways in which we may deal with the investor's likely frustrations and potential bitterness.

Intelligent information transfer and timely communication are my prescriptions for a continuing happy (or at least satisfactory), healthy, and nondestructive Angel/entrepreneur relationship. What I mean is very simple. The entrepreneur should prepare the Angel for realism, frequently spelled the same as disappointment. The entrepreneur should, better than most, know what the investor anticipates. Remember, the investor will take the entrepreneur's "best case" projections and think of them as the "most likely case" or even "worst case" projections. This is so, in part, because the entrepreneur will always tell prospective investors of how conservatively the projections have been made. The investor likes to think that entrepreneurs have been overly conservative in the projections they have given the investor. Entrepreneurial investors are like the rest of us. They most frequently permit their "wishes to become the parent of thought."

The entrepreneur recognizing this must constantly assert realism by discussing fully the problem areas and the areas wherein expectations are likely to be frustrated. I am certain that the management policy which permits only good surprises is not only the best way of running a company, but is certainly the best way of running a relationship with investors.

Specifically, the entrepreneur should establish a regularly scheduled series of communication elements with the investor. These communication elements should be both written and personal. I am a strong believer that monthly newsletters with charts should be sent to Angels. The charts should be the reflections of a living business plan. The charts display previously achieved results, current period results, and projected results, as well as new or amended projections.

Entrepreneurs should not be frightened by the need to constantly project. The need to project is part of the need to plan. Only those of us fortunate enough not to have had to rely on investing Angels in their business can afford the extreme and delicious luxury of having "blunder forth" as their corporate motto. Also, the entrepreneur making the projections should be the person best able to list the reasons why the projections may not work out as honestly expected. There is no reason why they should be reluctant to share the negative possibilities with those who are depending on them to enhance their investment and lives. Entrepreneurs should not, though they frequently do, think of themselves as being superhuman and having an ability to fully control their lives and environments.

The problem, of course, arises as a result of what has been told Angels in order to induce them to invest in the first place. Incidentally, I believe that the problem is not the honest presentation of expectations, but rather the failure of the deal to be structured in such a way as to equitably recognize the various interests in the event the situation works out better or worse than was anticipated at the time the deal was negotiated. In other words, Angels made certain assumptions as to their probable future profits. These assumptions were based upon information and semi-promises provided by the entrepreneur. I believe Angels are entitled to receive what they paid for, to the extent the entrepreneur can provide it. The entrepreneur can in fact frequently provide this result by adjusting the interests held in the company to accommodate the facts as they evolved versus the promises made to induce investment. In a well-structured deal (from the Angel's standpoint) entrepreneur largess or voluntary equitable treatment of the investor is not required, as it is already in the investment contract.

Back to communications. The entrepreneur should meet with the Angels at least quarterly, and probably monthly, for the purpose of keeping the investor within the family and delaying, for as long as possible, the development of the destructive, though perhaps inevitable, "we (the doers) versus they (the capital providers)" syndrome. Once the we/they thinking has developed and the camps become established, the problems begin. Entrepreneurs should do everything possible to have Angels play a role that keeps them feeling that they are on the entrepreneur's team and are in fact making a contribution. To the extent possible, the Angel's worst fear--that of being thought of as a sucker-source of funding--should never be permitted to evolve. The Angel is frequently more concerned with being thought of as a sucker or fool than of losing money. (I believe this is one of the reasons there is so little litigation brought by Angels, even where justified.) If the problems of the company in achieving objectives are fully and fairly understood by Angels and they feel that they are on the team, they will possible be available for additional funding and certainly not be as resentful of the need for it as would otherwise be the case.

The textbook "what if" list of things which can go wrong, kept updated, is another good idea. Certainly, the management has or clearly should have such a listing, formally maintained or not. Why then should the Angels also not have this list of possible horrors? After all, they are an owner of the company and before the closing should have been told it was for better or for worse. Should they not have the pleasure of relief when one of the horrors fails to materialize? Frequently Angels have no idea of how close they came to disaster.

Entrepreneurs can ask their Angels to help: help to gain information, help to gain customers, help with public relations and, on occasion, help with personnel matters. The entrepreneur should recognize that in most cases the Angle had to have been competent in some areas of activity which are, or can be, useful to the entrepreneur's company to have made the money which is being invested. A knowledge of the Angel's strengths should be in the entrepreneur's asset file.

A positive outcome is still possible when Angels fail in their appointed, or volunteered for, assignment. In the failing, they will be more understanding of the issues confronting the company and the entrepreneur. This does not mean that the Angel should be asked to do thing which are likely to fail. It does mean that the Angel's own failure can be carried by the entrepreneur as a future psychological credit and used at some point in the future.

Another suggestion for the entrepreneur is to have the Angel make occasional presentations on behalf of the company. These presentations can be to prospective employees, investors, customers, or suppliers. The point is to get Angels to publicly identify themselves as a team member.

When the entrepreneur/manager of a business travels, particularly to places the Angel may think of as desirable or glamorous, it would be well for the investor to be informed of the reason for the trip. No one likes to think they are being a patron for others' pleasure without their knowledge or approval. Sales trips to San Diego are difficult to explain to investors enduring northern winters. Similarly, overseas trips are frequently suspect, particularly when the company is not yet profitable in its domestic business. In these cases, it is worthwhile to make a special report to the Angels.

I can just hear some of you thinking "What kind of Angels are these who need all this babying?" or "How am I to run the company if I have to spend my time placating Angels? After all, if they had enough confidence to invest in me in the first place, then they should leave me alone to get on with running the business." Well, my friends, it ain't so. The average private company investing Angel wants, and needs, to feel loved, as the second reason he invested was to help the entrepreneur. That is a very dangerous and personal sort of thing. Angles can easily feel betrayed and forget the reason why they invested, which was to profit extraordinarily. One of my favorite sayings is "No good deed shall go unpunished." Imagine the venomous feelings generated when the Angel feels embarrassed, used, abused, disappointed, and betrayed.

I do not believe it possible for the recipient of early high-risk-funding to say "thank you" enough or to comment to others, within the earshot of the early Angels, how grateful the recipient is for their early assistance and the confidence they demonstrated.

If the entrepreneur has deceived the Angel in the early stage of the company's development, and even if the company subsequently becomes successful and the Angel is enriched, it is a mistake for the entrepreneur to admit to the Angel the deception. I once monitored a panel on which sat an entrepreneur I had financed and whose business was then widely believed to be very promising. The entrepreneur, in his opening remarks, told the audience how he had exaggerated the early prospects of the company (though they later developed) to impress the Angels. From that moment onward, I never trusted him and ceased to be his champion.

Christmas cards and inexpensive gifts for Angels make sense. Don't send expensive gifts, as the Angel is all too aware of whose money is being spent. Similarly, entertainment of the Angel charged to the business should be reasonable.

Another and final idea--why not name a room, conference room, or lab in honor of the investor? Who wouldn't be flattered? It only costs a plaque.

Dealing Successfully with Inventors

One of the more common business relationships, particularly in new technology-driven companies, is between inventors and entrepreneurs.

The inventor is concerned with developing a different, if not unique, method of creating a product or process. The methodology must be sufficiently different from what has been recorded as having been accomplished previously to permit the establishment of either a protectable patent or know-how which can be kept secret. Inventors are ever fearful of competitive discovery, and the resulting usurpation of what they believe are their earned rewards. Inventors are trained not to make divulgences, not to trust those offering assistance; they usually try to hold back key elements of information as insurance against the theft of their intellectual property. Inventors also have been known to withhold divulging elements of their knowledge to assure their future and continuing importance to and position with companies. The inventor typically is a solitary worker and thinker; seldom is invention a collegial effort. Inventors are concerned that those with whom they ultimately deal in the exploitation of their developments will not fully or adequately recognize the genius of the development and therefore not be motivated to invest sufficient effort or resources in commercializing, exploiting marketing the invention.

Entrepreneurs are frequently burdened by a need to prove something to someone in terms of succeeding in a project. They are driven to succeed. They are not necessarily themselves inventors, or even possessing of the right brain dominance associated with creativity. They are observers, surveyors, creators and exploiters of opportunity.

They are planners, even though they may not be able to fully articulate their plans and/or prepare a business plan. They are seekers of expandable and protectable niches.

The strength of the relationship between entrepreneur and inventor is based upon the significantly different personality characteristics. The commercial weaknesses of one are complemented by the strengths of the other. It is a natural relationship in terms of the personality characteristics usually found in those having such specific skills and tendencies.

Although inventors do not usually have the natural instincts of a business manager or entrepreneur, they are distrustful of how well others do and will perform these functions on their behalf.

Entrepreneurs, though they may have little technical learning or knowledge, are not shy about suggesting improvement and thus give inventors the impression of their having been taken over and controlled. Inventors find being controlled intolerable, as they are frequently concerned that "their last good idea will be their last good idea." It is this fear of non-future inspiration that creates the paranoia. The entrepreneur, on the other hand, believes that whatever happens in the activity in which he is presently involved, he will be able to create even greater opportunity in the future.

Both the entrepreneur and the inventor understand rejection. They deal with it differently. Inventors take it very personally, because the idea being rejected was the fruit of their brains, their babies, their egos. Entrepreneurs, on the other hand, have the business as their baby. It is the business which must succeed. Although there is great identification with the business on the part of the entrepreneur, there is not the same feeling of being personally rejected, of having their own ideas and beliefs scorned as being invalid when an order is not received or a contract not consummated. For the inventor, the rejection is, must be, taken very personally, because it is really the inventor, and not the product, who is being rejected. Even when inventors are successful in creating a relationship, it is usually, by its very nature, one where inventors receive only a small part of the selling price of the object representing or using their invention, and they are therefore in the position of often resenting, as being too small, their level or return versus what they believe they should be receiving.

It is this great sense of personal involvement and feeling of being not sufficiently appreciated that makes it so difficult for inventors to deal successfully in many business relationships. Here are some rules

I follow when dealing with inventors.

1. Recognize that the development is the brainchild of the inventor. They are proud of it and hold great hope for it. Never criticize the basic idea. If the idea is to be rejected, it is best to do so on the basis of a projected unfavorable economics or production or on a believed inability of the market to recognize and accept commercially the merit of the product.

2. Insist that the inventor be represented by a trusted and commercially sophisticated advisor of the inventor's selection. Do not negotiate a final agreement with an inventor who is unrepresented by an appropriate advisor.

3. Make an honest attempt to share with inventors the true economics of the development in which their invention is a part. Inventors frequently have an exaggerated view as to the level of profits that are derived by a manufacturer or distributor. The inventor should be made fully aware of the relationship between the royalty or compensation being paid to the inventor and the profit after all expenses, including amortization and depreciation, earned by the party paying the inventor.

4. Encourage inventors to be forward-looking and not retrospective in their viewpoints. What will be the next area of their focus? How will they be able to improve on the existing development, or will they be able to find other and better ways of meeting the same user need as the present product? The more inventors look forward, the more realistic they may be regarding the value of their last development. It is the fear that the last will be their last which requires inventors to place a high premium on the contribution. If they believe they will be as, or more, productive in the future, they will be easier to deal with.

5. Understand that inventors may actually be correct in their business, marketing, or production insights. They have probably thought about the specific problem, the One for which they have at least a partial solution, longer and more intensely than you have.

6. If possible, use the inventor's name in the promotion of the development. Provide inventors with as much positive recognition as is consistent with good business, recognizing that inventors are artists in that they create rather than reproduce. The major difference between the successful inventor and entrepreneur is the inventor's ability to continually develop new ideas, whereas entre-

preneurs probably make the most amount of money if they can continue to do something repetitively, unburdened by the need for continuing creativity.

7. Force the issue of freezing the design. Do not let the inventor delay production or distribution while tinkering to develop the perfect design or product. Plan an improved product before releasing the initial product, and have the inventor immediately focus on the next generation.

8. Be certain that inventors maintain an awareness of relevant developments. Use inventors as advisors, as they may be able to provide useful insights. An agreement to advise can be a part of the basic compensation package.

9. An ability, on some predetermined basis, to terminate a relationship is useful and can be addressed in the original agreement. The ability to terminate or buy-out does not indicate a requirement to use the agreed-upon basis if a more favorable one can be negotiated. The originally agreed-upon basis is simply insurance.

10. Do not promise anything to an inventor that you are not sure you can accomplish or provide. The inventor is frequently childlike in a willingness to believe and therefore subject to great disillusionment and subsequent contempt and bitterness if disappointed. It is always better to foster conservative expectations than ambitious ones.

These guidelines should be helpful to those structuring a contractual royalty, as well as a direct working relationship, with an inventor. They are based upon my experience and observation. There are no hard rules in dealing with any group of people. However, because inventors are often subject to the largely noninnovative industrial development process of larger companies, and therefore receive frequent "not invented here" syndrome responses, they share common characteristics.

Entrepreneurs and inventors need each other. Perhaps, through the gaining of additional insights, hopefully giving rise to constructive consideration of their individual and mutual needs, they can more successfully accommodate each other.

What Is the Investor Betting On?

Howard Stevenson of Harvard summed up this concept in his interview with me.

My personal opinion about investing, whether it be the stock market or startups or real estate, is that you need to know what you are betting on. You should be able to write down the five things you are betting on. These factors might involve the adoption of a new technology or the emergence of a new market; for example, in a real-estate deal you may be betting on your ability to rewrite the leases or a decline in interest rates or the passing of a new zoning law.

The investor might even imagine himself being asked to write a short account of his investment for *Fortune* or *Forbes* (or, of course, *Venture*). What exactly is he betting on? What does he consider to be within the control of his management? Can volume of sales or projected profits be undermined by lack of cost control and inventory control? How sound is the basic business concept?

Economic Potential of the Opportunity

The important aspect of evaluating an investment opportunity is how the economic potential of the opportunity relates to the amount of money and/or other resources to be invested and the risk associated with the investment. Angels must never lose sight of the fact that they must evaluate the opportunity relative to the *total* amount they will be called upon to invest, recognizing that they will in all probability have to choose whether to reinvest or suffer significant dilution. The amount of money invested in the startup stage will probably have to be increased 5 to 10 times to bring the company to a semi-mature stage. Angels will have to invest their time and energy, as well as their money. Will all this be better than earning a trouble-free return by investing in an aggressive mutual fund?

Investors must be clear in their own minds about what their interest in a company means to them, and how much they wish to be involved in the affairs of that company. They must not confuse their objectives, as the investor, with those of the entrepreneur, and they must maintain their vision of where the company can go.

The risk factor must be carefully examined by investors. Having accepted the risk levels involved in a private company investment, Angels should then compare the expected returns from that venture with those from another investment of equal risk but with a far lesser degree of involvement and greater liquidity.

Advice of Experts

Before investing in a business, all investors have to question their own level of expertise in the area. For example, if an entrepreneur claims to be an expert engineer, does the investor have enough personal knowledge to determine whether this is a valid and sensible claim? If they cannot decide themselves, do they know where to find the answer? Most Angels sooner or later will find their own managerial capacities brought to the test in judging the performances of entrepreneur/managers. To be a good investor in other people's businesses, you have to understand your own strengths and limitations. You should not permit yourself to make an investment in people without having the ability to make a valid judgment about them.

Many experts are willing to sell their time on some basis to investors. The more technical the subjects are, the easier it is to identify an expert. They are recognized authorities who contribute to journals on the subject, who teach the subject at universities, or who work in the field or a closely related field for other companies.

I always like to hear what someone who knows a particular business has to say about the person I am thinking of investing in. The "acid test" is the one in which the person knowing the subject of the investigation is asked if he would invest his money under the control of that individual. You won't find out if you don't ask.

An expert may be found or retained for Angels by their law firms, investment bankers, or management consulting firms. Many of the larger management consulting firms profess an ability to provide expert advice in almost any area. A well-known and respected academic's daily consulting fee ranged from $500 to as much as $5,000. Their total feel will probably be very small in comparison to the amount being invested in the enterprise, while their advice can go a long way in improving the decision-making process regarding the investment. The cost of such advice is generally tax deductible, as are most expenses incurred in investigating a possible investment, so long as the investment qualifies as being a business and not a hobby.

Academics are usually more available to Angels than executives in the same business area. The latter, of course, are the real experts but are often wary of those they think likely to be competitive with them. A retired executive who was well placed in a company with a business similar to the one of interest can contribute valuable advice, both on a one-shot and ongoing basis, and frequently on very favorable terms.

Legal Representation

I recommend that arbitration provisions be included in contracts rather than leaving disputes to be settled by litigation. Arbitration is frequently a more cost-effective procedure, although at times court litigation can yield a more favorable result. However, you may need advice on whether to go to a regulatory agency, a state body, or a courthouse, especially if you feel that a fraud has been perpetrated. The friend you went to college with and who is now such a cracker-jack tax lawyer will probably not be the person you really need. The Angel should avoid the general practitioner of law and go to a corporate lawyer with corporate finance expertise. Because it is a critical decision as to who represents the Angel, it is perfectly reasonable to ask attorneys whether they have previously represented Angels in the size of transaction in which the Angel is involved. As well as avoiding lawyers with too little experience, the Angel must avoid those accustomed to representing venture capitalists in deals worth millions of dollars, because such deals may have little relevance to the smaller scale problems of the typical Angel. Ideally, lawyers should be familiar with their client's investment from the initial decision to put money into the business and should have advised in preparing the contract. It is also reasonable to require that the entrepreneur accept the investor's attorney as attorney for the company after the deal, if the investor is providing the bulk of the funding.

For information on attorneys who specialize in these types of transactions, see Appendix H.

However, I think it is a mistake to ask for most lawyers for business advice. Lawyers are trained to search in the past for comfort-providing precedents and, therefore, tend not to be very forward-thinking. Typically, lawyers will find a reason to advise their clients against going into almost any transaction, because they are often exposed professionally to the problems rather than the joys of business, and therefore see the worst-case side of the deal. Lawyers' perspectives are affected by their awareness of the history of transactions that produce disagreements and losses. Lawyers must be regarded as useful servants by the Angel, but as nothing more in terms of investment decision making. An experienced lawyer's advice is invaluable to an Angel in how to go about becoming involved in deals upon which investors have already made their decisions. The extent to which a lawyer should be actually involved in negotiating the transaction is open to discussion.

For a discussion of legal documents of venture financing, see Appendix I.

An Entrepreneur's Guide to Dealing with Lawyers

The relationship between lawyer and entrepreneur client is difficult, especially for less-experienced entrepreneurs, to master. Because lawyers are so important to the entrepreneurs, it is important for entrepreneurs to attempt to find ways of working successfully with the person on whom they depend so completely, particularly in the early stages of a developing business.

Why is the relationship so difficult? What makes the level of customer of client satisfaction frequently unsatisfactory, and what, if anything, can be done about it? First, let's consider the psychological, intellectual, and financial self-interest points-of-departure distinction.

The relationship usually begins when clients contact lawyers for assistance in accomplishing a specific objective. Clients know what they want to achieve. If they are typical entrepreneurs, they want the objective accomplished very rapidly. Being controlling personalities, as are most entrepreneurs, they quickly become frustrated when confronted with obstacles and tend to blame the person pointing out the problems. Although intelligent entrepreneurs do not want a "yes" person for an attorney, they do not want to have to sell their attorney on their ideas or projects. The entrepreneur wants an advocate more than a counselor. Entrepreneurs usually see their situation with clarity, perhaps with oversimplification. It all seems so simple to them. They are frustrated when others cannot or will not see it their way. Remember that entrepreneurs, usually during the period they are spending the greatest amount of time with their lawyers, are in the fund-raising mode. In this mode, the entrepreneur is likely to frequently be on the more or less receiving-end of rejection. Such rejection and/or waiting for responses from funding sources, that seem to move with glacial speed, do not put entrepreneur clients in the best of moods to be told why things can't be the way they want.

Lawyers have both a responsibility to and a possible liability caused by their clients. Lawyers may want to be an advocate and emotionally the ally of their clients but frequently feel they can best be of service by remaining aloof, identifying the problems, and thereby effectively saying "no" to their clients' wishes. Lawyers have been trained to seek comfort only from precedent. They have been taught that if a body of competent authority, a court, has found a result to be "right," then it is right until a body of higher authority reverses the decision. Therefore, lawyers believe that what has been found correct is correct until otherwise decided. Entrepreneurs, of course, are in the business of looking into the future and feel they are very much a part of the future. They are more interested in causing future change than in being bound by the past. Almost by definition, lawyers and entrepreneurs are opposites.

Entrepreneurs must, to be successful, be creative; One has to reject established and authoritative source beliefs and, at times, facts. The creative person finds ways around obstacles, rather than simply identifying their presence and, perhaps, searching for paths others have used in circumvention. Lawyers' successes depend, in part, on being well organized, on being able to keep many different matters neatly in their minds and files. Their businesses depend upon their reputation, and one of the prized kinds of reputations is for dependability and practicality. For lawyers, there is more to lose than gain in seeking the brilliant but very different solution; it may subsequently prove indefensible, and even if it succeeds, their colleagues are likely to describe it condescendingly, and perhaps a bit enviously, as an "aggressive approach that happened to work." Lawyers live in a community of peers, and peer judgement is important to them. Entrepreneurs have forsaken community judgement to pursue what they believe is right, acknowledging it to be different and therefore probably better. Entrepreneurs know intellectually they may fail, but believe the odds, due to their skills and superior vision, favor their success. Their failure is that of a businessperson in a business. It is not as fiduciaries giving clients who depend upon them advice that turns out to be wrong and therefore damaging to both the giver and receiver of the advice.

Now we come to another significant problem area: time. Time is the commodity the lawyer has to sell. Time, itself, has no relevance for the entrepreneur. Entrepreneurs are prepared--no, want--to spend every waking hour pursuing their destiny, developing their project, managing their company. They know not from hours or schedules. They are compulsive, driving, and driven. They have one project that is vitally important to them. They really don't know psychologically how to deal with the professional who has other clients, especially during periods of their need. They view their attorney as their advocate, friend, ally, co-conspirator, father figure, and comrade-in-arms. It is therefore distressing to the entrepreneur when, at the end of the meeting, the next client appears, also demanding of the same intense attention.

On the subject of time, it should be noted that one of the problems is that some attorneys habitually underestimate, to the client, the complexity of an issue or process, partially as a means of selling their services. They recognize that the client wants the job done quickly and inexpensively. Therefore, a little like "bait and switch," they indicate that the process will be about 20 hours or $3,000, when indeed 100 hours is more likely to be the count and therefore $15,000. In all fairness, lawyers frequently have an almost impossible task in accurately forecasting the amount of time a matter is going to require. The client frequently withholds information that would have helped in the forecast, either out of ignorance or in an attempt to make the job look simpler than it is, and therefore less warranting of a high fee.

Another problem is one of the entrepreneurs. They read situations quickly and focus on finding solutions rather than problems. In their own minds they become almost as or, at times, more knowledgeable about relevant law than their lawyers. Not unlike prisoners in jail, entrepreneurs will actually study and become expert in the aspects of law that are important to them. They will be prepared to debate these aspects of law, and frequently the supporting decisions for the position they want to take. It is almost inevitable that as the lawyer explains the law to the client and describes the rationale for the adoption of positions, the client becomes more educated, but having a different mind-set than the lawyer, reaches different conclusions.

The client is frequently in the position of the "wish becoming the parent of the thought," since entrepreneurs are only focused on achieving their objectives, and the basis for boilerplate is of little interest to them.

Finally, money is a problem. Attorneys have only their time and, of course, knowledge and experience to sell. The attorney is not usually, by choice, a partner or shareholder in the client's business. This is not to say that attorneys do not frequently become interest holders in the client's business. They do, but frequently as creditors. It is to say that attorneys, as professionals, want to be paid, in cash, and within reasonable time after presenting their bills for the services rendered. However, putting cash availability as an issue aside, entrepreneurs are only objective- and achievement-focused. They are concerned with their own personal sacrifice and therefore and not likely to be impressed with the attorneys', or other of their associates', sacrifices made on their behalf. The word "associate" is key. Entrepreneurs see all who work with them as being team members. In their minds, team members win when the team wins, and it is almost against the best interests of the team for any of the members to take assets out of the game before it is over.

Of course, most entrepreneurs are too sophisticated not to understand intellectually the difference between fellow equity-owning team members and a professional advisor. Nevertheless, what I have described is how most entrepreneurs really "feel" about the relationship with lawyers and, to a much lesser degree, accountants. It is the lawyer who becomes so vital as the presenter of the views and wishes of the entrepreneur. It is the lawyer who is forced to be in the position of controlling people who have become entrepreneurs specifically, consciously or otherwise, because they couldn't stand the thought of being controlled by an employer or circumstance. If only the lawyers understood never to say "you can't" or "never" to their entrepreneur clients, they would keep some of those clients longer and the relationship would be more mutually productive.

It is really, however greatly emphasized, a case of entrepreneurs wanting to know "how" their wishes are going to be achieved, and not why they "can't" be. Lawyers might be well advised to team-advise their entrepreneur clients, with one partner, wearing a white hat, presenting possible methods for progressing, and the other, wearing a black one, presenting the negative or "can't do it" options. Of course, the firm should be prepared to supply a continuing progression of nay-sayers, because the entrepreneurs will usually wish to have "another" opinion and sooner or later another opinion-maker. The advocate is likely to keep the account longer even though they may not be as good for the client. The problem with the team approach is one of the increased hourly charges.

Incidentally, certain of the major Wall Street-type law firms have this gambit worked out to a science. During one negotiation, I remarked to a fellow board member that no one had ever seen a lone lawyer from one particular firm because they always traveled as a brace, pride, gaggle, flock, school, or herd. This law firm seemed to have a young briefcase carrier (and, at times, apprentice briefcase carriers) for each of their more experienced warriors, and also a senior medicine man for each of the specialty areas. Other than myself, no one seemed too upset by the specter of ten lawyers focusing on minutiae, because the company was publicly owned and responsibility was being shed at a fair price to those in the room.

77

In the case of public companies, where the owners are absent, the professionals have a field day, being able to exercise fiduciary responsibility in a most profitable manner. If senior management of publicly owned companies received bonus payments based upon professional fee economies, which are usually directly within their control, as opposed to being continually and willingly seduced by the professionals, fees would be much lower and the quality of decision making would remain at least constant.

The following suggestions are offered as a means of reducing the potential for friction and misunderstanding between entrepreneur and lawyer.

1. The entrepreneur should provide the attorney with a written statement as to what exactly is desired. The attorney then should respond, in writing, as to what is involved in accomplishing the desired result, estimating the associated costs. The entrepreneur must realize that additional work will incur additional fees and that changed or broadened assignments also change the original estimate. The nature of the relationship, being frequently dynamic and responding to unpredictable external stimuli, is one where hard estimates are difficult to obtain and should, in fairness, be viewed skeptically.

2. The attorney should keep the client advised as to the state of the billing meter. How many hours were spent or invested by the lawyer each week? Was there more or less time consumed than had been estimated? Attorneys know how the meter is running. They should let the client know. This is not to say that clients should be billed weekly, but they should know their own "burn" rates. The client should be aware of the hourly billing rate, and of all associated expenses, of the various people working on matters for them. A client can be "associated" to death by permitting the indiscriminate use of associates to "research" peripheral elements of a transaction. It is wonderful training for the associate and may possibly be of value to the client. It is also possible to find oneself in the position of using a partner to do work which a paralegal could perform. The client is the master, or should be; and the lawyer should remember that the client is the customer, and as such, must be satisfied as to both result and process. If lawyers believed that clients could themselves be sources of repetitive business if treated fairly, the quality of the relationships would, in many cases, be different. How many entrepreneurs continue to use the first lawyer with whom they came into contact? Why

haven't they? The lawyer's assumption that much of the business from entrepreneurs is essentially one-shot has something to do with the way the business is handled. Also, as the attorney is fully aware, once a matter has been commenced with an attorney, it is difficult for the client to move it to another lawyer.

3. There should be a specific understanding, committed to writing, as to any reduction or increase in fees if the desired result either does not occur or is achieved in some better-than-originally-expected fashion. Both project abandonment "kill" and greater than anticipated "success" fees are legitimate areas for candid discussion between client and attorney, before the event of representation.

4. The issue of attorney participation in the client's business is a difficult one. I argue from experience that it can work to the client's detriment to have the attorney as a profit participant, because then his focus is on the level of enterprise profit to be earned rather than on the level of risk being accepted. On the other hand, there are excellent reasons, mostly those of motivation, for clients to want their advisors to share in the same profit source as does the client. I think that it would be best to also use a non-profit-participating professional as advisor to the board in cases where there is an advisor involved who holds an interest in the company and who happens to be in that position due to having earlier performed professional services for the company or its principals.

5. Termination of service is also a fair subject for discussion between clients and professionals. The client should know if there will be any problems with changing lawyers of calling in other lawyers to help. Will the entrepreneur's lawyer insist on being fully paid before releasing documents to the client? If so, then perhaps it is better to keep only copies of original documents with the lawyer. The originals can be kept by the client in a secure place. Will the lawyer want to be fully paid before cooperating with the successor counsel?

6. Terms of payment should be agreed to. The seeking in advance of credit for legal service is acceptable if there is a good understanding, on both sides, of the magnitude of effort their client expects the lawyer to invest and/or speculate. Although a lawyer's bill does not necessarily have to be taken as the point of departure for a negotiation, the client should request a breakdown of the specific charges that went into the bill. Clients must come to understand how many hours they are buying every time they either

make a request or permit the lawyer to "look into" something.

7. Entrepreneurs do not do a good job of interviewing prospective legal representatives. They frequently do not ask for references of current clients or the identity of prior clients. They should. The retention of a lawyer is a vital step, and lawyers are critical to the success or failure of the effort. Their records should be reviewed with the same diligence and concern that would be used in the hiring of a senior associate, or in a manner similar to what the prospective investor would use to investigate the entrepreneur. There should be a very clear understanding of the level of responsibility being undertaken by lawyers in advising the client. Do lawyers have specific expertise in the area of all or most of the client's needs? How much experience have lawyers had in the required areas of the law? Will one or more specialist attorneys have to be used? Will they be from the same firm?

8. Conflicts of interest become increasingly prevalent in the case of clients wishing to use attorneys representing prospective investors or lenders, as well as competitive firms. The client should seek an understanding and possibly a commitment on the part of the attorney as to how conflicts will be resolved in case they arise. If the lawyer is offered the account of the bank from which the client is borrowing, will the accepting of the account give rise to a conflict? If so, which account will be cast aside by the lawyer?

9. I do not believe it unreasonable to request an undertaking from the professional to the effect that the professional agrees not to represent or provide assistance to any party with whom the client is litigating for a mutually agreed number of years after the attorney's retention has ended.

10. It may be important to determine, in advance, if attorneys will agree to serve as members of the board of directors. As important, will they agree to retire as directors if asked to by the person appointing them?

The relationship between client and lawyer has the potential to be extremely valuable to the entrepreneur. The value will be influenced by the candor and intelligence used in establishing and maintaining the relationship.

Chapter 5

Evaluation of the Entrepreneur and Management Team

Purchase Agreement Representations and Warranties by the Company

Angels have a right to believe what entrepreneurs seeking funding tell them. As a extension of this, Angels have a right to recover their investment, to the extent lost, if it can be shown that the entrepreneur misstated or failed to bring to the Angel's attention information that might have changed the angel's mind about the project.

Although it is the company that must provide the representations and warranties, I believe it is reasonable to require entrepreneurs to do so as well. After all, they are essentially the company and are going to be the primary beneficiaries of the funds the Angel is providing. It is also a good idea to get the entrepreneurs' attorneys to provide, to whatever extent possible, their "opinion" as to the factualness and completeness of the statements made by the company.

The headings for the following checklist were kindly provided by Jim Bergman, general partner of DSV Partners. They may be too comprehensive but provide an idea of the points to be covered.

Organization, standing, and so forth. The investor has to know that the company is empowered to be in business and do the things that are necessary to earn a profit. Articles of incorporation and bylaws will have to be provided and reviewed. The Angel has to be careful that all of the company's subsidiaries are accounted for, because an unmentioned subsidiary may have liabilities for which the company is responsible.

Qualification. A company should be licensed to do business where it does business, or a statement should be provided indicating that its lack of license will have no material adverse impact on the company's business, and so on.

Financial statements. All the financial statements (and footnotes thereto) that have been provided should be a form acceptable to the Angel or, more probably, to the Angel's counsel and accountant. If the Angel is investing in an on-going business, that company's accountants (actually their insurance company) have a good deal of liability in the event that Angels lose money and can show that audited statements presented them were inaccurate due to the auditor's failure to investigate and confirm. This is, of course, the virtue of an audited statement for the Angel.

The Angel should not, in my opinion, be a "nice guy" or "good loser" when losses occur. If it can be shown that any of the professionals providing service to the company, or to the Angel, failed in their duty, they should make good to the Angel. They received payment for professional service after having presented themselves as being professional. As a practical matter, if they believe they have any liability at all, most professionals will be pressured into offering a settlement by their insurance carrier and by the prospect of spending a lot of time in litigation. I believe that Angels generally do not protect their interests to the extent they would if those interests belonged to others and they were responsible as fiduciaries. For this reason, I recommend that Angels think of themselves as fiduciaries of their own money.

Tax returns and audits. The Angel does not want to invest in a company only to find out subsequently that the company has undisclosed tax obligations.

Changes, dividends, and so on. This is simply a statement of fact that since the date of the last financial statement provided to the Angel, no dividends have been declared or paid, nothing of significance has occurred without having been brought to the attention of the Angel *in writing*, and no agreements have been made which might change the Angel's decision to invest, including wage changes and labor problems.

Title to properties. The properties owned by the company are in good repair, and no other party has an interest in them. The

Angel should also know if the company is complying with local zoning laws.

Litigation. The Angel has a right to know if there are any legal actions pending or even threatened against the company. This is a very important disclosure area. All too frequently, Angels find a suit against their new company about which the entrepreneur either had knowledge or should have had knowledge.

Compliance with other instruments. The company and its officers have to state that they are running thebusiness in a manner which is consistent with the law and regulations to which they are subject and with agreements with other parties. It is not possible for an outsider to make these statements, because only those responsible, and the company lawyers, can or should know the details.

Debentures and conversion stock. All instruments issued by the company are authorized, valid, and enforceable.

Securities laws. No violation of securities laws is caused by this transaction, and the transaction is not conditional to its compliance with these laws.

Patents and other intangible rights. Investors must know if the company has the unencumbered rights to the patents and processes that are necessary to conduct the business. They must also know, and fully understand the implications of, the full details of any royalty arrangements.

Capital stock. This is the amount of authorized and outstanding shares, including shares reserved for the conversion of warrants and options. It is in this clause that a statement must be made regarding the existence, if any, of preemptive or similar rights.

Outstanding debt. A full description must be provided.

Schedule of assets and contracts. The descriptions in this inventory of assets and contracts must be full enough to permit the Angel to comprehend their significance.

Corporate acts and proceedings. The company's board of directors and shareholders must have done whatever is required to accomplish the transaction.

Accounts receivables. The accounts receivable on the balance sheet must be real, and the customers must have no valid reason for not paying within a reasonable period. An adequate bad-debt reserve should have been established, and there should be no offsets that would preclude payment of the receivables.

Inventories. Inventories should be fairly reflected in the financial statements and should be priced in a manner known to and agreed upon by the Angel. In this clause, there should be a statement concerning the continued availability of raw materials and so forth.

Backlog. The statement concerning the backlog situation should be of a date immediately prior to the execution of the contract.

Purchase commitments and outstanding bids. The Angel should be aware of commitments already in place that will, or may, require the company to spend money or incur liability.

Insurance coverage. An inventory and description of policies should be provided, including a disclosure of the company's previous relationships with the insurance companies with which policies are carried. As Royal Little advises, "Be sure that sufficient product liability insurance is being carried."

Brokers or finders. Unless otherwise noted, no financial intermediary fees will be paid by the company relating to this transaction. The company will have to indemnify the Angel against any claim by a party know to the company or the entrepreneurs involved for compensation as a finder or broker.

Conflict of interest. The Angel should know if any of the officers or directors of the company have any conflicts of interest due to owning interests or having a fee relationship with any organization or entity with which the company does business.

Disclosure memorandum. This is a statement to the effect that the memorandum provided to the investor describing the business contained only true and complete statements. It is up to the Angel whether he wants "projections" to be warranted and to what degree.

Relationship with employees. Labor difficulties and the potential for unionization of the staff are disclosure points which should be covered.

Disclosure. This is a catchall that reaffirms that all statements made to the Angel are true and complete and that all relevant information known to the entrepreneur has been made known to the Angel.

Investigating the Entrepreneur

Angels should be forthright with entrepreneurs and not wait until the last minute to put questions to them. Angels must be clear as to what answers they expect to their questions. For example, before asking entrepreneurs whether they smoke marijuana or snort cocaine, Angels should have considered their own attitude to the significance of this. In most cases, Angels will find themselves teaming up with a first-time entrepreneur who has no track record or failure and successes. Investigation of such entrepreneurs has to center, out of necessity, more on their personal qualities than business achievements.

Angels should make a list of the questions they intend to ask the entrepreneur. The following areas are worth considering.

1. The entrepreneur should be requested to provide a short biography. This biography need not extend more than four or five typed pages and should include personal, as well as business, data.

2. An investigative agency report of the entrepreneur should be secured. In a leaflet entitled *Investigative Services for Management*, Pinkerton's describes its procedure as follows:

Increasingly management is turning to Pinkerton's for help in investigating the background of job applicants as it becomes more difficult to judge or confirm data appearing on application forms-and even harder to detect the deliberate inaccuracies or omissions that often occur.

Pinkerton's offers two basic types of applicant investigations: *background investigation* for the more sensitive, responsible positions and *personnel investigations* for less demanding, high-turnover situations.

The *background investigation* encompasses the following:

- A thorough check of personal references to determine reputation, family status and other personal characteristics pertinent to the position desired.
- Verification of claimed education, school activities, and grades.
- A financial check to determine credit history, indebtedness and possible civil suits.
- A check on litigation records and criminal records where permitted by law.
- Investigation of past employment record including the determination of job stability, attitude, reputation among associates and superiors, and reason for leaving. Periods of unemployment are also checked.
- Neighborhood background, based on interviews with neighbors to ascertain reputation and conduct.

85

- Check on community activities, including affiliations with clubs, charity organizations and business groups. Establish social habits and reputations.

The *personnel investigation* would cover only three or four of the above areas as considered appropriate and is offered at a pre-agreed flat rate per item.

Because of our network of offices, it costs no more to check an applicant's background anywhere from coast-to-coast than it would on a local basis. Regardless of the city of origin, the investigation is considered "local" to the office responsible for the investigation.

3. Entrepreneurs must expect to find themselves in stressful situations. Have they performed well under stress previously?

4. The entrepreneur should be asked to provide personal, as well as business, references. Friends given as a reference should be queried about the quality of their relationship with the entrepreneur--that is, whether they consider themselves to be friends or merely acquaintances. Angels must make it clear to the friend why they are asking these questions--they and the entrepreneur are starting a new company. The Angel should also ask if the friend would like to invest. And if not, why not? Does this friend know other people who know the entrepreneur? Anyone with whom they have had a disagreement? Anyone with whom they have been in business? Any lawyer or accountant who has done work for them?

5. Does the entrepreneur like to go to Atlantic City or Las Vegas? Does he play the commodity markets? Most good entrepreneurs abhor speculating on random events, insofar as the game of chance of commodity market is random; they like to feel in control of the future. While it is possible for a gambler to make an excellent entrepreneur, a fondness on their part for high-risk speculation should tell the Angel something.

6. Are entrepreneurs willing to take a psychological test? If they object, would they be willing to do so under the condition that they took the test independently and showed the results to the Angel only at their own volition?

For an interview of two investigators of entrepreneurs, see Appendix J. See also Appendix K.

Checking References

Private company investors are buyers of people. They want to back an entrepreneurial manager who has flexibility of mind coupled with dedication of purpose. They need someone who can start a company (for instance, an appliance stare), see it not working out as planned, and in response switch the facility to one the rents appliances and starts a mail order business from the same location.

The entrepreneur the Angel wishes to find has a number of qualities, including a sense of ethics and an integrity fully consistent with those of the Angel. There will be an enormous difference in feeling on the Angel's part about a deal which failed for any number of reasons, and one which failed through malfeasance of its entrepreneur/manager. In one case Angels will feel foolish for having made a mistake, while in the other they will feel anger at having been cheated. Yet, they will know that they themselves could have done something to prevent themselves from being cheated, and, therefore, they have a much greater level of personal responsibility for the loss. They could have checked out the entrepreneur better.

I am not suggesting the fraud is prevalent among entrepreneurs. On the contrary, I know of very few instances of fraud being perpetrated by entrepreneurs who start businesses. They are too optimistic, too future-looking, and too secure in the belief in their own ability to cause future events to occur. The less motivated, more cynical businessman or corporate executive is more prone to take advantage of opportunities to profit at the expense of others and may be less concerned with the consequences. Entrepreneurs may well deceive, but it is usually themselves whom they deceive first.

Integrity is not the only quality required on the part of the entrepreneur, but it is the one always required. As far as I am concerned, when there is evidence of a background problem, I do not accept an explanation such as "I was young and made a mistake."

The Angel should require a list of references from the entrepreneur that the Angel can use as a starting point in looking into the entrepreneur's background. One of two things can emerge from a background check. One is the desire to be in business with the individual being investigated, almost regardless of the nature of the business. The entrepreneur just checks out wonderfully well. My advice is to go with him if you can find any justification for his project. A good person will make it work--even if not in the manner originally contemplated. The second thing that can emerge from a background check is a feeling of doubt. If Angels develop some doubt about the entrepreneur as a person, they should drop the deal. They should simply walk away from in. First and foremost, Angels are buyers of people.

Clearly, entrepreneurs expect strong recommendations from those they have listed as references. Through those listed as references, the Angel can find names of others who know the entrepreneur, and these may be the people who can provide the Angel with the most dependable information on the entrepreneur.

Burt Alimansky of the Alimansky Group asks the entrepreneur for five references, including one who dislikes him, without saying which. We can all think of someone who dislikes us and sometimes with cause. It may be someone we have fired, beaten in competition, or mutually dislike instinctively. From such an individual, a different picture of the entrepreneur may well emerge.

However, the key information to be gained from references is the names of others who know the entrepreneur. One of the outstanding advantages of professional venture capital investment managers is their ability to immediately check out people. It is an invaluable resource. Members of the Association of Venture Investing Angels (www.venvest.com) should find it easier to research individuals and companies. Background checking is very important, and Angels should probably check out the entrepreneur with a minimum of five and, preferably, ten individuals.

James Bergman told me, "In a reference check, most people do not want to say anything bad about a person. However, if you give them the opportunity, they are often willing to name someone who might have something unfavorable to say."

It does no good, or only very little, to ask for references and either not check them at all or not check them effectively. As Burt Alimansky suggested, it may be a good idea also to ask entrepreneurs for the name of one person who dislikes them. The value of the detractors is that they may lead the Angels to others and, thus, cause a more balanced picture of the entrepreneur to emerge. However, the fact that there are people who dislike the entrepreneur should not dissuade the Angel. Running a business is not a popularity contest. I think there is too much concern among executives for being liked; many seem to believe that leadership and popularity are in some way linked.

Integrity, in the fullest sense of the term, is the most critical element with which the reference checker must be concerned. Integrity includes being realistically honest with oneself. It also includes a whole spectrum of dealings with others, not being restricted to whether the subject of the review ever "stole" anything. The further back one goes into the life of the person being checked, the more reliable the results. The reference and background checker is seeking character flaws as indicated by acts, and should not be concerned with snooping into the acts themselves.

I once had the background researched of a prospective employee, whom I unfortunately hired. It was found that he, while in the military, had stolen (used without authorization) gasoline for personal purposes. Now that is not a big thing, especially since it had occurred 20 years earlier. However, I later came to wish I had then recognized the significance of this minor infraction. This individual ended up costing me millions of dollars, because he was basically contemptuous of authority and not terribly concerned with the use, let alone sanctity, of other people's property. He was also not very intelligent, and this I should have noticed, if nothing else, from the record of his mediocre school grades. Yes, school grades can be important in contributing to the whole picture of the individual.

I mentioned this individual's contempt for authority. Authority is an important concept for the Angel and entrepreneur to understand. They would in a perfect world have mutual respect for each other; the world, lacking in perfection, Angels should insist, by their bearing and deportment, on having authority. Authority in this case results from having something--money--that someone wants, whereas respect must be earned. This kind of authority is reflected in power. The Angel's power is their ability to say no.

All too frequently, the entrepreneur is contemptuous of money--or at least the present owners of the money. This is an understandable attitude inasmuch as entrepreneurs have a strong personal image of what they need to accomplish, of the value and merit of their ideas, and of the need for the products or services they wish to provide. After many instances of rejection by those with the money to invest, entrepreneurs naturally come to see themselves as being more intelligent, and those with the money they need as being either too stupid or too greedy to agree to whatever they are proposing. To survive and persevere, the entrepreneur must have many of the same self-protective qualities of the salesman who routinely suffers daily rejections. One can, of course, wade into deep psychological waters here by questioning whether they may have some need to be punished and speculate about that previously noted very strong relationship with their fathers.

89

Reference Check Questions

You should always first tell the person being queried the exact reason for your interest. For example, You are considering investing in a project in which the person about whom you are enquiring is likely to play a major role. Therefore, you, the angel, have to learn something about his background not only to find out whether you should, or should not, invest in the project but also to determine the person's relative strengths and weaknesses so you can try to create a situation and environment most productive for all concerned.

1. When did you first meet _____ and under what circumstances>
2. What was the nature and quality of the relationship?
3. Are you still in contact with _____ and with what frequency?
4. What bad things can you tell me about _____'s performance under pressure?
5. Does he seem to seek stressful or comfortable situations?
6. How does he handle failure or situations that do not develop as he planned or would have liked?
7. In instances of failure or problems, does he tend to blame himself, others, or circumstances beyond his control?
8. When he fails to succeed, how long does it take him to bounce back with an alternative means to accomplish the same goal or with another new idea? Does he get "frozen" into one approach?
9. What can you tell me about the family relationships of _____?
10. Can you think of anyone who might question his integrity?
11. Do you know any people who dislike or have had disagreements with _____?
12. Other than the names of such individuals, can you tell me anything about the problem or disagreement?
13. What are the best things or strongest points you can tell me about _____ from the perspective of a future partner or investor?
14. Have you been able to observe how _____ works with other people? Does he work better with peers of those he is supervising? How does he relate to superiors?
15. Does he complete projects undertaken or does he become distracted?
16. Who do you know who is closest to _____ or in a very good position to provide insights about him?

17. Did you expect this contact and have you had others of a similar nature? If so, from whom? did you tell them the same as you are telling me?

18. What do you think _____ will be doing 10 years from now? What do you think he really wants to be doing 10 years from now?

19. If you had the opportunity to invest, alone or with others, in a business to be managed and possibly controlled by _____, would you invest?

20. If you did not have the money to invest, would you borrow it if there were no interest payments and if you only had to repay, in the case of loss, 50 percent of the amount borrowed? If not, why not?

Although there are other good questions to ask--and still more will evolve from this list--these are key questions that will provide meaningful insights into the character and personality of the entrepreneurs and their relationship to the people whose names they have provided. Remember, it is important to get to talk to people who know the entrepreneurs and whose names they have not given as references.

It is a good idea to make notes during the interview, because it is easy to forget who said what and in which context. You will want to weight the responses as to the nature and quality of the relationships. You may also in the future wish to go back to the listees.

Reference and background checking are the areas of greatest amateur Angel weaknesses. The inherent and intentionally developed advantage of professional venture capital investors is that they are probably a working part of a well developed network of other investors and industrial, academic, banking, and professional contacts that can provide a very quick, detailed, and frequently accurate picture of the subject of the investigation. The informal investor, and particularly the Angel who has some sort of not-for-profit-only relationship with the entrepreneur, is in a disadvantaged position to check out the entrepreneur seeking funding. However, it is vital that the Angel do so because one never really knows another person until there is a shared common experience of stress or danger.

Confidentiality and Nondisclosure

It is only fair to both parties that the entrepreneur be accorded the right to buy from the Angel, at the Angel's cost, all investigative reports and so forth within a 60-day period from the time at which the

Angel and entrepreneur agree that no deal is imminent. During the period, Angels would agree to treat as confidential all such reports and other intelligence developed by them. Of course, material given the Angel by the entrepreneur can be provided on the condition that it remain the property of the entrepreneur, and that the Angel has no right to divulge it without the entrepreneur's permission.

Many entrepreneurs are convinced that they have top secret information and have made major discoveries. This, combined with the fact that rubber stamps marked CONFIDENTIAL are readily obtainable in stationery stores, can result sometimes in a somewhat paranoiac presentation by the entrepreneur to the investor. All too frequently, entrepreneurs request, or even try to demand, that Angels execute a confidentiality and nondisclosure agreement with them prior to their divulging certain aspects, or perhaps the major element, of the proposed business. Angels should not sign anything without adequate legal advice, nor should they, in my opinion, accept anything marked *confidential* without an understanding of what, if any, liability is being incurred. It is not unknown for entrepreneurs to allege that an Angel or prospective Angel damaged them by an unauthorized disclosure of confidential material.

Many major manufacturers require entrepreneurs and inventors submitting inventions to them to sign a "disclosure release." In essence, this release says that the only rights inventors have are those which are covered by their patent application and that are ultimately allowed.

On balance, I would be opposed to the average Angel signing a nondisclosure or confidentiality agreement without there being a very good reason to do so. Angels can always discuss with their attorneys any liability they might assume by discussing with others the results of an investigation they have undertaken, particularly one with negative results about an individual entrepreneur who has not given the Angel authority to make disclosures.

It may be constructive for all concerned if Angels inform the entrepreneur at their first meeting of the minimum investment objectives acceptable to the Angel, as well as the form of investment they usually find attractive. If there is too wide a chasm on broad points, it is unlikely there will be eventual agreement on the details.

See Appendix L for the "Statement of Policy and Procedure for Those Seeking Funding" used, at times, by the Arthur Lipper Corporation. See also Appendix M for the request for prospectus used by Continental Illinois Venture Corporation and Continental Illinois Equity Corporation.

Evaluating the Entrepreneur as Manager

The terms *entrepreneur* and *manager* are often used interchangeably in this book, because in a startup situation or development-stage company these titles are frequently borne by a single individual. Usually, the Angel negotiates with the entrepreneur on the understanding that the entrepreneur will be the company's first manager. In almost all cases, the entrepreneur is initially the manager and then, as the company grows, the managerial function is taken over by others. It is worth noting that one of the major problems of small companies, particularly those that are growing rapidly, is that entrepreneurs fail to recognize that others can do a better managing job than they can.

Many of the entrepreneurs an Angel meets have neither the background nor particular talent for managing a company. They will only rarely have experience as a chief executive officer and commonly will have never had the responsibility of personnel management. Being a good scientist, engineer, or marketing person is not the same as being a good chief executive officer of an entrepreneurial and developing company. It is critical for the Angel early on to determine the breadth of the entrepreneur's skills, and individuals having the experience and skills which entrepreneur lacks should be put on the payroll. The Angel can either suggest these individuals or propose to the entrepreneurs that the entrepreneurs find and attract them to their management team.

Most Common Mistakes of Successful Entrepreneur/Managers

While addressing a group of entrepreneurs, I suggested that many entrepreneurs had difficulty living with success. Afterward, a banker asked me what I considered to be the three most common mistakes made by successful, business-owning entrepreneurs. My answer? (1) Pressing for revenue growth when it no longer comes naturally; (2) failing to provide for succession; and (3) starting new endeavors, most often reflecting their need to prove that they can "do it" again (that is, it wasn't luck the first time).

Establishing Goals for Management

One of the requirements of any successful relationship in commercial terms is that managers, as well as members of the staff, know what is expected of them in the way of performance. Thus, appropriate goals and objectives should be established for management. The best approach is for each immediately senior person to discuss goals and objectives with each immediately junior person, giving the latter a chance to make his own input. When people whose performance is being measured play a role in establishing their own objectives, they will generally establish them higher than those that would have been imposed upon them by the senior person.

The objectives to be achieved by management are not only those of sales and earnings, but include things such as retaining the services of a certain number of engineers by a certain date, concluding the negotiations for a specific contract by a certain date, having a production line up and running by a certain date, and having a sales/marketing presentation package put together by a certain date. To insist on the completion of assignments on schedule is important, because the greatest losses or expenses in any new company are those which are caused by a failure to coordinate properly the use of resources, which include people.

The thought here is that there should be a staging, or scheduling, of expense items associated with specific company activities. To acquire space, people, and other items of expense prior to the time that one is fully able to utilize them is wasteful. A large wall chart showing clearly what is expected week by week is an extremely useful management tool.

Angels should be aware of the activities to be completed by agreed upon dates. If they are not, they will not be in a favorable position to judge the efficiency of management, and whether they should provide additional funding when and if it is needed. Further, only by understanding the scheduling of expenses will the Angel be able to judge the probability that the business-plan projected results will be achieved.

Measuring Managerial Performance

As in establishing goals for the management team, Angels should have more than simply net earnings as their gauge in measuring managerial performance. Lower than projected results in the face of negative factors not anticipated (or even anticipated) in the business plan may demonstrate superior management skills, because without these superior skills management would have achieved even lower returns.

Conversely, higher than projected results are not in themselves necessarily indicative of superior management, because the projected results could have been deliberately underestimated in order to assure management's ability to achieve them, or might have been boosted by a general price rise in the industry which was not anticipated. Measuring managerial performance is one of the big areas in which management consulting firms offer services, and many books have been published on the subject.

In relating to new companies, the Angel must demonstrate a realistic understanding of the problems, and it is up to management to make the Angel aware of the problems and not to blandly suggest that everything is just fine. Entrepreneurs are well advised to treat Angels as true partners, letting the Angel know problems as the entrepreneur and management sense them, rather than waiting for the problems to become fact.

Managerial Compensation

In my opinion, the need to provide monetary incentive for entrepreneurial managers is frequently exaggerated in the mind of the Angel. Of course, entrepreneurs will always present such a need in order to extract the best deal from their standpoint from the Angel. Entrepreneurs are primarily motivated by ego, need for recognition, and need to accomplish objectives. Their overall money interests in the enterprise are set out in the terms of the deal with the Angel, whether it be stock, a share of profits, or whatever. Their actual monthly paychecks (executives should be paid monthly and staff every two weeks) should reflect the amount which they *need* to have to live on a scale roughly equivalent to that on which they lived prior to funding of the company by the Angel. Incremental amounts may possibly be offered based on the achievement of objectives and, of course, also possibly as a percentage of profits earned. However, if this approach is used, the profits-earned factor should include only those profits over and above those that were projected in the business plan and that have already, therefore, been paid for by the Angel, since these were the profits used as an inducement to get him to invest. The entrepreneur should not be paid more than once for the same performance.

I believe that incentive compensation should be on a pool basis, shared among a number of members of the management team and not just exclusively for the entrepreneur. All too frequently, members of the management team other than the entrepreneur are not adequately or fairly taken care of in terms of stock distribution or whatever form the deal takes in the contract between the entrepreneur and the money interests. It is important to develop a team spirit and also not to become too personality-dependent. Therefore, I subscribe to the procedure of allocating perhaps 20 percent of the profits of a company over and above an agreed upon amount to an employed executive pool.

Martin Solomon, a very experienced and successful investor who has had lots of private company investment experience, had this to say:

> Normally an entrepreneur's salary should be set at a level so that he can continue to live as he has before. Only rarely has salary become an issue in negotiations I have conducted. I would wonder about the entrepreneurial qualities of someone who seemed overly interested in salary. He may be more interested in the perks and trappings of a corporate life than he is in creating an important company.

Employment Contracts

Employment contracts typically benefit the employee and seldom the company. In general, they ought to be avoided by the Angels, particularly when they relate to new companies. On the other hand, compensation agreements can be useful to define the basis for compensation. A compensation agreement of this kind is very different from an employment contract that agrees to employ an individual on certain terms for a specified period of time.

An employment contract should not be necessary when dealing with an entrepreneur who has a continuing interest in the form of equity in the company, except when the contract may be used in conjunction with the shareholders' agreement. For example, certain equity givebacks from the entrepreneur to the company will result in the event of certain objectives not being achieved.

Stock options, phantom stock plans, profit shares, royalties, bonuses, and so on, are all valid incentives to be used by the owners of a business to reward employees. These corporate lollipops should always benefit the money-investing owners of a business and not dilute their interests.

Chapter 6

SUCCESS AND FAILURE

The Successful Venture

Success cannot be judged solely in the amount of dollars earned. It must also be judged by the achievement of projections upon which the investment was premised. This means that entrepreneurs get where they say they were going within the framework of time originally laid down. Thus, in the rare case of an accurate projection, the success was really achieved when the projection was made. The resulting actual profit in dollars can come as an anticlimax. Success for the Angel is the achievement of maximum gain with minimum risk. But it is not for maximum gain alone--it's not just a matter of making a great deal of money. Success should always be evaluated as risk-related, and profit is not always quantifiable as the monetary return on investment. Also, the investment, which is frequently more than money, can be difficult to define.

With successful private companies, money is usually made through patiently staying with the company. The wise investor is in to stay, except in cases where the public or other buyers anticipate greater success for the company than is realistic. In general, when a private company becomes successful, the investor will regret in future years having sold out early.

Investor strategy may require selling off part of the holding, somewhat like cashing in the chips of one's original stake in a gambling casino while one is ahead and playing from that point on with the house's money. An investor managing a portfolio of private company

97

investments is more likely to do this than an investor in a single company. There are all sorts of emotional and psychological reasons for not wishing to sell one's holdings in a successful private company. After all, in part, it's the Angel's baby.

The Spirit of Success

The successful entrepreneur builds or rents business space, acquires business equipment, generates professional fees, rents money both to and from banking institutions, and pays taxes, among many other things that contribute to society. However, the most important result of a successful business in a community is the spirit of success which is transmitted to others in the area. Success builds and breeds success. The image of success quickly follows the fact of success, except in the case of some initial public offerings where the imagery precedes the success. As a result, more companies and entrepreneurs come to recognize the community to be a good place to build wealth. There are just no cases of entrepreneurs building successful companies without a natural sharing of the wealth that has been created. Successful entrepreneuring is really one of the few win/win situations in any free society. Successful entrepreneuring is not a zero-sum game where for every winner there must be an equivalent loser. Successful companies are not like commodity futures contracts. They have a positive community-wide ripple effect.

With Success, Further Opportunity

Assume that a private company venture is not only successful but is making a lot of money. Assume also that Angels have either control or an ability to substantially influence the management of the company. What should they do to maximize their success? Should they do anything at all? I like the farmer's advice: "If it ain't broke, don't fix it."

Going public and becoming paper-rich is an enormous temptation and frequently a very good idea. Besides this, there will be ever-present opportunities to sell out, and there is nothing wrong with a ringing of the cash register. The more dollars an investor possesses, the more progress he can achieve in both personal and societal enrichment. See Appendixes U and O for the valuation of a business.

Bill Berkley advises, "The best time to sell a company is when it is doing well and you are predicting it will do better. Never wait for a downturn. However, when earnings are increasing is the hardest time to sell, because things look as if they will go on like this forever."

However, there are some other possibilities to consider. The success of the investor's venture probably indicates the presence of a superior management team. This success presumably also brought about the establishment of significant executive-benefit programs. Such benefit programs can in themselves be an important part of the Angel's and entrepreneur's reward of success. For Angels to be included in these benefit programs, they or their spouses should be directors or consultants. Entrepreneurs should be willing to include Angel designees in the executive-benefit programs, to ensure their cooperation and generosity in situations where investors have sufficient control or influence. The benefit plans may include pension, profit sharing, stock repurchase, and so forth, and are all capable of playing a vital role in the estate planning of both Angel and entrepreneur.

What about using the successful private company as an investment vehicle? Investors in thriving companies will continually have other investment opportunities presented to them. Should they decide to invest in new ventures, they can probably finance them independently and with greater ease and probability of success than previously due to their experience with the already successful venture. But why not bring the opportunity to the already successful company? The singular advantage in doing this would be that the Angel has already identified, and perhaps played a role in creating, a group of proven successful managers who can not only assist in the evaluation process but also be of enormous assistance in helping the management of the new company.

What about the possibility of buying real estate or other assets through the successful company? Why not? Some appropriate losses can be charged against the earnings of the company for tax purposes-- most of the time--and whatever leverage is required may well be easier to obtain through the successful company. The critical consideration, however, in all these issues is whether or not the effort will prove to be a damaging distraction for the managers of the business. Nothing should be considered which will jeopardize that wonder of wonders--the truly successful privately owned company.

Highly successful private companies possess personal relationship strengths upon which further enterprises can be built. Such a company also has an invisible structure of professional advisors and availability of finance. While this cannot be valued on a balance sheet, nevertheless it is a very real asset and one which can be used.

The successful private company may invest in other ventures by becoming a joint venture partner. Such a company can also invest through loans, guarantees, and technical assistance programs.

The essence of being a good private company investor is to find truly capable people and to develop a mutually good working relationships with them. The more good people Angels have on their teams, the larger will be their estate. My advice is to *use fully the efforts of the few motivated and capable people you can identify and attract. Such use will be to your and their advantage.* That's what venture investing and being a great entrepreneur are all about.

Time to Get Out

As George Jessel used to say, it's not just a matter of deciding to sell--it's a matter of to whom. Buyers are easy to find for 100 percent of highly successful companies but will probably be difficult to locate for presently marginal or downright unsuccessful companies. Disposing of a minority position will probably be almost impossible. Thus, opportunity may well be the trigger to sell. Certainly Angels should try to sell when their associations with companies no longer bring them pleasure and satisfaction. If you're not enjoying it, get out if you can. Also, Angels should have the ability to compel the sale of an unsuccessful company in order to salvage a part of their investment.

Because investors in a private company do not have the luxury of calling their broker with a sell order and can get out only where a situation permits it, they could extricate themselves as soon as possible when they lose confidence in the entrepreneur, if Angels are unwilling or unable to replace them. Private company investment requires a much greater degree of uniformed reliance on management, by and large, than does investment in a public company, because of the greater information output a public company must give its shareholders. Once their trust is gone, so too should the Angels leave.

Declining profit margins are a tipoff to seriously consider exiting. The private company investor must be aware of profit margins on a monthly basis, not merely quarterly or annually. An effective way to do this is to keep a chart, which can also include a number of other operational elements of the company, such as order backlog, sales, cost of sales, profits, square feet used, number of employees, employee expense as a percentage of revenue, employee expense as a percentage of earnings, executive expense as a percentage of other staff expenses, rate of incoming orders, and debt maturity. Using a monthly updated chart and the notebook in which they have been recorded the entrepreneur's projections, the investors can readily see where they have been and probably where they are going.

Who has the right to sell the company is another thing Angels must keep in mind. Without a contract stipulating to the contrary, management of the board of directors is the group that determines when a company should be sold, to whom, and on what terms. Although the Angel may hold a 51 percent interest in the company, frequently a two-thirds or three-quarters vote of shareholders is required to sell. One of the safeguards Angels should consider writing into either the shareholder or loan agreement is that, under certain conditions (these conditions would be basically protective, such as failure to achieve earnings or failure to maintain a current ration), the Angels have the right to sell the company or to sell their shares in the company to the company. Depending on the provisions of the contract, management that has failed to meet certain projections can be excluded from voting.

Management may be given the opportunity, or first opportunity, to buy the Angels' stock. Indeed, in a troubled company, management may be the only market for it. Under these circumstances, angels may retain an appraiser or investment banker to estimate the value of their holdings. If the company has been successful, they will probably already have been the recipient of a number of offers and will have fair, though perhaps exaggerated, ideas of the value of their stock.

Angels also should remember that offers may have been made for the company of which they have not been fully informed. If management holds little or no stock, they may correctly see the sale of the company as a threat to their positions and turn down the bids, or bid overtures, without passing them on to the shareholders for consideration, or management may inform the shareholders only after the bid has been discouraged or rejected.

The value of a new company's shares will be affected by how far along it is toward its projected success. Obviously, the shares of a company that expects to be in the red for another three years will usually be sold (if they can be sold) more cheaply than the shares of a company which has shown a little profit in its fourth year and expects to show a big profit in its fifth.

Competitors in the same business are clearly one group that may be interested in buying out a company. The same business in a different geographical location may wish to expand by buying out the firm. Suppliers and customers may be interested. Personal contacts made by the Angels can be buyer candidates. Over the time period they are in a particular business, active investors open themselves to many contacts in that and allied businesses.

Finally, the investor who wants out may consider making a deal with management. In exchange for this stock, he may accept a certain sum and, say, 2 percent of sales over a specified period. He may prefer to be paid as a consultant to the company over an agreed time span in order to be entitled to certain corporate benefits.

Dealing with Failure

Failure can be defined simply as not achieving projected results. From the investor's viewpoint, a failed venture and a failed company are not synonymous. The Angel may even be able to get out at a profit in the case of disappointing results if the deal was well constructed. Because it is essential to investors to recognize a failure before it becomes common knowledge, they should rely on monthly updated charts to indicate danger trends. When a trend becomes set-- that is, when it continues beyond the third month--it typically becomes difficult to reverse.

The Angel's corrective action will depend upon what element of the company is in a downtrend. The radical surgery of a complete sellout may not be required. The trend may not be irreversible. Management or product may be changed. A plant may be closed or opened. Another important factor will be the investor's own freedom of movement. With success, one has significant control over one's destiny; the absence of success limits the amount of one's control and increases that of others over one's destiny. Thus, Angels using borrowed funds may find their options severely limited.

The Angel's primary concern in the event of failure must be to salvage as much of their investment as possible. Ideally, the contract should provide a means for this. It is my view that private company investors should always be in a preferred position until they recapture their investment with a time value for the period they have been investing. In negotiating an agreement on the future distribution of company assets to the interest holders, the point at which all interest holders rank equally must be identified. It's not necessarily from "dollar one." For example, if original investors had put $150,000 into the company over four years, they might qualify for a $200,000 settlement before anything was paid to the other interest holders.

If the company is to be sold, the Angel had better understand what salaries and perks the management of the company are going to get from the new buyer. A little conspiracy, or pseudo-conspiracy, can easily develop between the new owners and old management, particularly when management is advising the selling investors on the fairness of the deal. The manager of a troubled company, aware that the investors are anxious to sell, may approach a potential buyer and say,

"The investors are really fed up with this thing because it isn't going as they expected. I think I could persuade them to sell out at a big discount to their cost. Let me tell you, with another $150,000 in there, I could really turn this company around for a new owner. What about letting me stay on as president and giving me 20 percent of the stock or profits?"

Nothing is more frustrating for Angels than to end up having gotten out of a deal at a loss only to see some of the same people who were in the deal with them make a profit. Angels must retain control over the sale negotiation for their protection and never simply act as a ratifying agent for whatever management negotiates.

If a company still has any vitality and potential, its own management may be its most likely buyer. Certainly, entrepreneurs/managers are in a position to be most helpful to an Angel who wishes to get out. They can most easily arrange to have the investors paid either all or part of their money back or some of it now and some at a later time. Angels cannot demand much more than they are entitled to, and that will usually depend on what is in the original investment contract and shareholder agreement. Management should be informed of the Angel's intent to exit and be provided with a chance to structure it to everybody's benefit.

Circumstances other than failure may prompt the departure of the angel. The Angel may just realize his interests will be better served by his having a different relationship with the company than the one created by his original investment. Thus, Angels might purchase a small plant from the company for a $100,000 note. They might exchange their interest in the company for the patent rights to a single product manufactured by the company. Angels may wish only to change their relationship with the company; for example, they may wish the company to continue manufacturing a product, sell it to them at an agreed price, and give them exclusive servicing of a certain number of accounts. Management will often redouble their efforts to buy out Angels they think might sell their interests to a competitor. The parting does not have to end in screaming and crying. It can be a very amicable arrangement and mutually constructive.

If a company does close its doors, who gets the tax benefit? My position is that the entire tax benefit should go to those who invested money, not to those who invested talent and effort. Again, this is something which must be spelled out in the purchase contract and structured appropriately.

Most people lose all of their money when a private company fails. I think this is unnecessary in a lot of cases. If they did a better job of structuring their withdrawal, they would not lose so much. It can also be a matter of when Angels decide to throw in the towel. The earlier they recognize the result of a downtrend, the greater is the probability that they will be able to salvage something. The longer a business continues to lose money, the greater its losses, leaving less assets which may be available to investors, entrepreneurs, and subsequent owners. And the longer Angels are in losing businesses, the greater is the likelihood that they will believe it in their best interest to put more money into it.

Alert, intelligent Angels learn from their failures, and *all* investors have failures. These failures need not necessarily include a company's bankruptcy--any investment which generates less than the results anticipated, that justified the original assumption of risk, constitutes a failure.

All investors, will have their own set of rules. Some might be:

- Never go into a company unless it is adequately financed.
- Never invest in a company unless its management has had prior success in running a business.
- Never invest in a company that is dependent upon a small number of customers.
- Never invest in a company that is dependent upon a narrow range of technological developments.
- Never invest in a company in a geographic location which is not prosperous.
- Never invest in a company which is labor-intensive and unionized.
- Never invest in a company which is dependent upon government contracts, protection, or largesse.

- Never invest in a company which is dependent upon financing from a single financial institution.
- Never invest in a company in which an inventor is the chief executive officer.
- Never invest in a company that is in a business in which unsavory individuals are present.
- Never invest in a company in which the entrepreneur is experiencing marital discord or is a philanderer, drug abuser, or heavy drinker.
- Never invest in a company in which you can not be proud.

There are a lot of lessons to be learned, and the Angel learns a new one with each experience.

Necessity for Angel's Action on Downside

From the Angel's position, a critical point is reached when a company's trend toward failure seems set and the probabilities for failure outweigh those for success. Investors will not have time to argue with the entrepreneur at this critical point--they must have already put themselves in a position to take direct action. Typical of the measures the wise Angel will have taken are: control of an increasing number of the company directors in inverse proportion to the rate of company success; an irrevocable proxy that takes effect at a critical point, ratifying the sale of the company or its dissolution or whatever the Angel requested; and a signed but undated letter of resignation from the entrepreneur to be activated only at the critical point.

Although these measures are tough on the entrepreneur, Angels who ask for these contractual concessions know that most investments like these lose money, and they have no assurances that their's will be an exception. Also, being in possession of these rights does not mean that an Angel must exercise them. In practice, Angels often feel sorry for the entrepreneur and, in spite of their better judgement, allow the entrepreneur to continue running the company. But Angels must have these powers--restricted to the downside--if they are to be in a position to grant largesse.

When a Company Closes

Many things happen when a company closes. The reputation of everybody involved is damaged. The reputation of the product being offered is damaged. Competitors come in and fill the void left by the failed company. Creditors have to be dealt with if money is owed.

105

Does the failed company own the patent of the product, or does the entrepreneur own the patent and license its use by the company? Is it an exclusive license? Is it a limited license or a full license? Is the license terminable by the company's failure or by certain guaranteed ratios not being maintained? Is the license dependent on a certain level of sales being attained and maintained by a certain date? Entrepreneurs frequently get their holdings in the company through assignment of either the license to the patent or ownership of the patent. The intelligent Angel will probably take the patent interests or an assignment thereof as part of the collateral for a loan, or certainly as part of an overall transaction which may be triggered by certain events, such as failure to maintain certain ratios. Care must be taken by the Angel in structuring private company investments to be aware of the possibilities of creditor claims of "preference" and of the claims by either the entrepreneur or creditors of usury.

Angels should not think that the company can pass from the scene this year and come back at a future point. More likely, the assets of the company will be sold to satisfy creditor claims. If Angels have done a worthwhile job in structuring the original agreement, they will be one of the creditors who have to be satisfied--perhaps the primary creditor who has to be satisfied.

Litigation

Most Angels are reluctant to become involved in lawsuits, and, in most cases, the reluctance is well founded. However, there are exceptions. A loss can be considerably minimized by litigation or the threat of litigation when the Angel's loss is someone else's fault. Angels are considered to be fair game by many, and most Angels do not take sufficient action to ensure that other people treat them fairly. It may take only a couple of hours of a lawyer's time to investigate whether there is any liability on the part of someone for Angel's losses in a failing company. In many cases where this need not have been the result, the Angel is the only one to take a loss. Frequently, the greatest remaining asset of a failing or failed company is the potential liability of its directors and others who may have contributed to the loss. Angels are often too embarrassed to sue, having not listened to the advice of friends not to invest in that company, fearing that their reputation will be damaged by publicity, and wishing to forget these bad investments and move on to a good one.

The decision whether to litigate frequently depends as much on the defendant's ability to respond to a judgment as it does on the merit of the Angel's case. The vast majority of cases are settled out of court rather than litigated, and these settlements often involve the faults of others being translated into smaller losses for the investor. Attorney fees for litigation of this nature are probably best handled on a contingency-fee basis.

The following will indicate to investors facing losses the type of questions they should be asking:

- Did entrepreneurs have the assets they claimed to have before the investment was made?
- Did entrepreneurs spend the investor's money in the way the investor was told it would be spent, or did entrepreneurs spend it in a manner designed to benefit them in a way not disclosed to the investor?
- As an inducement to purchase goods or services from them, did suppliers lead the investor to believe that they could deliver their product at a specific point in time, and was the Angel's lack of success caused by these suppliers' inability or unwillingness to supply in time the product they had contracted for?
- Have the employees leaving to start their own competitive company stolen data which are the property of the investor's company?
- Is the Angel's loss a result of bad legal or accounting advice?

A lawsuit should not be brought by an Angel against entrepreneurs who have honestly failed to accomplish what they tried to do. However, inexperienced entrepreneurs are taken advantage of by other companies, and to the extent that investors have suffered damage by someone taking advantage of the entrepreneur/manager of the company in which they have invested, investors can do something about it.

Business Discontinuance versus Failure

Perhaps one of the most damaging cliches is the often heard statement that most businesses fail in their first five years. Most businesses do not fail in the first five years in the sense of bankruptcy or creditor losses. The fact that a business was discontinued does not mean that it failed, as is shown by this excerpt from the President's Report on Small Business:

90 percent of the approximately 400,000 businesses that dissolve each year do so for voluntary reasons, such as retirement of the

107

owner or desire to enter a more profitable field. 99 percent of "failed" businesses have fewer than 100 employees and over 80 percent are under 10 years old. Only 10 percent of businesses that annually cease operations do so for involuntary reasons. They may file for bankruptcy or be considered a failure if the organization ceases to operate and leaves outstanding debt.

Actually, bankruptcies are running about 60,000 per year versus more than 700,000 new incorporations. Many find it convenient to own assets through a corporation, and for all intents and purposes many such corporations can be regarded as dormant. There are more than fourteen million corporations in the United States and most do not have even a single active employee.

One type of business discontinuance is caused by the inability of a new enterprise to get credit in the first place. In all likelihood, the lenders denied credit because they believe most businesses fail in the first five years. Without unsatisfied creditors who are unpaid, there can be no business failure in the strict legal sense but rather only a discontinuance.

Frequently, even businesses which are marginally profitable are discontinued. It is not only losses which bring about discontinuance but also inadequacy of profit.

I would, however, accept without reservation the following statement: "Almost all new businesses fail ... to achieve the initial projected results of the entrepreneur and expectations of original investors (most frequently the entrepreneurs themselves)."

Chapter 7

WHEN YOU ARE THE LEAD ANGEL

Before they decide to become lead Angels in an enterprise, investors should carefully review whether they are willing to assume the responsibility of the role. As lead Angels, they will, in fact, be inducing others to assume risk by their very presence in the transaction and relationship. They will also be assuming a responsibility for most appropriately structuring the transaction to gain maximum benefit for the Angels. When the terms of the transaction are subsequently to be modified or additional funding is required, they can have another problem to contend with--that of finding themselves aligned with the management group, frequently almost becoming a part of the management team by virtue of the ongoing monitoring that they have been performing. They have probably become more aware of the company's problems than the other Angels, and certainly more of a believer in the entrepreneur's view of its potential. It is also possible that investors will have experienced such significant frustration in dealing with the entrepreneur that their judgement regarding the whole business opportunity will be distorted. Therefore, the possibility, or rather the probability, exists that their perspective and overall view of the company will diverge from those of other less involved investors.

Arthur Little, chief executive officer of the Narragansett Capital Corporation, had this advice for the lead Angels:

> If there are going to be others investing along with you in a venture, warn them to use their own judgement before committing themselves. When some people in Rhode Island hear that I am

investing in something, they decide to do it too. Sometimes that works out well for them, and sometimes it doesn't. I am very careful not to recommend ventures to people, but in spite of that they often go ahead and invest anyway.

On balance, I would recommend against the informal or individual investor becoming the lead investor of an investment group, unless the other investors are more sophisticated than he is, or unless the other investors have the ability to make more than simply a financial contribution to the company.

Bill Berkley had this to say to the lead investor:

In attracting or selecting appropriate partners or participants for investing in a venture, deal with people you think have the resources to invest and the knowledge to be able to make a decision. Knowledge is the greatest problem, because it is very hard to talk with someone who has no comprehension what the business really involves. When you try to discuss a supermarket proposal with someone who is knowledgeable only in the insurance business, you end up having to teach him the industry. My criteria for selecting partners would be, first, financial resources and, second, at least some knowledge of the business involved.

Attracting Participants

Angels or informal investors have already been advised not to accept the responsibility for soliciting investments from other nonprofessional investors, even though they may be tempted to tell their friends about this wonderful new company they have discovered and even offer them the same terms they are getting himself. Apart from the inadvisability of being gratuitously responsible for other people's money, lead Angels are assuming that the deal will work out as predicted. If the deal does work out as anticipated, and few deals do, the lead Angles will be heroes to their friends. If the opposite occurs, they may reasonably expect an opposite reaction from their friends. If the outcome of deals could be anticipated so easily, instead of asking others to join them, Angels should borrow from banks and mortgage their property in order to provide all the money themselves. The nonprofessional investor is not likely to understand all of the risk areas inherent in private company investment.

However, if informal investors, as lead Angels, can interest a successful provider of venture capital, someone with a wide business knowledge, or, ideally, a person with knowledge of the field in which the new company is situated, they should not hesitate to do so. Lead investors themselves will be called upon to contribute more than money to the enterprise, and all other sophisticated investors they find, who can make contributions over and above their financial commitments, will serve as an enlarged resource for the company.

The Board of Directors

The significance of a board of directors in a private company depends upon how the voting equity is distributed and upon shareholder and purchase agreements surrounding the financing transaction. If, in fact, the entrepreneur holds the vast majority of the voting equity, a board of directors per se is not particularly important, and many of its functions can be adequately provided by a board of advisors. After all, one of the primary functions of a board of directors is to evaluate the performance of the management of the company and to decide, when necessary, if management must be replaced for the benefit of all of the owners of the business. Therefore, if the management of the company controls the vast percentage of the shares and can elect their own directors or appoint themselves as directors, it does not make a great deal of sense to look to the board for investor protection other than as a source of entitled information. Also, there are meaningful personal liabilities associated with being a director, of which investors should be aware.

The qualities of a director that can be of value to a company are those of wide business experience. By and large, it does not make a lot of sense to put scientists on the board of directors, particularly that of a private company, because their contributions of skill and experience can be equally well made by them as an advisor. A director should have a sense of humor and perspective, the former being desirable and the latter important. Experience is the key word.

The number of director appointees an investor has is critical when a board votes. The board of directors is important in a company's life when there are controversial decisions to be made; then votes become very significant. Among the critical decisions that a company commonly must make are: whether to embark on a new project; whether to seek a financing; whether to accept the terms of a proposed financing; whether to buy another company; whether to sell or merge with another company; whether the compensation paid to the managers of the company should be increased; and whether the managers should be removed or transferred. As a rule, the directors representing

111

investor interest will usually agree with management proposals during periods when the company is doing well. It is during those periods when the company is failing to achieve projected results, or when things are otherwise not going well, that investor interests and entrepreneurial interests are likely to become divergent. At that time the natural adversarial relationship, which has been lurking below the surface all the time, will tend to become obvious to all. Then votes can be critical. For this reason, in structuring financing I frequently include provisions that grant to the investors the ability to appoint an increasing number of the directors upon nonachievement of projected results.

The Angel's interest can also be protected by the creation of bylaw provisions requiring approval for certain acts of an amount of outstanding shares which would have to include those held by the Angel, and thereby providing at least an effective veto ability. For instance, if the Angel holds 25 percent of the voting shares, shouldn't authority for borrowings, in a small company, exceeding $100,000 require the affirmative vote of 80 percent of the outstanding shares? Of course, it should not be possible to change the bylaws with less than a similar percentage of the shares being in favor of the change. Mergers, acquisitions, and so forth should require similar levels of shareholder approval. Therefore, it is not only through board memberships that elements of control can be created and maintained. Much the same control, negative or positive, can be worked into a shareholders' agreement. Needless to say, the level of control exerted by the investor can, and should, lessen with the positive achievements of entrepreneurs. There is little reason to rein in clear winners--let them run their hearts out once you have confidence in them, justified by results and not based upon hopes and expectations.

Angel interests, as opposed to entrepreneurial interests, must be protected, since it is the investor who typically takes the financial risk, whereas entrepreneurs benefit, and I believe appropriately so, in the case of success disproportionately to their dollar investment. The equitable offset to that position is that the Angel should be protected on the downside considerably more than the entrepreneur. This protection will in part take the form of increasing control by the Angel of the company the entrepreneur has started. When to sell, when to close down the company, when to stop a particular product line, and when to accept financing which may be opposed by the entrepreneur as being too dilutive are all areas in which Angel interests and entrepreneurial interests will diverge.

People with wide and relevant business experience should be invited to serve on the board of directors. That experience may be acquired either through having started new companies themselves or, in the case of an academic, through having observed a large number of companies in similar stages of development. I think that academics, typically professors or associate professors from business schools, can make very worthwhile directors, even when they are not investors in the company. Lawyers similarly are in a position of observing and being involved with a large number of companies and are, therefore, able frequently to make contributions. However, I question having the same lawyer who represents the company on the board of directors. Clearly, the lawyer representing the Angel would, from the investor's point of view, make a good director candidate.

I recommend that the board of directors of a private company, particularly a startup or development-stage company, be limited in number to perhaps five. As is the case with most committees, an inverse ratio exists between the efficacy of the unit and its size. The larger the board, the longer will be its meetings and frequently less will be accomplished. Five directors is a good number. In a situation where the Angels put up all or the majority of the money and receive approximately 50 percent of the equity of the company, which seems to be a more or less typical situation, the initial board could be composed of two directors from the entrepreneur's side, two from the Angels' side, and a fifth director who is agreeable to both sides and an adherent of neither camp. However, should the projections not be achieved, one of the entrepreneur's seats on the board, and possibly both, should be transferred to the Angel group.

Hired management need not always be represented on the board, but the entrepreneur should be represented, because he is a capital risk assuming equity owner or has, in some form, an equity or profit-related interest. I believe it is a mistake to view, as many young companies do, placement on the board of directors as an honor to bestow on members of the management team. The company can obtain from those same managers all of the contribution they can make without placing them on the board of directors or even a board of advisors. From the board of directors or a board of advisors, the company obtains benefit of the advice and experience of those not involved in the day-to-day management of the business and even of those who are not involved as direct investors.

Angels should have the right to appoint directors but need not serve on the board themselves. However, Angels must recognize that there

113

is liability associated with serving on any company's board of directors and that in all probability, they may, and certainly the company will, have to offer an indemnification to anyone serving at their request on a board. Director and officer liability insurance is not generally available to new companies; anyway, the premiums are extremely high.

This report from an article in *Venture* is an extreme example of director liability:

> In a decision handed down by the U.S. District Court for the Southern District of New York, the court found Roy Furmark, a former director of the Newfoundland Refining Co. (NRC), a privately held Canadian corporation, personally liable for $11 million when the company went bankrupt. Although there was no claim of fraud, Furmark was held liable because, according to the decision, "for a period of two years preceding the bankruptcy, NRC loaned $30 million to its sole shareholder and owner, John M. Shaheen, and other companies owned and controlled by Shaheen."
>
> Furmark appealed the decision, claiming that it means not only personal disaster, but disaster for corporate directors everywhere. The U.S. Court of Appeals for the Second Circuit did not see it that way, and upheld the District Court's decision.

In the Furmark case, the court is taking the position that the director had a fiduciary duty to the creditors. This is based on the old English legal concept that creditors, uninformed of a company's true state of finance, can look to members of the board of directors to personally make good the creditors' losses on the grounds that the director theoretically could have halted the acts of commercial deception. All of this assumes that directors had perfect vision and that they themselves were adequately informed as to the true circumstances of the company.

I suggest that directors be appointed and asked to serve for a two-year term. As with most consultants and advisors, directors will make the major portion of their contribution in the very early state of the relationship. It is always difficult when the controlling shareholders or management of a company determine either that directors are no longer serving a useful purpose or that there is another person they want in the seat. Someone then has the embarrassing job of suggesting to directors that they not stand for reelection or that, perhaps, they should retire. It is much easier to ask people to serve for a specific period of time and, if they prove unsatisfactory, simply not reinvite them. One can, of course, issue another renewal invitation to those one wishes to continue. But all find it easier when they know they are serving on a board for a specific period of time and it is not something that will go on forever. Of course, directors are always elected to serve for specific periods, but the election is a formalization of an invitation made informally. My suggestion relates to the issuance of the invitation by the controlling party.

Compensation for directors is understandably a consideration that should be focused upon. Whether independent directors should be compensated with equity, warrants, options, or anything that relates to equity, as opposed to simply receiving a per diem fee or retainer, is open to debate. Heidrick and Struggles, the executive recruiting firm, has prepared much survey material regarding the compensation of directors, as has Deloitte Haskins & Sells and a number of other accounting firms.

The real issue in the compensation of directors is whether they should have a vested interest in the rapid growth of earnings and, therefore, rapid appreciation in price or valuation. I believe it is better that directors be in a position to act as a restraining influence on an aggressive management, continually taking the side of prudence against that of overly ambitious expansion. Similarly in concept to this problem is whether investors should pay their attorneys, in part of in whole, in shares, warrants, or some other interest in the company. If investors give them a holding, attorneys will have as their central focus the growth of the company, or the growth of the company's earnings, and the enhancement of their vested positions--as opposed to functioning as traditional attorneys by indicating the areas of danger and risk and the problems associated with any transaction. Investors may be putting their board of directors in a similar position by giving them stock. If the directors will all benefit from increase in earnings and the price of the stock, then who will take the position of caution and prudence? All things considered, I think that directors representing investors should be paid cash fees on a per diem basis. If they choose to invest themselves, that opportunity should be made available to them on perhaps the same terms as the Angels. But it is probably a mistake, from the investors' standpoint, to offer the investor-appointed directors incentives similar to those of management.

The members of the board of directors often serve as window dressings for the company. The composition of the board of directors is one of the things a prospective customer, a sought-for employee, and even a prospective supplier looks at. At such time as the company is negotiating with an underwriter in terms of going public, the composition of the board of directors becomes more important. Everyone likes to see on the board, particularly that of a young company, names of independent directors which are recognizable, either because of individual accomplishment or because of the individual's associations. A senior vice president of a bank, a vice president of a well known publicly traded company, an astronaut, or a professor of business administration at a well-known university adds much luster to a private company's board of directors.

In terms of the contribution of the individual at board meetings, a distinguished name or title is less significant than the experience that the name or title *may* represent. If the individuals serve on a number of boards of directors, the chances are they will be in a position to make a meaningful contribution. If they serve on no other or only one other board, they are less likely to make contributions based on wide experience and observations of other companies.

One can usually rely on the integrity and intelligence of experienced directors not to permit themselves to be appointed to the boards of companies in direct competition with one another so they would be placed in a position of having a conflict of interest. A more difficult issue is where the director of a company is also affiliated either with a supplier of goods or services to the company or with a customer of the company. By and large, I believe that directors on the board of a company should not be either vendor- or customer-affiliated any more than they should be affiliated with a competitive company. However, in many cases, a key supplier or an important customer may wish to have a director on the board and may even be an investor in the company.

Selection of the Board of Directors

Legally, directors represent all of the shareholders without distinction. In practice, directors have special loyalty to those shareholders or corporate officers responsible for their appointment to the board. In private companies, a *we* and *they* situation frequently develops--we the entrepreneurs, they the money; or we the investors, they the managers. Accordingly, directors often wear team colors.

While directors' votes reflect their views as to what is in the company's best interests, what those best interests are can be a matter of viewpoint. These problems are resolved in real life by certain individuals and factions retaining the right to appoint a certain percentage of company directors to protect their own interests. Thus, it is well understood by all concerned that when investors have the right to appoint 50 percent of the board and do so, those directors will be primarily representing those investors' interests, since they have the ability to replace them with those who will. In most cases, there is a commonality of shareholder interest, and it is usually only during periods of stress that the interests diverge.

However, directors should not be mere puppets. They should not be totally controlled, or at least should not usually be, by the interests they represent. Some of their decisions occasionally will be in opposition to the wishes of the individuals who appointed them. They have legal obligations to all of the shareholders, and, as intelligent people, they must vote what they believe to be in the best interests of all of the company's owners. Their obligation is, however, only to the owners, and not the managers, of the business.

The following report appeared in *Venture*.

"No one around here ever asks the boss a tough question--so I decided to form a board of directors to give myself a few peers to talk to," says Ray Peterson, owner and president of Industrial Fabricating Co. in Stratford, Conn. If he worked for a large corporation, he says he'd have six or seven "equals" to swap ideas with; his board helps provide similar feedback.

"The best thing about the board is that it makes me think," he says. His board has already made an important contribution to savings; in response to board probing, Peterson was forced to admit one of his products was unprofitable. He dropped it immediately.

Any question can be brought up at a board meeting, but it's wise to concentrate on business objectives and performance. A wisely chosen board will give your business expert guidance in areas where your own knowledge is weakest. "Most small businesses are started by people with technical or service expertise who don't know enough about business and finance," says Robert A. Howell, clinical professor of management at New York University's Graduate School of Business Administration. "I've seen cases where a board has taught an owner to multiply earnings tenfold," he says. Most states require all corporations to form a board but companies often create boards "in name only"

117

that seldom meet and don't make serious contributions to the firm.

In order to find the best board members for your company, you should isolate your weaknesses and look for people who are strong in those areas. Howell recommends that you choose five to seven members (if you have an odd number of directors, you eliminate the possibility of a tie vote); too many people can stall a decision with too much discussion.

A hypothetical board might consist of a venture capitalist, an investment banker, a business school professor, and an owner of a similar business, provided there is no conflict of interest. It may be desirable to find someone with a strong background in accounting, although this person will most likely not be a CPA-- most members of "big six" firms are forbidden to join corporate boards. Some owners also find it useful to appoint an attorney well versed in business law. Select directors who are likely to serve for an indefinite length. "The longer, the better," says Howell. "Look for commitments of 10 to 15 years, so that they get to know the company." Peterson advises that you look very carefully at the prospective members" personalities too. "Make sure that they're straightforward," he says. "Get people who can be counted on to ask tough questions."

There are a number of ways to make board membership attractive. In smaller and younger enterprises money alone rarely serves as a major incentive. But many companies hold annual or semiannual all-expense-paid conferences at posh vacation spots. Others give their board members equity in the corporation. But even if you can't offer either of these things, you may be surprised by how many people accept your offer. "I only pay my board $200 a meeting--but they do it for the experience," says Peterson. "They gain as much knowledge and insight as I do."

Most important of all is to learn to be completely candid with your board and accept its guidance. Howell says that too often owners of small businesses are used to making all important business decisions by themselves and can't break the habit. "After having spent a lifetime being self-reliant, a lot of business owners find they can't open up as much as they would like to," Howell says. "I've seen a lot of unnecessary problems occur because of this, and it's always sad when someone who could have prevented the difficulties was sitting on the board all along."

118

Fully Independent Board of Directors

Effective, conflict-free corporate governance is frequently not easy to achieve. A particularly difficult situation often occurs when the senior managers, including the chief executive officer (CEO), are also substantial, but not controlling, owners of the business. Difficulties can arise because one of the primary functions of a board of directors is to continually assess the efficacy of management, and to take corrective action if necessary. Since those involved in the company's management cannot always be objective about their performance, the solution would be to have a fully independent board of directors, excluding even the CEO, to represent the interests of the owners. The owners who are also managers of the business could appoint directors to represent their ownership interests. It is possible that a director representing the interests of the owners would not agree with all of the views of the CEO. Using their perhaps more objective judgement, such independent directors might perform a service for all the owners by, in a closed executive session, voting against the recommendations of the CEO, for the CEO's own good as one of the owners of the business. Owners elect directors; directors appoint managers. It's a good system if the directors recognize and remain faithful to their masters.

Advisors and Consultants

For the purposes of this discussion, a differentiation is made between advisors and consultants. Advisors tend to serve on a long-term basis; they will probably form an advisory board and have a lasting concern with the company. They may be investors, people with banking or technological experience, or retired members of a board of directors or of a management group. Advisors, of course, may also perform consulting functions. Essentially, advisors are continuously available to the management of a company to give advice.

Consultants are typically retained on a per diem basis to address a very specific area of the company's activities or to solve a particular problem. The professional consultant is essentially a butterfly that flits from company to company in an act of cross-pollination, taking experience gained in one company and applying it in another. Although a consultant will often try to establish a long-term relationship with a company, the attempt should probably be rejected in favor of a number of short-term consultants. The consultant will probably settle for periodic assignments. As with directors, the company is likely to get the major percentage of the consultant's total contribution very early in the relationship. Although consultants are extremely useful sources of information as to what is going on in the industry generally, and as to what is happening in other companies of special interest, small-company management is conspicuously backward in making use of them. Investors may be useful to the managements of companies by suggesting, or perhaps even imposing, specific consultants with whom they have had prior experience.

Managerial Change and Intrigue

No one likes to enter a marriage with a prenuptial agreement. However, recognizing that more than 50 percent of all marriages end in divorce or separation, such an agreement may be appropriate when there is a disparity of financial assets prior to the marriage. The relationship between Angel and entrepreneur is a marriage of sorts, with the investor almost by definition having the greater personal asset base. Added to this is the fact that the Angel most frequently will end up eventually investing more than had been originally expected at the time of the initial investment. Finally, there comes the time, all too frequently, when Angels believe that the company will fare better with a new manager and that the very protection of their capital in fact requires a change in management. At this point, Angels will find it extraordinarily useful if they have provided the necessary protection for the owners of the business of a contractual agreement stipulating that, upon nonachievement of projected results, entrepreneur/managers will resign some, or all, of their positions. The Angel or the board can always decline the resignation or reappoint the entrepreneur.

In practice, most entrepreneurs will not want to stay with the company if not in the top position. Entrepreneurs rarely recognize the situation where a developing company requires new or different skills in its management than the entrepreneurs themselves possess. The entrepreneur ideal for the initial startup may be totally unsuitable to the company at later stages in its development, especially during periods of stress and disappointment.

The agreement as to role change can, of course, be part of a buy out package where entrepreneurs have agreed to sell *all* of their stock to the company or to the Angel at, say, book value under certain conditions. In startup companies, this in effect means that entrepreneurs will simply surrender their stock under certain conditions, because the stock will probably have little or no book value or net worth at the time the agreement is triggered. The triggering of the agreement might be a third consecutive quarter in which projections of revenues have not been achieved. The trigger might also be a shortfall by 50 percent or more over a give period of time of the cash flow, or a combination of sales and earnings. Whatever the trigger point, the period to which it is related should be relatively short-term. This protective device for the Angel should be used much more often than it is.

In many new companies, management struggles result in intrigues, some against and some for Angels. With entrepreneurs, Angels are dealing with people who have enlarged egos since otherwise they probably would not be entrepreneurs. The entrepreneur, in turn, has to deal with Angels who are fearful of losing their investment, and who will quickly seek to blame someone other than themselves when something goes wrong. The entrepreneur is the logical person to blame. Thus, it is not unusual for a private company to have struggles, intrigues, secret meetings to which not all of the board members are invited, meetings within the management group, meetings among Angels, and meetings between various parties and their attorneys. These things have a way of escalating as the groups tend to panic with impending problems.

On the subject of Angel protection, I suggest that the Angels recognize that the position of secretary of the company, so frequently thought to be titular, has at crucial moments a real significance. The Angels' attorneys are the most advantageous people for them to have as secretary of the corporation. Similarly, investors might consider having the company use their attorney as corporate counsel or certainly as co-general counsel. A further precaution would be for Angels to arrange for the selection and appointment of auditors, rather than the company or entrepreneur do this.

Key-Man Life Insurance

In the event of the entrepreneur's death, key-man life insurance can spell the difference between a recovery of the investor's investment and a certain loss. This article, by Kathleen Mirin, appeared in *Venture*.

Whether it happens with a plane crash, an automobile accident, or a heart attack, the sudden death of a company's founder can also mean the death of the company. But young companies can be protected from an early demise by life insurance policies for the key employees who make the business run.

121

Key-man insurance, as it is called, is a high-stakes insurance policy purchased by the company, which is also the sole beneficiary. If a top executive should die, key-man benefits-- often amounting to several million dollars--buy valuable time to adjust to a new scheme or to find a successor, provide funds to buy out the stock of the deceased partner, or reduce debt while the company reorganizes. "The purpose of key-employee insurance is to keep the business in business," says Michael L. Abruzzo, corporate vice-president with New York Life Insurance Co.

Key-man insurance is also standard in venture capital contracts. "The venture capitalists' reward for backing an enterprise is the growth of the company," says Stan Meadow, a small corporation specialist with McDermott, Will & Emery, a Chicago law firm. "That type of growth depends of the entrepreneur."

How much should an entrepreneur be insured for? The central question is, what would it cost to replace the founder or key executive? Formulas based on a multiple of the person's salary or a percentage of the company profits--common measures in established companies-- are useless in the case of a startup, where the founder may take stock in lieu of a big salary and the company may not turn a profit for several years.

The most common way to gauge a founder's worth is to "calculate what it would cost to bring in someone of equal skill," Meadow says. In most startups, that almost always means a six-figure salary, since the newcomer will lack the personal commitment to the company and will not receive as much compensation in equity. "If you have to go out of the house to hire, it's almost inevitable that you have to pay a higher salary," Abruzzo says. "And it may take a number of years to bring that person up to the level of the lost employee."

Most young companies opt for term insurance rather than whole life policies because term policies are lower. For example, a $1 million term policy from New York Life on a 45-year-old, non-smoking executive in excellent health would cost $1,400 the first year. A comparable whole life policy would cost $21,500. "In the early years, they buy term," Abruzzo says. "When the picture gets rosier, they convert to whole life so they begin accruing equity."

Jim Liautaud, a Chicago investor who has started a number of high-technology firms, says he also considers the company's rate of growth in deciding how much key-man insurance to buy. "The faster the company grows, the more critically it depends on one man," he says. "Every time I start these things up, I have a high horsepower guy who is vital to the company. During the first two, three, or four years of the company, these guys are critical."

In his interview with me, Arthur Little told me,

"I always insist on very substantial life insurance -- for a million or 2 million dollars--for key people in new private companies. The insurance is taken out in favor of the company in order to protect my investment, even though this is not a tax-deductible expense."

Chapter 8

STRUCTURING THE DEAL

Before Angels can structure a deal--and I believe it should be the Angels who do the structuring--they have to make an attempt to really understand the motivations and needs of the parties to the agreement. Just how high a money motivation do the entrepreneurs have? How much risk can they stand? What are their long-term goals? Are they empire builders? Do they want, and perhaps actually need, complete control over their lives and, therefore, over the company? Can they accept direction? Do they need social status? Do they want to prove to a prior employer or associate that they were right and the latter wrong? Is making the most amount of money while using the least important to them as a game? How will they work under stress?

I, as the investor, must review my own objectives in this project. Do I truly want to hold control and is that my principal objective? How much involvement do I really want in the company? Is the product or service area one which I find interesting or fun? How much risk can I really accept? Do I want to take a total risk in this particular venture? What if some of my other ventures need additional financing at the same time as this new pet needs a second feeding? It always happens that way. Do I have the capability to manage the company if something happens to the entrepreneurs or if I have to replace them? Are their talents readily found elsewhere and at similar cost? What other investors could make this a better and safer investment for me? How much board of directors' representation do I real-

124

ly want or need? What is the best return on investment I am currently earning, and what is the best currently available to me? What is the minimum return on this investment necessary to make it attractive to me? How balanced in terms of risk is my overall portfolio? How much do I know about the entrepreneurs or the business they are proposing that I get involved with? Am I interested in heightened visibility in the community? Do I want to have my spouse or children involved?

As indicated elsewhere, I believe strongly that Angel provided funds take precedence over promotional or entrepreneurial interests. The only question in that area is whether or not investor funds should earn while waiting for the business to be successful. This is not to say that the actual payment for the use of the funds cannot be deferred until the company can afford to make the payments. Since the entrepreneur in all probability will be paid a current wage, it seems reasonable for the investor's dollars to earn a wage for their owner while they are being put to work.

Risk level assessment and containment by the Angels must be considered next. If Angels wish to limit risk -- to the extent that it is ever possible in a private company investment, let alone a startup -- they should be willing to accept a lessened upside potential. It is only fair to recognize that Angels cannot have it all their own way. They cannot expect to be fully secured and to have 100 percent of the equity. Once Angels accept that fact, it is only a matter of establishing the appropriate tradeoff points. How much risk is fair for how much profit potential?

My view is that investors are better off in early stage investments in taking a heavily secured (to the extent possible) and senior position. In other words, they should let the entrepreneur have more of the initial equity and take a lesser profit play but on a maximally secured position. My reasoning is that investors will likely get chances to improve their position once the company develops further, since entrepreneurs have, in all probability, underestimated the amount of funding required. Angels, therefore, will be in a natural, and perhaps inevitable, position to improve their potential profit participation later with little sacrifice of ranking. The Golden Rule of business becomes increasingly operative as Angel-financed businesses need additional funding. Also, the more senior the investment positions of Angels, the more deals they can do, as they can then use leverage more effectively themselves. Therefore, investing through providing the use of assets, to which title is held, might be the best way to invest in a private company. The ownership of the assets can always be exchanged for equity later in the company's development.

Since it has been concluded that the Angel's investment should take precedence over that of the entrepreneur, and that the Angel should initially take a lesser reward potential in exchange for a lesser risk burden, the questions remain of how much, and of what. In many cases, the question of "what" is more difficult than that of "how much". What is the reflection of the Angel's anticipated to-be-profit-generating interest in the project? Debt (with appropriate incentives), stock (share of profits) or royalties (share of revenues)? My own preference is for a share of revenues - which can always be converted to equity, either by the entrepreneur under certain circumstances or by the Angel. My least favorite reflection of investor's interest is that which relates exclusively to profits.

I have two reasons for my aversion to profit-only related inducements to invest in private companies. First, the *reported* net profit (in the instance of success) of a privately owned company is highly controllable by the management. It also may well be in the best interests of the owner's of the company, or its managers, to take actions which reduce current profits for the sake of either increased future profit or for other reasons. Second, I see no virtue in any investment structure which unnecessarily places the company management in the position of having to report and pay income taxes on the highest possible amount of earnings.

The way I like best to share in a business is through a royalty on revenues. I do this through the medium of what I call Revenue Participation Certificates ("RPC").

Revenue Participation Certificate

A number of industries have found royalties to be a useful means of permitting a participation by one party without creating a full partnership between the parties. Frequently, the reason for isolating the interests of one party was a limitation of the level of contribution that party could make to the total effort. In some cases, royalty holders are wholly passive. Another good reason for the party not in control of the business or project to want a revenue-based interest is the difficulty in some businesses in agreeing on the fairness of accounting or level and description of appropriate, and directly related, expenditures. It is easier and therefore much faster to get, and give, a good accounting of the number of objects manufactured or sold than to determine the profits made.

Some industries which traditionally have used royalties as a means of compensation include; publishing, entertainment, oil and gas, mining, timber, real estate, and, of course, a broad range of companies dealing with patent and copyright holders.

I use the term Revenue Participation Certificate (RPC) rather than simply revenue participation because I believe it important to continually note that the entitlement can be represented by a document, much like a stock or bond certificate. The RPC should be freely transferable. The RPC entitlement is not some vague agreement to be negotiated at a later date after results occur. Since I am usually the holder of the RPC, I want it, at some point, to be fully negotiable and therefore prefer using a term which usually connotes transferability. Although the RPC is not equity, as it does not vote or have an ownership interest in the issuing company, it is probably a security for purposes of the holder making a public distribution. It has always been my thought that an investment broker underwriting and trading in fully SEC registered RPCs would make a lot of money.

Many circumstances occur in which a company and/or non-incorporated provider of goods or services might make use of a RPC; for example, providing and compensating professional services, gaining and permitting the use of equipment or real property, or obtaining and providing finance. RPCs have no residual interest in a liquidation of a company, except for fees due. The RPC is not a share of stock. Were it a share of stock, federal and local taxing authorities would assert that payments made were dividends and therefore were not deductible as an expense to the company. Therefore the RPC should probably not be sold by a company directly for capital raising purposes, but rather be issued as a part of transaction. In my case, I usually structure the RPC to be, in part, as a consulting fee. The payments received by the owner of the RPC are, in any case, income to that party, and must be structured in such a way that they are an ordinary expense item to the paying company.

Although the RPC has many applications, the one on which we will now focus is the financing of companies, particularly companies in their development stages. The RPC is an ideal method of compensating a company's loan guarantor, and it is in this connection that I have made the greatest use of the technique. I much prefer to earn my right to share in the success of a venture through being a guarantor, or direct lender, rather than through the purchase of equity. My reasons for the preference are based on my wish to use maximum leverage and also to avoid conflicts with management.

The following considerations should be reviewed. There is no "right" or "best" set of terms, since each transaction differs with the circumstances of the Angel or financier and of the entrepreneur. However, one should bear two important facts in mind: most entrepreneurs truly believe their projections, and very few projections are ever achieved. My own use, and advocacy, of the RPC as a device for investors is based upon my experience relating to these two "facts" of venture investing.

Guarantees

The Angel/guarantor's single most important consideration is to recognize the probability that the guarantee will be called upon by the lender funding it, owing to the company not being able to repay the loan as agreed. In many, if not most, cases, the difference between being a direct lender to a company and guaranteeing that company's obligations is only one of time.

Guarantees can take many forms. They can be full and unconditional, and it is this form that most lenders demand. In this form the guarantee agreement also usually obliges the guarantor to be liable for all interest charges and costs of collection, all without reference to time. The lender is in complete control and has no risk, assuming the guarantee is "good." Therefore, I strongly recommend that the guarantee document be fully reviewed, understood, and negotiated with the funding lender.

Other forms of guarantees should be considered. Guarantors and others involved in the borrowing process should bear in mind that banks and other lenders want to make loans. They do not make money by saying "no." They are in business to lend at rates which are sufficiently higher than their own cost of money to yield a profit. The role of the guarantor is to provide sufficient comfort to the lender to permit a "yes." It is also worth noting that guarantees can be used with all suppliers of credit, not just banks.

Indemnifications

Indemnifications are not guarantees but have some of the same attributes and can be used by entrepreneurs in some of the same circumstances as guarantees. Also, the issuer of the indemnification can receive as compensation a RPC. In the case of an indemnification, the indemnifier undertakes to pay the indemnified party an agreed upon amount in the event the indemnified party incurs a loss in dealing with the subject of the indemnification. The indemnification agreement usually requires the indemnified party to take normal actions to protect his own interest. Most importantly, the indemnified party *must* seek payment from the primary obligor *before* seeking redress from the indemnifier. This is very different from the case with a guarantor. A guarantor or endorser of an obligation is as fully liable as the primary obligor. In other words, the lender can come directly to the guarantor of the loan without making any attempt to obtain payment from the borrowing company which was guaranteed.

Forms of Guarantees and Related Considerations

Partial guarantees. A company I started in Singapore issued "first loss guarantees" to banks on behalf of companies. The company accepted the risk on the first loss, either in percentage terms, which I preferred, or in absolute amount, which the banks preferred. Obviously, the first loss guarantor is in a better position if the risk is reduced by repayments rather than always being liable for the maximum fixed amount. In this case, the banks referred business to the company since they wanted to rent their money to the borrower at attractive rates of interest, from their perspective, but still required the comfort of additional support for the loan. The first loss guarantee issuing company charged the guaranteed borrower a fee based upon the same rate of interest which the bank charged on the amount of money which was exposed to risk by the company's issuing the guarantee. This resulted in the borrower effectively paying double interest on the portion of the loan guaranteed, which was usually one-third to one-half of the full loan, and only bank interest on the balance. Although the borrower was paying double interest on the guaranteed portion of the loan, the alternative for the borrower was one of seeking nonbank financing on the full loan, which would have resulted in significantly higher overall charges.

Conditional or contingent guarantees. Contingent guarantee liability can either be activated by the occurrence or nonoccurrence of events or released similarly by some achievement. For example, the guarantor could become liable if the company failed to have an audited net worth of at least X amount by Y date, or conversely be released from the guarantee in the event that by Y date the net worth exceeded X amount. Earnings and/or current ratios of assets to liability tests are also possible. The guarantee could be released were the company to

129

obtain agreed upon additional financing or a contract, or upon the occurrence of some other event which, were it present at the time of the loan negotiation, the bank would have made the loan without the guarantee. It is important that the bank specifically agree to the terms and conditions for releasing the guarantor from liability. The bank will resist specific release conditions, asking the guarantor to rely on the bank's goodwill and its need to meet the terms which will be offered by competitive lenders once the borrower is in a better condition. Guarantors should resist the appearance of reasonableness by the bank, since obtaining release from guarantees is very difficult.

Collateralization of guarantees. In some cases it may be possible for the guarantor to simply execute a guarantee agreement with a lender without providing the lender with collateral to assure performance of the guarantor. In most cases, the bank or sophisticated lender will want some form of collateral. There should be a negotiation with the bank by the guarantor as to the amount and form of collateral. Clearly, the guarantor might simply place with the bank U.S. government obligations in an amount in excess of the amount of the loan being guaranteed. The bank would like this situation almost as much as the guarantor making and pledging a deposit with the bank. However, the guarantor might also offer to lodge with the bank unregistered shares of some publicly traded corporation, or an interest in a privately owned corporation, or another nonmarketable asset. The asset collateralizing the guarantee can be whatever the guarantor and lender agree upon. Also, the amount of collateralization can vary.

The guarantor might ask why the bank should not be satisfied with a 50% collateralization, especially from a creditworthy guarantor. It should be understood that the bank is not in a position, and does not want, to immediately liquidate the collateral to resolve an indebtedness on the part of the guarantor. The bank will simply want *cash* upon calling the loan, and the company's inability or unwillingness to make the repayment is not of concern to the bank since the bank will have the guarantor's commitment and collateral.

Collateral value maintenance is also a point to be negotiated. What happens if the value of the collateral declines, or advances, during the period of the guarantee? Should the guarantor be required to maintain a specified level of value? Will the bank permit withdrawal in the event the value increases? Will the bank permit substitution of collateral, and under what conditions? Of course, the guarantor is in a better position, as is the borrower, if the loan can be repaid at any time without penalty.

The form of guarantee collateral I suggest is a Letter of Credit ("LC"). Further, I propose the specific guaranteeing entity have no assets other than the LC or that the bank agree to make the loan on a basis of having no recourse to the guarantor other than to the pledged collateral of the LC. The guarantor can own the shares of the corporation actually issuing the guarantee and can either have the RPC or other guarantee fee paid to himself *or* to the guaranteeing entity. In any case, the guarantor is in a much better position if the bank has as their only collateral a LC with a fixed maturity date than if the bank holds assets having a value which extends past the period of the guarantee. The guarantor is better protected if the bank calls the loan should the borrower fail to make timely payments or breach other elements of the loan agreement. It is only upon the guarantor assuming the position of the lender, through subrogation, that the guarantor will be in a position of being able to protect his capital.

Subrogation. The guarantor obtains, if the contract so provides, all of the borrower's collateral held by the lender once the guarantor pays the lender the monies owed under the guarantee. The guarantor is really buying the loan from the lender and is therefore substituted as the lender. Therefore, the guarantor is potentially the net beneficiary of all of the demands for collateral the bank imposes upon the borrower and, in fact, the Angel can suggest to the bank the collateral necessary for the guarantor to issue their guarantee.

Terms of guarantee. Guarantees are usually issued for the entire term of the loan. I suggest the guarantor limit the term of the guarantee, and therefore limit the period of the loan. Guarantees, as loans, can always be reinstated and rolled over, providing satisfactory progress is made on the part of the borrower. For instance, the guarantee could be for one year, with an agreement that if the borrower made an agreed upon amount of progress the guarantee would be available for another year.

Guarantee Fees

Guarantee fees can be paid in cash, or by transferring an asset of the guaranteed party or of some other party, including shares and/or debt of the guaranteed corporation. Guarantee fees can also, of course, be paid in the form of RPCs.

131

Fixed fees. RPC considerations and the revenue participation fee entitlement represented by the RPC can be fixed as to percentage of revenues, with or without a threshold level and/or a cap or upper limit of participation. There can be a maximum and/or minimum amount of fee agreed to be paid over an agreed upon period.

Currency and jurisdiction. Payments made pursuant to obligations of a RPC can be made in any currency and directed to any depository upon which the parties have agreed. The agreement can be subject to any jurisdiction agreed. Similarly, the parties to the agreement may agree to submit differences to binding arbitration in any jurisdiction.

Scaled fees. Fees may be scaled to reflect the needs of the guaranteed party and guarantor. The guarantee fee can be for a lower percentage at lower sales levels and rise with the level of revenues. Conversely, the percentage participation can reduce with increased revenues. It depends on the type of business and the particular transaction. If the business being invested in through the acceptance of risk in issuing guarantees is operationally highly leveraged, it might be better to have a low, or perhaps no, participation until the revenues are at a level which would generate profits; participation could then increase with the projected profit margin in order to provide a return which would be the equivalent of an ownership position. On the other hand, if the business is one in which personal service of the entrepreneur is a primary factor, and therefore the ultimate size of the business is limited, the guarantor would naturally want a larger piece of the earlier revenues. An arrangement where the RPC entitlement scales down in percentage terms provides the guaranteed party with an incentive to expand the business.

Assignability of fees. There is no reason why the fees received by the RPC holder should in any way be restricted as to assignment. This is important, since the RPC owner may wish to use the future revenue flow from the RPC as collateral for borrowing or other purposes.

Transferability and Negotiability of RPC

The owner of the RPC will want to have as unrestricted an asset as possible. In theory, as noted previously, there is no reason why RPCs cannot be offered publicly by either a company or by the owner of RPCs. The lender will not release the guarantor from the guarantee without satisfactory substitution of guarantee and/or collateral. Nevertheless, subject to the obligations to the lender, and certainly

132

after the loan has been repaid and/or the guarantor is relieved of liability, the owner of the RPC may want to be able to profit from disposing of the RPC if it has not been terminated - rather than just collecting the negotiated revenue participation.

Term of RPC Entitlement

Although the guarantee for which the RPC is awarded will be for a specific period, and usually in connection with a specific transaction, there is no reason why the RPC entitlement should have any specific maturity. The matter is purely one to be negotiated between the guarantor and the entrepreneur. As a guarantor receiving the RPC fees, my favorite term is somewhere between forever and perpetuity. As an entrepreneur issuing an RPC, I would see no reason why any fees should be paid once the guarantee liability was extinguished. Fairness, and fairness is good business, will place the term of entitlement somewhere between the two extremes.

Termination

As the requirement to pay RPC fees is burdensome, as is the requirement to pay rent, taxes, and other fixed costs of doing business, the entrepreneur will seek a basis for terminating the payments. This is particularly true as in many cases the owner of the business will find the presence of an RPC an impediment to selling or merging the business and/or going public. The termination payment can be in the form of debt or stock, of an agreed upon minimum amount or percentage basis, or of cash. If in stock (which can be a convertible preferred as well as common stock), the shares can be either registered or registerable. I believe that it should be the owner of the business who has the option to convert, not the owner of the RPC. In any case, termination should not be even a remote possibility until after the owner of the RPC has been relieved of *all* liability and has received *all* payments due. The termination schedule should take into consideration the amount and timing of RPC fee payments received, as well as the maximum amount of capital which was exposed to risk. It makes no sense for the RPC owner to negotiate termination while either under the pressure of a possible loan call or when there are open account items.

Financial Reporting

Owners of RPCs do not have a specific interest in the profits of a business in which they have a revenue participation fee entitlement.

As guarantors, they are interested in the ability of the borrower to meet obligations which otherwise will become their obligations. Therefore, once the guarantee liability has been extinguished, the RPC holder's right to receive audited financial statements may be lessened or relieved. The RPC holder is solely interested in the level of revenues, and the difference between gross and net revenues if the contract makes that distinction. Therefore, an attested statement of revenue is all that should be necessary if the attestation is made by a party acceptable to the RPC holder. Of course, if the RPC holder is being asked to consider some change in status or if the issuer of the RPC is taking some corporate or structural action which will have an impact on the value of the RPC in terms of the level of revenues or fee entitlement, then there should be a requirement for the provision of full information.

Monitoring Performance of the RPC Issuer

Depending on circumstance, the RPC holder may wish to have the right to a flow of information similar to and at least as much as that which a director of the company is entitled to. The RPC holder should be careful, as should the issuer, that actions are not taken which would permit taxing authorities to assert that the RPC was sufficiently similar to a share as to attempt to disallow the fee payment deduction as being but a disguised dividend. Nor does the RPC holder want to be in a position where it could be claimed by other creditors that he was a creditor in control of the issuing company or that, in the event of bankruptcy of the issuing company the payments were a preference. One solution might be for the RPC owner to also have, perhaps in some other entity than the one issuing the guarantee, an amount of the RPC issuing company's stock. The RPC owner, as justified by the shareholding in the non-guaranteeing entity, could then place a person on the board of directors of the RPC issuing company. This is an area where counsel for the guarantor should be especially aware of the relevant bankruptcy laws.

Security

The issuer of the RPC may secure the provider of the guarantee and owner of the RPC with a pledge of assets unencumbered by the primary lender, or by assignment of a subordinated interest in assets already pledged to others. Second, and even third, mortgages do have value. The guarantor can also be secured by an endorsement of a third party and/or pledge of assets owned by others. It is important to recognize that issuers of guarantees can also be indemnified as well as be the beneficiary of third party guarantees.

One technique I have used is to require that the entrepreneur become a personal guarantor of the loan, and in some cases the entrepreneur's spouse as well, in the event the company fails to achieve some event which the entrepreneur had predicted would occur as an inducement to persuade me to accept risk.

Revenue participation certificates are not new. Only the phrase is new. Royalties have been used successfully for centuries by a wide range of enterprises. I predict that in the future, increasing numbers of Angels and entrepreneurs are going to be involved in transactions which use revenue sharing or royalties, rather than profit sharing or equity, as a basis for one party gaining use and control of the capital of the other party. Profit determination is frequently a subjective exercise in which the objectives of various constituencies have to be balanced and dealt with. A broad range of management and accounting options have an impact on reported profits. As an Angel and financier, I prefer to have my return on risk acceptance and capital employment based upon a factor about which all parties can agree. The RPC is one way of accomplishing this objective as revenues are non-ambiguous.

Example of RPC Technique

The following is a letter to a lawyer who asked how to use an RPC technique in providing what otherwise would be equity in a venture capital investment.

Dear _____,

Thank you for the opportunity to review the material regarding KDI. Assuming that one accepted the premise of sales increasing more than 8-fold and profits by more than 2000-fold within four years, there exists an extraordinary opportunity for an investor.

However, the investor should also be aware that the $1.0 million sought is *PURE* risk capital, regardless of the form it takes, unless guaranteed in some way by other than KDI, because there is almost no balance sheet protection.

Therefore, the following structure is believed fair in terms of balancing risk and reward from the perspective of the investor. From the perspective of the present owners of KDI, they will profit handsomely should the projection be achieved and will not have to put at risk more than is already committed.

1. I suggest that the investor(s) obtain a one-year letter of credit from a credit worthy institution in the amount of $1.0 million. The issuing institution should agree to renew the letter for additional one-year periods, at the request of the investor(s), assuming that the investor(s) have provided the level of collateral or other comfort the issuing institution requires.

2. The investor(s) can then propose to KDI the guaranteeing of a loan, from a bank selected by KDI, on terms to be negotiated. The investor(s) will agree to collateralize their guarantee by the pledging of the letter of credit.

3. The arrangement I propose is for the investor(s) to receive, as an inducement to accept the risk of guaranteeing a $1.0 million loan, for a stipulated period, a revenue participation certificate (RPC) entitling:

   1% of the first $10.0 million of annual revenues

   2% of the next $5.0 million of revenues

   3% of the next $5.0 million of revenues

   4% of the next $5.0 million of revenues

   5% of the next $5.0 million of revenues, and of all additional revenues.

Based upon the projections provided the following table reflects the results of the above:

| | Projected | | | | |
Year	Revenues	Pretax Profits	Resulting cumulative annual RPC payments	Gross RPC ROI	% of KDI's Pretax
Year 1	$ 7.25	$ .583	$ 72.5	7.25%	12.2%*
Year 2	13.2	1.2	100+64=164	16.4	13.7%
Year 3	19.6	2.08	100+100+138=338	33.8	16.3
Year 4	26.0	3.43	100+100+150+240=590	59.0	17.2

*A deferral of all or part can be negotiated

4. The term of the guarantee should not exceed 2 years and there should be a threshold level of achievement required for the second year of the guarantee.

5. Were KDI to wish relief from the RPC obligation, the following is proposed ONCE the investor(s) have been relieved of ALL guarantee liability and KDI has met all of its RPC payment obligations:

   A. Cash payment of $5.0 million within 2 years and increasing at 35% per annum thereafter: or

   B. Conversion, only at KDI's option, into a senior redeemable convertible preferred stock of KDI on the basis of the amount of preferred having a similar value to the cash payment option at the time of issue. Both the preferred and common stock, into which the preferred is convertible, should have registration rights. The conversion price and maturity of the preferred can be addressed later.

6. The term of the RPC should be 35 years, though KDI can shorten the period through using the above formulas.

There are a number of other considerations, including: third-party endorsements, collateralization required by funding bank, personal guarantees of the primary promoters, pledge of shares of KDI, signed undated letters of resignation of KDI executives to be used (by dating) only upon certain agreed circumstances, consulting role of agent of RPC holders, auditing rights, etc., which should be addressed.

The net of the above is that were the projections to be achieved, KDI would be worth more than $15.0 million in Year 3, assuming a modest p/e. KDI would in all probability seek relief from the RPC payments, and the worst-case (from KDI's perspective) deal is still a good one. From the perspective of the RPC-holding investor(s), a good deal is achieved even without the achievement of the projected events as long as: 1) KDI survives and can refinance the guarantee or repay the guaranteed loan and 2) revenues increase to exceed $15.0 million.

I hope this is useful to you. In any case, it provides an insight into the use of RPCs.

Sincerely,
Arthur Lipper III

Deal Structure Can Be More Important than Pricing

The structure of a deal can be much more important than the apparent or stated pricing. The example here is real estate, but the approach is equally applicable to private company investment.

BUYER: I'd like to buy your house. How much are you asking?

SELLER: $90,000.

BUYER: You have a deal.

SELLER: (taken aback): Aren't you going to negotiate?

BUYER: No, I never negotiate price. But *we* have a problem.

SELLER: What's our problem?

BUYER: I don't have $90,000.

SELLER: What are we going to do about that?

BUYER: I have $15,000. I'll go to the bank this afternoon and find how much of a first mortgage they'll give me, and you're going to give me a five-year second mortgage on the difference.

SELLER: I am?

BUYER: You are, since we both want me to buy this house for $90,000.

The deal was struck for $15,000 in cash from the buyer and $55,000 from the bank, with a five-year second mortgage of $20,000 from the seller, and this is how I bought our White Plains, New York home in which we lived for 27 years. The property, described as an estate for sale purposes, after lots of investment and improvements, was appraised at several million dollars. All that may be needed in a deal is a single element of initial agreement:

ENTREPRENEUR: My company needs a million dollars for 90 days, until the public offering becomes effective.

INVESTOR: I like your people and I like your company. What do you want to give me?

ENTREPRENEUR: A 5-year warrant on 25,000 shares. The stock will be offered at 16.

INVESTOR: I'll take that. But you're also going to give me, as well as the 5-year warrant, a put so that at the end of five years I can put the stock back to you 20 points higher. In other words, I am going to buy the stock at 16 and have the right to sell it to you at 36 at the end of five years.

ENTREPRENEUR: That's a $500,000 minimum profit over five years!

INVESTOR: You say the price of the stock is going to climb, that earnings will increase significantly. Won't the stock be selling at way over 36 in five years' time?

ENTREPRENEUR: Of course, it will be. Our earnings are going to quadruple.

INVESTOR: Terrific. So what do you care then if I have a right to put the stock to you at 36 as I am obviously not going to do so if the stock is selling at more than 36?

There is a potential tax problem for the investor accepting both the warrant and a put, in the same entity, in that the IRS may ascribe a higher value to the warrant than would have been the case absent the European style (exercisable only at maturity) put. Angels to be successful have to be very tax-aware.

This agreement, which was concluded with a company on the verge of going public and described in the company's prospectus, was based on the entrepreneur being willing to accept a single element around which a deal could be constructed. The investor did not argue with the entrepreneur about the number of shares being offered. He simply took what was offered him and locked the entrepreneur into what the entrepreneur himself proposed.

Thus, investors can let the entrepreneur propose the deal as they see it, and then take the elements they can work with from that proposal.

Lipper Equitable Distribution Formula for Financing Startups

In many cases, entrepreneurs approach investors with an excellent idea for a business and appear to be qualified to manage it. There is only one problem: Entrepreneurs do not have the money and choose, typically out of concern for their family, not to incur personal obligations. Otherwise, everything seems great -- the idea, the market, the product, the staff, everything.

My proposal in such a case is that Angels receive 100 percent of the initial equity of the business (perhaps structuring to qualify for the benefit of S or Limited Liability corporation status), and that entrepreneurs receive an option from the company to acquire within 5 to 10 years 50 percent of the then-to-be outstanding shares at 150 percent of the Angel's cost, with, of course, the money going to the company. The Angel could permit a lower exercise price if the option was exercised earlier than agreed or could adjust the exercise price to the performance of the company. The important feature is that the Angel initially owns all the shares and the entrepreneur none.

If entrepreneurs suggest that this (or any other proposed deal) is too tough a deal, I usually ask if they have any friends or family members who would like to participate with me in this overly unfair deal favoring the Angel. They can have any part or all of it. I also suggest to them that it probably *is* too tough a deal if they are only going to build a small company, but that it is a great deal if they are going to build a big company, because the company is getting well funded at the outset. Entrepreneurs can subsequently borrow money, sell some stock, or sell some of the options (they may even be registered if the company goes public) in order to buy the rest. Thus, for example, they could have an opportunity to buy half of a company worth $8 million for $300,000--the ultimate value of the company being dependent upon their own efforts. I also point out to the entrepreneur that if Angels own all the stock initially, the Angels will likely be less reluctantly forthcoming with more money when it is needed and will be all the more motivated to contribute whatever assets they have.

This arrangement does not affect entrepreneur salary, employee stock option plans, or any other conventional means of motivating the entrepreneur and management.

There are a number of variations on this approach. The option price and/or number of shares optioned can vary with projected result achievement levels. The arrangement can, and should be, structured to recognize additional shares issued for capital or acquisitions. Angels should think through what they want to happen to what may become a block of shares equal to, or by that time, larger than their own in the event of the entrepreneur's death or divorce. Should the shares be equally voting if held by other than the entrepreneur? Any restriction on voting will, of course, reduce the value of the shares and, therefore, of the option. I always provide an incentive in the deal for the entrepreneur to invest earlier than the option's maturity.

Profit Margins

The essence of business planning is estimating future revenue levels and accurately determining the cost of being in business at various levels of volume.

In reviewing projected financial results, Angels are obliged to constantly challenge assumptions in order to understand the dynamics of the project's profit margins. Are the profit margins realistic compared to other companies in the same field? Will they be maintainable once competition enters? Can they be attained with the funding being sought or with what is available? It is in this area of profit margin analysis that the Angel's accountant can possibly be most helpful. I would not ask an accountant for general business advice, nor would I seek his counsel regarding the reasonableness of the projected revenues. I would, however, want to have the benefit of his experience regarding the likelihood of the projected profits evolving if the revenues were as projected. The accountant is more likely to be blessed with the "pessimism of reason" than either the entrepreneur or the prospective Angel.

When Angels read the business plan for a venture, generally it should be the revenue and profit margin attainability upon which they focus. The accountant can be most helpful in the profit margin assessment area.

Many of us read business plans, hundreds each year, by glancing at the summary and quickly reviewing the five-year projections. If the business concept seems at all reasonable *and* if the five-year projections are of sufficient magnitude to be interesting to me, and appear reasonable in relationship to various elements, then, and only then, do I think about reading the entire plan. This may be a little like reading a murder mystery by looking at the last chapter first. I want to know what "happened" and then go through the drill of reading to see (1) how it happened, and (2) if it was a reasonable conclusion to reach based upon the facts presented. Also, the section in the plan which is critical and which really important in my assessment of reasonableness of the projections is the backgrounds of the directors, officers and advisors displayed.

An all too frequent business plan failing is that I find myself still wondering what the business is the entrepreneur believes he has described after reading the first page of the Executive Summary. If the story can't be summarized on one page it's probably too esoteric to be of interest to me. It's very simple. Describe who the customers are or will be and the unique selling proposition or advantage to the customer in purchasing the goods or services being offered. Then describe how those goods or services can be produced and marketed for less than the sales price.

141

Stock versus Assets

Angels are most frequently offered opportunities to invest in or lend to (if there is a difference) existing corporations and, thus, do not have the flexibility and comfort of forming their own corporations for the project. They are specifically being asked to buy stock rather than assets.

What is the difference between stock and assets if the values are comparable? The answer is known and unknown liabilities. Although liabilities can also be stated as being comparable, investors do not know how fully stated they are in the case of the already existing corporation. An ongoing business can present investors with many unwelcome surprises; for example, entrepreneurs may have promised to give the finder (of the Angels) a lifetime consulting contract at $2,000 per month, or there may be a dispute about the creation of the product or ownership of the patents, or a claim may be threatened by an ex-associate or employee for damages of some kind. The pending action may not even have reached the stage yet where the company has become aware of it.

Angels are much safer from unknown or under disclosed liabilities in completely new corporations where future claims involving the entrepreneur, for acts committed previously, will probably focus on, or likely can be contained within, the entrepreneur's interest in the new corporation. Of course, a reader of this book will have already learned to obtain an indemnification from entrepreneurs for legal actions relating to their prior acts.

Investing in assets, rather than stock, in the form of buying shares of a newly formed corporation which acquires the assets and none of the liabilities of the predecessor corporation, is better than investing in the original corporation, because of the unknown liability issue. Included in such a transaction are the assumptions that the assets can be cleanly transferred for consideration -- the consideration being available in a form satisfactory to the owners and known creditors with prior interests in the assets -- and that there is not a significant tax-deductible loss being left behind in the original corporation. It is also being assumed that suppliers and customers will not be upset by a change of ownership -- the business being the ultimate asset -- even though the name of the enterprise has remained the same (being one of the acquired assets).

With a new corporation, Angels can create bylaws and structure the companies to suit their purposes, rather than undertake the sometimes more difficult task of altering and amending the details of an already existing situation. Another benefit of forming a new corporation is being able to produce a net worth statement for lenders that without question can fairly and completely identify assets and liabilities. (There may, however, be a question as to the valuation ascribed to any particular asset or liability.) The investor is comforted to know there is no skeleton in the closet, because the closet was just built today.

For a short article on this subject, see Appendix P.

Entrepreneur Guarantees

Most venture capitalists require some investment on the part of the entrepreneur in the venture being financed. The Angel similarly has reason to feel more comfortable if the entrepreneur has something tangible to lose if the Angel is likely to be faced with financial loss. The question is the amount and form of the entrepreneur's risk, and what the Angel should do if the entrepreneur is without financial assets. After all, some of the best qualified and most creative people -- the very kind Angels want to run a company in which they have a major interest -- have no money available for investment or other significant unencumbered assets. However, these same people will be making the projections as to future events on which the Angel will be relying both as to the basic decision of whether to invest or not and the appropriate valuation to place on the business.

James Bergman, of DSV Partners, pointed out,

The investor largely has to force the entrepreneur to attach his signature to his representations. At this time, the investor may discover that the entrepreneur has not done all his homework; for example, he may not have completed a thorough search to ensure that his patent will be accepted and does not infringe on the rights of another. This is the time for the investor to make such discoveries. When something incorrect is discovered after a closing, the investor's money is gone.

The normal way of handling the issue of projections is through the Angel discounting them in reaching a decision as to whether to invest or not, through valuation and in the allocation of rewards (equity). Yet, what can be done to spread the possible pain in the event of Angel loss?

Why be concerned with sharing the pain of loss? The reason is to equalize the risk/reward relationship. Entrepreneurs should not have

143

only upside potential. If they have nothing to lose, they have every reason to gamble and not bother with taking a measured view of management decisions and their likely results. Always betting to win is not prudent, and prudence is a requirement in the management of other people's money. Too few entrepreneurs consider these responsibilities, perhaps because too few Angels make the point to entrepreneurs that they are in a fiduciary position and must act accordingly. This is not to say that risk should not be accepted, because that is the expectation of the Angel. It is to say that the risks taken should not be total. One does not "bet the farm" on a single hand of cards, unless *all* of the owners of the farm agree and understand the possible consequences.

The basic question remains of how to have the entrepreneur share present and future risk intelligently. One way I have done it is to require the entrepreneurs making the projections to personally guarantee the same bank loan I am guaranteeing, to the extent that the retained earnings or book value results fall short of their projections. In one case, I provided a $100,000 bank guarantee in consideration of receiving ten percent of revenues of a service business. The business had a number of contracts from major customers in hand and was growing rapidly. The money was to be used for increased marketing efforts, such as having more salespeople and producing a brochure describing the company services. The entrepreneur represented that the contracts already in hand were certain to produce minimum revenues of $1 million the first year, $2 million the second, and $3 million the third. Therefore, I could expect to receive a guarantee fee of at least $100,000 (which, of course, is income to the guarantor and fully taxable) by the end of the first year. I told the entrepreneur, "You are making these projections while having no personal liability to me or to the bank, because the bank is lending your company money on my guarantee. You will have to guarantee that I will receive the fees anticipated or, in the event of a shortfall in fees paid to me, co-guarantee the bank." The significance of having the personal guarantee of the entrepreneur/manager is that the Angel-guarantor of the corporate loan will, if called upon by the bank to make good on the guarantee, inherit through subrogation all of the assets (including the personal guarantees of the entrepreneur) held by the bank to secure the loan in the first place. This assumes the bank is fully guaranteed and has agreed, as has the borrowing entity, to have the pledged assets subrogated to the guaranteeing party. The entrepreneur then owes the amount guaranteed to the bank to the Angel-guarantor.

144

It is also possible for the Angel to require of entrepreneurs that they obtain, under certain conditions, the guarantees or investment of others. If the entrepreneur is without friends or acquaintances who, for profit expectation or friendship, will not expose themselves to any risk, the Angel might have some second thoughts as to why this should be so.

As a matter of principle, I believe that the entrepreneur should be at some risk. However, I am flexible as to quantum, timing, and circumstance.

More on Entrepreneur Guarantees

It is all well and good to conclude that entrepreneurs will manage a business more prudently if they have something tangible to lose if the business fails or even if agreed upon objectives and projections are not met. The question is how to structure the penalty payment or penalty risk assumption, which may never result in any payment. A guarantee of a portion of the Angel's potential loss is an appropriate means of accomplishing risk sharing. Let's say that the entrepreneur now agrees he "will make up half the investors' loss if sales are not X by Y date." Now let's assume that sales are less then X, and investors look to the entrepreneur for compliance with their undertaking. As entrepreneurs often have little, if any, real money, the statement was empty in the first place, and there never was any real sharing of risk. As there was not the risk reduction anticipated by the investors, there was in fact an increased risk over what the investors had agreed to accept. Of course, the interest held by the entrepreneur in the company having been guaranteed might be transferred to the Angel so that, at least, the Angel then owned more of a company having a Net Operating Loss carry forward which conceivably would have a future value to the Angel.

The fact that the entrepreneur says "Sorry, investor, I just don't have the money to make good on my promise" does not mean that the Angel is necessarily out of luck or permanently out of funds. There is always the future; entrepreneurs have a way of making repetitive tries for the gold ring and frequently--for periods, at least--succeeding in gaining wealth. Also, because entrepreneurs are very human, they frequently forget the pain for which they were previously responsible. Therefore, a point to consider is that the Angel's return of capital may come from a future business enterprise. Accordingly, the terms of the entrepreneur's obligation should not be an unchangeable impediment to the entrepreneur's future. It may make sense for guaranteed Angels to subordinate their future interests in the profits (or whatever) of the entrepreneur to those financing the entrepreneur's new venture in the future. The guaranteed Angel wants the entrepreneur to get into business again and to succeed. Similarly, the Angel has a vested interest in seeing that the entrepreneur's credit rating is not damaged more than the facts justify. In a surprising number of instances, people who have gone bankrupt (and legally, therefore, have no further obligations to creditors) have repaid in full all previous creditors from money made in subsequent businesses. Angels, however, will not be hurt by attempting to "insure the conscience" of the entrepreneur by obligation. Incidentally, I would almost always back entrepreneurs who made good on prior obligations when they were not required to do so. Successful Angels invest in good people.

Therefore, I suggest taking entrepreneurs' notes as evidence of their intention to pay at a specific date in the future or whenever possible. The earlier the Angel attempts to get the note, the easier it will be. The correct time is before the Angel's money passes to the entrepreneur's control.

One last thought regarding promises to pay Angels by entrepreneurs: The Angel can treat a note or promise to pay as a sort of foreign debt or even debased currency, because as an asset it has a possible or probable value, but it may not be easily ascertainable by either the holder or the party to whom the Angel is trying to assign or sell it. A note is like a large yacht: the more people you have on it the more fun it is--for the holder of the asset. Of course, depending on the situation, the Angel can properly seek or insist on third-party full. partial or conditional endorsements on the guarantee or note. These endorsers (or co- or sub-guarantors) can be the spouse, the sibling, or other family and friends of the entrepreneur, or just those from whom the entrepreneur bought an endorsement for a fee or for the prospect of reward sharing. The endorsers can have a limited or full liability for the amount involved. Also, the personal obligations being undertaken in an unendorsed guarantee can be, for, say, ten percent (or more) of the entrepreneur's future earnings over Z amount per year, up to some amount. All of these protective devices should be instituted before the Angel permits the seduction to be consummated, as afterwards ardor and reality sets in--that is, few entrepreneurs assist Angels in subsequent fund recapture unless so obliged.

The very idea of the Angel (or lender) requiring (extracting) the guarantee of the spouse of the entrepreneur will offend some readers.

146

I do not suggest that obtaining the spouse's endorsement is always a must. However, there are at least two reasons why it is a good idea.

The first is illustrated by the story of the advice given by a London merchant banker to the King of England during one of the bleakest periods of World War II. The advice was, "Put Canada in your wife's name." Business owners and entrepreneurs frequently, and at times with perfectly valid reasons, separate assets between themselves and their spouses (and children). This asset division should be reflected in the personal net worth statement the entrepreneur is required to prepare for the Angel. An understatement of assets (where there is an obligation) can be just as misleading, and therefore fraudulent, as an overstatement. Angels can never really be certain if they have been fully informed or if the situation will remain constant. The spouse could inherit money after the execution of the guarantee, as could children (from their grandparents, perhaps). If Angels are intent on recapturing their money to the extent "possible," then they must think through all of the disaster scenarios and position themselves accordingly. Angels must remember that after the honeymoon, attitudes and perspectives change; Angels are not likely to be in as good a position to protect themselves after the check passes as before. If the reason for the guarantee is to get money back, make sure the document is drafted and executed appropriately.

Second, the spouse is an integral part of the total picture, or make-up, of the entrepreneur. They will share in the rewards of success whether or not they remain married after the success is achieved. To assist in achieving success, they are going to have to continue to positively motivate the entrepreneur and make personal sacrifices of attention. They will be more understanding of the pressure the entrepreneur bears if they are a direct participant therein. They may also hold an initial interest in the company and most probably will through inheritance. Although a co-signer is sometimes described as a "fool with a fountain pen," I believe that the act of co-signing between married partners can be a relationship-strengthening indication of confidence and participation. Let the spouse sign. As with all of the other protective devices suggested in this guide, holders are not required to use the rights granted in the documentation even though they hold the rights to do so.

Justification of Penalty for Nonachieved Projection

Because it has been stated that projections are almost always wrong, or at least highly suspect, the thought may have occurred to some that the purpose of requiring entrepreneurs to provide projections is to trap them into a performance-based deal. This is absolutely not the case.

The purpose of Angels' requiring entrepreneurs seeking funding to prepare and provide projections is twofold.

First, the reason for being in any business is to earn profit, and the amount of profit believed possible justifies the amount of the investment of time, talent, money, and risk of loss. Whether or not entrepreneurs actually put a business plan on paper, every successful entrepreneur who has built a business has had a plan. The purpose of committing a plan to paper is to better share it with others. Projections of results are an integral part of such a plan and must be developed to determine the steps the business manager will take. A business plan is simply a road map used to plan a trip. Without such a map, getting lost is almost inevitable. Getting lost can sometimes be fun, but it can also prove fatal. In starting and running a business -- any business-- the Angels, entrepreneur, and managers must know what is expected around the next turn. To know this, they must also know where and when the turns are placed along the path they intend to travel. As the Dun & Bradstreet business failure statistics show conclusively, and as has every other study I have heard of, it is lack of adequate planning that is the major reason for business failure. Therefore, entrepreneurs must prepare plans and make projections to reach conclusions themselves as to whether they have valid business ventures or just ideas for new products or services that might well be attractive to some company already in business with many of the required elements in place. By seriously studying the plan with entrepreneurs, the Angel will come to understand (1) the business being proposed and (2) something of entrepreneurs and their talents and weaknesses. The entrepreneur must be able to defend satisfactorily, to the Angel, all assumptions and premises made which have an effect on the financial results projected. If it doesn't make sense on paper, it won't work in practice.

Second, Angels can estimate a projected return on their investment in the project only through learning from the entrepreneur or through the entrepreneur's business plan and its projections. Only after calculating such a return on investment (assuming that the entrepreneur has fairly presented the facts and assumptions) can the Angel compare the return on the private company investment with that available by investing in publicly traded companies, which may be in the same

148

area of business activity and, thus, have a similar potential from the same macroeconomic trends predicted or assumed by the entrepreneur.

A thought that presents itself here is that investors would be well advised to specifically identify those publicly traded securities which are most directly related to the private company being considered. A detailed study of these several publicly traded companies may yield ratios and performance measurements applicable to the private company. It may also be a very good idea for the investor to invest in the public companies, since it is very possible that the private company entrepreneur's knowledge of the industry and his predictive capabilities concerning new developments are superior to his ability to run a business or even to obtain the necessary funding to start one. Investing in publicly traded Internet-related companies would have been a good idea for those considering funding companies having an Internet product which were not public. The industry's macroeconomics were great, even if a large number of wanna be's didn't make it. Such a public company investment could yield much information and insight and possibly offset the results of the private company investment if that does not work out a hoped. Certainly, the added intelligence gained from studying and coming to know the competition can only help in the decisions the Angel will be called upon to make. Of course, if both the idea and the private company investment work out, the Angel will really have a great parlay.

I believe it to be a fair supposition, and a basis for negotiation, that the entrepreneur knows more than the Angel about the proposed business. Therefore, it seems only fair to burden entrepreneurs with the responsibility for their statements and projections, because Angels are forced to rely on them for the prospect of profit and apprehension of loss. I would agree that entrepreneurs should not be penalized if they are also risking capital on the same basis as the Angel, or if they will place themselves in financial risk in the event that what they have projected is not achieved. In the absence of a financial risk undertaking by the entrepreneur, penalization through withdrawal of reward seems a logical offset.

Motivating the Entrepreneur

Because most entrepreneurs are motivated by a need to achieve, to be recognized, and, most importantly, to prove something, money tends to be more important to them as a symbol than as buying power. Most of the successful entrepreneurs I know do not live at the level their income or net worth would permit. Thus, investors who wish to motivate entrepreneurs must consider how best to do it and not simply throw money at them by way of reward.

In structuring the deal, Angels have to be clear themselves how the entrepreneur's greater effort can accomplish the desired goal. Do Angels want sales to increase over budget, or do they prefer that expenses be kept to an under budget level or to a set percentage? Do Angels want debt levels reduced, or do they want an increased subordinated debt that does not have to be guaranteed by them? Do they want a new group of executives? A reduced unit cost in some manufactured item? A merger completed? The sale of a division? The completion of a certain task? Once Angels have decided what exactly they want and how the entrepreneur can best help them get it, they should set up a bonus plan which can involve cash or stock, or stock equivalents.

Angels have to understand the business well before they can expect to know where the efforts of the entrepreneur/manager are best focused. As a partner, the Angel may well be in a better position than the manager of the business to point out the areas that most need improvement. It is Angels' money that is being used to pay people, and it is their profit which is either being increased or diminished by more or less attention to specific areas than would otherwise be the case.

I believe in specific project bonuses and not in general performance rewards. Entrepreneurs are already motivated in the general performance area by virtue of their holding an interest in the company and receiving a salary. Specific project bonuses mutually agreed upon by the Angel and entrepreneur/manager can be highly constructive for a company. When a management team is involved, its key members should be included in the bonus plan.

You, as the Angel, can think of your dollars as green slaves -- the more you have of them, the less you have to do yourself and/or the more you can accomplish. Thus, the interest on your money is equivalent to rental of your green slaves in the form of more green slaves. It seems reasonable that the owner of these green slaves should be willing to pay a premium for their early release for reassignment to other jobs. After all, the owner of the green slaves is going to be paid more proportionately for their showing up for work on the first day than for any other part of their effort. In venture capital terms, I structure deals in such a way as to give entrepreneurs a benefit if they can replace and thereby free up my money at an earlier than anticipated date.

The wish of Angels to recapture their money for redeployment in this way must be distinguished from the approach of most professional venture capital investment managers. They are paid to employ the money under management rather than to achieve the highest possible total return. Normal venture capital money managers are not financial-leverage-oriented, because if they are successful (in raising money), they already have all the money they can use for current investment purposes. This is not the case with individual Angels investing in private companies. They need their green slaves back as soon as possible...and in good condition. They cannot, somewhat smugly, take the position that venture capital investing is a process that requires seven years to know performance results. If you ever wish to upset a venture capitalist, suggest the need for an interim term performance measurement service, such as those I created in the New York Stock Exchange member firm, Arthur Lipper Corporation, in 1967 for mutual funds.

Paying entrepreneurs a cash bonus or reducing the revenue participation certificate (royalty) rate, either in percentage or maturity, are other ways Angels can motivate entrepreneurs to replace their money.

Individual Angels fortunate enough to have a flow of deals to consider should be willing to pay a premium for earlier than contracted fund recapture. More sophisticated entrepreneurs will probably, of their own accord, suggest such an arrangement if more attractive funding becomes available to them. However, it is more advantageous for Angels to offer entrepreneurs an incentive early on, because their offers will appear more attractive in the early stages of the business before actual profits have been generated.

Bill Berkley told me,

By and large, I don't think that partnerships are the best form of structure for a new or very young company. A corporate structure that involves a convertible, redeemable, voting, preferred stock held by the investor often provides a big incentive for management when the conversion ratio is tied to the achievement of objectives. If the entrepreneur/manager does not redeem the stock, the investor ends up with a big piece. If the entrepreneur/manager meets certain objectives, the preferred stock gets redeemed out and the combined equity owner ship balance changes. I do not give a particular incentive for early redemption, and there's no penalty for late redemption, either in the cost of the interest or the accrued earnings.

Dan Lufkin had this suggestion to make. "One very useful formula goes like this: the investor puts up all the money and gets 100 percent of the equity; if entrepreneurs pay back all the money in one year, they get 80 percent of the business; in two years, 60- percent; in three or more years, 40 percent."

Dangers of Overcapitalization

If I were writing this book for the purpose of advising entrepreneurs rather than Angels, I would advise them to seek the maximum amount of money they could get while keeping as much equity as possible. The advice I offer to Angels is not the reverse image of this. I do not believe that Angels should necessarily invest as little as possible in return for the greatest amount of stock they can get. Entrepreneur and Angel must not lose sight of the fact that there is a business to be built and managed. The real issue is the very difficult job of estimating the true amount of Angel funds which will be required and the timing of the need for the funds. The scheduling of investment, with appropriate go/no go points, is a large part of the art.

The question of how much money is required must be answered by the added question of from what source. It is overly simplistic to answer "from the Angel." Which Angel? The one who took the seed-capital risk, or the one who came in for the startup phase? Then, there are also Angels who at the time of seeking seed and startup money decided that although the project interested them, it was too early for them to come in. They may be the ones to put up the money now. It is understandable for entrepreneurs to want to put the painful, tiring, and disagreeable chore of money raising behind them once and for all. Nevertheless, Angels have different risk tolerances and greed-level thresholds, and entrepreneurs will retain more of their companies if they raise the money in tranches. They will also be able to maintain more control over their Angels if they have different Angel groups rather than a single one.

Early Angels should have the right to provide additional funding on terms negotiated by other investors. Early Angels should also be delighted if and when other investors make commitments on less advantageous terms than their own and should not feel a need to participate simply to maintain their position in the company. So what if the Angels' percentage holdings decline? The purpose of the investment is not for investors to be able to tell their friends that they own 33 percent of Robby Robot Corp. The purpose of the investment is to make money for the Angels, to have each of their invested dollars work as hard as possible for them, and for at least the minimum returns they have established.

The dangers of overcapitalization will readily be seen in the similarity of the Angels" giving their teenagers too much of an allowance or granting any young manager of a division too much of an operating budget. Once funded, entrepreneurs are off and running. Being goal- and achievement-oriented and not necessarily profit-oriented they are likely to become walking examples of the laws of Northcote Parkinson.

The point is that in the case of startup investing, Angels are most often financing those who have not previously built a business or made a lot of money themselves, and, of course, therein lies a major part of the risk and the reason for high startup rates. It is up to Angels to supply some of the missing experience that often translates into restraint. The Angel should challenge the entrepreneur's stated initial personnel and equipment requirements, with particular emphasis on the timing of the need for them. I do not really accept the premise-- although I have been persuaded many times into accepting and financing it--that good people should be hired when they become available, and that business will follow. If they bring business with them (salespeople, for instance), that would be different.

In the act of "growing" a company from little to big, the measured growth will likely be profit growth. Angels will remember that entrepreneurial enthusiasm is catching, and that the wish is often the parent of the thought. A Lipper rule for the investor who is in a position to influence the entrepreneur: "Do it smaller at first, then do it larger when you know enough to do it better."

Typical entrepreneurs need to prove something. This results in their being more concerned with being the biggest and best at something than with being conservative and prudent managers. Being biggest and best at almost anything is an expensive undertaking. As an Angel, and frequently sole financial risk-taker in young ventures, I opt for a lesser early growth. As with a sports car, it's easy to get going so fast that operating control is jeopardized. Perhaps a good road sign for entrepreneurial investors would be: *go slow--learning curves ahead.*

153

For a review of an actual case affected by overcapitalization, along with other mistakes, see Appendix Q.

Voting Trusts and Proxies

Under certain conditions, more frequently than many suspect to be the case, entrepreneurs can become a serious hindrance to the business and the Angel. At times of corporate stress and problems, entrepreneurs are frequently motivated differently than the Angel. Also, entrepreneurs may act irrationally (1) if "their baby" is being threatened, or (2) if they feel they must vindicate their original judgements. In either case, they need, and the Angel needs, a mechanism which permits decisions to be made in a non-emotional, businesslike manner. The establishment of a voting trust, into which all or a significant portion of the entrepreneur's shares are placed, is a worthwhile consideration.

The trustee can be a person unaffiliated with either the entrepreneur or the Angel or can be chosen by the Angel. The trust can terminate on the achievement of certain objectives, such as four consecutive positive earning periods, sales reaching a certain level, or net worth reaching a stipulated level. Any number of termination points can be used other than simply a moment in time. Of course, if the company goes public or if Angels are offered an agreed upon minimum amount for their investment, the trust can also be terminated.

Some of the benefits of a trust can be created, with less formality, by the Angel holding the proxy on the entrepreneur's shares to vote either on all matters or on specific ones, such as merger, liquidation, or recapitalization, in the event of certain things having occurred or not occurred. The problem of holding a proxy versus establishing a trust is one of the mortality of the proxy holder. When the individual invests through the medium of a corporation, the investing company holds the proxy. The immortality of the corporation conveys benefits frequently worth the administrative expense and possible double taxation concerns. Of course, the use of Limited Liability and S corporations ameliorates the concern for double taxation.

Private company investors can invest though trusts established for their own benefit or for that of others. One very wealthy family that has been highly successful in entrepreneurial investment has invested principally through the medium of trusts. I have been told that in terms of tax management, it has worked out wonderfully well for the family.

Interest

Most Angels lose sight of the reason why they are investing when it comes to interest on their money as the form of return on their investment. If maximum current return coupled with apparent safety of principal are the Angels' true objectives, second mortgages may be their best investment. They might also consider the factoring of accounts receivable. Indeed, in both of these areas, it is at times possible, in the case of commercial borrowers, to work into the loan equation some sort of equity or warrants to buy equity participation.

Angels who wish to participate in building a new company must structure their deals so that the rent the company pays on their money will not stunt the company's growth. By all means, they should calculate the interest return they expect as being necessary to justify the private company investment. Angels must be aware at all times of the value of their money. But they should not extract interest from the company at the stage where money is worth more to the company than it is to them. If Angels need the income currently, they should not be investing that money in a private company in the first place.

There are a number of ways in which investors can defer or offset the rent due on their money. The simplest way is for them to accept zero coupon notes evidencing the accrual of corporate obligation. This technique unfortunately gives rise to an income tax obligation for Angels. Another technique is for them to add the amount of money rent to an exit or a buy-back formula, which will be discussed. They can also accept the rent in the form of additional equity or warrants to acquire equity.

The point the Angels have to remember is that it would be silly for them to deprive an infant of nourishment if they expect it to grow and develop into something that can serve them in the future. They can structure a fair deal while recognizing that growing a company is an exercise in the allocation of resources. To use another metaphor, don't drown the plant with money and don't let it die of thirst. Angles can think of funding as a water-feeding device that provides water as the plant needs it but only as much as they determine are really needed by plant.

The problem with a buoyant new issue market can be that too much money is made available to entrepreneurs, not that prices are too high or bad deals are being financed, but that instances of great waste occur as entrepreneurs get too much money without sufficient restrictions or controls on their use of the funds.

Since private company investing Angels are in a position to dictate the terms of the deal to their advantage, they should make a special attempt to understand the company's cash flow projections, instead of concentrating on projected profits. Cash flow is the critical issue in young companies.

Acceleration of Principal Payments

Acceleration of principal payments--if installments are not paid when due, then all money becomes due--is an important clause to have in any investment purchase agreement (loan or stock repurchase), because it gives Angels an opportunity to gain more control, more quickly, when the situation arises of the company not being able to meet an obligation to them or others. Angels must remember that the creditor who gets in control fastest is the one most likely to achieve the greatest recovery. Angels have to remember, and entrepreneurs recognize, that the Angel's gaining of control does not in itself mean that it will be used unfairly or in an adversarial manner vis-a-vis the entrepreneur. A company being obliged to accomplish something difficult or even impossible, such as paying Angels all of the money it owes them, gives Angels power they would not otherwise have, but that power is a result of the Angels' being placed in unexpected jeopardy.

Contrasts in Private and Public Company Investing

Figure 1 is an effort to graphically display the three most critical considerations in the rational investment decision-making process. Of course, far greater reliance on the Angel's predictive abilities are required when dealing with private companies, particularly early development or seed capital stage companies, than when comparing mature, publicly traded company shares. These comparative analysis elements are:

1. The period of time it requires for a company to "earn back" the amount originally invested. In other words, if a company's stock is purchased at $10 per share and the shares earn an aggregated average of $1 per share per year for the next 10 years, then there would be a 10-year earn back period. A price-earnings ratio is simply another way of expressing a similar concept in that the P/E indicates the number of years of the current (or a projected) year's earnings which are represented by the current price of the stock. An earn back estimate is used by anyone buying 100 percent of

the shares of a business in determining whether or not the price asked for the company is reasonable. In other words, the buyer of a company must have a view as to the future levels of cumulative earnings, and not those of only the current year or the year ahead.

Figure 1   Number of years of projected earnings required to equal amount invested in a private company on a comparable basis as company having similar projected earnings and trading publicly at the price-earnings ratios indicated.

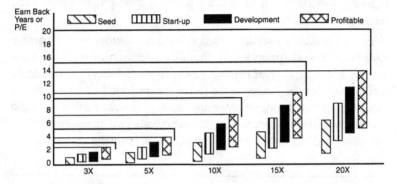

Price-earnings ratios of publicly traded shares using projected cumulative earnings for the same period as for the private company.

Note: Assumes required ROI increased to recognize illiquidity of private company investment on basis of: Seed 5-10X, Startup 3-6X, Development 2-4X, and Profitable 15-3X.

2. The value of liquidity is reflected in normal securities markets pricing by the magnitude of the discount applied to various price-related ratios. The more liquid the security, the more generously will the market usually value the comparable ratios. In other words, if a widely held and broadly traded issue sells for twelve times current earnings, shares of an otherwise comparable private company should logically be valued at a lesser price-earnings ratio level. There is "exit safety" in liquidity, and the absence thereof usually justifies, and normally imposes, on price-related ratios a discount from that of a comparable company that has the Angel benefit of marketability or liquidity.

3. The earlier the stage of development in a company, the further in the future normally are the earnings that may be expected to recoup the original investment. The fact of business that "time is money" is represented either by interest charged (or paid), or in the discount factor applied to the price-earnings ratio based upon

157

current or projected earnings. Very significant cumulative future earnings are required to analytically justify paying a high price-earnings ratio based upon current earnings. The buyers of stocks selling at low current P/Es usually have better long-term investment results than those who buy high P/E stocks, because predicting future events accurately is so difficult.

Clearly, these comparative factors, as they relate to one another, have to be thought of as ranges and not as absolutes. The purpose of Figure 1 and Table 1 is to indicate possible appropriate ranges when relating the elements.

Table 1 forces a user to consider the three factors of comparable earn back period (price level), liquidity premium or discount (exit value), and proximity of earning power (predictability). It should be recognized that the further in the future the projected earnings are, the more that can go wrong in achieving them. Also, the further away the cumulative earnings are, the greater the money cost factor (interest or discount) that has to be applied to make the investment comparable to

Table 1

Stock Price	Current per Share Earnings	P/E	Earnings Yield	Years to Earn Back* 0%	5%	10%	15%	20%	25%
6	1.00	6	16.7	6	5.4	4.9	4.6	4.3	4.1
7	1.00	7	14.3	7	6.2	5.6	5.1	4.8	4.6
8	1.00	8	12.5	8	6.9	6.2	5.6	5.2	5.0
9	1.00	9	11.1	9	7.6	6.7	6.1	5.6	5.3
10	1.00	10	10.0	10	8.3	7.3	6.6	6.0	5.6
11	1.00	11	9.1	11	9.0	7.8	7.0	6.4	5.9
12	1.00	12	8.3	12	9.6	8.3	7.4	6.7	6.2
13	1.00	13	7.7	13	10.3	8.7	7.7	7.0	6.5
14	1.00	14	7.1	14	10.9	9.2	8.1	7.3	6.7
15	1.00	15	6.7	15	11.5	9.6	8.4	7.6	7.0
16	1.00	16	6.3	16	12.0	10.0	8.8	7.9	7.2
17	1.00	17	5.9	17	12.6	10.4	9.1	8.1	7.4
18	1.00	18	5.6	18	13.2	10.8	9.4	8.4	7.6
19	1.00	19	5.3	19	13.7	11.2	9.6	8.6	7.8
20	1.00	20	5.0	20	14.2	11.5	9.9	8.8	8.0
22	1.00	22	4.5	22	15.2	12.2	10.4	9.2	8.4
24	1.00	24	4.2	24	16.2	12.8	10.9	9.6	8.7
26	1.00	26	3.8	26	17.1	13.4	11.4	10.0	9.0
28	1.00	28	3.6	28	17.9	14.0	11.8	10.4	9.3
30	1.00	30	3.3	30	18.8	14.5	12.2	10.7	9.6

*Number of years required for earnings to equal price paid if earnings increase at annual percent compound rates of growth shown.

158

currently available and already profitable liquid investment alternatives. Of course, that is what professional investing is all about, the constant comparison of available capital use alternatives. What successful Angels must focus upon is their assessment of ultimate, time-related risk and reward-related elements. Use and study of these exhibits will, it is hoped, be found of value in comparing dispassionately price-related factors once there exists the basis for an assumption of future earnings for the companies being compared.

For example, if an investor used Figure 1 to gauge the comparability or attractiveness of a private company investment, the investor would determine the level of cumulative earnings which are expected to develop over, say, the next five years for the publicly traded comparable company. Let's assume that amounted to $12 per share, and that the shares were currently selling for $36. Therefore, the stock is selling at a multiple of cumulative earnings of three times. If we assume that a currently profitable private company should be valued at a discount to yield the investor between one and a half to three times as much as the investor would receive by investing in the publicly traded shares, then the private company would be valued at one top two times the cumulative five-year earnings level, whereas the shares having the benefit of liquidity were valued at three times. Such range is indicated by the bar at the lower left. Not that the line immediately above the group leads to the left scale at the three times or three year level.

Now, let's assume we are comparing a private investment with a publicly traded share selling at 20 times the projected earnings (also, if current earnings and not cumulative earnings are used, then 20 years are required to achieve earn back). Of course, a multiple of 20 implies the expectancy of future earnings increases. Actually, much of the securities analytical "science" involves the projection of *rates* of earnings growth. In this example, we will assume that we are considering investing in a development-stage private company which is not yet profitable. If the appropriate premium to the investor is two to four times the return, the market anticipates for the publicly traded share and then only 5 to 10 times the projected earnings should be paid for the private company. Note that the discount is greater for earlier stage (than the already profitable company used in the first example), and that the range is greater in absolute terms.

By studying Table 1, the investor can determine the arithmetic basis for the Figure 1 graphic presentation and also calculate the specific values derived from the table which may be applicable to a specific investment opportunity.

159

As a further example for use of Table 1, assume that investors require a minimum earnings yield (the inverse of a price-earnings ratio) of 12.5 percent (a P/E of 8), as that is the amount investors believe they could earn with only the acceptance of a minimum amount of risk. In this case, investors would have to convince themselves that the current per share earnings level of at least $1 per share would increase by 5 percent for each of the next 6.9 years, as this is necessary to earn back the price paid for the stock if purchased at $8 per share. It is also true that the earnings would have to increase at an average annual compound rate of 10 percent for 6.2 years, or at 15 percent for 5.6 years, or 20 percent for 5.2 years, or 25 percent for 5 years...all to provide an earn back assuming a cost of $8 per share and a current level of earnings of $1 per share.

The above simply "follows" the line across the "8" level and indicates that the longer a compound annual average growth rate is assumed to continue, the lesser may be the annual rate of growth to achieve a required level of cumulative earnings.

The art of investing requires an appreciation of compound interest tables...and this is a fact which should not escape any student of the market or investment opportunities.

Definitions and Investment Return Guidelines for Use with Tables and Figure

Seed Capital

This is the inspiration, idea and frequently pre-incorporation stage. Money is used for feasibility studies, business plan development, product investigation, and marketing surveys.

As this is the most speculative stage, at least a 500 percent better return than that expected from publicly traded securities is warranted. In other words, if investors expect to double the value of their publicly traded securities portfolio in five years (a 15% annual, average, compound return), then seed-capital investments should have the realistic potential for a tenfold return in the same period.

Startup Phase

This is the stage where money is used for renting offices, hiring personnel, developing products or services, and initiating sales. A 300 percent improvement in projected return over publicly traded securities is warranted by the illiquidity and usual risk levels assumed.

160

Development or Second Stage

This is the stage where the company is in business but not yet profitable. Additional funds are used to further the activities of the business. Depending on the financial assets and liability relationships, a level of return of 200 percent of that available from liquid investments of a similar nature is reasonable.

Profitable but Private

Funds at this stage are needed to expand the business. At least 50 percent premium seems warranted to compensate the investor for the illiquidity inherent in private company investment.

The Price of Illiquidity

What is the fair or appropriate relationship between the price one is willing to pay for the future earnings of a private company versus that of a company the shares of which are publicly traded? The question assumes that the Angel recognizes that a current or projected price-earnings ratio, or earnings yield, is a reflection of the number of years of future earnings which are represented by the current price of the shares, or valuation of the company.

Table 2 provides the Angel with a possible scale of comparability. The illiquidity penalty is for illustration purposes only, as there are many factors to be considered before reaching any conclusions as to the level of penalty to be applied. The only point to be certain of is that the returns anticipated from the illiquid investment must far exceed those available from marketable securities. The chart reflects that which should be a very much lower price-earnings ratio paid by the Angel for the same level of future earnings achieved by a publicly traded company.

Table 2

Private Company Investment Stage	Expected or Required Increased Return (or Illiquidity Premium)		Public Company Cumulative P/E for same Number of Years*				
			3x	5x	10x	15x	20x
Seed	5 to 10 times	=	1.6-0.3	1.0-0.5	2.0-1.0	3.0-1.5	4.0-2.0
Start-up	3 to 6 times	=	1.0-0.5	1.67-.83	3.33-1.67	5.00-2.50	6.67-3.33
Development	2 to 4 times	=	1.5-.75	2.50-1.25	5.00-2.50	7.50-3.75	10.0-5.0
Profitable	1.5 to 3 times	=	2.0-1.0	3.33-1.67	6.67-3.33	10.0-5.00	13.3-6.67

*Range of price-earnings ratios (based upon cumulative projected earnings) for marketable securities which a private company investor could use in calculating appropriate private company valuation of P/E.

161

Perks and Rewards for the Investor

Perks as a return on investment is an area not generally contemplated by Angels or entrepreneurs, or even by many professional venture capital investors. (However, some underwriters approach this area of reward through imposed management consulting contracts.) After all, one of the advantages of having one's own business is the exercise of personal discretion over the spending of monies in a manner beneficial to the owners of the business.

Entrepreneur/managers of business will expect to have funds available for travel and entertainment. They will also expect to be able to use discretion as to the hiring of staff. They may expect the company to provide them with a car and, as the business grows and prospers, even with a plane. But what about investors? To the extent that these expenses are really nontaxed dividends and are not truly "required" in the daily running of the business, shouldn't Angels also have some available to them?

Angels can discuss openly with entrepreneurs their feelings on the subject of perks. Whose son or daughter is hired for the summer? Shouldn't the Angel have a company American Express card with an understanding as to charge limits and purposes? Shouldn't the Angel have the use of a company car when on company business? Should annual meetings, or even quarterly meetings of the board of directors, be held at restors? I have pointed out elsewhere that the Angel may be served when the entrepreneur's spouse is involved with the business. Similarly, the entrepreneur may be well served if the Angel's spouse is interested and well informed about the business. Therefore, shouldn't consideration be given to naming the Angel's spouse as a director or an advisor of the company? After all, if the Angel were to die and be succeeded by the spouse, the entrepreneur will fare better with a survivor well informed about the business and its demands and potentials.

Perhaps the best approach is for Angels to discuss with entrepreneurs the level of travel and entertainment expense allocations expected, and then to assign some percentage of that amount to Angels for them to spend in promoting the interests of "their" company. When a company prospers, it is not only the entrepreneur who should benefit from its success in ways generally associated with the owning of private businesses. Private company investors should think of themselves as partners or owners of (a part of) the business and not as shareholders. The connotation of the term shareholder is, or should be, one of being able to sell to an ever-present buyer, such as is usually the case with publicly traded securities and rarely with private companies.

Consideration may also be given to the company hiring the Angel as an advisor or consultant on terms known at the time of the investment. It is not unusual for underwriters to insist on an agreement by the company, as part of their underwriting package, that the company retain the underwriters, or their designees, for advising and consulting services at $1,000 to $5,000 per month for one to five years. Professional investors also at times charge fees for consultation. The Angel is advised to read the prospectuses or offering documents of low priced and speculative offerings to obtain an idea of the amounts extracted from company owners for access to other people's money. The reading of many prospectuses is a good education for Angels, and they should pay close attention to the sections headed "underwriting compensation" and "certain transactions." They will remember too that the underwriter is typically getting the stated rewards without having to assume the risk of investment. Other rewards for the underwriter may include added undisclosed compensation areas, such as pension fund management and brokerage business derived from the employee benefit plans of the underwritten company.

One great reason for investing in a private company seldom gets attention to print--to obtain a job. This way Angels have the opportunity to employ *both* their skills and money. If this is one of the Angels' motivations, they should get it out on the table quickly to gauge the reaction of the entrepreneur. Angels should not be surprised if entrepreneurs are less than enthusiastic about the idea. From their standpoint, they are being saddled with another personality with which to contend, and one which is unlikely to be as receptive to their commands as others. Entrepreneurs may also have no reason to believe that Angels really have anything more than their money to contribute. From the Angels' standpoint, they get a chance to participate fully in the new company and watch how their money is being utilized. The Angel must understand that such an investment can be very expensive and result in a less than great job. On the other hand, it can be a great investment and a great job--if it all works out as projected.

Angel employment is a difficult area. One of its basic aspects is that Angels understand their own motivation. In making the investment, are they simply putting their dollars to work for them? Or are they willing to accept a lower return on their dollars in exchange for employment and recognition? Two questions can be asked as a measure of such a situation. Would Angels have put their money into this company without the promise of employment? Would entrepreneurs have hired or associated with their Angels if they did not have money to put in the company?

An agreement can be reached that the company will retain consulting services from the Angel (or the Angel's company) once the company has reached a certain revenue level or achieved certain profits or some other agreed upon measure of progress. A prior understanding should be reached of the services to be performed and the amount of time to be devoted to providing these services. The duration of the services should also be discussed. Perhaps the services will continue until dividends are paid, until the net worth of the company reaches an agreed upon level, or for as long as the entrepreneur/manager receives a salary above a certain amount.

Although Angel employment or retention can be very constructive, there is a good chance of misunderstanding. There is a risk too of Internal Revenue Service claims of "dividend" declaration, whereby they deny deduction of amounts paid by the company but still require the individual receiving payment to treat it as income. This situation is only likely to arise if the compensation is unwarranted by effort or excessive in amount.

Investment through the Provision of Property

Although I have touched upon this subject elsewhere, I cannot stress enough the logic of the approach. Leasing property to the company is so much simpler than lending the company money and then having to worry about security on the loan or fighting with other unsecured creditors in the case of loans made to the company or payments due for one thing or another.

Suppose a company with which you are favorably impressed asks you to invest equity money to build a plant. Tell them that instead of giving them the money, you will build a plant for them and lease it to them for a consideration that will include an ability to acquire an agreed upon interest in the company. Suppose the company wants to use the money for the development of a new process. Have all rights to the new process assigned to you in exchange for your money and give the company back conditional rights to use and/or market the process for an interest in the company. One of the conditions might be for the company to be profitable or have a stated level of sales or net worth. Whatever the proposed use of proceeds, Angels can find elements to own. That ownership can be structured in such a manner as to make the benefits, as long as everything is going well and as projected, accrue to the company much as if the company had simply gotten the money from the Angel and then itself acquired the assets.

The difference in the arrangement becomes apparent only when the company runs into trouble. In a troubled company, the burden of debts and other pressures tend to confuse and make difficult the life of the entrepreneur and any unsecured creditors. Having unencumbered title to tangible assets provides protection for Angels in such situations. The Angel in this position of strength has *options*, and it is this availability of options which permits private company investment and Angel survival as well as capital enhancement possibilities.

Much of commercial life is a zero-sum game in which for every winner there must be a loser, as in the commodity trading business. Things are not always this way, but they are frequently enough to make Angels aware that they are the ones who must protect themselves, since no one out there is going to do it for them. Anyone who doubts the reality of this should observe some creditors' meetings (particularly the first one) and witness an enlightening display of greed and fear, righteous indignation, and jousting for position and advantage.

Assets as Loan Security for Companies in Debt

Angels are frequently requested to advance funds to companies already in debt. Usually earlier lenders have acquired as protection the traditional asset classifications of the company such as property, plant, accounts receivable, and inventory. In many cases, the lenders have also obtained the personal guarantees of the entrepreneur and, perhaps, even a pledge of all the shares of the company. Thus, the lack of available assets to secure a loan can be a major problem for Angels entering an already debt-burdened company.

Another problem for Angels in lending to companies already in debt is the possibility that the debtor will resist payment at the time the loan matures. It is also possible that other creditors will be claiming the same assets as pledged to the Angel, and that at the very least there will be a delay in collecting monies due, as well as an incremental expense of legal action.

Angels should always try to lend through the medium of asset acquisition and contributed use thereof with the thought that they will make a profit on the sale or subsequent use of the acquired property if the loan is not repaid.

One technique for avoiding the necessity of getting a "judgement note" (though that is not a bad idea for the investor) and of obtaining a claim on assets is to purchase them at the time the loan is entered into. The purchase can be made for a nominal amount and other good and valuable consideration--namely, the making of the loan. The assets purchased may include the right to use the name of the entrepreneur's company, the patent or the rights to it, exclusive rights to use the customer list, full distribution rights to the product, and the rights to any product improvement--the list can be as long as one's experience and imagination permit. Obviously, entrepreneurs will not be willing to sell these rights to the Angel for a nominal amount unless they can also recapture them for a nominal consideration. Thus, entrepreneurs are given the right to reacquire these assets for the same sum as they are paid for them *if prior thereto the loan has been repaid.* A profit can be built into the arrangement by increasing the exercise price of the option with the passage of time, thereby providing the entrepreneur with an incentive for early repayment of the obligation. These techniques should not be considered foolproof and may be attacked by creditors. Therefore, whenever possible the contracts should be executed before there are any other creditors. The answer to the entrepreneur who questions the amount of the loan in relation to the value of the property is that the relative value is of no consequence *if the loan is repaid* as the entrepreneur has promised. To protect the entrepreneur from the possibility of Angels having their own financial problems that might prevent the exercise of the purchase option, an escrow agent or trust may be used.

In looking beyond traditional asset classifications, Angels may have to do their own creative thinking. I was asked once to provide funds for a heavily leveraged hotel project in Singapore. Having been told that every conceivable asset of the hotel was mortgaged, I proposed to the owner that I would provide funds through acquisition of two assets were they to be unencumbered. One was the elevators. My thought was that I could control all convenient access to the floors above ground level if my loan was not repaid, regardless of who had claim to the other assets. Clearly, if anyone was going to operate the hotel, my claim would have to be satisfied. The second asset I wanted to acquire was the large neon sign on top of the hotel and unrestricted use of that sign. The owner was puzzled. Why did I want the sign? The name of the hotel management company on the sign was very well known, being associated with more than twenty other hotels in Asia. I told the owner that if my loan was not repaid, I intended to take the sign off the roof of the very imposing hotel and place it on top of a squatter's hut on the airport road, visible to all using the airport. As it happened, we were able to arrange a full financing of the property without my acquisition of either the elevators or the neon sign.

As with all techniques discussed in this book, Angels should check with their lawyers before proceeding. The laws of the land are frequently drafted to "protect" the borrower(particularly in Texas and some of the Western states having "frontier" mentalities and differ from state to state) and, therefore, may disadvantage the lender. In lending through the acquisition of assets, investors must be certain of their rights to the title and use of the acquired asset. The same acquisition techniques can be used to gain or secure equity interests in houses and companies. The Angel should ensure that the costs of registering title and the possible tax consequences are well understood by all concerned and paid for by the seller/borrower/entrepreneur.

Angel acquisition of assets, with a leaseback or license to the selling company, is frequently a good way for the Angel to participate in the developing company. The lease payments can be geared to reflect revenue levels or unit throughput as well as the fixed minimum rental. A capital gain may also be anticipated if the terms are such that the company leasing the assets has an incentive to reacquire the assets at a premium price to avoid the payment of high and/or increasing lease payments.

Usury Laws

"You charged me and I agreed to pay an amount that I now find to be too much, so I won't and don't have to pay back anything at all."

Usury laws, which vary from state to state, can frequently be accommodated by providing for the payment of services that the Angels are prepared to offer and that are reasonable in terms of the size of the payments. The Angel may also buy property from the company for a nominal consideration and lease it back to the company; of course, the Angel has to be sure the property acquired is vital to the continuation of the business. Such vital items could include

167

patent rights, customer lists, key pieces of equipment, property essential to the company, or the rights to certain developments of the company.

Exit Formulas

Exit formulas or prearranged takeouts are the Angel's equivalent to a prenuptial agreement. Their importance is probably the least understood and least focused upon element of informal investor deal making. Why is the recapture of the Angel's funds so frequently left to chance? Just as it is hardly the most optimistic (though possibly realistic) of attitudes a loving couple demonstrates before marriage in executing a prenuptial agreement, perhaps many investors think of exit formulas as bad luck or self-fulfilling predictions of failure. There is no room for such queasiness in the business world. Angels must have the option of recapturing their funds under certain conditions.

What are those conditions? They are time-and/or progress-related. The Angel, and perhaps the entrepreneur, should have a means of breaking the relationship on a least painful basis. Equity investments of course are being discussed -- debt repayment scheduling is a different matter, although some of the techniques are similar in both areas.

As an approach to exit, the Angel can (or can be required to) tender or put to the company some percentage of the shares of the company held at a price that relates to either book value or a multiple of earnings or cash flow. Revenue levels can also be used as a determination of value for shares repurchased or put. As previously indicated, entrepreneurs may wish to have a call at, say, a multiple of book value, but they should be required to have achieved some level of earnings or cash flow for the call to be exercised. In most cases, the Angel should get, and not grant, the options.

An agreed upon percentage of a company's earnings can be dedicated to purchasing an agreed upon segment of securities issued by the company. Further, the company can also agree to use a portion of earnings for the redemption of preferred stock; this preferred stock can also be convertible or have common stock purchase warrants that are attached and that may be detachable initially or at a later stage.

Overall, the most effective exit formula is no formula at all, if there is in place a buy/sell agreement which permits either party--or perhaps only the angel -- to initiate the offer to purchase. Recipients of the offer can either accept it or require the initiator to accept the same deal as they proposed.

It is important to remember that the existence of a binding agreement does not necessarily require its application, since the parties to it can modify it or cancel it at any time. The purpose of agreements protecting the Angel is solely that of protection. Such agreements do not have to be put into effect. Just because one has a loaded shotgun in the closet does not mean one has to take it out and use it. One can, but one does not have to.

Right of First Refusal

The Angel should insist on a right of first refusal to reinvest in the company on the same terms, and up to an agreed upon amount, as any other subsequent investor making either a new or follow-on investment. The reason for the Angel to insist on this right is that subsequent investors in the company will probably drive a harder bargain than will one of the original investors. Added to this is that all investors seek good investment opportunities and, thus, the original Angels should retain the right to make new investments. The entrepreneur will almost certainly not resist the Angel's requirement for a right of first refusal.

However, Howard Stevenson of the Harvard Business School presents another point of view:

> An investor's right of first refusal very often prevents good negotiation with a new buyer. The buyer is put in the position of having to spend his time and effort on what he knows may end up as the investor's deal. A right of first refusal denigrates the value of any property. I think people forget that a preempted right to invest has a cost.

Recognizing the validity of Professor Stevenson's observation could cause Angels to insist only upon a right to participate in new financings to the prorated extent of their original interests. Professor Stevenson's point is, and was, more directed to the possibility of a sale of property than to financings. Also, he is focussing more on the entrepreneur's or company's perspective and not that of the Angel.

Most new issue underwriters will ask for a right of first refusal as to future sale of securities by the company, and even by the company's shareholders. My advice to companies is not to give such a right, because the underwriter will probably do the deal without it and, hopefully, the company will grow sufficiently to be able to attract a larger and more prestigious underwriter in the future. Also, why should the company commit itself to deal with a firm that may itself change and be controlled by different owners, that may suffer financial or reputational reverses, that may simply be less attractive than another underwriter who then wants the company's business? As Angels will probably have to agree to the terms of the underwriting, they have a veto, which can be used effectively at times.

Buy/Sell Option

I always insist on a buy/sell option in situations when I am providing funds to an individual or buying into a deal, and when I will end up with an equal number of shares as, or an interest of equal proportion to, the other players in the game. The buy/sell option is indeed a thing of beauty in that it keeps all players honest.

It works as follows. The initiator can at any time (or at a previously agreed upon time--for example, two years into the deal) propose the purchase of the other participant's stock on any terms and for any price. Other participants then have the right, within a specified period of time, either to accept the offer to compel the initiator to sell them all of their interest on the terms and at the price the initiator originally proposed. A six month's delay in closing (with extreme penalty for non-closing) may be provided to give a less wealthy party time to arrange financing of the transaction, if necessary. Of course, if recipients of the offer choose to take over the property on the terms bid, they can elect a shorter period to closing.

The buy/sell option's great attraction is its mutuality and symmetry. What's fair for one is fair for the other. Having said all that, I must admit to never having used a buy/sell option in the form in which it appeared in the contract. Since both sides know that the option is there, they negotiate around it and propose something that does not permit or require it to be put into effect.

Years ago, while negotiating a deal with COMSAT for one of the companies I owned, I proposed a buy/sell option and the financial vice president involved said, "Oh yes, a Texas option." I have not heard it called that before or since, but whatever you call it, it remains an effective safety valve in many fifty/fifty deals.

Do the Deal--Then Investigate

The late Jack Whitehead, one of the early venture capital industry practitioners, negotiated the deal before investigating the opportunity. As one of the very shrewdest venture capital investors, he regarded time as one of his most valuable assets. In order to avoid wastefully investing his own time and that of his associates, he established a preliminary understanding with the entrepreneur before the time-consuming process of investigation is put in motion. I frequently do the same thing as I am reluctant to make the time investment if the entrepreneur isn't prepared to share my view of reality and equity.

Angels should be aware that many entrepreneurs seek funding from more than one capital source at a time. On occasion, entrepreneurs will also "shop" the deal finalized between them and Angels with other potential funding sources. Whitehead and the entrepreneur agreed on the basic terms of the deal "should Whitehead Associates decide to proceed within thirty days." In other words, the entrepreneur offered Whitehead a 30-day option in return for Whitehead's seriously investigating the deal. Of course, only a person with the experience, knowledge, and reputation of Jack Whitehead could (1) know by limited exposure to an investment opportunity and only a few meetings with the principals if the deal has sufficient potential to make the investigation effort worthwhile, and (2) legitimately persuade entrepreneurs to tie up their deal for thirty days without a commitment.

One benefit to entrepreneurs is that other venture capital investors tended to view any deal on which Whitehead had "bid" as being sufficiently attractive to pay slightly, or even significantly, more attention than what was originally offered.

A slightly different approach designed to achieve the same result as the prenegotiated deal (which less experienced Angels may not be ready to make) is as follows. Applicants for funds agree to pay the investors' cost of investigation and review if investors in turn "offer" them a deal, within certain broad parameters, within a specified time period, and this deal is then rejected by the entrepreneur. In a way, this is a better arrangement for entrepreneurs, because they are still free to continue their money-raising efforts while Angels are doing their research. All that the entrepreneur is committed to do is pay for, and perhaps purchase, the work product of Angels' investigations if investors decide to go forward and the entrepreneur has found a better deal. Of course, an entrepreneur's simple agreement to pay an "investigation fee" to the investor may be sufficient insurance for the Angel.

Entrepreneurs must beware of the payment of investigation and commitment fees, and frequently prepaid expenses, to con men who masquerade as Angels or financial agents and who have neither the intention nor ability to make investments. Blind ads in the classified sections of publications offering money on terms which appear to be overly generous may be bait for unsophisticated or overenthusiastic entrepreneurs.

Certain underwriters of speculative public offerings also make money by requiring the up-front payment of fees "to cover expenses" without a commitment to provide funding for the entrepreneur. This practice is also found in the case of some "best efforts" commitments, if that is not a conflict in terms. My problem with this unattractive practice is not related to legitimate underwriter expense reimbursement but rather the profit element frequently bundled into the arrangement. Specifically, the company agrees to the payments being for "nonaccountable" expenses and that leaves room for the functioning of rampant greed. Higher quality investment banking firms do not usually have this up-front payment requirement, as they are dealing with established companies. There is a positive correlation between the fairness of the arrangements and the strength of the securities-issuing company. Such is the way of the financial world, and it should surprise no one that weaker companies pay more for less.

Chapter 9

REFINANCING AND ITS NEAR INEVITABILITY

Are the Angel's Pockets Deep Enough?

In creating their original business plan, first-time entrepreneurs frequently under-project the amount of money the proposed company will need. Being born optimists, they do not allow sufficient room in the business plan projection for the almost inevitable delays. Entrepreneurs are also aware the more money they ask from the investor, the less likely the deal is to get financed. They also realize too that in exchange for large sums of money, their own interest in e company will be diminished. Entrepreneurs projecting a need for a million dollars may suggest that they get half the stock of the company and the Angel the other half, whereas entrepreneurs projecting a need for five million dollars clearly cannot suggest with the same degree of confidence that they should get half the stock with little or no investment. Thus, there is a strong tendency for entrepreneurs to minimize continually the amount of money that is necessary in the development of their projects.

A consultant, perhaps an accountant, can be of assistance to both the Angel and entrepreneur in studying the basis for business plan projections as they relate to the need for additional investment.

Arthur Little told me, "When it comes to refinancing, investors have to let entrepreneurs know they are someone who must be reckoned with. Then, entrepreneurs will be willing to negotiate and make a bargain. But investors should not be objectionably tough with them; otherwise, they will go elsewhere first the next time."

If Angels put in only a quarter of the funds available for private company investment, they most likely will find themselves the position of being able to adequately refinance their holdings in a new company. Thus, were Angels to set aside 20 percent of their available investment funds for the purposes of private company investment and use only 5 percent of their available investment funds in their initial investment in the new company they would be able to diversify their portfolio. They thereby avoid the principal mistake made by many investors--that of getting in too deep, too early.

When to Say No

For Angels trying to salvage part of their investment in a situation that is not working out as anticipated by the entrepreneur, the critical decision is when to stop the game. Who must take the initiative? If things are allowed to drift, a point will be reached where the payroll cannot be met or suppliers cannot be paid, bringing the game to a stop. However, there is almost certainly a point prior to this when most dispassionate observers would realize that the game has to end. This is the point where the probabilities of failure far outweigh the probabilities of success and is certainly the latest time at which Angels should begin to reduce to a minimum their further risk exposures and view investment salvage as their primary and overriding objective.

Left to their own devices, entrepreneurs will typically run the company right up to the moment the phones are removed. After all, they have enormous investments of ego in the project and frequently cannot bring themselves to admit to themselves or others the failure that is so apparent to those not involved. There is likely to be much conflict between Angels and entrepreneurs who still believe in the project and in their ability to pull it off. Here comes into play the Angel protection mechanism of having a preponderance of the board of directors, of having a proxy from entrepreneurs on whatever stock they possess, and of having the contractual right to sell or terminate the business.

When the call for more money comes, the first question Angels must ask themselves is whether this is a chance for the making of an attractive investment or simply a financial contribution toward delaying almost inevitable failure. The answer should be clear. The investor should only invest more money when the balance of evidence suggests success, and this success should be achievable with the amount of money the Angel is prepared to invest anew in the situation (as opposed to only the "possibility" of the new investment bringing success). I suggest making a list of the possible good things and bad things that may occur within the period of time the new investment permits as a means of tallying the possibilities..

In the absence of clear indications of failure--such as the fact that the invention did not work or the contract did not come through-- management often comes to believe that the only obstacle to success is the reluctant Angel. Management may readily admit that they have incorrectly projected their need for money but point out that success is within their grasp with a new infusion of funds. The management reasons that *if* only Angels would have confidence in them and believe their current projections rather than dwelling on their prior projections all could work out. Further, the entrepreneur will come to believe that the Angels may very well *cause* the failure of the project due to their fears and stinginess. Nothing has gone wrong, in management's view. It's simply that they have run out of money. At such a point, Angels must realize that, in all probability, neither they nor management have the ability any longer to make dispassionate judgments regarding the situation.

Yet, Angels have to make a determination. They must deliberately seek to make a rational, rather than emotional, decision. One mechanistic approach would be: If the management of the company cannot persuade any other investor, one not already involved in the company, that an investment should be made, be it for only a part of the money that is needed, then present Angels probably should simply take their loss, or cause the loss (if that is the way management presents it) by failing to put in the additional funds.

Such subsequent or involuntary investment, made in part for the purpose of vindicating earlier judgment, is frequently the worst kind of investment--one which causes investors disproportionate pain, because they are in further than they wanted to be, and because it seldom works out. The original Angel is probably best served in not investing more money in situations where the required reinvestment is caused by disappointing results.

The best kind of reinvestment to make in a private company is what is required because the company has grown either according to plan or better than planned, and needs the money for expansion and delivery of goods and services. This kind of second-stage investment is what all venture capitalists seek; indeed, some venture capital organizations are only interested in making second-stage investments, because so many companies die after the initial investment without ever getting to the second stage level.

An Incident

The entrepreneurs had already started, using their own resources, a company manufacturing office partitions. Prospects were bright, but they were having some cash flow problems and needed an infusion of new money. They asked the Angels to guarantee a $25,000 bank loan in exchange for a 40 percent holding in the company, with an agreement that the company would buy back that 40 percent holding in two years for $25,000. The Angels said to themselves that all they had to do was guarantee the note, put no actual money in the company and collect $25,000 in two years' time -- a fifty percent annual return on money they did not even have to invest. Among the things the Angels should have known I that a doubling of money in 2 years is a 41% annual average compound return, not a 50% return.

When the Angels went to the bank, they found they had to put up $25,000 worth of Treasury bills as collateral. They signed the loan guarantee without worrying about the clauses that said they were also guaranteeing interest on the $25,000 loan and costs of collection. The business began to fail, and the Angels decided to cut their losses by getting out. The Angels wanted the bank to call the loan so the Angels could become the direct creditor of the company and take some action which would protect their interests or to close it down At this point, the bank refused to demand full repayment of the loan, thereby shutting down the business, as the Angels requested. The bank had made a guaranteed loan, was collecting interest, and had no incentive to terminate the arrangement. Ultimately, the Angels found themselves liable for $50,000, double their original guarantee, when the company finally closed.

Dan Lufkin says,

What hurts people is that they make a distinction between a guarantee and actual investment of money. They think it's much easier to make a guarantee, that it's not money out of their pockets. Never sign a guarantee without having in mind that you are signing a check. And as you would when writing a check, look closely at what you sign.

Realism in Cash Flow Projections

The entrepreneur and management team which lacks a great deal of experience in projecting the time period, and, therefore, funds required to reach and maintain positive cash flow, is in for a difficult task. Angels should be aware of their level of expertise, and they must remember that most things take longer than originally anticipated, and that this extra time is going to cost money in salaries, rent, insurance premiums, and so forth. The chief cause for the underestimation of monies that will ultimately be required by a new company is the inability or unwillingness of the entrepreneurs, in preparing their business plans and their associated projections, to make allowances for an adequate passage of time.

Angels can take mechanistic approach by substantially increasing the amount of estimated expenses and pushing back the date of income receipt expectation, or they can halve the amount of income they expect to receive. However, none of these approaches is truly satisfactory. Angels, therefore, must study and question all the key numbers in the projections themselves.

It is not wise simply to look at the profit figure projected for the fifth year, assume the company will be worth, say, a multiple of ten times earnings at that point in time, and feel that a position acquired today at a fraction of that sum is an investment bargain. I suspect that this is a normal thought process and series of events with many Angels. They take the highest earnings figure, apply a price/earnings multiple to it, and then regard their investment as the price of admission to that wonderfully high figure.

Angels can evaluate a situation only by taking the time to understand the numbers generated by the entrepreneur. Are the salaries full and complete? If the office or plant space requirement realistic in size with what has to be paid for it? Are professional fees realistically portrayed? Has an adequate time allowance been made with provisions for delay? Have interest and financing charges been adequately provided for? Will sales be as projected in the time frame projected? Are sales commissions and discounts adequately reflected?

I suggest that Angels spend a minimum of several hours with entrepreneurs and have them defend, month by month and year by year, the projections presented. Angels could have someone, perhaps more knowledgeable than themselves, attend the meeting with them to question the entrepreneur further on each of the numbers used to reach the projected bottom-line result. Notes should be taken by

Angels and their representatives during this meeting. These projections are really the inducement to make the investment, and it is important for Angels to have a record not only of the projections, but of how they were put together by entrepreneurs. These notes may be of great assistance to Angels later in strengthening areas of weakness in the company and in reaching reinvestment decisions.

Underestimating Financial Needs

All Angels and entrepreneurs would like to make a lot of money by having to use only a little Entrepreneurs, in making projections, and Angels, in reviewing and evaluating them, often permit "the wish to be the parent of the thought." The making of money usually requires time and money, and time is money.

One unpleasant result of underestimating the need for sufficient financing in a new company is that the need for more money will arise before the company has achieved clear success and that, therefore, the new Angel providing the needed funds will impose terms unattractive to the previous Angels. Also, it is at the time of such an unexpected refinancing requirement that the relationship between entrepreneurs and Angels is most likely to become strained. The only solution to this problem is to do a better job of estimating the financial needs of the company before the Angel commits to the venture.

Entrepreneurs and Angels, once involved, must provide for the needs of the company, since estimating them alone is not sufficient. The company's future financial requirements can be met by pledges from Angels or from others, pending certain developments or achievements. Whatever arrangements are used, the entrepreneur would be well advised to promote the acquisition of the predictable needs of the company during the initial period of buoyant optimism, before reality sets in. It is always easier for entrepreneurs to raise funding before they have a shortfall on projections to explain away.

Actions Planned if Schedule Slips

As anyone who has been in the military understands, contingency plans are vital to ultimate success and, frequently, to survival. Although no one expects things to work out exactly as planned, most people find it difficult to make constructive alternative plans. For Angels, contingency planning should focus on assuring themselves that their control and influence in the company will increase, rather than decrease, as problems develop. With increasing failure of original plans to materialize, the role of Angels should increasingly change from that of observers to that of controlling factors. This shift in the balance of power, if it does not save the company, can greatly reduce loss to Angels.

A contingency plan is normally made to anticipate a lower than projected level of revenues and profits but can equally well be made to anticipate a level of revenues greater than had been projected, resulting in a strain on production facilities and delivery mechanisms, or service aspects of the business. Contingency plans include cutting back overhead unless revenues reach a certain point, and closing a plant or aspects of an operation if revenues fail to reach a certain point. Contingency planning really involves scheduling the use of resources, which is perhaps what business is all about, in that it is the meshing of resource and opportunity.

Contingency Commitments of Other Participants

In some companies, investments are staged. Sometimes they are staged simply by time; this was frequently the case when research and development limited-partnership tax shelters were prevalent, although there are still good reasons to stagger the investment. Perhaps a third of the money goes in at the time of the original investment, a third is due in January of the following year, and the final third in January of the next year.

Wise entrepreneurs seek a Letter of Credit to represent the commitment of Angels, because entrepreneurs must assure themselves as to the availability of the committed funds as scheduled. Wise Angels keep a string on their investments and have some sort of hurdle or measure that warrants the incremental payments, such as the completion of a development, the attainment of a level of sales, or the obtaining of a customer order--something as evidence of progress. Should Angels become dissatisfied with the progress of the enterprise as being different from that which was projected, they should be able to refuse, if performance standards have been previously agreed upon, to make incremental payments.

In a company where there is a group of Angels, one Angel who fails to provide the monies committed, for whatever reason, can jeopardize the position of all the other Angels. Therefore, the Angels should have an agreement whereby failure to perform as committed, which in itself places a burden on the other Angels, entails the immediate loss of interest of the defaulting Angel. Of course, unless agreed otherwise, the defaulting Angel has liability for damages to the other Angels.

Perhaps the most equitable way of handling such a default is that the defaulting Angel gives up that portion of equity, or whatever form the original investment has taken, to the extent needed by the remaining Angels to obtain a new, replacement Angel to stand in the defaulting Angel's place. In other words, if the original Angel has a five percent interest in the company and defaults on a $20,000 incremental payment that would have entitled the investor to another five percent of the company, the remaining Angels should, by agreement, have the right to use part or all of the original five percent holding as an inducement to attract a new Angel. In order for the Angels to avoid having to threaten or plead with a defaulting Angel at the time money is needed, contingency arrangements should be worked out in advance.

Chapter 10

NEGOTIATING
THE INVESTMENT

Techniques of Negotiation

I do not intend to give advice such as "Always sit with your back to the window or light source," or "Arrive first at the meeting and take the chair farthest from the door so that your opponent has to walk to you," or "Put your watch on the table to let your opponent know that you have only a limited amount of time for this matter," or "Spread out your papers to intimidate your opponent with the depth of your study and knowledge of the matter." Incidentally, *Power*, by Michael Korda, is a very funny book on negotiating and power plays. It should be read with Woody Allen in mind as the practitioner of what is being advised.

That the other party is an *opponent* is the key word and thought of most how-to-negotiate books. While this is always true to some extent, Angels investing in private companies must not lose sight of the fact that they are entering into a partnership and will probably not be able to extricate themselves (or their money) unless it works out well for all concerned. Because of the intensely personal nature of most private company investments, it is a mistake for Angels to think in terms of buying a security. They should, however, know the elements they must have in a deal to make it work for them. The making of a list of such points can be helpful.

A technique of negotiating with entrepreneurs I have found to be effective is to view and, perhaps present yourself, the prospective Angel, as an intermediary or investment banker responsible for investing your own funds and perhaps those of others. In other words, think of representing your interests as a professional or fiduciary and not of being the Angel. Think of being held accountable yourself by the owner of the money for the deal you are negotiating and subsequent developments as they affect the company, and therefore, the investment. Think of having to answer to the owner of the money as to why you made the investment and why you "permitted" the terms as they developed. Note the use of the term *permitted* in reference to contractual terms. Because Angels do not have to do the deal, any concessions they have made during the negotiation have occurred only because they have been permitted. The Angel must always remember there is no requirement to invest and there will be other opportunities for them to employ their dollars. They should also remember the Golden Rule of business: Those with the gold make the rules.

Angels must never allow themselves to be hurried into a deal. They should be wary of any deal which must be closed at short notice, remembering how much easier it is to get into a deal than out of one.

In response to a question of when life begins, a priest said "at the moment of conception," a minister said "at birth when the first breath is taken," and a rabbi said life begins "when the dog dies and the children leave home and go to college." There is no question as to when an Angel's involvement and risk exposure begin. For Angels, the life of their investments starts *only* at the closing of the transaction. All of the negotiations that go into the decision-making process are unimportant, in terms of risk exposure, until that point where Angles commit themselves.

Being Represented in Negotiation

Several schools of thought exist about whether Angels should negotiate directly with entrepreneurs or should use a representative. If Angels use an attorney, entrepreneurs are likely to use one also--so that at least four people are now involved in the negotiation, which will be expensive and take a longer time to complete. If Angels and entrepreneurs can agree upon a single attorney, the attorney can play the role of arbitrator in working out a fair agreement.

Needless to say, it is important to have an attorney put on paper the agreement reached between the principals; the attorney also ensures that the principals understand the consequences of their agreement as to possible developments in the future. After all, much of the boiler-plate in a contract is a result of experience in prior transactions, and few people are better qualified in this regard than seasoned lawyers. The fact that the boilerplate typically favors the side that prepares and presents the contract is something that should be remembered by Angels.

Apart from attorneys benefiting investors through their experience, the use of an attorney to negotiate a deal can also give investors a second bite at the apple in that they can moderate or change what the attorney has negotiated or enhance their position by insisting that certain terms be renegotiated. However, Angels must bear in mind that in private company investments, they are, in effect, entering into a partnership and it may not be to their ultimate advantage to deal in a manner which might be considered unfair or overly grasping by their future partners.

The following opinions were given independently.

Howard Stevenson said,

An attorney's fundamental role in negotiating contracts is to make sure that the deal which is agreed upon is the deal which in fact gets down on paper--that there are no time bombs sitting there in what has been termed *just boilerplate.* Every investor has to remember that boilerplate is put in documents because it closes loopholes in favor of the one who put it in, which can have important consequence. Anytime someone says to me "It's only boilerplate," I grow wary.

Investors who use an attorney as a negotiator will generally wind up in a much more adversarial position than they would if they had used a neutral middle person or negotiated for themselves.

Harold Bigler, of Bigler Investment Management Company said,

Rather than have attorneys negotiate on their behalf, I think the investor and the entrepreneur should do their best to understand what it is they want to accomplish, put that in writing and then go to a lawyer to have him draw up a term sheet. It is a mistake to get lawyers in the negotiations too early, because you'll get lost in trivia.

And Howard Arvey, my friend of many years and one of Chicago's most competent attorneys, said,

For an upcoming negotiation, I recommend that investors go over the base parameters with their attorneys or consultants or advisors and review the transactions principle by principle. If investors are the type of people capable of negotiating for themselves, then they should do so, after first having gone over the ground in consultation.

Angels are not striving to strike the hardest or toughest bargain. They are striving to create a fair deal, but fair and yet favoring themselves. Fair favoring investors means that their interests are protected during periods of disappointment.

It has been suggested that any experienced business person, or indeed any intelligent individual, can serve as an umpire in a negotiation. An investment banker or a professional deal maker, neither burdened nor blessed by a law degree, may serve both parties equally well. Nevertheless, an attorney should always be used to prepare the final documents. Appendix R shows a term sheet used by Whitehead Associates.

Howard Stevenson added, "Negotiation is always easier with some sort of middle person. They help avoid a clash of egos, and such clashes are a characteristic difficulty of negotiations. The role of a middle person can be very important here."

Antidilution Protection

While potentially a contract's most treacherous terms, Antidilution clauses can yield extraordinary benefits for both investors and entrepreneurs. For an article on antidilution protection, see Appendix S.

Warranties from Promoters

One of the first things Angels should ask the promoters or finders of a private company investment opportunity is how much of the deal promoters are taking themselves. And if promoters are not themselves investing in the deal, Angels should ask why not. The Angel should also seek terms equal to, or superior in protection of capital than, those of the promoter.

Promoters and agents of deals need the ability to make their opportunities sound attractive, and one of the simplest ways to attract Angels to a deal is to make it sound like a sure thing. If the promoter of a deal plays down its risk to Angels, the latter are entitled to suggest that the promoter give them a warranty in exchange for their cash investment. For example, Angels are told that if they invest $200,000 in a company, it will earn $100,000 next year and $200,000 the following year. This clearly is an investment opportunity that could be structured into an attractive investment--whether it is a good invest-ment will depend on the deal the Angels negotiate. Angels should ask promoters for an affirmative warranty regarding the $100,000 guaranteed profit the next year. If this is not forthcoming, Angels can test promoters by asking for a lesser amount, say $25,000, guaranteed by the promoters and undertaken as a personal liability. My guess is that the finder will decline the opportunity to warrant any earnings, and there may be a message in that for Angels.

In the case of entrepreneurs also being promoters or finders, Angels could ask for a warranty in the form of additional stock. Suppose the Angel's $200,000 investment originally entitles them to a 25 percent holding in the company; the warranty might provide Angels with an additional 50 percent holding if the $100,000 "guaranteed" profit next year fails to materialize. Such an approach is probably best handled through the terms of conversion of a note or preferred or the issuance of the penalty shares, which can be held by an escrow agent pending the report of earnings of the company.

Another form of warranty is one that requires the guarantor to make up the shortfall to the company rather than directly to the Angel. Thus, if the shortfall amounts to $50,000, guarantors, instead of writing a check to investors, are required to buy $50,000 worth of common shares in the company. This assumes Angels hold a senior convertible security that has antidilution protection. The advantage of this form of warranty is that it provides the company with additional working capital. The disadvantage is that it provides the guarantor with a block of shares that may be a nuisance if votes become important. Of course, non-voting shares might be issued to the guarantor. A warranty requiring the entrepreneur or promoter to lend money, subordinated to interests held by the Angel, interest free to the company, in an amount equal to the shortfall, may be even more advantageous to the Angel than one requiring the promoter to buy equity.

The forms that warranties take vary enormously from industry to industry with the financial circumstances of the entrepreneurs, with the size of the company, whether it is early or late in a company's development, and so on.

Most of these warranties intended to be protective of the Angels' capital should disappear when the company becomes profitable, or when it has attained its projected level of activity for two or three consecutive periods, because it would not be fair to have Angels protected from unforeseen developments forever. In my view, Angels should be protected from unforeseen developments, vis-a-vis those holding promotional (not paid for with money) interests, only during the early stages in the development of a company.

It is easy for promoters or entrepreneurs to let their enthusiasm run away with them and persuade the Angel, sometimes described by some old-hand oil stock promoters as "mullets," that their project is a sure thing, almost risk-free, with the result that Angels put in more money than they can afford or even borrow funds in order to invest them. This is the scenario which is frequently the cause of much money being lost, perhaps unnecessarily so in many cases, by private company investing Angels.

Fees

When a finder's fee for locating investors is paid by a company, in effect investors in the company are paying the fee, or at least their proportionate share of it. Angels should not object to the company in which they are considering an investment paying a finder's fee to someone who located them so long as (1) the fee is reasonable in terms of the total, and (2) the fee does not significantly increase the amount of money necessary for Angels to provide. For example, a company-paid fee of 20 percent of the investment, leaving the company only $80,000 out of a $100,000 investment, would certainly be looked upon unfavorably by any experienced Angel. Likewise, a fee that gives finders (who perform only that service) a 20 percent holding in the company, compared to the Angels' 50 percent and management's 30 percent, is clearly unreasonable. Of the reasonable standards of fairness for a finder's fee, the so-called Lehman formula of five, four, three, two, one formula has stood the test of time: five percent of the first million, four percent of the second million, three present of the third million, and so forth.

A distinction should be made between the simple finder and advisors or consultants to the company. My use of the term *finder* refers strictly to the introductory agent between the entrepreneur and the money and not to the individual who is providing other services on an ongoing basis to the company, or who may have provided services to the company before the financing. That individual is really just another part of the management team that the Angel is acquiring.

The consulting fee charged the issuing company in many low-priced new-issue underwritings is frequently not a consulting fee at all, but rather an element of incremental underwriter profit taking the form of a contractual relationship with the National Association of Securities Dealers member firm underwriter and the issuing company. I believe it is outrageous for underwriters to propose that they or their designees be paid, say $4,000 per month, for a period of 36 months after a deal has been completed. This is frequently a way of attempting to avoid NASD regulations that limit the amount that can be charged by an underwriter in a public offering. It is unfair to the investors and equally unfair to the management of the company. I strongly believe that, between the underwriter and the company, there should be a strict limitation on, or possibly even exclusion of, contractual commitments entered into prior to the receipt of funds which require services to be rendered after the receipt of funds.

If, in fact, the management of the company wants the advisory services of the individual or firm that has been responsible for having raised the money for the company, they can acquire those services or contract for their provision after they have the money in hand and not as a condition of its receipt. I suspect that few companies would otherwise retain these services on the very steep terms described in many new-issue offering documents.

Incidentally, investment bankers and intermediaries frequently charge ongoing management consulting fees to companies for which they raise funds from Angels. Angels, therefore, should be aware of all the profit elements that may affect the judgment of the party recommending the investment to the Angel.

Expenses of Review and Negotiation

Investigating investment opportunities in private companies is an expensive pursuit. One needs lawyers, private investigators, accountants, and technical experts. The question of who pays for the investigation is best divided into the two subsidiary questions of who pays for it in deals that close, and who pays for it in deals that do not close. Angels are always best served by an agreement that the company will pay the expenses of investigating the deal and their attorneys' fees. This is becoming much more usual than has been the case.

In the case of a deal that closes, it perhaps should be agreed that the company pay the costs of negotiation and investigation, considering these expenses to be part of the deal. In the absence of the company's undertaking to pay these expenses, Angels should probably increase their expectations of the amount they are to receive from the company, either in equity or some other form.

In the case of a deal that does not close--the assumption being that it does not close because the Angel has decided not to go forward--certain expenses should be borne by the company. For instance, if the company makes a projection of earnings of $100,000 and Angels, in analyzing all the projections, reach the conclusion that the earnings projection is absurd and without basis, then these Angels should receive reimbursement for their expenses if they are clearly in the right. Certainly, Angels should be contractually entitled to reimbursement if any material statements made to them are found to be inaccurate.

Most frequently these days, underwriters of low-priced issues require a company for which they have not issued securities before to present payment in advance for a certain percentage of the underwriter's compensation and to be responsible for all the underwriter's expenses. In one case I recently negotiated, a $25,000 payment was expected at the same time that the underwriter's non-binding letter of intent was executed; this sum was simply to cover the underwriter's legal fees involved in the early stages of prospectus preparation and the underwriter's "due diligence" research.

In the case where an Angel retains an advisor or a consultant, the fact that the company pays the expenses does not mean that the company selects the professional retained to assist the Angel. The company is simply the party the bill is sent to. The consultant or advisor can have only one master, and that must be the Angel. However, if the company pays the bill for a feasibility study and the Angel elects not to proceed, clearly the feasibility study should become the property of the company. They then will have the right to use the study again as they see fit and as is permitted by its author.

When to Spend on Investigation

The costs of investigating a private company for the purpose of investment are high and may vary little in relation to the size of the company. Thus, investigation of a small investment costs about the same as investigation of a big one, which is one of the reasons why venture capitalists shy away from small deals. Angels who see a high flow of deals cannot afford to investigate more than a small percentage of them, because each serious investigation can easily cost them a minimum of $5,000-7,000.

Wise investors wait until all other elements of the deal are in place before actually spending any real money on the investigation--that is,

Angels should have already made up their mind, on the basis of other factors, to go ahead if the investigation results turn out to be favorable. It is reasonable for Angels at this point to seek an agreement from entrepreneurs that if the entrepreneur cancels the deal from this point on, they should pay the costs of the investors' investigation. If the deal is closed and the investment made, then it is an open question as to who pays for the investigation. Typically, the business pays, which, of course, amounts to Angles indirectly paying some of their own expenses.

What if ...

All investors, and most particularly private company investing Angels, should understand that anything that can go wrong, will go wrong. Especially when it comes to maintaining schedules.

Therefore, a "what if" list of things that can go wrong can be reviewed, item by item, by the Angel and entrepreneur. The corrective actions agreed upon should find their way into the shareholders' agreement or memorandum of understanding in order that they may be implemented if the circumstances arise. Not all contingencies can be envisioned, and one certainly does not wish to have a team of lawyers preparing a 100-page document. This is meant as nothing more than a suggestion that it is constructive for investors and entrepreneurs to try to look forward into the future together. Anything agreed upon can later be changed with the consent of all parties. Investors should not be afraid to get it on paper. Even an informal note or memo of an agreement, initialed by both parties, is better than no "paper" agreement at all.

The entrepreneur's reaction to these questions, or others like them, will provide the Angel with insights into that entrepreneur's personality. How entrepreneurs handle the stress of answering "what if" questions can provide Angels with insights as to how entrepreneurs will handle the stress of being faced with real-life problems. In fact, Angels should keep in mind that entrepreneurs will probably make better decisions in the simulation than they will in real life. If they cannot respond intelligently to the following sort of questions, in all probability they will not be able to handle such problems.

1. What if the company fails to achieve projected results for four consecutive months (or quarters or years)?

2. What if the product the business depends upon cannot be produced at anything like the cost anticipated?

3. What if certain key executives are found to be incompetent?

4. What if the investor is unwilling or unable to fulfill future finding commitments to the company?

5. What if the chief executive officer dies or becomes incapacitated? Incapacitation must be defined to the satisfaction of both parties. Is a stroke incapacitating? Is alcoholism? What about a spinal injury that keeps the chief executive officer in a hospital for more than three to six months? What about a psychiatric report showing advanced paranoia (not an uncommon affliction of both entrepreneurs and Angels)?

6. What if the company is sued for patent infringement and counsel advises that the company's case is not strong?

7. What if three of the top engineers or scientists on whom the company depends leave to start their own competitive company?

8. What if a competitor makes a bid for the company? At what price and under what conditions will the investor and entrepreneur agree to sell out? (A buy/sell agreement can resolve this.)

9. What if the financing promised by the bank (or underwriter) fails to materialize? What fall-back financing positions exist, in terms of both source and the deal, that might be acceptable under the worst conditions? How much interest can the company really afford and remain a viable business entity? What is the maximum amount of equity that can be given up as a sweetener and still leave enough to justify the participation of the Angel or entrepreneur or both?

10. What if the plant burns down, or a flood sweeps the office records away? What other natural disasters can be jointly imagined and planned for?

11. What if a divorce takes place and either the Angel or the entrepreneur is faced with a hostile ex-spouse as major interest holder? Do shares become nonvoting in the hands of an ex-spouse? What about survivors? Does the control of the company change, or only the profit participation, with change in personal circumstances of the Angel or entrepreneur?

12. What if the Angel (or entrepreneur) files personal bankruptcy?

13. What if embezzlement is discovered? Is it company policy that where a law is broken, the authorities are informed?

14. What if a union attempts to organize the workers?

15. What if a competing company becomes available for purchase?

16. What if the use of drugs by executives or workers becomes prevalent?

17. What if supplies of raw materials become hard to obtain?

18. What if a competing company already has some of the dire problems being considered possible for the new company?

19. What if an underwriter suggests taking the company public?

20. What if a competitor has a problem with production or integrity of executives? Will the new company publicize the problems of its competitors?

21. What if the entrepreneur intentionally exceeds budgeted expenses?

Checks and Balances

After the entrepreneur has presented the company budget to the Angel, and the Angel has approved it, the question remains of who will ensure that the budget will be adhered to. One answer is monitoring by the Angel of all major expenditures and of all borrowings. As suggested elsewhere, the investor can have the right to co-sign or at least review all company checks made out for more than a certain amount, for example, $1,000. The entrepreneur should not have the right to borrow additional funds without the Angel's prior approval.

The initial budget approved by the Angel may have to be changed to reflect changed business conditions. The Angel should retain the right of approval of all budget changes over a certain amount.

Who Speaks First?

I usually insist that the other parties in a negotiation set forth their side of the deal first. Whoever speaks first is merely suggesting an initial point of departure. They may not realize this, but that is all it amounts to. For me, it is mandatory that entrepreneurs put out on the table what they think the deal consists of and what they think their relationships with Angels should be. This then becomes the point of departure for Angels to improve upon.

This way Angels find out quickly what the entrepreneurs' parameters are. If entrepreneurs are overestimating the value of their company by 50 percent, perhaps entrepreneurs and Angels can solve their differences through discussion and deal structure. But if entrepreneurs are overestimating their companies' value by 500 percent, it would probably be a waste of time for Angels to discuss it with them. Rather than hurting the entrepreneurs' feelings by speaking their minds, Angels are better off sending them to speak with other investors, telling them to come back after they have had some specific offers.

A Dialogue

ENTREPRENEUR: I've no money but I've put a lot of time and energy into this project.

ANGEL: Certainly, you have. Just as I've put a lot of time and energy into making the money you need for your project. So I don't think your prior effort is any more significant than mine. But I recognize that this business is your idea, and that there would be no deal if it were not for your efforts. How much money do you need?

ENTREPRENEUR: $150,000 for a year.

ANGEL: Why don't we do this then--I'll take 80 percent of the company and you'll take 20 percent, and I'll lend $150,000 to the company. The day that you repay me my money, if it's within the next fifteen months, our positions will reverse. You'll own 80 percent of the company, and I'll own 20 percent. Does that sound fair?

ENTREPRENEUR: (Pause) What happens if the schedule slips a bit?

ANGEL: You said you wanted the money for a year. I've already given you fifteen months--three extra months. What do you mean by the schedule slipping a bit? Give me the number of months.

ENTREPRENEUR: Maybe two years instead of one.

ANGEL: In your presentation of the enterprise to me, you said I'd get my money back in a year. That's what I based my thinking on. Now you're saying two years...

ENTREPRENEUR: I'll pay you interest the second year. Maybe both years.

ANGEL: That isn't always a fair trade. How are you going to get me paid? I think I should have some form of guarantee. Initially, you will own 20 percent of the company, and I will put in $150,000. Can you guarantee $30,000 of that personally?

ENTREPRENEUR: After two years, you will have all your money back and have 20 percent of the stock. I won't have all my time and energy back.

ANGEL: Isn't your 80 percent holding going to be worth a great deal of money then?

ENTREPRENEUR: Yes, I guess it should be.

Note how the entrepreneur was attracted by the symmetry of the Angel's deal, which may or may not have turned out to be fair. In deal-making, symmetry frequently gives the appearance of fairness and can result in increased equity for the Angel.

Of course, the two-year deal, even with interest payments in the second year and a $30,000 guarantee, is not nearly as attractive as, though it may be more realistic than, the one-year deal. Therefore, a greater equity retention by the Angel would seem fair.

An Entrepreneur's Unrealistic Offer

ENTREPRENEUR: I need $50,000 to establish my restaurant business, and I'll contribute my services free for a year.

ANGEL: But that's not a good deal for you. How can you live without income for a year? Because you would need at least $30,000 to survive for a year, your offer indicates to me that you already have at least this amount in a bank or in your spouse's name or whatever. Yet, here you come asking me for money. If it's such a good deal, why aren't you putting your own money into it?

ENTREPRENEUR: I have no money. My spouse works. We'll live on that income.

ANGEL: Your joint income will be reduced for that year. Are you sure that you're one of those very remarkable people who can go back to living on much less than what they earned the previous year?

Angels must be warned against entrepreneurs who are contributing their services without charge or making other offers Angels consider too generous, because this can lead to a wholly unrealistic set of financial projections. A business must be viewed on the basis that Angels are paying a market price for all the necessary elements of the business. Angels must be able to lure a replacement for entrepreneurs who die or become disabled.

When Entrepreneurs Think They Can Find a Better Deal

ENTREPRENEUR: I have to consider looking for someone who will give me the money I need in exchange for a smaller amount of equity than you demand.

ANGEL: Go right ahead. By the way, how many people have you gone to for the money before you came to me?

ENTREPRENEUR: I went to the bank. They turned me down. After them, you're the first person I came to.

ANGEL: It's very reasonable for you to want to have alternatives. Why don't we end this meeting now. I'm interested. You look to me like a winner. I think I'd like to be in business with you, but I must suggest that you go out and spend some time talking t other investors and other sources of money. Come back and talk to me when you find what other sources are available to you. Without your making these comparisons, you will probably think that whatever deal we might agree on now is unfair to you if the business is successful.

The Angel here is not trying to rush the entrepreneur into a deal, any more than he would wish to be rushed into one himself. The Angel realizes that if his future partnership with the entrepreneur is to be harmonious, the entrepreneur must not feel coerced by the Angel's terms. If the entrepreneur said he had seen several investors previously, the Angel here should ask him what was their reaction, if any had made him an offer, and if any had asked to check into his background.

Deals Passed Over

At some time or another, all Angels will pass up what later turns out to be a good deal. Yet, they must remember that, for any number of reasons, that deal might not have turned out to be a good one for them. One common way of missing out on a deal is to be uncompromisingly negative on the whole deal, because certain parts are unacceptable. An example of this occurred to me recently. I took a deal in which a company was seeking a million dollar guarantee in return for a five-year warrant on 25,000 shares to an investment banking firm, which I will call Smith & Co., suggesting to them that I would participate jointly with them. Smith & Co. liked the company but not the deal and turned it down on the grounds that the rewards for providing the million dollar guarantee were not lucrative enough. I offered to pursue this with the company to see if I could get a higher level of return, but Smith & Co. were not interested in considering under what conditions they would change their decision, and, thus, they decided to simply pass.

I went back to the company and told them what Smith & Co. had said about the rate of return they were offering, telling them that Smith was a knowledgeable firm whose opinion I respected and that had to be reckoned with, which was true. The company immediately offered another 15,000 shares of free stock, and, thus, I picked up $240,000 worth of stock at no change in risk simply through an improvement in the deal. If Smith & Co. had asked for a change in the deal instead of simply saying no, they would have obtained a better deal.

Instead of saying no, Angels should tell the entrepreneur under what conditions the deal would be acceptable to them. I never say no to someone I want to do business with, because I know that in reality I am investing more in people than in businesses. I say "Not on these terms" or "Not in this business," but I finish by telling the entrepreneur, "Come back to me again, because I want to do business with you. Together, we'll find a basis that makes sense to both of us."

If you like people and have confidence in them as entrepreneurs, invest something with them--even if you do not like the deal. If they ask for $100,000, suggest that you will participate with others to the extent of $10,000 on whatever terms are negotiated. They will almost certainly run out of money and need a refinancing, and, by that time, you will know more about the venture than you can now. You can always then come in on the second-stage financing, if it looks good. Sprinkling money amongst talent is a good program for entrepreneurial investors.

The entrepreneur may be initially disappointed in being offered a $10,000 participation instead of $100,000 but will usually accept, realizing that with one investor committed, for whatever amount, others will be easier to attract. Even if you lose this deal, the entrepreneur will come back to you with his next project.

Obviously, Angels putting in a small fraction of the whole are not in a position to dictate terms to the entrepreneur, although they should try to get the same terms as the major investors. If they do not get the same deal as the major investors, perhaps they can get a different deal rather than a lesser one.

Mentioning Specific Cash Amounts

Investors should not make an offer of a specific amount of money or percentage to entrepreneurs unless they feel they are close to making a deal. If the Angel has suggested a particular sum of money for an agreed upon interest in the company and the entrepreneur then asks for a delay in their discussions, the Angel should make it clear to the entrepreneur before the Angel leaves the room that this sum of money is not a firm bid, that it is not something the entrepreneur can always return for and be assured of getting, and that it most certainly is not a sum the entrepreneur can quote to other prospective investors in hope of raising the bidding. This is not to say that knowledgeable entrepreneurs should not seek a firm proposal for a set period of time. They are certainly entitled to seek the best deal possible. But why should Angels give away such an option when they can sell it? It is not unreasonable for the investor to propose to the entrepreneur that, in return for an agreed upon dollar amount or interest in the company, the investor will agree to be committed to a specific deal for, say, 30 days.

Entrepreneur as Angel's Protector

The highest rate of return available to investors is in the pre-development, or seed-capital investment, stage. The earlier investors go into a company, the more equity they can demand in return for their investment, because the risk is greater at this point than later in the company's development. While it is true that later investors often take priority over the original investors, original investors can structure their deal so that they do not suffer a dilution relative to entrepreneurs--that is, so that entrepreneurs cannot dilute the angel's interest relative to their own along the way. Original Angels can be given the benefit of sharing in the entrepreneur's compensation (over an agreed amount) and warrants, shareholder appreciation rights, phantom stock plans, and so on. They can have a contractual relationship with the entrepreneur that if the company is sold or its control changes hands, the entrepreneur will share pro-rata with the Angels the benefits of the shareholder-appreciation rights, stock plans, and employee stock-option plans. Angels can force the entrepreneur to be a guardian of their equity interests in the future--in other words, give the entrepreneur fiduciary responsibility in preserving the position of the Angels--not as a percentage of the total shares outstanding but vis-a-vis the shares or interests of the entrepreneur. This approach on the part of the Angel can be of assistance to less financially sophisticated entre-preneurs, who may not be thinking in terms of protecting their origi-nal holding in the company. Such a relationship preserves the con-cept of partnership, even though one party is more directly involved in the day-to-day affairs of the company.

Worst Case Projections

When entrepreneurs come to see me with their business plans, I tell them,

> Give me your worst case projection. Don't give me your middle or best case. We'll negotiate the deal from the worst case, because my shortfall is going to be from your pocket and not from mine because you are the one making projections. Now, if you do better than your worst case projection, you should have a bonus. But I shouldn't have to pay you anything for achieving the projections you tell me you are going to achieve, because I'm already paying for those in the terms of whatever deal we may make today.

Projections are not a matter of symmetrical percentage variance--in other words, if the projection is 100 and the best case is 120, the worst case is not necessarily 80. The basis for arriving at worst case must be an analysis of individual elements that can go wrong, causing a halt or a delay in the production process: a delay of three months in this department, a delay of five months in another, periodic shortage of a raw material, and so on. These realistic elements must be used in working toward the bottom number. Thus, a business plan in which there is symmetry between the best and worst cases is probably not based upon realistic or seriously contemplated factors.

Questions by Entrepreneurs

Angels should not have to prove themselves to entrepreneurs. Entrepreneurs typically have come to Angels simply for money. Entrepreneurs have not come to Angels, though they might have been more successful had they done so, as a money partner. When the entrepreneur approaches the Angel with the attitude that the Angel's only value is his money, the entrepreneur has no justification to demand personal data about the Angel.

However, entrepreneurs often approach Angels with the line, "Your money is incidental, what I really want is you as a partner in the busi-ness." Angels beware!

197

If entrepreneurs have other, approximately equal offers, it is reasonable for them to determine which of the investors is going to be easy to live with. Is the Angel's motivation to increase their visibility and influence? Is their purpose really to grab control of the business? Is the Angel a user, in the negative sense, of people? What has been the Angel's history of dealing with people?

On a moral basis, entrepreneurs should be concerned with how much of the Angel's net worth is being invested in their enterprises. There are obvious issues of morality when an entrepreneur persuades investors to invest more than they should in a venture that is clearly speculative.

Angels should look upon entrepreneurs' questions with a view to having a balanced relationship with them. The entrepreneur has a right to know what will happen if the Angel dies. Also, Angels may have skills, contacts, or so forth that could help entrepreneurs in the business and, thus, give entrepreneurs more to work with in their efforts to make the business successful.

Disclosure of Angel's Net Worth

On occasion, I have been asked to provide a net worth statement to a lender. This has come about either because I was borrowing directly, or because I was guaranteeing the obligations of some borrower with whom I had a relationship. I have always declined to provide the requested data, because I only borrow on a fully secured basis, pledging collateral. I do not seek unsecured credit. If unsecured credit is sought, personal net worth information is clearly a valid request by the lender. My reason for declining the request mostly has to do with my not wishing to have on record the extent (or lack) of my own wealth, or that of a private company which I control Such information on an investor in the files of a financial institution, especially in this country, can be, and frequently is, made available to the institution's many employees and to its officers and directors, and possibly their friends, without the investor's permission or even knowledge.

In any case, the reason why lenders want the information in the case of secured or guaranteed company loans is not so much to form a judgment as to credit-worthiness as it is to have something to which the supplier of the information can be tied in case of a default. If a lender can show, even remotely, that a misstatement was made by the seeker of credit, the latter can find himself in a much more difficult situation than otherwise. It may be almost impossible for active business people to accurately describe *all* their assets and liabilities. Assessments made to the best of their abilities at one time may appear incomplete and even intentionally inaccurate years later, when in all probability their assets and liabilities will be much changed.

Years ago, Dr. Henry Jarecki, the then chairman of Mocatta Metals, provided a direct, simple, and fair solution to the problem. I was at the time seeking a line of credit in commodity dealing for a company I controlled. He asked me for a financial statement for the company, and I told him that we did not, as a matter of principle, distribute them. He then asked me for my personal net worth statement. My answer was the same. He next asked if the current net worth of the corporation was in excess of a certain amount. I said that it was. After that, he asked if my personal net worth exceeded a certain amount. I said that it did. Then he simply asked if (1) I would attest to those statements, and (2) I would agree to be personally responsible for informing him if either the company's or my net worth fell below 80 percent of the amounts stated, in order for him to take steps to protect his company in terms of the credit being extended. Henry knew that as long as he had me personally liable, without (please note) my technically guaranteeing any obligation, he had all of the real benefits of a net worth statement and personal guarantee. I have used his brilliant solution many times since learning it.

Chapter 11

MONITORING AND MANAGING THE INVESTMENT

Scope of Angel Involvement

One assumption made in this book is that Angels are going to be active rather than passive. Another assumption--when it is not being spelled out as a warning--is that entrepreneurs' projected results will not be achieved, and that the Angels' degree of involvement in the new company will probably involuntarily increase as they become more concerned with the protection of their capital than with its enhancement. If Angels are not prepared to be involved with the company and to spend at least several hours a month, and perhaps considerably more time than that, in monitoring the progress made by the company in absolute terms (as well as progress made by the company relative to its projected rates of progress), then investors are well advised to seek capital and income opportunities in publicly traded securities.

Private company investing requires time, diligence, and intelligence--but lots of time. This is not to say that the time invested has to be viewed negatively, because working with private companies can be extremely rewarding, both in terms of the ongoing process of learning and of the satisfactions to be derived from helping someone create a successful and viable enterprise. Nevertheless, lots of time is required--weekends and nights usually, because private company investors normally have their own business affairs to look after during working hours.

The amount of time required to look after their investments may cause friction in the family life of Angels. In extreme cases, Angels' families come to resent the private company investments and the entrepreneurs and management involved in the private companies. This resentment can result in pressure on Angels to disengage themselves from the private companies.

I think it important that the spouse of the Angel be fully aware of the potential of the company, as well as the problems as they develop. Investing in private companies, particularly within smaller communities, is very much a family affair. There are going to be a lot of hard feelings and resentment if the investment does not work out well, and, sometimes, they are there even if it does. However, pressures can be minimized by the family having a better understanding of what is involved.

It is a fact that successful entrepreneurs, and also, I believe, active Angels as entrepreneurial investors, create the additional time necessary to be successful in their commercial pursuits at the expense of what some describe as the "quality" time spent with their families. The emotional demands, let alone physical demands, on individuals building a business are urgent and frequently all-consuming. Angels, not having the ability to make their loss (or profit) whenever they choose, have this additional anxiety over that of investors or speculators in publicly traded securities. Angels are burdened at times with a feeling of impotence and loss of control. They may not be able to get out of an investment that threatens their financial security, because they have put more money in than they had anticipated or was prudent by making follow-on investments to protect what was already invested. Their spouse in the meantime may well have suffered the natural fear of loss of family assets and security, combined with having been ignored or at least having received less attention than previously.

When a company or investment works out well after a period of anxiety, spouses are mindful of "their sacrifice" and can be resentful of the success of their spouse. Thus, family pressure can result from success, just as it does, in a different and more intense way, from failure. I am suggesting here that successful entrepreneurs, and often successful Angels, pay a generally unrecognized price for their successes.

Angels who are not burdened with their own domestic troubles may have to contend with those of entrepreneurs. A point worth noting is that with success comes a financial incentive for separation due to the

201

increased wealth available for division. In some cases, Angels may have to consider the entrepreneur's ex-spouse as well as the present one.

Angels should think through, with their attorneys, what happens to the business in which they are considering an investment if there is a contentious divorce proceeding during the period of their lock-in investments. At this time, consideration should also be given to the disposition of the entrepreneurs' shares, and votes, in the event of their death. Do Angels want to be in the position of dealing with the survivor's attorney or next spouse? Similarly, from the entrepreneurs' point of view, do they want to be dealing with the ex-spouse or survivor of the Angel? These contingencies can, and should, be discussed openly between the entrepreneur and Angel and can be provided for in much the same way as for a partnership. In covering the possibility of a change in principals, a buy/sell option and/or voting trust arrangement can be helpful.

Timing and Degree of Angel Involvement

Angels must determine their own timing and degree of involvement in a private company, because entrepreneurs will have the natural reaction of wanting to be left alone to "let me run my business" without the "assistance" of Angels. It is true that simply having the money available for investment, and the courage and/or greed to make the investment do not mean that the individual has the ability to assist in the management of the enterprise. And down deep, entrepreneurs frequently have contempt for individuals with resources to invest. Sometimes that contempt is well deserved. Nevertheless, Angels must have the ability to gain as much information as they wish about the company, its problems, and its prospects. Angels must be in a position to increase their influence and control, and, therefore, involvement, as their investments become increasingly jeopardized. The entrepreneur will usually not welcome the involvement of the Angel, and this may become a friction point between the two.

The involvement of Angels may take the form of requiring the company to hire a management consultant or an officer, perhaps even a new chief executive officer. Their involvement does not mean that Angels are going to step in and physically manage the company's affairs on a day-to-day basis. Time is money for angels also, and although they have the right to be increasingly involved in the company, they should view the investment of their hours in the same way they viewed the investment of their money. They may be better of putting the same five or eight hours on a weekend into studying new investment opportunities than in working with one already made. As with money, one should not throw good hours after bad.

Angels make money with their minds (using their memory and their intuition) and their time; skills can equally well be focused on new opportunities as on one in which they have a present involvement. They must consciously decide how to expend their energies. Years ago, Maurice R. "Hank" Greenberg, chairman of the American International Group, whom I think of as one of the most outstanding executives I have known, told me that the most important thing for executives to do is to determine how they are going to use their own time and not give up control of it to others--right down to which telephone calls are returned, which letters are answered, and which meetings are attended.

Effective investors, like effective executives, cannot be in a position of simply responding to the needs of others. They must dictate their own areas of focus and priority, based on their own objectives.

Consultants as Overseers

It is perfectly reasonable for a consultant to be retained to review, on a periodic basis, the progress of a company. An accountant hired to review the monthly financials is likely to see things in them that the Angel would have missed. Technical and marketing consultants are regularly employed by companies to oversee developments periodically. While the Angels' perspectives are usually different from that of the management, they too can benefit from these consultants' findings. Periodic management reviews by a consulting firm can be of particular benefit to Angels.

Angels must really view themselves, at times, as part of management and, at times, as one company investing in another company. They must in fact try to act as their own financial consultants or fiduciaries viewing themselves as if they were accountable to the owners of the money invested, even though of course it is their own. This will force them to be more decisive and to take provisions for unpredictable events, just as professionals do; if they didn't, they would be criticized for their omission. All too frequently, Angels, when dealing with their own money, act as if they do not understand that dollars lost have to be recreated. Frequently, the dollars were earned at a time when they were easier to make than at the time when they were lost. Money made in a bull market and lost in a bear market must often be replaced by money made in that same bear market, which may not be an easy feat to accomplish. When Angels lose their money, it is likely to be at a time when it is most difficult to re-earn it. Also, and it is the premise and reason for my writing this book, when Angels lose their money we all lose as then there is that much less money and willingness to finance new private companies. The pool of Angel capital is a national asset, one which I am dedicated to trying to preserve and enhance.

Entrepreneur Extravagance

Angels are frequently bothered by what they regard as the personal extravagances of entrepreneurs. While unauthorized loans to officers and similar transgressions should require the instant dismissal and perhaps prosecution of the entrepreneur, many other expenditures amount to gray areas. Did the entrepreneur's office have to be redecorated in such lavish style? Perhaps, as the entrepreneur will rationalize, it will impress customers and pay for itself many times over in higher orders. If the Angel feels that the entrepreneur tends toward extravagance, it should be an easy matter to draw up an agreement giving the investor the right to co-sign every check for over $1,000 or some other reasonable amount relative to the size of the business or to, at least, see a record of them.

By agreement, the Angel can also review a synopsis of every new contract entered into by the company, including a description of the relationship with the other company, the financial condition of the other company, how the contract came about, who is responsible for it, whether there are friends or relations of the entrepreneur in the other company, the profit margin at which the sales contract was figured, and how it compares with the profit margins of other sales contracts.

By and large, I have found entrepreneurs to be honest to a much greater degree than executives who are employees, especially of publicly owned companies. I know of very few instances of entrepreneurs being con men--they may fool themselves but, typically, they are not crooks. They do not start out with the purpose of taking advantage of the Angel. A number of them have bad habits left over from their days as employees and expense reimbursement and allowing hope to be reflected in projections are obvious problem areas, so it is important that the Angel lay down the guidelines as to what is expected. A policy memo, approved by the Angel, regarding entertainment, first class travel, and so forth may be necessary if there is not to be future unhappiness.

Although investors cannot police entrepreneurs, they can let them know what is expected of them and what the probably results of a breach of agreement are.

One of the reasons I like to use the revenue participation certificate method of investing in private companies is that matters of management perks are then of no concern to me. Entrepreneurs should be free to live well "on the company" and spend as they feel justified without fear of shareholder or profit-interest holder criticism. That's fine as long as every week, month, or quarter I receive the agreed upon shares of revenues. I fly economy class, and I expect others spending my money to do so also if my interest (and reason for my assuming financial risk) in their activities is profit-related. The RPC works wonderfully well in lots of deals.

Enforcement of Agreement between Angel and Entrepreneur

One of the facts of commercial life is that people agree to almost anything suggested or required by a source of funding prior to obtaining the money. The most troubling problems likely to confront the Angel are those relating to the entrepreneur not adhering to agreements made prior to a period of problems. Entrepreneurs under stress frequently feel cornered and trapped by circumstances beyond their control and see their agreement with the Angel as being the part of the closing circle that is the weakest. After all, entrepreneurs may reason, the Angel is really either their partner or someone who is trying to take advantage of them anyway, and, therefore, their obligations to the Angel are of lesser concern than those to others, who are typically imposing greater pressure at the time of stress. Although it may be easy to understand how entrepreneurs may reach such erroneous conclusions, it behooves Angels to protect themselves by having the means already at hand with which to enforce their agreement with entrepreneurs.

Perhaps the most common means of ensuring compliance is for the Angel to hold as security, and have the right to vote, the shares of the company owned by the entrepreneur. Although this sounds onerous, it really is not inasmuch as all entrepreneurs have to do is what they promised to do, and on which premise Angels risked their capital. A less direct method would be for the shares of the entrepreneur to be held, and voted under certain circumstances, by a third party acceptable to both the entrepreneur and Angel.

Another technique of assuring the cooperation and compliance of the entrepreneur is to have a money obligation, perhaps secured or collateralized with property or third-party guarantees, that becomes effective only in the event of the entrepreneur breaching the agreement with the Angel. Such an agreement could call for the entrepreneur, in the event of certain previously stipulated developments, to purchase non-voting shares or to lend an agreed upon amount of money to the company on a non-interest-bearing subordinated (to the investor) basis.

Developments warranting either a forced provision of funds to the company or a surrender of complete control to the Angel might include threatened bankruptcy, asserted by creditors or demonstrated by the Angel and confirmed by the auditors; loss of an agreed percentage of the company's sales; the denial of patents; or entering into contractual relationship or borrowings unauthorized by the board of directors or the Angel. The entrepreneur may agree that these would be important eventualities but point out that the chances of their happening are remote. The Angel can reply that because the chances of their happening are so remote and because the agreement is important to the Angel and costs the entrepreneur nothing, there can be little risk in accepting the agreement.

Shareholders' Agreement as Management Tool

Martin Solomon, in his interview with me, summed up this technique:

I use the shareholders' agreement to define the terms and conditions of the management of the business. The agreement specifies that investors are to be financially reimbursed before the entrepreneur/manager. Rights of first refusal are given to both sides. Whether investors do or do not have board representation, they must, by the force of their experience and judgment, as well as by their contractual agreements, maintain a method of exerting influence on all but the day-to-day details of running the company.

Chapter 12

THE ANGEL AS CORPORATE ENTITY

Serious private company Angels should give consideration to whether they, as individuals, should be doing the investing. Circumstances may make it more advantageous for them to invest as corporate entities. Here they are faced with another question: Mirror, mirror, on the wall, which is the fairest entity of all?

Corporations, trusts, and partnerships--foreign and domestic--are all worth study. Angels may wish to keep relatively small investments on a personal level. There is liability to almost anything Angels do in business, and tax consequences too, for both winning and losing situations. The use of well-designed entities can reduce potential loss and maximize retention of benefits.

The tax situation, marital status (and the likelihood of its remaining unchanged), and other activities of Angels all will affect their decisions as to the best and most appropriate investment vehicles to use.

One of the most attractive investment vehicles is certainly the Limited Liability Corporation (LLC). It used to be the S Corporation. LLC corporation shareholders can deduct corporate losses from their personal income for tax purposes and, once profits exceed losses, still have the ability to elect to be taxed as a corporation. Besides this, the membership interests or shares of the LLC can be held in the names of various individuals, directly or through certain trusts.

For further material on LLCs and S corporations, see Appendixes T and V.

I believe it is better to invest in private companies as an active

Angel through the medium of a corporation. There are clear advantages to owning a corporation when it comes to estate planning, taxes, insurance, business expense allocations, and permissible tax deductions. There are even real advantages in the employee benefit plan area which can be of major significance. In most cases, the majority owner will also be an employee of the corporation. However, it is possible for the Angel's children or spouse to be the founding shareholders, directly or through trusts, and for the Angel (who may also lend to the business on either a secured or unsecured basis) to be the paid employee. Of course, the manager of the investing corporation can have a profit-sharing arrangement with the corporation. In establishing such a corporate entity, care must be taken not to create a personal holding company and to preserve LLC status.

Persuasive as all these reasons are, it is not primarily because of them that I recommend the use of a corporation to Angels. Successful investing in private companies is a serious business and will be accomplished with a higher level of success if it is conducted as such. The following are some of the functions Angels representing a corporation (that they own totally or nearly so) will find easier to perform than Angels acting as individuals: considering and researching an investment opportunity; structuring a deal; and negotiating contracts, in which, of course, the Angels' decisions must be ratified by their boards of directors, providing a chance to change a position previously adopted or to decide not to proceed. The creation and use by the Angel of a bona fide board of directors in the investing entity is also not a bad idea.

Angels representing a corporation find these functions easier to perform because (1) they are acting as fiduciaries, which is in itself an advantage, because it is always easier to represent the interests of others than one's own; and (2) those with whom they deal take them more seriously and cooperate with them to a greater extent in their investigations, monitoring, and, perhaps, collection efforts.

Angels find that financial institutions will take them more seriously, in most cases, as corporate representatives, than as individuals, as will entrepreneurs and company employees. This will be the case even when it is recognized that Angels own the corporation, and that there is not much more capital in it than that invested in the entrepreneur's company.

In instances where Angels use borrowed funds or guarantees, a corporate vehicle is desirable even when the lender to the corporation requires the personal guarantee of the shareholder of the corporation.

The ability to be flexible and imaginative in the disposition of the shares of the Angel-owned corporation is an advantage in tax and estate matters. In addition, in the case of a pending or possible marital dispute, arrangements can be made to specifically exclude the shares of the investing corporation from what may be later claimed as marital property. The corporation can have shareholder agreements which can be useful in estate planning.

There are too many considerations to go into detail here, and Angels should only consider these matters in conjunction with their attorneys. All wealthy Angels should consider ownership or control of foreign corporations and/or ownership of their domestic corporations by friendly foreign entities. "If it is not illegal, it is legal" is a doctrine appropriate for those intent on maximizing returns and retentions at all levels. For many, however, the possible savings will be offset by the concern that they are doing "something wrong." So be it. I am not advocating or advising on tax minimization or avoidance techniques. No doubt the reader is already aware that many very rich people do not seem to pay a lot of taxes and that there must be reasons why this is possible. The intelligent use of domestic and foreign corporations and trusts is one of the ways to achieve a minimization of tax burden for the wealthy and well advised.

An important benefit was pointed out by Dan Lufkin. "Angels who invest as a corporate entity will have less of an ego problem in reviewing troubled ventures than those who have invested in their own names, and they will be less likely to feed things that should be let die."

Chapter 13

STRUCTURING THE FINANCING

Stanley C. Golder

> *Stanley C. Golder is a consultant in the firm of Golder, Thoma, Cressey, Rauner, Inc. in Chicago. Founded in 1980, the company currently manages $695 million in four venture capital funds. For the prior nine years, Mr. Golder was president of the Equity Group of First Chicago Corp., one of the largest and most successful bank holding company business development investment affiliates. He is a past chairman of both the National Association of Small Business Investment Companies and the National Venture Capital Association. Golder, Thoma, Cressey, Rauner, Inc. is an active investor in consolidating fragmented industries.*

The structure of venture capital investments follows no set formula nor does it fit into a perfect structure: the objective is to reconcile the differing needs and concerns of the venture capitalist and the entrepreneur in a way that is satisfying to both parties. Since each situation is different, structures vary widely.

One issue that relates to the process of formalizing a venture investment is the financial structure; in other words, the form of securities instruments used. These securities instruments have certain advantages and disadvantages and can be used to provide a fair an equitable structure.

210

Needs and Concerns

The needs of the venture firm and the company will vary based on the company's stage of development, the risk and the ultimate potential as well as the requirements and the philosophy of the individual venture firm. However, there are a number of factors for venture capitalists and entrepreneurs to consider when creating any investment.

Primary considerations for the venture capitalists include:

- Reasonable reward given the level of risk.

- Sufficient influence on the development of the company, usually through board representation.

- Management's relative contribution to capital. (This assures that managers have more at stake than just their egos.)

- Minimization of taxes resulting from various types of cash flows to investors (dividends versus interest, versus capital gains).

- Future liquidity in the event that the company is successful or stagnates.

- Voting control, which is particularly desirable if performance is substantially below expectations and the management team must be replaced.

- Protection from having any remaining investor dollars split with entrepreneur in the event that the company is unsuccessful and dissolves.

- Current yield in the case of an SBIC (Small Business Investment Company), which has debt to service.

Primary considerations for the typical entrepreneur include:

- Ability to lead the creation of the business that they have conceptualized (operating and strategic control).

- Financial rewards for creating the business.

- Adequate resources needed to achieve their goal.

- Minimization of tax exposure for buying cheap stock.

- Value of substantive contribution from board members.

Common considerations for both sides include:

- Flexibility of structure that will allow room to enable additional investments later, incentives for future management and retention of stock if management leaves.

- Balance sheet attractiveness to suppliers and debt financiers.
- Retention of key employees through adequate equity participation.

The structuring process includes laying out the needs and concerns of both parties; evaluating all alternatives; and choosing and negotiating a structure that is consistent with the company's financial needs and capabilities and that will provide liquidity and, in extenuating circumstances, control for the investors.

Securities Instruments Commonly Used

The structure of a venture capital financing uses a range of securities instruments, from straight debt to debt with equity features (convertible debt to debt with warrants) to common stock. The following is a summary of the securities that are often used in combination with one another:

- Senior Debt -- Generally used for long-term financing for low-risk companies or for mezzanine (later stage) financings.

- Subordinated Debenture -- This is a type of debt that is subordinated to financing from other financial institutions such as banks and may be unsecured. It is usually convertible to common stock or accompanied by warrants to purchase common shares. Senior lenders accept this as equity and therefore allow increased debt from other sources.

- Preferred Stock -- Generally convertible to common stock, preferred stock gives the venture capitalists "preference" over common shareholders and some rights while from the entrepreneur's perspective it improves the company's debt-to-equity ratio. One disadvantage is that if dividends are attached, they are not tax deductible.

- Common Stock -- Generally the most expensive in terms of ownership given to the venture capitalist because it has the most risk. But from the venture capitalist's view it is also the least flexible. If affords no protection, allows the least amount of control over management and since there is generally no dividend, provides no return until the stock is sold.

Choosing the "Right" Instruments

The advantage to debt instruments from the venture capitalist's perspective is that they can be designed to provide (1) preference in case

212

of liquidation, (2) some current income and (3) remedies in case of default. An SBIC that has used its leverage and thus has debt to service will prefer an income bearing security. For the company, however, excessive debt can strain its credit standing and make future long-term financing difficult and, in case of default, places the venture capitalist in a position of control. On the other hand, common stock or (as it is often termed) straight equity provides no protection for the venture capitalist and as a result will ultimately be very costly for the entrepreneur in terms of equity give-up.

Entrepreneurs, venture capitalists and their respective attorneys can be creative in modifying traditional securities to meet the needs of a particular situation. Most venture capital financing structures are a combination of debt and equity that satisfies both parties. The often used preferred stock structure is a compromise between common stock and not structures for several reasons. First, preferred stock has more protection than common stock, but less than subordinated notes.

Second, preferred stock usually carries a dividend, but it can only be paid if the company is profitable. Also, preferred stock is a separate class of stock, and accordingly, has certain rights established in the articles of incorporation which are stronger than the rights of common shareholders, but usually not as strong as noteholders. Finally, preferred stock may be redeemable, which would allow investors to obtain a return of principal, assuming that sufficient capital is available for redemption.

Other combinations and unique hybrid structures can often provide preference in sale, liquidation or merger; and current income plus capital gain for the venture capitalist without weighing the balance sheet with too much debt.

A no-load convertible preferred, for example, has no dividend attached; has liquidation preference; converts to common at the option of the holder and automatically at a public offering; votes as if common stock; is considered equity; and requires a board seat, monthly reports, registration rights and a right of first refusal for future financings. This is typically used for startup and early-stage financings and is attractive to the entrepreneur because there is no dividend obligation.

Common stock may be used in a larger successful company while senior debt with warrants may be more appropriate in a turnaround situation.

Flexibility of Structure

The structure adopted initially affects the ability to take actions subsequently and there fore should be as flexible as possible. Firstly, the rights of initial investors to participate in subsequent financing rounds should be established so as to provide as little obstacle as possible to their being completed. Secondly, there needs to be provision made for providing stock that can motivate key management brought in subsequent to financing. Thirdly, if management members leave, some or all of their stock should be retained by the company. These last two issues can be dealt with by having a class of stock of management differing from that issued to investors. Reserves can be established for additions to management and stock issued can be escrowed. Care needs to be paid to the tax implications so that members of management are not faced with unexpected liabilities in connection with their holding this stock.

Another point on structure of transactions, which seems obvious, but is often ignored, is that an investor in an early stage company who puts in considerably more dollars than the entrepreneur should generally not lose money on their investment, while an entrepreneur makes money. This, again, mitigates toward using a senior instrument so as to protect the investor's position.

Obviously, it is in the best interest of both the investor and the entrepreneur that the instruments used be considered equity and be leverageable as the company grows. Preferred stocks should cause no problems as they are clearly equity, even though they may have redemption requirements. These are easily handled by senior lenders if and when the company is capable of acquiring debt. Subordinated debt can be accommodated to this need, but has a few more problems vis-a-vis senior lenders as a company grows. In either case, however, these instruments should be equity as far as any senior creditors are concerned, so that appropriate leverage can be obtained when necessary.

Many venture capitalists prefer not to make outright purchases of common stock except in cases where the majority ownership is in the hands of an investor group. Even then, there are many arguments for preferred stocks. Before taking a common equity position, there can be a waiting period to determine if the company performs as expected and to see if management's objectives are similar to those of the investors and will protect the investors' interest.

The question of ultimate liquidity is also very significant. While there are differences in various parts of the country, an ultimate maturity on investments is preferred, which either provides liquidity or the ability to negotiate toward liquidity when the company has not reached its objectives, but is viable.

In most cases, investments are thought of only in terms of success or failure, but it is very possible that a company will move relatively sideward (sometimes called the living dead) or plateau in its growth and therefore be unable to achieve a public market. Even if companies go public, the market will not usually accept a large amount of stock from inside investors, unless the company makes major progress. The only way out for the venture capitalist is the company's sale or merger. At this point, the goals of the entrepreneurs or managers of the company may differ from the investor's objectives. Consequently, contractual arrangements to achieve liquidity become most important and can be best achieved at the inception of the investment.

Control

Another problem that is handled by appropriate structuring is the very serious aspect of control. Business people approach venture capitalists with the idea that they should control their own business, but history has shown that many entrepreneurs do not have the desire, may jot have the ability and certainly do not have the experience to run a business as it grows. Most venture capitalists do not want to run companies, but they feel that it is their basic responsibility to see that the companies in which they invest are well run and if management changes are appropriate, they can be achieved.

Various types of senior instruments can give investors the opportunity to have their interests protected as these types of problems develop. This is not a means to financially disadvantage the equity interest of the entrepreneur. In fact, it is designed to help that interest and to enable a board of directors to make changes in management if they deem appropriate.

There are major differences between investors and not all of the companies in the industry have the same philosophies. Having been involved with many successful companies and having heard many successful entrepreneurs speak who have been backed by venture capitalists, I think entrepreneurs will find that control may be an issue with inexperienced investors and entrepreneurs but not with those

215

who have been successful. De facto day-to-day control needs to be distinguished from voting control.

Keep in mind, appropriate structuring of a transaction cannot make a bad investment good; it can, however, influence the results of investments that are not meeting the initial expectations.

In making every investment, the parties presume a high level of success. Over the years, the record proves that only a small percentage are truly successful. Therefore, achieving liquidity and/or return of capital and the possible remedies available by using instruments other than common stock can be helpful to the investment process and beneficial to both the entrepreneur and venture capitalists.

Avoid inflexible structures. More often than not, an inflexible structure will exaggerate a strategic problem rather than provide a simple solution. For example, there have been situations where an inflexible deal structure enabled one very small player to obstruct an entire round of badly needed financing. Therefore, the best advice for both the entrepreneur and venture capitalist is to keep the structure simple and flexible and to be sure to understand the terms so that they have a good, constructive relationship.

See Appendix N.

Chapter 14

BENEFITS OTHER THAN FINANCIAL OF INVESTING IN PRIVATE COMPANIES

What I have said so far in this book has not been a full and honest reflection of my true feelings about investing in private companies, because I have emphasized mostly the negative aspects, leaning heavily to the side of caution. I have felt it my duty to do this in order to not encourage the reader to make investments that inherently have high probability of loss. Now, I must counter this and come out of the closet by saying that I know of no more exciting and fulfilling role in the commercial world than that of playing a part in the creation of successful enterprises.

Exciting, frustrating, fulfilling, frightening, rewarding...along with the possibility of making a fortune, in both relative and absolute terms, when it works out well. When it works out poorly, investing in private companies can result in financial ruin and the destruction of personal and family relationships. My greatest hope is that this book will be helpful in providing readers with ideas that will enhance their gains and minimize their losses.

Most of the good things (and some of the bad) result only from the Angel's active participation in the business in which there is financial involvement. There is no doubt in my mind that the active role is preferable to the passive. The rewards of success for the active Angel are much more than money alone, and the passive Angel is denied these most of the time.

217

The major risk of Angels' active involvements in companies is that they will encourage them to make follow-on investments that may not be warranted in terms of the availability of comparable investment opportunities or justified in terms of their own resources. The reason for this is obvious. Angels become full or quasi-entrepreneurs, sharing the hopes and, worse, the beliefs of the managers of the business. As they become "one of them," they cultivate friendships with the managers and, still more unadvisedly, perhaps even with their families. They then do a terrible job of negotiating adequate return or security for their follow-on investments

The actively involved Angel is much more likely to fall prey to "hostage" or "ransom" investments than the passive Angel. These are investments made by Angels in attempting to recoup by making further investments in the belief that the company will succeed "if only we could keep at it a little longer." When a private company is significantly behind business plan-projected levels, most follow-on investments do not work out well for the Angel. Nevertheless, and unfortunately most of the time, active angels are indeed likely to play check writing angel up to the point where they can no longer do so.

The real and potentially tragic problems come from the use of leverage by Angels to fund ventures. For follow-on investing, the original Angel is, in all probability, initially going to use personal guarantees rather than cash. I strongly urge the original Angel to invest follow-on funds in a company *only* after the deal has been negotiated by another noninvolved, and, therefore, more dispassionate, investor. If no other investor can be found, there must be a reason. Angels must never place themselves in jeopardy simply to be a nice person or a team player. Angels must remember who they are. They are the Angel and not the entrepreneur. Switching roles seldom benefits Angels.

The destruction of the entrepreneur, in both financial and personal terms, is an unfortunate and occasional by-product of the current high levels of corporate formation and entrepreneurial activity. There is a lesser need for Angels to share the same fate. They must remember that their investments are a business opportunity and not a cause. Although they may have to suffer the embarrassment and remorse of a failed venture, they can come back to finance a new idea or company so long as they have not permitted themselves to lose all their money. *The psychological need to vindicate the initial judgement, by breaking even, is the single greatest cause for all investor losses.* How often one hears amateur investors say that they are going to sell "as soon as they can get even," which makes total nonsense as a plan. The question investors in publicly traded companies and Angels financing private companies must ask themselves is, if they were not already holding a position would they recreate it. If not, why consider any follow-on investment? It is possible, and perhaps probable, that Angels would be better served by assuming a comparable level or risk in a different situation than the one in which they are presently embroiled. The result of deciding that further, follow-on, investments are not likely to be made in a private company is one of mandating the initial arrangements contain all of the necessary protective covenants. If the agreements are properly negotiated the Angel will have to be consulted and approve any further financing which is asset-based or which causes a dilution of the Angel's position.

On balance, risk-accepting (or relishing) Angels are best off sprinkling money on patches of talent in seed-capital investments. Doing this, they will get greater play for their dollars in terms of percentage interest, even after all the subsequent dilutions that occur as the company acquires the funding necessary for its development. The nearer in development a private company approaches profitability and the probability of going public, the lesser its discount in value from comparable public securities. Therefore, in spite of their greater risk, very early-stage speculations are frequently the most appealing.

Most venture capitalists seek second stage investment opportunities rather than startups or, certainly, seed investments. The risk involved is one reason for this, and another is the amount of time required of an investor, particularly one acting in a fiduciary capacity, in monitoring and assisting the entrepreneur. Thus, this is one of the few areas where the individual investor has a modest advantage over the professional investor.

Another possible advantage Angels have over the professional is that their livelihood is not going to be threatened by admission of a venture failure. Some venture capitalists are likely to keep throwing money at a problem company for no better reason than to keep it and their reputations afloat. One of the true luxuries associated with being wealthy is that Angels do not have to apologize for their financial mistakes to anyone--except perhaps their spouses.

Traders in commodities and securities say "The trend is your friend" and "Don't fight the tape." The same can be said for private company investment. If the company in which you are invested is going well, then invest more in it. If the company's performance is disappointing, try to extricate yourself--or at least do not become

219

more heavily involved. If you have structured your investment intelligently, your interest will be protected. Let someone else be the hero.

When a successful enterprise results in a cash bonanza for me, my wife asks me what I will do now with all this new money. She already knows the answer. I am like the Australian pastoral property owner who was asked the same question when he won a big lottery and answered, "I guess I'll just put it into my property until it's all gone."

Starting and financing young companies is the activity of which I am a willing captive. And I believe there is no more constructive and rewarding way to live a business life. I wish well those involved in entrepreneurial investing in private companies--our country needs you. To those who have not had the experience, I suggest that it can be a wonderful adventure.

Chapter 15

THE MAKING OF
AN ENTREPRENEUR

The issue of training people to think more creatively is an important one for any society. Modern societies depend upon innovation for society to grow and prosper. Motivation and intelligence usually lead to innovation, but finding better ways to achieve a result can be hastened by those who see things differently--at times, radically differently. I do not believe that such divergent thinkers--that is, entrepreneurs--can be created through education, any more than artists can be created. They can be encouraged and assisted, once identified as having entrepreneurial tendencies; but created, no.

Large companies seek more highly motivated and innovative employees. They seek those who will work more independently and assume greater levels of responsibility. For the most part, however, they do not want the rest of the entrepreneurs' characteristic impatience with structured or bureaucratic decision making or their willingness to stumble in search of a "better way." They confuse result and process. They want the former and do not understand the latter. I suggested to a senior executive of a major electronics company recently that his employees be permitted to make suggestions for change anonymously and only claim them if they worked out. They should be permitted to run a project without the burden of having disclosed the authorship for the idea. The reality of being an employee is that the penalty for failure is greater than the reward for success. Those with the qualities to be effective entrepreneurs are well aware of this fact.

The only political mandate I know of to "create entrepreneurial activity" is, strangely, in an area where one would least expect such effort to be successful. The culture and tradition of that area demand strict adherence to conformity at all levels. Failure is penalized in the most extreme ways. Total loyalty to an employer is traditional, the ideal of leaving a job almost unthinkable, and starting a company to compete with a former employer tantamount to treason. That area is, of course, Japan. In Japan today, the Ministry of International Trade and Industry and Ministry of Finance wage a not so subtle campaign to increase the incidence of entrepreneurial activity.

I am not proposing new government programs for the United States, because I have not seen the old ones work. I am not leaning toward tax incentives, because I believe their impact to be marginal. I am not suggesting the breakup of large companies, because it is the existence of these dinosaurs that creates competitive opportunity for entrepreneurs. I am not proposing that any functional department of local, regional, state, or federal government, save one, assist communities in fostering entrepreneurship. That government function, where not privatized, is education.

Why should a society trouble itself to give special assistance to budding entrepreneurs? Because entrepreneurs cannot be successful themselves without bringing benefits to others (in the form of employment, at the very least). The creation of wealth, as a by-product of entrepreneurial success, enriches far more people than is the case when a fortunate or skillful stock or commodity market speculator makes a lot of money. To many people, the elements of entrepreneurial and speculative risk-taking and success appear to be the same. Among the more obvious differences between the entrepreneur and speculator is that speculators can change their minds at any time and close out their positions--perhaps even reverse the positions and bet on the opposite of what they originally believed. The hallmark of many great speculators is just such an ego-denying flexibility. The single greatest cause for loss in stock and commodity market speculation is the individual's ego need for vindication of the initial judgement. In the case of entrepreneurs, a similar ego need is seen as constructive, because motivation, determination, and persistence are usually necessary to the successful venture. The successful speculator gets rich or richer; this is very different from the wealth of jobs, careers, services, and product innovation that are created by, and accompany, the success of entrepreneurs. If the difference between entrepreneurs and speculators was more widely recognized, it would be wonderfully constructive for entrepreneurs specifically, and for the country generally.

A definite bias against capitalism, perhaps unintentional, is present in our society. What do young children learn about work and reward? They learn that one "has to go to work." Most entrepreneurs do not feel that they have ever "worked" when working for themselves. How do average teachers feel about the profit system? They frequently feel abused by it, and certainly, in most cases, do not really understand the workings of capital markets and the operation of the system of free enterprise. How then are average teachers going to present a positive view of what they neither understand nor favor? They are not likely to do so. We need to create the means of providing economic education to children before their attitudes are formed in negative perceptions of what is responsible for their well-being.

We are neglecting our human resource raw materials in this country. Our competitors in Japan have the finest educational system in the world at the elementary and secondary levels. Their high school graduates are better educated than our college graduates. Education, especially education relevant to our country's needs, may be too important to be left in the hands of educators. The business sector may have to become involved and deal with the problems of "tenure versus excellence and community longer-term benefit versus the current demands of today's parents who lose interest in education as their children pass through the process.

Unfortunately, such an approach would be a long-term solution to what, in many communities, is an immediate problem. I have no quick fix to offer. We Americans are going to have to adjust to the result of our having squandered the advantages we had in the late 1940s and 1950s. We wanted comfort and convenience, and many achieved them. We wanted easy wealth, and inflation provided it to many who had assets. We wanted to work less and enjoy life more. We did - and now the piper has to be paid. We didn't have the money to do what we wanted, so we borrowed it. We borrowed it to a point where it can never be repaid but only rolled over, and that will become increasingly difficult unless the government, regardless of which political party label it bears, can get long term inflation under control. All governments, when faced with a choice between repudiation of debt and inflation, have opted for inflation. I doubt ours will be different.

The objective of *Venture* magazine was to provide profit education. The publication informed its readers about events, trends, and developments that may helped them earn more money, or sometimes (and of equal importance), lose less. In part, *Venture* also created positive attitudes toward commercial creativity. But, to a great extent, *Venture* was preaching to the converted or at least to the favorably inclined. Instructors dealing with students in entrepreneurial education get to the students too late, or when there is no longer any need for attitude affecting instruction. Educators must get to the students earlier, before their attitudes have formed. These educators have to compete with the effective pounding of television on the minds of the young. The Dallas TV series character J.R. Ewing and other negative portrayals of businesspeople and entrepreneurs should not be permitted to be the accepted image of free enterprise.

What then can most effectively be taught to student entrepreneurs? The answer is simple--relevant skills. Students already know "why" and perhaps even"where"; they need to know "how." Students having entrepreneurial tendencies are likely to be impatient with anything whose relevance is obscure to them. Some will criticize the teaching of skills as being too narrow an educational approach; indeed it would be for nonentrepreneurial students, but emerging entrepreneurs have different needs from those who will function as followers and employees rather than originators and employers. Entrepreneurial students do not need to be motivated or to have their imaginations stirred. What they need is to be shown how to put their already existing motivation and imagination to work for them in practical ways-- they need skills, not theory.

The areas of study most necessary for entrepreneurial success are; planning, cash flow projection and analysis and profit margin analysis. Entrepreneurs must learn to understand cash. The best business advice for young entrepreneurs is "Don't run out of cash." Entrepreneurs must come to understand that it almost always takes longer than expected to create sufficient critical mass of revenues to offset expenses. They must also understand specifically where the profit is coming from, and on which aspects of the operation they are not making money. Planning is critical. However, it is the planning of cash which is *the* most critical aspect of business planning. If nothing was done other than to impress young entrepreneurs with the need to forecast accurately their business cash needs, they would be saved lots of pain. Then they would better understand the risks inherent in attempting to go forward on a severely undercapitalized basis.

224

Ethics

Business educators are generally not in a position to teach morality, because they gain admittance to the minds of their students too late in their development to make a significant impact on their system of basic values. My guess is that basic values distinguishing right from wrong are formed well before puberty, or at least during the very early teens.

Fortunately for all of us, ethical behavior is good business. Those who have a reputation for honesty and competence obtain financing more readily and on more attractive terms than those without such a good reputation. Students may not fully realize just how vital is the need for obtaining the use of other people's money in the founding, development, and operation of almost all businesses. When one recognizes that all borrowing is the renting of other people's money and that the ability to do so--and the amount of rent or interest charged for the use--is directly related to the lender's perception of the likelihood of timely repayment, the importance of reputation becomes clear. Similarly, the investors' willingness to permit their capital to become captive to the will of the entrepreneur is largely determined by their belief that the entrepreneur will treat them fairly in their joint pursuit of profit, and that the profit justifies the risk and loss of liquidity.

Ethical behavior, or, too cynically perhaps, merely the appearance of being honest and of treating people fairly, is also demonstrably important in a number of other vital aspects of developing and managing businesses. If students come to understand the benefits of ethical behavior, educators do not have to be too concerned about their student's value systems. Educators need to teach, because it is true, there is ultimately more profit to be earned from right than wrong acts. They should also inform their students that, in an age of advanced communications, news travels fast.

Manufacturers enjoying a superior reputation for product quality (in many cases, this factor is also thought of as the manufacturers' integrity) have an ability to charge more for their products and can therefore earn greater profits. A reputation for treating people fairly allows employers to gain greater positive participation from their employees and also to hire people on better terms. Dealing fairly with suppliers--and that includes telling them when it will not be possible to pay them on time--permits the creation of better relationships, which can translate into the gaining of more credit on more favorable terms.

If educators simply can help their students to understand that ethical behavior-- treating others as they themselves would wish to be treated--is good business and, conversely, that taking short cuts results ultimately in profit reduction, they will have made a major contribution to their students' and the nation's welfare.

Early Education

I have long wished to promote a "Sesame Street" type of television program, using a lemonade stand as the point of departure for understanding, to teach business principles and entrepreneurship to young children. Using the lemonade stand business, one could easily, and in understandable terms, demonstrate such arcane concepts as inventory control, site selection, competitive pricing, credit extension, promotion and advertising, and personnel management.

Dr. Marilyn Kourilsky, a Consultant to the Kaufmann Foundation and formerly director of teacher education at the UCLA Graduate School of Education, has developed an experience-based or debriefing method of instruction used in conjunction with her participative model economy simulation. More than 100,000 teachers in 38 states have been trained in this approach and program. In this program, the students role-play various occupations and functions in a society. Some play it safe, some are aggressive in their economic pursuits, some fail, and some gain wealth and power. For more information on her program, see Appendix W.

Gifted Children

We should understand why we should be interested in helping gifted children. The usual motivation to assist with gifted children advocacy is based upon the natural desire of parents to gain an advantage for one of their children. I understand this motivation, though it is not the basis for my interest. I have my own children to love and am not seeking other people's children with whom to be concerned and love. Gifted children advocacy is vitally important to me because I believe it is vitally important to our country. My advocacy is based on a pessimistic view of critical future societal needs and not as it relates to assisting any one of my own children.

We do not have to look too far to realize that we who believe in the need to identify and develop superior assets in children are in a minority, and increasingly one which is being viewed as a threat by those with opposing views. (It is, of course, a matter of perspective to

226

whom the assets of gifted children belong--the individual exclusively, the family unit, the community, the state, or society.) Because fear is one, and perhaps the most important, factor in determining human (as well as animal) reactions and behavior, we must try to understand the fears of those antipathetic to helping gifted children.

With fear, there is also envy. The parent of the "normal" or "average" child is naturally envious of the child perceived by them to be better.

Of course, the term "better" is relative, and one which is a result of a perception. Is smarter better? Is more creative better? What about more artistic? There can be little doubt that healthier is indeed better. But what about being more responsive and affectionate--are these better? Parents of nongifted children need to understand that advocates of gifted children are focusing their concern on a difference of specific potential and *not* on superiority of the whole person, be it child or parent. *Difference* is the key word.

Why is it so easy for parents of non-gifted children to accept difference in the case of physically handicapped children and children with learning disabilities? Why have advocacy groups for the learning disabled been so successful in terms of eliciting public support and federal dollars, and advocacy groups for gifted children so unsuccessful? Is it because the former do not, through their children, represent a threat? Is it because the learning-disabled child will be less likely to compete with other children for college, jobs, or even favorable peer or teacher attention? As selfish, and perhaps petty, as these reasons are--insofar as they reflect a myopia about the broader needs of our society at large--we must acknowledge the all too human realities that are operative here.

What can be done? Perhaps advocates for gifted children can offer some assurance and demonstrate that, through the achievements of gifted children, the standards for all children can be increased. Advocates have always maintained that gifted programs are the spawning grounds of future problem-solvers whose contributions will help to secure and enhance our country's way of life. Such programs are often akin to research and pilot studies in other fields. Ultimately, through their innovations, today's programs for the gifted and talented can become tomorrow's general education.

Some of these general areas of innovation include developing creativity, building a challenging curriculum, enhancing student motivation and productivity, recognizing the importance of learning style, developing higher-level thinking skills, and making schoolwork relevant to individual needs and abilities.

If these things are not at the core of a commitment to excellence, nothing is.

The fallacious thought is almost omnipresent that there is no need for incremental assistance to the gifted child. Doesn't cream float to the top? Sure it does. Of course, I am referring to what remains "cream" after the homogenizing process of a society that worships child superiority only in the single area of athletics, and that conversely encourages a parent or teacher to say to a child demonstrating divergent thinking or behavior, "Why can't you be like all the other children?"

There is no more deadly force in the limiting of our country's greatest potential natural resource (that of achieving gifted people) than the demands for normalcy placed upon very young gifted children. Not being stupid, after all, the children soon understand that it is easier to appear to be like all the other children, and to stop trying to use their minds or learn differently or faster than the other children.

The hard and disagreeable facts are that the gifted and the handicapped are engaged in an inevitable conflict over allocation of public funds. Predictably, the handicapped will win and have already done so by a 400-1 margin. The parents of the handicapped have efficiently organized themselves. Advocates of the handicapped have orchestrated the sympathetic reactions of voters and legislators to a point where they are a real political force. How ridiculous it was for the long defunct Federal Office for the Gifted and Talented to be in any way associated with, let alone housed within, the Bureau of the Handicapped. The term "severely gifted" is heard, with only semi-irony, at education conferences with describing an extraordinarily gifted child.

Profit-making corporations are the logical major future employers of the gifted. Corporations are the consumers of the products of education; therefore, they should be the parties most concerned with the future supply and quality of the product. Support should take the form of assisting with identification and enrichment programs plus, in some cases, direct involvement in the education process.

The gifted are the only disadvantaged group that must publicly prove their need for assistance. Advocates of the gifted must create a public awareness of special need and societal benefit before seeking funding. Popular, and even institutional, attitudes must be changed.

228

We must celebrate excellence. We must honor achievement. We must recognize human potential. We must create and celebrate competitive heroes as role models. We must develop human potential. Gold in the ground--even discovered and proven reserves of gold-- enriches only those perceived to have the ability to mine it in the future. As time passes for each nonidentified and/or unaided gifted child, society loses the ability to mine the resource represented by that child, and we all lose.

The Straight Story for Spouses of Many Successful Entrepreneurs

In preparing for a workshop I presented to the spouses of chief executives, many of whom were also the owners of businesses, I was confronted by a dilemma. The dilemma was simply: do I tell them like I believe it is, and in so doing probably alienate many of their spouses, or do I give them the usual "how to read a balance sheet and income statement" sort of talk? The latter was easy and safe, whereas the straight story required considerably more thought and involved some risks. I chose the more difficult, interesting, satisfying, and useful (to the participants) course, thereby risking the loss of some executive friends.

I began by making a number of observations about entrepreneurs that are found in the second chapter and elsewhere in this book. I also suggested that many successful entrepreneurs have great difficulty in producing children who develop characteristics that the entrepreneur abstractly wished for or even predicted. Assuming that these observations are valid--and of course there are many exceptions-- what practical advice can be offered to spouses of such entrepreneurs?

Most successful entrepreneurs are married. In dedicating *The Larry and Barry Guide to Venture Funding* to "Anni, my wife of 33 years, to whom I am indebted (as our auditors will confirm)," I noted that "most entrepreneurs are indebted to their wives, either during or after their marriages." This section is intended to be for some spouses a view of their future, an explanation of the possible causes, and, for some, hopefully a prescription for avoiding that which may befall others.

Because entrepreneurs wish to control their lives, there is a need to exercise control over the lives of those who are in a position of affecting the life of the entrepreneur. Charlie Revson, Revlon's entrepreneurial founder, used to say, "I don't get ulcers, I give them" Most successful entrepreneurs have controlling personalities.

The conceiving, funding, and managing of a growing enterprise is, certainly in the early years, a grueling and often frustrating and frightening experience. Of course, it is also rewarding and exciting. It is so exciting that the same excitements required by others to spice up their lives are not required by the entrepreneur. During the early periods of company growth, the entrepreneur needs a safe emotional harbor.

Entrepreneurs require extra supportiveness and reassurance. Entrepreneurs, on one psychological level, assume they will become wealthy, much as they assume they will be operationally successful, but they do not have becoming rich as their primary objective. On another level, they report having inordinately high fears of failure. They want--no, rather have to--prove something. They are much more ego-recognition and power driven. Power is, of course, one of the important needs that propels highly successful entrepreneurs. The need to prove they were right, and their prior superiors or just the "establishment" wrong in not accepting their views, is a big part of the entrepreneurs' makeup, particularly in the case of those with technological or academic backgrounds.

Entrepreneurs suffer frustrations daily as they continually encounter those who do not share their visions or recognize their needs. As they are goal-oriented, and likely to be very impatient, they suffer. This frustration, even though it may be wholly self-imposed, takes its toll on any and all personal relationships.

So what do we have so far? People who are excited, stimulated, frustrated, frightened, rewarded, and consumed by their business. How much emotion or energy can be left for a spouse or children? How much "quality time" is there left in them after the 16-hour days and six to seven day weeks it takes to build a successful business? Remember, they are high-energy people and probably off to do battle at dawn's first light. How much patience will they really have left in the evening for the home front problems? Not much, in most cases.

But they want a home and a family. They just don't want to invest, or cannot invest, energy and emotion to the same extent as their nonentrepreneurial counterpart. In much the same way, the entrepreneur does not usually want to invest energy in having affairs, although of course it does happen. Extramarital involvements are not as enticing to the younger entrepreneur as to the nonentrepreneur, because there is to much else generating excitement in the entrepreneur's life.

Once successful, however, entrepreneurs find themselves with two things not usually available previously--money and leisure. They also may feel somehow less of a person, in that one of the results of their success may be the feeling, or reality, that they are "out of the battle" or at least away from the front lines. They then may have to prove to themselves, and others, that they can do it again, and that their first success was not just a fluke or due to luck. This is one of the reasons why so many entrepreneurs go into a succession of businesses.

Another manifestation of the same need to retain or reassert manhood, or the associated imagery, is the need for the company of a younger woman, most probably considerably younger. Frequently the new woman is someone with whom the entrepreneur has had or presently has a work-related relationship, that is, someone who "understands" and shares the pressures and requirements of business. Many second wives were involved in either the entrepreneur's business or had a business background of their own and could relate to the entrepreneur's needs, frequently having something to prove themselves.

How can a successful entrepreneur's children understand the time and emotional demands of business? How can they understand their parent's lesser (than their friends' parents') involvement in their school activities? How can they feel other than resentful of, and competitive with, the business of the parent, especially since these are probably, at least partly, the true emotions of the other parent that have been, intentionally or otherwise, communicated? Though frequently they do, it is not realistic for parents to expect children to have the same drives and needs they remember they had at their age. This cannot be reasonable expectation of children who have had the material benefits associated with entrepreneurial success. In most cases, successful entrepreneurs themselves do not come from families of wealth.

"How can I ever be as successful as you?" an entrepreneur's child may often ask.

"Why aren't you working harder, like I did when I was your age?" many entrepreneurs ask their children, with some frequency.

Neither question reflects what any parent would want to hear or say. Does the child's natural pride in a successful parent change to envy if there is an unusual amount of competitiveness in the relationship (and entrepreneurs are very competitive people)? Are the children at times embarrassed by the very success of the entrepreneur? Would not the children, who themselves need structure and predictability in their lives, rather have a parent who conforms to the pattern of the parents of their peers, and who is not different?

Are the pressures and demands on children by the entrepreneur different than those of the nonentrepreneur? Probably, because the entrepreneur is excessively aware of "quality control" and has a daily need for, and awareness of, "produced excellence." Being just "good enough to pass" is not good enough for a growing company in a competitive world. The company and its products have to be better to even maintain market position and certainly to grow. The nonentrepreneur also knows this, but doesn't live it the same way a business-owning entrepreneur does. The pressures on the children of entrepreneurs are, and must be, different and probably greater than on those having parents who work for others than themselves. In many cases, I am sure it is easier for the children to live with less controlling, less demanding, less successful, though not necessarily less loving parents than those being described.

In contemplating the future, the spouses of entrepreneurs should take inventory. That inventory should include both a review of the entrepreneur's present and prospective assets (and, of course, liabilities) and the spouse's own. In considering assets, one way of taking inventory is to stand in front of a full-length mirror naked and consider what the assets being reviewed will look like in ten years, when the spouse's business will, it usually is predicted, be more successful, and the spouse therefore more attractive to other people, regardless of how that spouse looks in that same mirror now or then.

If the wife and the husband think of the business as belonging to only one of them, rather than shared, a problem already exists. That problem is both psychological and financial. In terms of estate planning, as well as for the future financial security of the spouse (and children), the time to allocate and distribute the ownership of a business is early in its development, when the value is primarily prospective.

There are a number of valid reasons why the shares of a business should be controlled by those actively involved in building that business. However, there is, or can be, a difference between ownership and control. I favor the entrepreneur maintaining control, which really means the share-voting rights to stock in the business but not necessarily the benefits of full ownership. If spouses are going to be required to contribute to the success of entrepreneurs, perhaps through sacrificing the attention of those same entrepreneurs, should they not be directly rewarded, both financially and emotionally, through direct ownership and participation in the business? I believe they should.

A more difficult question is raised when spouses are asked to co-sign or guarantee an obligation of the business. What happens to their liability if they are no longer the spouse of the entrepreneur? Can the contingent of actual liability be written in such a way as to relieve them of the liability if a divorce occurs? Obviously, if they become widowed, then their liability remains. The lender might agree to release them from obligation in the event of divorce; this is not likely, because a divorce of convenience could preserve exactly what the lender is attempting to prevent. It is my view that spouses should accept the same risks as other owners of a business, but not unless they are in fact (and in name) an owner of the business. Spouses should think of themselves financially as individuals, and not merely as an extension of the family unit. Many of them will, in the future, find themselves to be again individuals.

The surest way for spouses and entrepreneurs to maintain their relationship is for the spouses to become involved in what they cannot effectively compete with--the business. Spousal involvement in the business is, in most cases, a very positive development. The spouse then truly understands the operative pressures, as well as being able to fully savor the delights of success, the latter being equally important as the former. Bearing only the pain is no fun. Participation is a very important concept and terribly difficult to fully achieve through other than direct involvement. The usually boring (to the spouse) nightly recounting of the day's events is not the adequate substitute for the spouse's having been there. I know that children have to be taken care of. That, of course, is a fact of life and has to be dealt with. Perhaps the spouse's full participation has to be delayed. Perhaps the children will have to be taken care of by another. Perhaps the children will have to receive less of both attention for the benefit of the entire family unit. In a survey of *Venture* magazine subscribers, it was found that 64 percent believed spouse involvement helped their marital relationship (only 9 percent believed otherwise). In 43 percent of the cases, the spouses served as members of the company's board of directors, while 39 percent served as company officers and 35 percent as part-time consultants. The form of involvement may be less important than the reality of the involvement. The spouses of entrepreneurs should be knowledgeable about the affairs of the company and have an input into the decision-making process. It is also desirable for spouses to be in a position where they can participate in the companies' employee benefit programs.

In considering either divorce or widowhood, spouses should understand that there are a limited number of people whom they are going to be able to rely upon and trust. The more successful the business, and the wealthier they therefore become, the fewer the number they should trust. A wealthy lone person is the target for many individual professional advisors and financial institutions. It makes sense to decide in advance of either divorce or the spouse's demise, with the thoughtful assistance of the spouse, on the identity of those whose advice and counsel should be sought. As an individual, the spouse has interests that are distinct from, and may even be in opposition to, those of the other partner. In a happy and constructive relationship, these differing needs and considerations can be balanced in terms of the mutual desires and needs of the parties. However, when the relationship becomes other than constructive, spouses had better be in a position to protect their separate interests.

In the management of money, either arising from an estate or divorce settlement, spouses have a distinct advantage over the entrepreneur "who made the money." That advantage is that they are unburdened by the need to prove anything. They do not have to prove that is wasn't luck, or that they are still as smart and/or vital as they used to be. They can simply invest for financial return without additional, and frequently counterproductive, motivations.

For a wealthy person, profit is really income maintenance. They do not have to, and should not normally, accept the incremental risks associated with estate enhancement efforts. Preservation of capital is their logical investment objective. In today's world, zero coupon bonds are probably their best bet other than mutual funds. They do not have to get richer. Understanding one's required objectives is a large part of assuring their achievement. A person, particularly a lone woman, should keep as many options open to her as possible. Options create an ability to respond to circumstantial changes. Therefore, they should avoid situations in which their funds are, or become, illiquid. Private company and real estate investing are not, in my opinion, appropriate for non-wealth-producing individuals. I also believe that mutual funds are the best investment medium for those with assets to invest, because the performance records and current (daily) results are so readily available. There is also an easy ability to diversity assets, another certain element of wisdom offered for passive investors. It is easier, and less emotionally wearing, to change mutual fund holdings than to disengage and retain investment advisors.

Spouses inheriting a controlling interest in a business should probably sell their interest. Alternatively, they should sell at least enough of the business to those running it on terms that provide an incentive to them to continue the business as it has been operated or to sell it advantageously to others. The usual situation, where the widowed spouse has not been appropriately briefed by the departed entrepreneur, is for a panic sale of the business for less than could have been achieved by a sale conducted differently. They may never have liked, or understood, the business and now need cash, almost any amount of cash, to assure the continuation of their lifestyle. The other extreme is where the widow tries to step in and run the business "as her husband would have wanted her to do." If that was the wish of the deceased entrepreneur, and consistent with the abilities of the widow, that *may* be fine. But what about the interests of the other managers of the business? Shouldn't they have an opportunity also to achieve wealth through enhancing the wealth of the founder's estate? I think the answer must be yes. Therefore, selling them shares sufficient to provide motivation will probably in the end provide greater wealth for the widowed spouse.

Significantly more than half of the spouses of successful entrepreneurs are divorced or widowed, and therefore they have to learn to fend for themselves, and on occasion against their spouses. Preparation is the key to successful confrontation of any problem. Getting advice from someone whose experience includes similar situations is one logical step to take. Spouses frequently have their own doctors, and there is no reason that they should not also have their own attorneys. On occasion, spouses' interests and those of their mates will differ, and even be in direct conflict. The conflict of interest may also be between them and their children, who usually come to think of themselves as the rightful heirs to most, if not all, of the rewards of successful entrepreneuring. Owing to the children's being unaware of the early contributions to the family's success made by the surviving spouse, they sometimes regard him or her as being just "lucky" or conniving in marrying so well. The financial desires and needs of the spouse and offspring are not automatically identical.

Chapter 16

How to Borrow More Effectively and Other Matters of Concern

How to Borrow More Effectively

If there is one characteristic element that binds those in business, particularly those in business for themselves, it is the need for ever-increasing amounts of capital. The need for increased capital is caused either by the business being not as healthy as had been expected or better. Few are the business situations that permit the growth of a business funded exclusively from investor funds or retained earnings. Borrowing, in some form, is the usual bridge between the business and those who must be paid.

Let us define broadly the act of borrowing. In my definition, borrowing is the act of one party using the assets of another party in return for the promise of either, or both, the return of the assets or payment for their use at some point in the future. It follows then that employees who are paid at the end of a period of labor, rather than requiring payment in advance, are lending the employer their services in much the same manner as the doctor or lawyer who bills the client after performing services. Therefore, it can be considered that the vast majority of borrowing takes the form of credit extension in return for services, as well as for goods, and then, in order of magnitude, monies. The fair and intelligent use of credit lines, be they formal or involuntary, can be thought of by the entrepreneur as "vendor equity."

In cases where there are only two parties to a borrowing transaction, what is the motivating element for the lender? The answer must be the same as that for the borrower: profit, either realized or prospective. Whether the loan is of services or money, lenders are utilizing their stock in trade in pursuit of profit. Lenders' concerns are utilizing their resources profitably and receiving the highest possible return consistent with the risk they are willing or able to accept. Most employees assume that they will be paid at the end of the pay period.

Professionals also assume that they will be paid the amount of their bill shortly after it is rendered to the client. However, the experienced professional knows that in a number of instances the client will not pay promptly and in some cases not willingly pay the full amount billed. A negotiation must then occur.

In much the same manner, entrepreneurs who work in their businesses for less current compensation than they could earn from others are lending their talent and energy to the business in the expectation of it ultimately being a profitable transaction. For this to be the case, they must eventually receive profit as a result of their ownership interest.

Angels investing directly in a business, as distinct from those who buy shares from another investor, place their assets at the disposal of the managers of a business in the expectation of profit. Conceptually, does it really matter whether the transaction is describable as a loan or purchase of equity if the owner of the money assumes that at some point in the future the money will be returned, either by the company or through the medium of selling the acquired instrument to another investor? I think not. (I am ignoring here the balance sheet effects, which may influence future investors when they analyze a company.) All investors have an ability, after the recapture of employed funds, to calculate the annualized return received on their investment. Some more sophisticated investors have the ability to project accurately the future return on investment, assuming the timing of the return of their funds and the amounts to be received are as expected.

The elements which distinguish investments, be they thought of as pure loans or "borrower profitability related," are the length of time the resources are employed and the relative risk accepted regarding the return of assets and relative magnitude of the lender's profit potential. How long is the asset, be it labor or cash, going to be tied up and therefore not available for better or alternative utilization elsewhere? How certain is the asset's recapture and profit that prompted transaction in the first place?

One of the important considerations for a borrower is the availability of lender alternatives. If there is only one employer in a town or only a single borrower seeking the funds of a lender, then both the worker and the lender's decision-making process is made easier by the lack of local competitive users. The alternative for the asset owner is either not to employ the asset or not to earn a return on the asset. In a world of instant communications and mobility, people and money quickly will find, and gravitate to, areas of capital and employment shortage.

The owners of resources, or the agents of the owners, have various reasons for accepting risk and/or seeking gain above what represents the balance of least risk for the most secure return. Not everyone wants to be a civil servant or invest in government bonds (perhaps "invest in government bonds" is an oxymoronic phrase depending on the particular government and inflationary cycle timing). Many people either wish, or are required, to seek a greater return, even at the cost of accepting a greater risk.

In most instances, the party requiring the use of the assets of others attempts to acquire the use of the assets on the most advantageous terms possible, that is, at the lowest net cost. Such cost is determined in many ways. The simple interest paid on a loan is only one cost factor. Others, frequently of greater importance, are loan maturity, compensating balances or other lender benefits, prepayment penalties, and cost of collateral associated with the transaction. Similarly, an employer paying the lowest hourly rate to workers is not always obtaining the best value. The same workers could frequently produce more if they were more highly motivated, or had better tools, or were better organized. If there is a single truth in any asset utilization cost analysis, it is that analysis is not a simple matter.

The art of borrowing is more than getting a "yes" and signing a note. To be a good borrower, one must recognize the risk-aversion characteristics of the prospective lender, be they imposed or natural, and find or create an appropriate accommodation. The creation of an attractive inducement to the lender will permit more favorable terms to the borrower. To determine the most desirable terms, borrowers must understand their own probable cash flow and the financial dynamics of their businesses.

238

Interest, the Least Important Factor, if...

The rate of interest paid by a borrower to a lender is the negotiated, or imposed, factor over which many borrowers anguish the most. They should not. The rate of interest paid is not a meaningful consideration *if* the borrower can repay the loan without being charged a significant prepayment penalty *and* if the borrower can replace that loan with another at an interest rate that is more favorable to the borrower.

The *if* and *and* in the previous sentence are of vital importance. No person, having an option, would want to borrow at a rate of interest higher than they thought reasonable unless they believed that they could shortly replace the loan with one that was more attractive. Therefore, such a loan should be repayable either without a penalty or with a fair penalty that, when included in the overall cost of money for the replacement loan, still makes the replacement loan more attractive than the original loan.

The problem for many borrowers is that they are not able to find the replacement loan they believed would be available to them because the event upon which they depended to make their situation more attractive to a lender fails to occur. (For example, such an event could be the receipt of a purchase order relating to a large sale.) When borrowers find themselves burdened by loans that cannot be repaid or replaced and that carry an interest expense in excess of the amount being earned by them on the borrowed funds, they may be in serious trouble. Such a predicament is not unusual, because many, if not most, borrowers frequently find themselves borrowing at rates of interest greater than they are earning. Most businesses--due to their size and credit standing--borrow at interest rates higher than the then-current market rate of interest, and most businesses, I believe, are other than highly profitable. I further believe that the majority of businesses do not earn, after paying a market-rate wage to the owners, a return on equity of as much as the going interest rate.

How can a business survive and pay a higher rate of interest than the rate of profit the business earns on the funds borrowed? The answer must be that the borrowed funds represent only a portion of the total funds used by the business. Some form of equity must make up the difference. The borrowed funds represent the leverage most businesses use to increase the amount of business that can be done only through using the funds invested by the owners or earned previously, and retained, in the business.

To illustrate, a business could be successful if it borrowed at 20 percent and earned only 10 percent on sales, if the total amount of the borrowing were relatively minor in terms of the total funds employed in the business. The issue facing a business manager, therefore, is not whether to borrow but how, how much, and when.

The determination of "a fair rate of interest" to be charged for any particular loan is a combination of factors that include: the current rate of interest available to the lender for which the lender believes there is no risk of nonrepayment (that is, "riskless return"); the lender's perception of the level of risk represented by the subject loan; the lender's perception of the potential for additional business that could result from the same or associated borrowers; the pressure on the lender to rent money to borrowers having the same characteristics as the borrower seeking the loan; and the maturity of the loan under consideration.

The lender's assessment of the character of the borrower is the most critical consideration. Few lenders wish to deal, on any terms, with those they do not trust. The need to deal with parties who are trustworthy is as much a reflection of the lender's fear of embarrassment as it is one of being concerned with return of the funds. For the most part, lenders are agents and not principals. This fact is important to understand, because the borrower should recognize that loan officers have a great deal more to lose in terms of their careers from a bad loan than they have to gain from making a good loan. After all, the definition of a "good loan" to the lender is one on which the money is repaid on a timely basis and that carries a rate of interest sufficiently higher than the lender's own cost of funds to provide a net profit. Borrowers must understand that most commercial lenders are themselves borrowing or renting the money they are lending, and are only in business to profit from the margin or spread between their cost of raw material (money) and manufacturing (administration) and the sale price (interest received). To be a good borrower, one must appreciate the position of the lender. This is, of course, true in any business, or perhaps personal, relationship. One of the reasons I am successful in negotiations is that my first and most important undertaking is the effort to really understand the needs and pressures of the other party. It is not always possible to accommodate these needs and pressures, but the understanding of them at least permits a mutual attempt to solve the other party's problems. A negotiation is so much easier if both of the parties are, or at least appear to be, attempting to solve the problems of the other party.

240

The rate of interest charged by a lender will be directly affected by the rate at which that same lender can obtain alternative investments or activity. If short-term government obligations, for which there is instant liquidity, are trading at a 10 percent yield to maturity, then competitively priced demand loans to businesses will carry a somewhat higher interest rate. Similarly, if the loan to a business is for a fixed term and does not have any provision for a floating rate of interest, the interest rate can be either at a higher or lower rate than the short-term government rate. The rate in that case will depend on the creditworthiness of the borrower (as perceived by the lender at that moment) and the lender's prediction as to the course of interest rates over the period of the loan. Borrowers should always ask lenders their predictions as to future interest rates, because this knowledge can be useful in negotiating both rate and structure.

Most lenders try to keep a mixture of loan maturities on their books. Only a few professional lenders are so confident of their own ability to predict future interest rate levels accurately that they wish to have major percentages of their loan funds out at whatever the then-current interest level is and out on maturities that are "bunched." Professional lenders want a portfolio of loans with "staggered" maturities in which, at all times, there is a positive and, to the extent possible, trouble-free spread between their acquisition costs plus administrative costs and interest revenues.

The accompanying table of compound interest rates should be required reading in every elementary school in the country. If the powerful workings of compounding interest were recognized, there would be a greater desire on the part of people to create businesses and make investments designed to provide a secure and predictable margin that could be reinvested constantly (that is, compounded) at the same rate at least. As is more frequently the case, people and companies seek to earn unrealistically high returns through the process of overreaching, only to fail.

One of the great values of zero coupon bonds is that they have the effect of dramatizing the working of discounted interest. Even on a simple, rather than compounding, basis, the results are dramatic. The compounding of "interest on interest" is a fine situation for any lender to be in, if the interest and principal are paid as expected.

Compound Interest: $1 at an annual effective rate of 10 percent compound interest yields the amount shown in the second column for the number of years shown in the first column.

Year	Yield	Year	Yield
1	1.100 000	26	11.918 177
2	1.210 000	27	13.109 994
3	1.331 000	28	14.420 994
4	1.464 000	29	15.863 093
5	1.610 510	30	17.449 402
6	1.771 561	31	19.194 342
7	1.948 717	32	21.113 777
8	2.143 589	33	23.225 154
9	2.357 948	34	25.547 670
10	2.593 742	35	28.102 437
11	2.853 117	36	30.912 681
12	3.138 428	37	34.003 949
13	3.452 271	38	37.404 343
14	3.797 498	39	41.144 778
15	4.177 248	40	45.259 256
16	4.594 973	41	49.785 181
17	5.054 470	42	54.763 699
18	5.599 917	43	60.240 069
19	6.115 909	44	66.264 076
20	6.727 500	45	72.890 484
21	7.400 250	46	80.179 532
22	8.140 275	47	88.197 485
23	8.954 302	48	97.017 234
24	9.849 733	49	106.718 957
25	10.834 706	50	117.390 853

Another aspect of interest that is seldom addressed effectively by borrowers is the timing of their interest payments. It may be worth it to the borrower to pay a higher stated interest rate if the interest payments are delayed or are payable only at the maturity of the loan. The lender will almost always prefer to collect interest on a daily basis or even in advance of making the loan. Prepaid interest loans can (though they usually do not) work to the benefit of the borrower. Such was the case when prepaid interest was deductible for U.S. income tax purposes. Prepayment of interest may also permit the lender to charge a lower stated rate of interest, which can favorably affect the rate charged by other lenders to the same enterprise. Lenders may wish, for their own financial or cosmetic reasons, to be able to receive the interest for the entire period at the beginning. The money to prepay the interest is borrowed from the lender, so in effect borrowers are borrowing more than they need or receive.

Interest-related negotiations occur most frequently in the instance of loans for specific periods of time and at fixed (nonfloating) rates, and where there is security for the loan. In the case of unsecured demand loans, there is very little room for interest rate negotiations, because both parties are free to adjust the terms through repayment on either a voluntary or demanded basis. This is not to say, however, that the borrower should not attempt to obtain a better than initially offered rate of interest. Borrowers may point out that there is less risk than is perceived by the lender; there may be a prospect for increased business which borrowers can provide or use their influence to provide; or the borrowers may know of others in similar circumstances who are borrowing more economically from the same or competing lenders.

Polonius was wrong in his advice to his son in *Hamlet* of "neither a borrower nor a lender be." A well-secured, high-interest-rate lender can be well rewarded. Being a borrower may be less fun and more stressful--but it is necessary for many of us who wish to do more business than our current resources permit.

SOP Company Builder Loans

We are going through a new period in America's industrial history. For the first time, those judged to be heroes of the financial world are engaged in what the British call "asset rationalizations," known to us as leveraged buyouts (LBOs). Whatever it is called, the exercise is still the same: making businesses more efficient users of capital by initiating actions which are, by definition, expedient. But where have the company builders gone?

Inherently, the business of buying businesses, or initially the control of businesses, is less socially productive than building a company. Seldom are more workers employed after the control of a company changes from traditional management, however poor it may have been, to the control of owners requiring increased cash flow and earnings to justify the funds used to take over a company. Because acquirers almost always borrow funds, their management decisions are more likely to be based on current market rates of return than on what may be best for the growth of the company. Also, the primary concern of new owners is less likely to be perks and pensions.

The current increase in large company reported earnings and resultant buoyance of the stock market is a direct reflection of downsizing and asset rationalization programs.

The situation reminds me of the imaginary animal that starts eating its tail and eventually devours itself. Of course, it is reasonable to believe that a different work ethic might be imposed on a divested property, and that it will actually be managed smarter and run leaner than before. That's the upside--the creation of smaller, more efficient units of production. Perhaps the greatest benefit of downsizing to smaller units is one of senior executives in the smaller units being closer to the customers.

The downside is that with all the media attention, glamor, and profit expectation focused on buying and borrowing, less attention and fewer resources are available for those wishing to amass wealth the old-fashioned way--by developing new products and services that meet with consumer acceptance.

Why not have the government give incentives to those who want to create and develop new businesses? The easiest, or at least most frequently recommended, means of rewarding company building is through some form of tax break. I suggest, however, that there is a better way: a program where a public body makes available Success On-Pass (SOP) loans, or loan guarantees, on an attractive basis, to companies that have already proven their success. The specific purpose of these loans would be for the successful companies to invest in nonaffiliated, newer, developing companies. Such a privatized, government-backed program could be much better than the Small Business Administration's type of loan and loan guarantee program-- or even Small Business Investment Company loans--because the loans would be "hard" and require repayment by companies that had proven their mettle.

Who better to select, administer, and monitor loans to developing companies than the management of successful businesses? Who better to offer and perhaps even impose, really meaningful advice and practical assistance than a company already able to demonstrate its own success? By requiring developing companies to interact with successful ones in order to get capital, the SOP company builder program could have an imposed mentorship result.

In my recommended program, the lending or guaranteeing agency would also profit, since the losses of money loaned to companies that already were successful would be minimal. And the loans made by the successful companies to developing companies would be less likely to go bad than if they had been dispensed by a government bureaucracy. Which successful companies would qualify for an SOP loan? Perhaps only those that are able to demonstrate they really didn't need the money--like those the banks want as loan customers. It would not be difficult to define "success" or the desired profile of recipient companies in such a program. The incentive to borrow the funds might come from attractive interest rates or tax credit on losses.

LBOs Based on Insider Information

Thinking as an owner, I found myself expressing a minority view recently when I learned that a major retailer, having gone private through a leveraged buyout (LBO), was scheduled to go public shortly after the LBO at a price that would yield a sixty times profit to the current shareholders. My view was one of revulsion and disdain for the disservice done to the prior public shareholders by the management group, soon to be so brazenly enriched. At a dinner party, I asked the company's banker and others who knew the details, "How did they do it?" The banker couldn't stop bubbling about how pleased they were that the loans were being paid off ahead of schedule and about how much money the bank was going to make. "But how did they do it?" I asked. "By turning off the lights and using pencils till they were shorter," my host replied. He added, "They were working harder and managing better."

Although I understand the higher level of motivation of the owner/manager versus the hired manager, one must question where the old board of directors was in representing the owners during the prior period of relative managerial sloth. The management is actually the same. The business activity is the same. The economic climate is not that different. What changed? Why didn't the directors require management to cut costs when they represented public owners? Why didn't management and the directors have an obligation to inform the shareholders being asked to approve the LBO terms that profits were going to be significantly higher under the LBO plan? When the company was anticipated to be public again, earnings would be many, many times higher than when the company's shareholders were effectively sold out at a discount to the price reflecting the more enthused management. Shouldn't the previous shareholders have been privy to the projected profits and the entire plan for restructuring? After all, it was shown to those who financed the LBO. Whose management was it who developed these plans? Who was paying their salaries? Who was paying fees to directors to represent their interests?

Would the directors have disapproved of a plan that now generates such high levels of earnings? Would the directors have rewarded management with bonuses had such a change in earnings occurred? Shouldn't a staff always "turn off the lights" and be mindful of the use of supplies?

The public shareholders/owners of the business were badly ripped off by those who either were inept or clearly put their own interests ahead of the interests of those who paid their salaries. I think it is disgraceful and deserves equal legislative and regulatory attention as other recent examples of the financial community's greed. I believe it is simply dishonest, and certainly immoral, for those paid to represent and serve to use their "inside information" to enhance the value of the property for their own enrichment at the prior owners' expense.

What about the customers of the retailers? How are they being treated? I don't know, but I'd bet better than before, since the firm's employees are being more closely and intelligently supervised. What about suppliers? Again, I don't know, but I'd be surprised if the store wasn't buying tighter and better, and, as a result, dealing more profitably with the same suppliers as before it became owner/managed.

The point is that we as business owners have an advantage in running our businesses that we sometimes forget. The advantage is that we care. Our disadvantage is that there is no one we can rip off and deceive by withholding information. Oh, well, we'll just have to go along turning off the lights and hope that our children will become the trusted executives of public companies not being managed for optimal profits and then be in a position to.... What would you want them to do?

IPOs--Friend or Foe?

When considering what to look for in a prospectus for an initial public offering (IPO), the question must first be addressed of why one should even think of buying such stock. The investor's answer has to be to make money; and the belief, therefore, must be that the shares will not in the future--or at least not while they are held by the investor--sell at a price below that of the initial public offering price. Such a premise, as relating to the broad spectrum of IPOs, is invalid. Most shares offered in an IPO do indeed sell subsequently at prices below that of the initial offering.

246

This fact should not surprise those who understand the system and workings of the market. Stocks are sold by those who profit from the process, rather than bought by investors without the stimuli of brokers and underwriters. Those involved in distributing newly issued securities receive far more compensation than they would for persuading an investor to purchase an equal dollar amount of securities already traded publicly. The cost of going public must be borne by someone. That someone is ultimately the buyer of the securities, in that the price paid includes an underwriting spread and selling group concession. The company issuing the securities receives less than the investor pays. Would sophisticated managers of businesses accept less for shares the company was selling than the maximum they thought available? Unlikely. I believe a study would show that, in most market periods, an aggregate profit would result from selling short every new equity issue, particularly those offered at a price of $10 or less at the IPO price, and covering the short positions 90, 180, and 360 days after the IPO.

There are, of course, exceptions, and some IPOs are priced at levels that are attractive to the investor. What is the likelihood of the average investor obtaining an allocation of IPO shares if the deal is hot and if, therefore, institutional and professional investing clients of the firms want to have positions? The likelihood is not good. Therefore, the average investor is able to buy shares in IPOs that are not generally thought to be great values by professional investors, and not in those IPOs that professionals find attractive. What do I, as a professional, look for in a preliminary prospectus?

Underwriter. Underwriters have had opportunities to study companies more carefully than any prospective investors. Underwriters have their firms' reputations on the line with each new issue. They need to have a record of successes if they are to attract subsequent underwritings and purchasers for subsequent deals. The reputation and the track record of underwriters are important considerations and should be known or researched by prospective IPO share buyers. Has the underwriter had experience with companies in the same or similar fields? Will the underwriter be the major market maker in the shares once they are publicly traded?

The underwriting of IPOs invariably affords participating underwriters and brokers a much higher compensation than is the case when the public buys, through them, publicly traded securities. In addition to underwriting fees, underwriters often require certain other opportunities to profit from companies they help launch publicly.

247

Therefore, IPOs are frequently distributed to the public at times and on terms for which there is less than a natural demand. Such broker incentive is not, however, present in the aftermarket. Therefore, to profit, the IPO buyer may have to await either the development of projected earnings or the market's recognition of the stock's attractiveness. When the new-issues market is euphoric, the IPO buyer will have an opportunity to take a fast profit and probably will be able to buy the position back cheaper later. In any case, the list of recent and pending IPOs is less "tech-y" and more businesslike. With greater current cash flow consideration and a lessening of aggressive underwriter pricing, the IPO buyer is currently getting a better deal.

Business. The business of the company issuing the securities should be understood. How profitable an industry is the IPO company competing in? What has been the business experience of the other companies in the same field? How good are the industry's profit margins? What size is the IPO issuer relative to similar companies in the industry? What competitive advantage does the issuer have? What are the price/earnings ratios of competitive companies versus those that are anticipated for the IPO issuer? What has been the revenue and earnings growth experience of the IPO issuer versus those of companies already publicly traded? If I had the resources, is this a company I'd like to own 100 percent of at the price at which it is being offered? Why is the business going to prosper in the future, or are the present levels of earnings the highest they are likely to be in the reasonable future? Is the business going to prosper through capturing a greater share of market or because the market will grow, or both? How well has the company done already, both in absolute and relative terms? Will the profit margins in this type of business expand, contract, or stay the same as the company grows?

Management. What is the character of management? What are their backgrounds? How committed are they to the business in terms of holdings in the company, and what is their share cost versus the IPO price? What salaries are they taking? How do the wages and perks offered compare to those of comparable companies? How dependent is the business on any of the management groups, and what are the risks associated with the demise or defection of that person or those persons? Is there any indication, by virtue of prior experience, that management has the experience and will to build a much larger or more diversified company than the present one? What are the relationships and experience of those on the board of directors? Have they been associated in the past with winners or losers? What is their relationship with the underwriter or other investors in the company? How are the directors being compensated? Does the company use consultants, and what is their reputation and basis of compensation?

Deal Structure. What are investors really buying? What are the structural preferences and priorities of which they are either a beneficiary or potentially disadvantaged? How much instant enrichment is the investor facilitating for the existing shareholders? What is the book value dilution being suffered instantly by the IPO investor? What rights, such as warrants, does the investor have, and what are their significance? How many shares will be available in the float for trading after the IPO? What is the amount of stock that can be sold in the market by existing shareholders and over what period of time? Are there any earnings or book value tests? What management incentive compensation plans exist? Does the underwriter hold warrants? Does the underwriter have a position in the company? How much net money will the company have after the deal closes? Will it be enough to achieve the objectives of the company? Is there any antidilution protection for the investor? Does the underwriter have an ongoing consulting or other relationship with the company? What are the shareholder voting arrangements?

Supporting Players. Who are the accountants? How long have they represented the issuer? Have they given a "clean" opinion of the financial statements upon which the underwriting is based? Which law firm has prepared the offering document? Is it the same law firm that normally represents the company? How long has this law firm been counsel to the company? Are there any conflicts of interest? What has been the record of the law firm in terms of affiliation with successful corporate clients? Does the company use the accountants for other than auditing services? Does the company use other consultants? Who? And on what compensation basis? Has the company retained public and/or investor relations counsel?

Other Investors. What types of investors are buying the shares of the IPO? Are there any professional investors? Have any firms of repute expressed interest in becoming involved as market makers and/or other supporting roles? What is the reputation and track record of other members of the underwriting and syndicate or selling group?

Pricing of the Issue. Is the price of the issue reasonable relative to the market measure indexes in terms of the price/earnings ratio and/or dividend yield? How does the P/E compare to other companies with a similar earnings record? What is the indicated level of market capitalization compared to companies already having shares in the market? At what price would the investor be willing to sell the shares purchased in the IPO, and what must happen for that profit to be achieved? What is the likely risk/reward relationship? How much can the shares decline in price before being supported by either a dividend yield or book value relationship comparable to that of similar companies versus the conceivable appreciation in the same period of time?

Inherently, there is no magic to the pricing of securities in an IPO. Intrinsically, after a $3 million offering the net worth of the company is the same whether a stock is priced at 10 cents or if fewer shares are offered at $10. But the 10 cent stock appeals to less sophisticated investors who may believe, based upon limited understanding of the factors, that they can enjoy the same rewards as more educated investors who have profited in what are made to appear as similar investment opportunities. Big fish eat little fish, and the unsophisticated new issue buyer is awfully tempting for the sharks of the investment world.

Much of the above information is available to the informed investor directly through the prospectus or when the prospectus is read in conjunction with information on companies already publicly traded. Some of the questions can be answered by the company at due diligence meetings or during road show presentations.

Intelligent IPO investing takes as much work as investing in securities generally. Those unable or unwilling to make the effort are advised to avoid new issues, because in the market, value is usually forged through the pricing mechanism of more knowledgeable sellers accommodating the orchestrated enthusiasm of less knowledgeable buyers.

Management Deception

When a company gets caught doing something improper or illegal, how should it--and its management--be judged? Do the owners really condemn such actions if they were made in pursuit of maximized profits? I hope so. But I doubt it. Isn't it appropriate for management to inform shareholders of its philosophy, especially as it relates to controversial areas? If shareholders knew the guiding principles of companies, they could choose whether or not to back those that had a policy of maximum profits at all times. Then, if the company subsequently follows a different philosophy from the one professed, shouldn't management be dismissed and, perhaps, sued? Deception of customers or suppliers by management is shortsighted and therefore bad business judgment. A management's not informing or lying to the owners of a business is inexcusable. Yet owners who fail to assert their rights to control or be informed deserve the surprises that lie in wait for them.

"Young" Businesses

It is generally accepted that one of America's most pressing problems is that of underemployment and unemployment. The problem is particularly acute because it affects both youth and minorities. Unemployment is at its most socially disruptive when found in combination, when minority youth are unsuccessful in their search for meaningful employment.

It is also generally recognized that our country's largest companies' primary management objective is increased productivity, which is reflected as an ongoing attempt to reduce the number of employees per unit produced. Only the most optimistic of future-tellers would predict that, in aggregate, the larger U.S. companies will ever again create a single net new job. At best, only replacement jobs will be created and their number, in the case of many companies, will decrease as managers allow attrition to function as the most painless and politically acceptable means of accomplishing their objective.

It is a fact that, of the net new jobs created, more than 66 percent will be created by companies employing fewer than 20 people. More than 75 percent of net new jobs are created by companies that have been in business for less than five years.

It is broadly believed that most new companies fail during their first five years to achieve the financial predictions and objective of their founders and frequently, particularly in their first year, fail financially. Further, it is known that most small companies are only marginally profitable after compensating their owner-managers.

Therefore, it can be observed that one of our country's major socioeconomic problems is being addressed, albeit inadequately, by companies that themselves are financially frail. Obviously, this is a dilemma of national significance.

251

Two questions arise: Is there anything the federal government can do to help? Should government even try to help? I am of the view that the government *must* attempt to help young businesses. The future economic, and perhaps social, stability of this country rests not only with small businesses, but even more so with young businesses. These young businesses usually start small but frequently do not remain so. These soon-to-be-*not*-so-small businesses are of special interest to entrepreneurial investors.

The federal government can assist in at least three areas. The first is by legislating that, in the first five years of a company's existence, retained earnings be tax-free. The second is that the government adopt *Venture* magazine's policy of sponsoring "profit education" by encouraging teacher training in free enterprise economics. The broader the understanding of the principles of profit making, the more positive will become the popular attitudes regarding free enterprise. The third area of assistance is a recognition of the essential role performed by entrepreneurial investors. In accepting the risk of total financial loss, they provide the fuel to set the process in motion. Such positive recognition could take the form of deferring a capital gains tax for funds reinvested in other new businesses within a specified period. A similar capital gains tax deferral is already available to homeowners purchasing a new home with proceeds from the sale of their former home. Certainly company formation, which is reflected in job creation, is as worthy of tax relief as individual residential upgrading.

To further induce owner-managers of businesses not only to hire but also to educate youth, particularly those who may be socioeconomically disadvantaged, tax incentives could be offered to companies for employees who can demonstrate significant skill enhancements, to the point that they are worth more to their employers and to themselves. In other words, a tax credit for promoting new workers *on the basis of demonstrated merit and contribution* specifically over those with greater seniority. This would create a significantly increased competition by entry-level employees in terms of striving for excellence, which can only benefit the enterprise and establish a continuing positive attitude by rewarding extra effort. Managers should be assisted in their need to continually improve the quality of available human resources.

In certain cases, Angels should be rewarded for their risk assumption by sharing in an investee company's revenues (rather than, or in addition to, profits) by holding a Revenue Participation Certificate (RPC). The Treasury could propose that such payments be classified as long-term capital gains rather than income and yet still be deductible to the company. In this way, companies could negotiate a lesser percentage payment due to the more favorable tax effect for the recipient. In any case, Congress should legislate approval for small business participating debentures. These instruments could provide lenders with a fixed return, plus profit participation, and a long-term capital gains tax result, while allowing the companies to deduct the payments.

Delegations of Independent Businesspeople

When the President and members of Congress received their copies of the final report of the Second White House Conference on Small Business, they also got the following letter from me.

October 15, 1986

The President
The White House
Washington, DC 20003

Dear Mr. President:

It has been suggested that an informed observer's reflections and recommendations, intended for both the participants in the Second White House Conference on Small Business (who will be intense readers of this Report), and yourself, would be an appropriate inclusion in this Report. Accordingly, the following is respectfully submitted.

First of all, the Conference was a success in terms of the stated mission. It was a success because the delegates were finally able, within the confines of the process, to develop and agree upon 60 recommended actions which represented the priorities of their delegations.

There was, however, one overriding fear and concern. That concern was that there was not going to be a sufficient subsequent reflection and administrative and legislative action to justify the significant effort and expense (time, as well as the cost of travel and lodging, to a business owner is money) the delegates had invested in the creation of the recommendations. None attending wanted to feel their investment was a waste.

253

Mr. President, the time and the efforts of the delegates will not have been wasted, almost regardless of the immediate response to their well considered recommendations, if they come to understand that the Second White House Conference on Small Business can be a beginning, a point of departure, rather than a conclusion. The objectives of the delegates, to improve our country's economic well being by improving the economic environment in which America's independent business owners must function, can be furthered by maintaining the presence of such delegations. The profit education and networking benefits of such a structured caucus would be most positive. The potential political strength of these delegations could be meaningful as business owners are such community role models and influential opinion leaders.

Were the state delegations to be made permanent, they would also focus their attention on assisting state and local elected representatives in understanding the needs of their most important and societally productive, in terms of employment and innovation creating, constituents.

Naturally, the delegates' greatest concern is for the implementation of the recommendations. Is it not logical, therefore, that their best interests would be served by their staying together as a group, having shared experiences that create the basis for their common vision as to the recommended action?

It is within your power, Mr. President, to cause the creation of a permanent body of independent business owners representing those in America on whom America so depends. As was the case in the delegations to this conference, some of the delegates could be elected and some appointed. Such a body could be a force for constructive liaison between legislators and administrators, at all levels of government, and business owners. Officially sanctioned and administered business owner representative bodies would, perhaps for the first time, permit independent business owners to have both a clear voice and a feeling of participation equal to that of large and established businesses in the process of democracy so important to us all.

Finally, the focus of the Conference recognized the ever increasing, as well as traditional, importance of entrepreneurs to the country. Many of the recommendations reflect the needs of developing businesses. Developing businesses (those of less than five years of age) are both the major source of employment creation and innovation. These developing companies are also, however, the most delicate of our enterprises. These are the entrepreneurial efforts requiring the greatest amount of assistance and encouragement. The economic realities are such that newer businesses operate at a disadvantage. Those in positions of affluence and influence would serve their country well by actively seeking ways in which to assist those entrepreneurs on whom we all depend so much for our collective future.

The Second White House Conference on Small Business was a success. Thank you for making it possible.

Respectfully,

Arthur Lipper III
Chairman & Editor-in-Chief

Trustee:	Institute of Private Enterprise
	University of North Carolina at Chapel Hill
Director:	International Council of Small Business
Ex-director:	Small Business Foundation of America
	Securities Industry Association - Economic
	Education Committee

In 1995, there was another White House Conference of Small Business, with many of the same recommendations made as in the prior two Conferences. President Clinton referred to the 1995 Conference in his 1996 State of the Union address. Unfortunately, very few of the recommendations of any of the Conferences have ever been adopted, and entrepreneurs will have to continue to look to themselves and Angels for the resources required.

Developing Business Administration (DBA)

I propose the establishment of the Developing Business Administration (DBA) as a new agency for state and federal governments to assist young as opposed to "small" businesses. It is the developing companies, those formed within the past five years, that account for the bulk of net new job creation. Younger companies have the greatest need for and willingness to accept economic education, consulting, and other nonmoney services from such an agency. By definition, it is the emerging growth companies on which society depends for innovative progress. Such a DBA could show dramatic results, whereas the Small Business Administration--mired in focusing on size rather than merit or maturity--has had difficulty demonstrating efficacy.

Military Real Estate

The Defense Orientation Conference Association (DOCA) is a little-known organization, composed mostly of civic and business leaders who are actively interested in the intelligent preservation and enhancement of our national defense system. DOCA members are invited, at their own expense, to visit defense installations. At one meeting, many of us--business owners, corporate executives, and professionals--visited Marine Corps Air Station El Toro and Marine Corps Base Camp Pendleton, both located in southern California on land worth many billions of dollars.

One of my first reactions to the visit was that consideration should be given to relocating many military installations. Only a portion of the hundreds of billions of dollars that could be raised by the government by selling these properties would have to be used to build new and improved facilities, including much needed affordable housing for service personnel and dependents. The government already owns more than 30 percent of all U.S. land, and many existing military bases are located where they are because of historic reasons that are no longer valid or economically defensible. Once civilian communities begin to encroach upon a base, it becomes difficult for the military to carry out most training missions. Because the Marines are required to be in a state of constant readiness, their training problem is particularly acute. Marines need a lot of land. But not, I suggest, land that includes nearly 17 miles of some of the world's most valuable beach front property, nor 5,700 acres for air bases in increasingly congested areas where nearby land has a current price tag of $1 million an acre, as is the case with Camp Pendleton, Miramar, El Toro, and neighboring Tustin, all favorably zoned.

For some of my recent talks and articles on various subjects, see Appendix X.

Conclusion

In flying over our country, particularly at times when the cultivated fields are of a different color than the raw land, I think of the vast amount of hard and lonely labor that has gone into clearing and working the land. I think of the sweat and tenacity required of the farmer, and the enormous financial difficulties which have been, and will be in the future, the farmer's lot. I know of no tougher job than trying to make a living from the land. Nevertheless, many of the most positive of the traditional American values are derived from our farming, grazing, and trapping heritage. It would be a shame if the urban, mercantile, quick-return-on-investment focus of many businesspeople today became the sole basis for our future values. Much can be learned by entrepreneurs and investors from the farmer's patience. Too many of us cause problems for ourselves by trying to force change and growth. Entrepreneurs share a similar frustration with farmers, however, in that capital is like rain: There's never enough of it when it's needed most.

ANGELS: PERSONAL INVESTORS IN THE VENTURE CAPITAL MARKET

JOHN FREEAR, JEFFREY E. SOHL, AND WILLIAM. E. WETZEL, JR.

The writers are members of the Center for Venture Research, Whittemore School of Business and Economics, University of New Hampshire. This paper appeared in the July 1995 issue of *Entrepreneurship & Regional Development*.

Introduction

Evidence is mounting that the late 1970's marked the end of an era in U.S. economy - the so-called industrial economy - and the beginning of a new era - the entrepreneurial economy (Birch 1987; Birch 1988; Huey 1994). In 1979, output of the Fortune 500 peaked at 58% of GNP, up from 37% in 1954. Employment reached 16 million and political economists foresaw a new industrial state dominated by large firms (Hale 1992). Between 1979 and 1993, Fortune 500 payrolls fell by over 25% to 11.5 million. In 1993 total employment among the 500 fell for the ninth straight year, from 11,802,133 to 11,546,647, while median employment dropped 5.3% to 10,136 (Fortune 1994). Simultaneously, largely invisible entrepreneurial ventures created over 20 million new jobs (Hale 1992).

Today the restructuring of America is well underway. More and more of the nation's work is being done by entrepreneurs and the fast, focussed, flexible ventures they lead. As the Fortune 500 continue to "build down," entrepreneurs and their investors are leading the US out of recession. Despite the compelling evidence of their job generating power, today's entrepreneurs face a daunting task in their search for equity financing, the fuel for the engine that creates jobs and moves technology from the laboratory to the marketplace. Founder's capital, sweat equity and bootstrap financing alone cannot provide the necessary equity for the most promising technology-based ventures.

During the late 1980's and early 1990's, most entrepreneurs came up empty in their search for venture capital. Seed and start-up financing by professional venture capital funds, the best-known source of venture financing, virtually disappeared (Bygrave and Timmons 1992). But even in the best of financial times, venture capital funds are not the place to look for early-stage financing. Entrepreneurs have been knocking on the wrong doors in their search for funds.

Research on early-stage investing has identified the informal venture capital market as the major source of equity financing for entrepreneurial ventures (Wetzel 1983). This informal venture capital market consists of a diverse set of high net worth individuals (business angels) who invest a portion of their assets in high-risk, high-return entrepreneurial ventures. Like most of the ventures they bankroll, these private investors are a nearly invisible segment of the venture capital markets. There are no directories of business angels and no public records of their investment transactions. Research has, however, clearly established the importance of the informal market in the United States and Canada (Riding and Short 1987; Haar et al 1988; Gaston 1989a; Freear, Sohl and Wetzel 1994). More recent research has extended the findings on the US informal venture market to the United Kingdom (Mason and Harrison 1992; Harrison and Mason 1993) and Sweden (Landstrom 1992; Landstrom 1993).

In an attempt to add to the knowledge base of the informal investor market, this paper examines the venture capital market for new technology-based firms. The research views this market from both a demand and supply perspective and attempts to delineate the role of the private investor with respect to the more visible venture capital funds. The research also focuses on the entrepreneur's perceptions of raising venture capital.

Venture Capital Markets

A sense of the scale and structure of demand and supply in the venture capital markets provides useful background for an examination of the role of angels in these markets.

Demand for venture capital.

Venture investors look for opportunities to back entrepreneurial companies that offer the prospect of long-term capital gains substantial enough to justify the risks and lack of short-term liquidity inherent in venture investing. There are no hard data on the number of these high potential start-ups and high growth private companies or their annual capital requirements. Educated guesses place the number of private companies growing faster than 20% per year at about 500,000. David Birch's research indicates that 4% of U.S. firms account for 70% of all job growth (Birch 1993). The 1993 INC. 500 fastest growing private companies are obvious examples (INC. 1993). The number of start-ups with attractive capital gains potential for investors is estimated to be 50,000 per year, less than 5% of total annual business start-ups. The equity financing requirements of these high growth and start-up ventures is somewhere in the neighborhood of $60 billion per year. Sixty billion dollars per year of high risk, patient, value-added capital is one measure of the capital formation challenge confronting the U.S. economy.

Supply of venture capital.

There are two primary sources of venture financing for entrepreneurs - one visible and one invisible. The visible venture capital market is composed of over 500 venture capital funds that manage about $35 billion. In the early nineties, venture capital funds were investing between $2 and $3 billion annually in entrepreneurial ventures. Considering the demand for this capital, three billion dollars per year represents a significant shortfall in the capital requirements of high growth entrepreneurial ventures. Compounding this capital gap is the fact that venture capital funds bankroll less than two thousand companies per year and two thirds of these financings are for ventures already in their portfolios. A typical round of financing from a venture capital fund is a later-stage deal in excess of $1 million.

The invisible venture capital market is the oldest and the largest segment of the U.S. venture capital market. It is made up of over two million individuals with a net worth in excess of $1 million, excluding personal residences. The majority of these individuals are self-made millionaires (first generation money) - individuals with substantial business and entrepreneurial experience (Gaston and Bell 1988; Postma and Sullivan 1990). While estimates of the scale of this informal venture capital market vary considerably (Gaston and Bell 1986; Arum 1987; Ou 1987; Gaston 1989b) conservative estimates suggest that about 250,000 angels invest approximately $10 billion every year in about thirty thousand ventures.

For ventures with competent, committed management and a convincing business plan, the odds of raising angel financing are much higher than the odds of raising capital from venture capital funds. A typical angel deal is an early-stage round in the $100 thousand to $500 thousand range, raised from six or eight investors. These co-investors usually are trusted friends and business associates. Find one angel and you have found five or ten.

The Data

The data used in the present study of the financing of new, technology-based firms (NTBFs) were collected from 284 companies founded in New England between 1975 and 1986. The 284 companies represent 27% of 1,073 firms in CorpTech's Corporate Technology database (CorpTech 1986). The data were collected and analyzed in two stages.

In the first stage, financial histories were collected from the 284 NTBFs. Financial histories included the year of each round of financing, the source, the amount and the stage of the financing. One hundred seven firms (38%) were launched and grew using only founder's capital, sweat equity and bootstrap financing. The other one hundred seventy-seven firms (62%) raised $671 million in 445 rounds of equity financing (Freear and Wetzel 1990).

In the second stage, entrepreneurs who had raised equity capital were asked about the process of raising funds and the characteristics of their investors, particularly individual investors (business angels) and venture capital funds. Data included methods employed for locating investors, the length of the search process, perceptions of investors' required rates of return, expected holding periods, relationships between investors and the management of the firm and entrepreneurs' perceptions of the value of these investor relationships (Freear, Sohl and Wetzel 1990).

261

In drawing inferences from the data, it is important to note two points. First, the data were collected from ventures that were founded during a period of rapid growth in the capital under management by venture capital funds. Second, most of these venture funds were invested in new, technology-based firms, NTBFs. Therefore, the relative size of the capital invested in NTBFs by private investors and venture capital funds should not be extrapolated to the population of all ventures that obtained capital from these two sources.

Financial History

The financial histories of the technology-based firms in the sample provide insights for today's entrepreneurs. To highlight what appear to be the most compelling implications of the data, angel financing is contrasted with financing provided by venture capital funds. The data provide valuable insights when segmented by the size and the stage of the investment during the early life of a venture.

Sources of equity financing included private individuals (business angels), venture capital funds, non-financial corporations, public stock offerings and other general sources. Of the 177 firms that raised outside equity, 124 firms (70%) raised one or more rounds from private individuals (excluding members of the founding management team and their relatives). Ninety firms (51%) raised one or more rounds from venture capital funds. Fewer than 40 firms raised funds from any other single source. Of the 445 rounds of financing, Table 1 indicates that angels provided 177 rounds (40%) and venture capital funds provided 173 rounds (39%). The remaining three sources collectively accounted for 95 rounds (21%).

The sample firms raised $76 million from angels and almost five times that amount, $370 million, from venture capital funds. When the data for angel and venture capital funds are segmented by the size of a round of financing (Table 1), the distinctive role of angels in smaller deals is apparent. For the 213 rounds under $1 million angels accounted for 56% of the dollars and 75% (160) of the rounds, compared to 44% of the dollars and 25% (53) of the rounds for venture capital funds. An examination of rounds under $1 million reveals a boundary area between angel financing and financing by venture capital funds in the neighborhood of $500,000. Angels provided 93% of the rounds involving less than $250,000 and 75% of the rounds between $250,000 and $500,000. In rounds under $500,000, angels were dominant in terms of dollars as well as rounds, providing a total of $23 million compared to $6 million from venture capital funds, a ratio of four-to-one. Thirty percent of angel dollars, as opposed to two percent of the dollars from venture capital funds, were invested in rounds under $500,000.

In financings over $500,000 the role of angels diminishes rapidly. Between $500,000 and $1 million, angels accounted for 33% of the rounds and for rounds over $1 million only 14%. As the size of a round of financing increases, angels are replaced by venture capital funds as the dominant players.

When investments are segmented by the stage of the financing, a second distinguishing characteristic of angel financing is evident. The stages investigated include seed, start-up, first, second, third, and bridge financing (Morris, Isenstein and Knowles 1990). In total dollars, angels were the largest single source of seed financing, accounting for $12 million (48%) of the $26 million invested in seed capital deals (Table 2). Their role declined sharply at the start-up stage, accounting for $29 million (20%) of start-up investments. At the first and second stages, angels accounted for only 8% of the capital raised. By the third stage, angels provided only 2% of the dollars raised.

Venture capital funds provided almost as much seed capital as angels, $11 million compared to $12 million (Table 2). At the start-up stage, venture capital funds were the largest single source of capital, providing 45% of the $144 million invested in start-ups, compared to 20% from angels and 19% from public stock offerings. Venture capital funds were the dominant source of first, second and third stage financing, accounting for 69%, 58% and 52% of the total capital, respectively.

The central role of angels in early-stage financing becomes more apparent when rounds, rather than dollars, are used as the measure of activity. As indicated in Table 3, angels provided fifty-two rounds of seed financing, representing 83% of the sixty-three seed deals. Angels also provided more rounds of start-up financing than venture capital funds, fifty-five compared to thirty-eight.

At the seed stage, the evidence suggests that most entrepreneurs should seek funds from angels, especially when the financing is under $300,000. At the seed stage, angels invested more funds, in more rounds, for more firms than any other single source. In a very real sense, angels are "seeding" ventures that will require larger rounds of follow-on financing as well as ventures that never raise equity from other sources. The median round of angel seed financing was

263

$100,000-$199,000. The median round of seed financing from venture capital funds was $400,000-$499,000.

At the start-up stage the business angel continues to be an important player, especially when the capital required is under $500,000. Angels provided 42 rounds of start-up financing under $500,000. Only two start-up rounds under $500,000 were raised from venture capital funds. For rounds above $500,000 the angels are replaced by the venture capital funds as the dominant source of funding. The median round of start-up financing from angels was $100,000-$199,000, compared to a median start-up round of $1-$2 million from venture capital funds.

Angels clearly are more active in seed and start-up financing than venture capital funds. Fifty-four percent of angel dollars and sixty percent of angel deals were invested at the seed or start-up stage compared to twenty percent of the dollars and twenty-eight percent of the deals from venture capital funds. Early-stage financing entails both greater risks and longer holding periods than later-stage financing. In their venture deals, angels exhibit less risk aversion and more patience than their professional counterparts. Avery and Elliehausen (1986) provided insights into the risk and liquidity attitudes of high income households. Compared to all U.S. families, high income households displayed a significantly higher propensity to assume above average financial risks in order to earn above average returns. High income families also displayed a significantly higher propensity to tie up funds for long periods of time in order to earn substantial returns.

In later-stage financing, the size of the round is the characteristic that distinguishes angels from venture capital funds. The size of the rounds provided by these two sources drifts further apart as the stage of the financing advances. For angels, the median size of the round of first stage financing was $200-$299 (thousand), and for second and third stage financing the median size (in thousands) was $100-$199. In contrast, for venture capital funds, the median size of the round of first and second stage financing (in millions) was $1-$2 and for third stage financing the median size (in millions) was $2-$3. Given the investment criteria of venture capital funds, this pattern is not surprising. Firms that can support expectations of a public stock offering or acquisition by a larger firm within five years typically require multiple rounds of financing in excess of $1 million.

The financial histories of the technology-based firms in the sample contain two fundamental lessons for today's entrepreneurs. Angels are the primary source of funds when the size of the deal is under $1 million and angels typically invest earlier in the life of a technology-based firm than other sources of outside equity capital. These findings suggest that angels and venture capital funds play complementary roles in the financing of new, technology-based firms. Angels are deciding which entrepreneurial ventures merit the equity financing and, in turn, are providing the market for the venture capital funds.

Raising Venture Capital

The second stage in this research was the collection of data describing entrepreneurs' perceptions of the process of finding investors and raising funds, investors' expected rates of return, expected holding periods and the nature and value of working relationships between entrepreneurs and investors. This stage in the study also focussed on differences between angel financing and financing by venture capital funds. Seventy-four firms, 69% of the 177 firms that raised outside equity capital, participated in stage two of the study.

The Search for Investors

Entrepreneurs were asked who was most helpful in locating investors. Since the names and addresses of venture capital funds are readily available, this question dealt only with finding individual investors. Sources of leads included friends, business associates, other entrepreneurs, attorneys, accountants, commercial and investment bankers, customers/suppliers and paid advertising.

Entrepreneurs reported significant differences in the effectiveness of sources of prospective investors. Eighty-three percent of the entrepreneurs found friends and business associates helpful. The next most helpful source was other entrepreneurs (31%). The ratings of the remaining sources ranged from 26% for attorneys to 2% for paid advertising.

To test for significant differences between angels and venture capital funds in the time it takes to raise equity capital, entrepreneurs were asked how long it took to secure financing from the two sources. The fund raising process was divided into two stages: the elapsed time between the decision to raise funds and the first meeting with an angel or managing partner of a venture capital fund, and the elapsed time between the first meeting and the receipt of funds.

In stage one, the median elapsed time was one month to find and meet the first angel and 1.75 months to find and meet the first managing partner of a venture capital fund. This result seems counterintuitive, given the relative obscurity of angels. Although venture capital funds are easier to find, it appears to require

more persistence to arrange an appointment with a managing partner than with an angel. An alternative explanation for the shorter period of time to meet an angel is that for private investors self selection by entrepreneurs may play a significant role. This type of pre-screening may in turn hasten the time needed for the entrepreneur to secure a face to face meeting with a potential private investor.

A more significant difference was reported in the elapsed time between the first meeting and the receipt of funds. The median elapsed time was 2.5 months for private investors and 4.5 months for venture capital funds. The shorter deliberation time ("due diligence") for angel deals may be due to the smaller number of people involved in the decision process or to the fact that angels tend to invest in fields with which they are familiar.

The Cost of Venture Capital

Significant differences existed in entrepreneurs' perceptions of the rates of return required by angels and venture capital funds. Median returns expected by angels were 32.5% per annum compared to 40% for venture capital funds. This difference is also counterintuitive, given the propensity of angels to invest more often than venture capital funds in high-risk seed and start-up deals. One explanation may be a factor unique to angel financing. In addition to competitive financial rewards, individual investors often consider the non-financial characteristics of their investments and thus part of their return is in the form of psychic income. Previous research (Wetzel 1983) indicates that fifty percent of angel investors reported that they accept lower returns or assume higher risks when the ventures they back are expected to create jobs in their communities, commercialize socially useful technology (such as medical, energy saving or environmental technology), assist women entrepreneurs or entrepreneurs from ethnic minority groups. The most influential non-financial factor was the satisfaction derived from assisting an entrepreneur build a successful business. Entrepreneurs sensitive to the match between the characteristics of their ventures and the personal tastes of angels should be able to raise funds on terms that are attractive to both parties. While the explanation may depend on the specific investment, entrepreneurs perceive angel financing to be less expensive than financing by venture capital funds. Although differences exist in the required return, both angel and venture capital fund investors are perceived to have similar exit horizons. The median holding period expectation for angels was 4.75 years and 5 years for venture capital funds.

Value-Added Investors

Both angels and venture capital funds invest their know-how as well as their capital in the ventures they finance (Ehrlich, De Noble, Moore and Weaver 1994; Harrison and Mason 1992). Entrepreneurs reported that 80% of angel investors and 81% of venture capital funds maintained a working relationship with their firms. For both groups, the most common form of this working relationship was representation on the board of directors. Although not as prevalent as board representation, a majority of the private investors and venture capital funds also served as consultants to the entrepreneurial venture. In addition, individual investors participated in ways not open to venture capital funds, with nearly a quarter of the private individuals working in a full or part-time capacity for the firms in which they had invested.

In addition to capital, entrepreneurs recognize a significant value-added component in their investor relationships. Table 4 summarizes the evaluation by entrepreneurs of the quality of this value-added component. Almost three-quarters of the entrepreneurs who had a working relationship with their private investors consider this relationship to be productive. Similar results were found for venture capital funds, with nearly eighty percent of the entrepreneurs rating the relationship as productive. Thus, both angels and venture capital funds add a significant value to their equity investments through a productive working relationships with the firms they bankroll.

Conclusions

The invisible angel segment of the venture capital markets appears to play a central role in maintaining the vitality of the US entrepreneurial economy. It appears that for new technology-based ventures angels are the most common source of seed and start-up financing, especially if the round of financing is less than $500 thousand.

Despite the fact that there are no directories of business angels, entrepreneurs report that it takes less time to find and close a deal with angels than with venture capital funds and the financing is perceived to be less expensive. The value angels place on the non-financial characteristics of the venture they back is a distinguishing feature of the angel segment of the venture capital market in the U.S. Both angels and venture capital funds add value to their investments through the establishment of working relationships with the ventures they finance, and entrepreneurs perceive these working relationships to be a productive component of the deal.

The history of business in the United States is the history of equity financing. For entrepreneurs, raising equity is arduous. Multiple rejections are part of the process. However, business history and the stock market pay tribute to the entrepreneurs who stuck it out. The vital role played by business angels is slowly being recognized, but their know-how and their capital are still largely untapped entrepreneurial resources. Entrepreneurs who understand the distinctive roles of angels and venture capital funds can save time and increase the odds of raising capital from the right source at the right time.

References

Aram, J.D. 1987 *Informal Risk Capital in the Eastern Great Lakes Region*, Washington DC: Office of Advocacy, U.S. Small Business Administration.

Avery, R.B. and Elliehausen, G.E. 1986 Financial Characteristics of High Income Families, *Federal Reserve Bulletin*, 72 (3) pp 163-177.

Birch, D., Haggerty, A., Parsons, W., and Rossel, C. 1993 *Entrepreneurial Hot Spots*, Cognetics Inc., April 1993, p. 4.

Birch, D.L. 1988 The Hidden Economy, *The Wall Street Journal*, June 10, 1988, p. 23R.

Birch, D.L. 1987 *The Atomization of America*, INC., March 1987, p. 21.

Bygrave, W.D., and Timmons, J.A. 1992 *Venture Capital at the Crossroads* (Boston: Harvard Business School Press).

Corporate Technology Information Services, Inc., 1986 Woburn, MA.

Ehrlich, S., De Noble, A., Moore, T., and Weaver, R. 1994 After the Cash Arrives: A Comparative Study of Venture Capital and Private

Investor Involvement in Entrepreneurial Firms, *Journal of Business Venturing*, 9: pp 67-82.

Freear, J., Sohl, J.E., and Wetzel, W.E., Jr. 1994 Angels and Non Angels: Are There Differences?, *Journal of Business Venturing*, 9: pp 109-123.

Freear, J., Sohl, J.E., and Wetzel, W.E., Jr. 1990 Raising venture capital: Entrepreneurs' views of the process. In N. Churchill, W. Bygrave, J. Hornaday, D. Muzyka, K. Vesper, and W. Wetzel, eds., *Frontiers of Entrepreneurship Research*, Wellesley, MA: Babson College.

Freear, J., and Wetzel, W.E., Jr. March, 1990 Who Bankrolls High-Tech Entrepreneurs?, *Journal of Business Venturing*, 5: pp 77-89.

Gaston, R.J. 1989a *Finding Private Venture Capital for Your Firm: A Complete Guide* (New York: John Wiley & Sons).

Gaston, R.J. 1989b The Scale of Informal Capital Markets, *Small Business Economics*, 1: pp 223-230.

Gaston, R.J., and Bell, S.E. 1986 *Informal Risk Capital Investment in the Sunbelt Region*, Washington, DC: Office of Advocacy, U.S. Small Business Administration.

Gaston, R.J., and Bell, S.E. 1988 *The Informal Supply of Capital*, Washington, DC: Office of Economic Research, U.S. Small Business Administration.

Haar, N.E., Starr, J., and MacMillan, I.C. 1988 Informal Risk Capital Investors: Investment Patterns on the East Coast of the USA, *Journal of Business Venturing*, 3: 11-29.

Hale, 1992 For New Jobs, Help Small Business, *The Wall Street Journal*, August 10, 1992.

Harrison, R., and Mason, C. May, 1993 Finance for the Growing Business: The Role of Informal Investment, *National Westminster Quarterly Review*, pp 17-29.

Harrison, R., and Mason, C. 1992 The Roles of Investors in Entrepreneurial Companies: A Comparison of Informal Investors and Venture Capitalists In N. Churchill, S. Birley, W. Bygrave, D. Muzyka, C. Wahlbin and W. Wetzel, eds., *Frontiers of Entrepreneurship Research*, Wellesley, MA: Babson College.

Huey, J. 1994 Working Up to the New Economy, *Fortune*, June 27, 1994, pp. 36-46.

INC., October, 1992.

Landstrom, H. 1993 Informal Risk Capital in Sweden and Some International Comparisons, *Journal of Business Venturing*, 8: pp 525-540.

Landstrom, H. 1992 The Relationship Between Private Investors and Small Firms: An Agency Theory Approach, *Entrepreneurship and Regional Development*, 4: pp 199-223.

Mason, C.M., and Harrison, R.T. 1992 The Supply of Equity Finance in the UK: A Strategy for Closing the Equity Gap, *Entrepreneurship and Regional Development*, 4: pp 357-380.

Morris, J.K., Isenstein, S., and Knowles, A. eds. 1990 Pratt's *Guide to Venture Capital Sources* (Needham, MA: Venture Economics, Inc.) pp 2-3.

Ou, C. 1987 *Holdings of Privately-Held Business by American Families: Findings from the 1983 Consumer Finance Survey*, unpublished manuscript, Office of Economic Research, U.S. Small Business Administration, Washington, D.C.

Postma, P.D., and Sullivan, M.K. 1990 *Informal Risk Capital in the Knoxville Region*, Unpublished report, The University of Tennessee.

Riding, A., and Short, D. 1987 Some Investor and Entrepreneur Perspectives on the Informal Market for Risk Capital, *Journal of Small Business and Entrepreneurship*, 5: pp 19-30.

Teitelbaum, R.S. 1994 Hats Off! It was a Heck of a Year, *Fortune*, April 18, 1994, p. 210.

Wetzel, W.E., Jr., Summer 1983 Angels and Informal Risk Capital, *Sloan Management Review*, 24: pp 23-34.

TABLE 1
ROUNDS INVESTED IN NTBFs

Size of Round	Private Individuals		Venture Capital Funds		Total
<$250,000	102	58%	8	5%	110
$250,000-$499,999	43	24%	14	8%	57
$500,000-$999,999	15	8%	31	18%	46
≥ $1,000,000	17	10%	120	69%	137
Total	177	100%	173	100%	350

TABLE 2
DOLLARS INVESTED IN NTBFs
(millions of U.S. dollars)

Stage	Private Individuals	Venture Capital Funds	Other	Total
Seed	12	11	3	26
Start-up	29	63	52	144
First Stage	13	118	39	170
Second Stage	15	111	65	191
Third Stage	2	59	46	107
Bridge	5	8	20	33
Total	76	370	225	671

TABLE 3
ROUNDS INVESTED IN NTBFs

Size of Round	Private Individuals		Venture Capital Funds		Total
Seed	52	29%	11	6%	63
Start-up	55	31%	38	22%	93
First Stage	29	16%	56	32%	85
Second Stage	26	15%	46	27%	72
Third Stage	10	6%	19	11%	29
Bridge	5	3%	3	2%	8
Total	177	100%	173	100%	350

TABLE 4
QUALITY OF THE WORKING RELATIONSHIP

	Angels	Venture Capital Funds
Very Productive	44%	39%
Moderately Productive	30%	39%
Neutral	22%	13%
Moderately Counterproductive	4%	8%
Very Counterproductive	0%	2%

THE PRIVATE INVESTOR MARKET FOR VENTURE CAPITAL

JOHN FREEAR, JEFFREY E. SOHL, AND WILLIAM E. WETZEL, JR.

The writers are members of the Center for Venture Research, Whittemore School of Business and Economics, University of New Hampshire. This paper appeared in the May 1994 issue of *The Financier: ACMT*, vol. 1, no. 2.

Introduction

Entrepreneurial ventures may be distinguished from the population of small businesses by their growth potential, their vision, and their plans to achieve that vision. An entrepreneurial venture seeking external equity capital has essentially two choices - one visible and one invisible. The visible venture capital market is composed of over five hundred venture capital funds that manage about $35 billion, roughly equal to the total assets of one large regional bank, the Bank of Boston for example. Pratt's Guide to Venture Capital Sources (1993) is a comprehensive directory of venture capital funds in the United States. In the early 90's, venture capital funds were investing between $2 and $3 billion in about two thousand ventures per year - not a lot of capital in the grand scheme of things. More funds change hands before noon every trading day on the New York Stock Exchange. A typical round of financing from venture funds is a later stage deal in excess of $1 million (Freear and Wetzel, 1990). About two-thirds of these venture investments were additional investments in ventures already in their portfolios.

The Invisible Venture Capital Market

The invisible venture capital market is the oldest and the largest source of venture financing. It is made up of a diverse and dispersed population of private investors, commonly referred to as business angels. Using data from the 1983 Survey of Consumer Finance, Charles Ou (1983) estimated that two million U.S. families held equity investments totalling $300 billion in privately-held businesses in which they had no management involvement, an average of about $150,000 per household. By comparison the 1983 portfolios of venture capital funds amounted to about $20 billion. Gaston and Bell (1988) examined the rate of informal venture investing based on a sample of 435 private investors identified through a sample of business enterprises, stratified by employment size and region, drawn from Dun's Market Identifier file. Gaston and Bell estimated that 720,000 investors annually made 489,000 informal venture investment with a mean dollar value per investment of $66,700. These numbers imply an annual flow of informal equity capital of $33 billion. During the same period, venture capital funds were investing about $3 billion annually, with an average investment of about $1 million.

Focussing on self-made private investors with a net worth in excess of $1 million provides a better comparison of the private investor and the venture fund capital markets. According to TIME magazine (1988): "An estimated 2 million U.S. men and women are millionaires, and nearly 90% of them earned their fortune by starting their own firm." In a 1986 cover story, "Ordinary Millionaires, " U.S. News and World Report (1986) claimed that the typical millionaire is a self-made entrepreneur and that 85% of America's millionaires own their own business or a share in a private company. The most visible examples of self-made mega-millionaires can be found on the 1993 Forbes Four Hundred Richest People in America (1993). The top five names (net worth in excess of $5 billion each) were Warren Buffett (Berkshire Hathaway), William Gates (Microsoft), John Kluge (Metromedia), Sumner Redstone (Viacom International) and the family of the late Samuel Walton (Wal-Mart Stores). As a group, the Forbes Four Hundred commands an estimated net worth of $328 billion.

Avery and Elliehausen (1986), using 1983 data, found that the net worth of 1.3 million U.S. families (about 2% of all households) was at least $1 million. Their data suggested that most of the wealth was saved from accumulated earnings, not inherited. The wealth, income and asset distribution of the top 1% of U.S. households (840,000 families) indicated that 37% had invested $151 billion in non-public businesses in which they had no management interest. The Avery and Elliehausen study also provided insights into the risk and liquidity attitudes of high income households. Compared to all U.S. families, high income households displayed a significantly higher propensity to assume above average financial risks in order to earn above average returns. High income families also displayed a significantly higher propensity to tie up funds for long periods of time in order to earn substantial returns.

These glimpses into the invisible world of angel financing suggest that, conservatively, the informal venture capital market is made up of several hundred thousand high net worth individuals, most with business and entrepreneurial experience, who invest at least $10-$20 billion in over thirty thousand ventures per year.

Angels and Technology-Based Firms

For technology-based firms, financing from private investors typically is a seed or start-up round in the $100 thousand to $500 thousand range, raised from six or eight investors (Freear and Wetzel, 1990). Co-investors usually are trusted friends and business associates.

The respective roles of professional venture funds and individual investors tend to be complementary rather than competitive (Freear and Wetzel, 1990). This complementary relationship has two dimensions - size and stage. First, at all stages, venture capital funds tend to invest substantially more dollars per round than private investors. Size differences become more pronounced as the stage of the financing advances. Second, private investors exhibit a significantly higher propensity to invest at the seed and start up stages than other investors. These investors also appear to have longer exit horizons and less risk aversion than their venture fund counterparts. Private investors are providing the seed capital that spawns new ventures. As the venture grows, it begins to outstrip the ability of individual investors to supply adequate equity capital. At this point, somewhere in the $500,000 to $1,000,000 financing range, professional venture capital funds may take an interest in the venture, particularly if the venture has demonstrated some success and has moved beyond the highly risky seed and start up stages of its development towards sustainable growth.

Market Efficiency

Imperfections in the informal venture capital market are well documented, for both North America (Riding and Short, 1987; Haar, Starr and MacMillian, 1988; Gaston, 1989; Freear, Sohl and Wetzel, 1994) and Europe (Landstrom, 1992; Mason and Harrison, 1992; Harrison and Mason, 1993; Landstrom, 1993). Imperfections are in part due to the largely invisible nature of the informal venture capital market and are manifested in the difficulty identifying the components of the market. There are no directories of private investors, no public records of their investment transactions, few vehicles for bringing together potential investors and ventures seeking funds, and transactions costs are high. In other words, seed and start-up financing for entrepreneurs is a scarce resource traded in an inefficient market.

Efficient markets allocate scarce resources to their most productive uses. Efficient markets are characterized by fully-informed buyers and sellers of capital and by low transactions costs. The visible venture capital fund segment of the capital markets is relatively efficient with respect to the informal market. However, neither the full information nor the low transaction cost criteria is fulfilled in the invisible angel venture capital market.

Researchers have identified the existence of at least two inefficiencies in the equity financing market for entrepreneurial ventures (Obermayer, 1983; Wilson, 1984). One is the "equity financing gap" between the needs of ventures seeking equity funds and the requirements of potential investors. These capital shortages include product development financing for technology-based inventors, start-up and early-stage financing for ventures that fail to meet the size, stage and growth criteria of venture capital funds and equity financing for closely-held firms growing faster than internal cash flows can support. Institutional investors may perceive a venture investment to be too small, too illiquid and too risky, particularly at the seed and start up stages. The debate over capital gaps overlooks the record of individual venture investors - business angels. Angels not only exist, they tend to invest in precisely the areas perceived as gaps in the capital markets for entrepreneurs (Wetzel, 1983). The second market inefficiency, however, now becomes significant.

275

The second market inefficiency arises when market mechanisms fail to match suppliers of equity capital with needy ventures in a timely way. An efficient market implies an unrestricted and timely flow of reliable information about financing sources and investment opportunities, and relative ease of market entry and exit. Venture capital funds are easier to locate than individual investors. Entrepreneurs have ready access to names, addresses, phone numbers, fax numbers, and descriptions of professional venture capital funds. There are no such public lists of individual investors, who, to avoid being swamped by would-be entrepreneurs seeking equity financing, tend to seek a degree of anonymity consistent with the need to maintain a reasonable deal flow. Consequently, the individual investors with the means to fill the "equity financing gap," -- the first market inefficiency, operate in an informal venture capital market in which information flows very inefficiently -- the second market inefficiency.

Characteristics of Angels

Given the position of high net worth individuals as the key source of early stage equity financing for technology-based ventures and the inefficiencies in the informal venture capital market, it is imperative to understand the characteristics of these business angels. Only through an understanding of these characteristics can one be in a position to develop effective policies that are designed to increase the efficiency of the equity financing market. In the context of the current research, two distinguishing features of angels are studied. First, the source of investment opportunities and the efficiency of each referral source is examined. Second, the locational characteristics of venture investing is summarized. In the discussion that follows, the basis for the majority of the conclusions was gleaned from a survey of high net worth individuals who have experience in venture investing (for a discussion of the survey methodology and additional characteristics of venture investors see Freear, Sohl, and Wetzel 1994).

Sources of Investment Opportunities

Recent studies have identified the dominant role of friends and business associates as sources of investment opportunities for would-be investors in entrepreneurial ventures (Freear and Wetzel 1989; Postma and Sullivan 1990). As early as 1970, the Panel on Venture Capital of the U.S. Department of Commerce Technical Advisory Board (1970) cited the informal network of people, institutions and relationships that are significant in the process of financing new enterprises. The Panel found that the informal network does not operate with the same degree of effectiveness in every geographic region of the country. Early in the development of the venture capital industry in the United States, Rubenstein (1958) reported that private investors were even more dependent on informal networks than venture capital funds. Rubenstein found that the fraternity of individual backers of small enterprises is rather close knit, at least on the local level, and that a good deal of information is passed about by word of mouth. The current research supports these conclusions concerning the role of friends and business associates in the informal venture market, but also provides evidence as to the importance of additional sources of venture investments.

Several measures are developed to ascertain the relative merits of various sources of investment opportunities for business angels. Information concerning the venture investment activity of one hundred and fifty angels over a five year period (1987-1991) indicates that this group of angels seriously considered 1577 investment opportunities in new technology-based firms (Freear, Sohl, and Wetzel 1994). From this group a total of 525 investments were made, resulting in an overall yield (or efficiency index) of thirty-three percent. In the context of the current study, yield is defined as investments made as a percentage of investments seriously considered for each referral source. Of the 1577 investment opportunities considered thirty-five percent (558) originated from business associates, followed by fifteen percent (240) from friends, and twelve percent (183) from a lead investor A lead investor is defined as an individual who committed funds and took the initiative to find additional private investors.

For those opportunities that resulted in a commitment of funds by an angel, the largest group (thirty percent or 159 investments) originated from business associates, followed closely by friends (twenty-five percent or 133 investments). Taking the investment considered/made dichotomy collectively indicates that friends were found to have the highest yield factor, over 55 percent, followed by a yield of 42 percent for entrepreneurial ventures seeking funds. Business associates and venture capital funds, with a yield of approximately 28 percent, were the next most effective source of investment opportunities, closely followed by lead investors. The remaining sources most often cited by active equity investors, attorneys, investment bankers, accountants, active personal search and commercial bankers, all showed yield factors below twenty percent.

This information concerning the total volume of venture investment activity and total yield per referral source appears to support earlier research findings on the importance of friends in facilitating the flow of worthy investment opportunities. In addition to supporting the existing research, the yield factors indicate that this network of "personal contacts" is extended to include both business associates and lead investors. The relatively high yield factors (based on volume) of both entrepreneurial ventures that are seeking funds and the more formal venture capital funds suggest that the deal flow may be capable of expansion beyond the local network.

To investigate further the efficiency of the source of investment opportunities, the study restated yield factors on an individual investor basis. In this context all investors are weighted equally, in contrast to the previous analysis where the volume of investments was the weighting factor. These investor yield factors are an acknowledgement of the distinguishing features of the individual's investment approach (source of investment opportunities) and attempt to discern the similarities among individual investors, regardless of the volume of their investment activity.

Using the individual investor as the unit of measurement the data support and emphasize the unique position of the personal network in the deal flow. In this context, the 558 investment opportunities that originated from business associates were considered by seventy-nine investors, indicating an average of 7.1 investments considered per individual. From this group of potential investments a total of 159 investments were made by sixty-seven investors, or an average of 2.4 investments (that originated from business associates) per investor. Similarly, for venture investment opportunities that originated from friends, an average of 4.1 investments were considered, resulting in 3.02 investments made per individual investor.

While these data indicate a sense of the activity of each investor, yield factors based on individual investors are more revealing. In this context, business associates were found to have the highest average yield factor per investor (forty-six percent), followed closely by friends (forty-two percent) and lead investors (thirty-eight percent). The role of the "non-personal" originators of the deal flow is somewhat diminished when yield is based on the individual investor. Specifically, venture capital funds and entrepreneurial ventures seeking funds both have yield factors of approximately thirty percent. While these factors are not trivial, they are smaller, on a relative basis, and indicate a lesser role of these sources in the individual's investment approach.

Analysis of the yield factors for the informal venture capital market reveals several interesting implications concerning the efficiency of the market. These yield factors underscore the importance of friends, business associates, and, to a somewhat lesser degree, lead investors. In situations where the investment opportunities originate from friends or business associates, one investment is actually made, on average, for every two investment opportunities seriously considered. For lead investors this ratio is approximately one in three. These factors taken collectively indicate the importance of the informal "personal contact" network in the exchange of information regarding early stage technology-based investment opportunities. It is widely held that the imperfections in the informal market are in part due to the invisible nature of the market, which results in a lack of the free and open exchange of information regarding investment opportunities. The possibility exists, however, of some local efficiencies within the network of trusted friends and business associates. The challenge facing both entrepreneurs and business angels is to develop mechanisms that facilitate the transfer of this information in a more efficient manner and to a wider audience.

Locational Considerations

An analysis of the locational characteristics of the informal venture investing market reveal several distinguishing features and interesting implications. Information concerning the location of the venture investments made by one hundred and forty-six angels over a five year period (1987-1991) indicates that half (fifty-two percent) of these angels invested in entrepreneurial ventures that were located within fifty miles of their primary residence (Freear, Sohl, and Wetzel 1994). In addition, for nearly one-third of the angels the venture was located between 50 and 300 miles of their home. On the investment activity side, these angels made thirty-seven percent of their venture investments within the fifty mile zone, and sixty-five percent of their completed deals were within 300 miles of their primary residence. As these geographical boundaries increased, the investment activity exhibited a dramatic decline, with only six percent of the investments and five percent of the angels investing in ventures outside of North America.

These locational characteristics indicate a distinguishing feature of the informal venture investment market. It appears that this local focus may support the notion of the importance of non-financial factors inherent in the business angel investment decision. These non-financial factors include the value-added component and the intrinsic satisfaction derived by angels investing in entrepreneurial ventures. Value-added identifies the situation where angels provide more than financial backing to the venture in which invest, through the establishment of a working relationship with the venture (Freear, Sohl and Wetzel 1990). Intrinsic satisfaction may lead angels to accept lower returns or assume higher risks. Wetzel (1983) identifies the intrinsic benefit that angel investors derive from ventures that are expected to create jobs in their communities, commercialize socially useful technology (such as medical, energy saving or environmental technology), assist women entrepreneurs or entrepreneurs from ethnic minority groups. The most influential non-financial factor was the satisfaction derived from assisting an entrepreneur build a successful business. Taken collectively, these non-financial factors inherently require a proximity to the venture in order to be in a position to take advantage of these unique features of venture investing.

These non-financial factors and the high investment yield rates of local networks of friends and business associates combine to suggest that limited market efficiency may exist at the local level and that venture investments tend to be local. In addition, these factors suggest that limited information about opportunities further from home may be inhibiting investment activity. Although these factors may indicate some limited local market efficiency, more effective methods of identifying opportunities further from home should have a positive impact on the rate of angel investing. Thus, a goal of researchers is to provide mechanisms to maintain the local efficiencies of the informal venture investing market and facilitate the extension of these limited local efficiencies to a broader range of entrepreneurs and business angels.

Venture Capital Networks

A better organized and more formal network would serve to improve efficiency by bringing investors and entrepreneurs together without breaching the anonymity and confidentiality requirements of either. The experience of the Venture Capital Network, Inc., (VCN), provides a case study on the operations, financing, and performance of such a network.

In 1984, VCN was established as a not-for-profit corporation affiliated with the Center for Venture Research at the University of New Hampshire. In the light of early, pioneering research into the informal venture capital market (Seymour and Wetzel, 1981), VCN defined itself as being in the information business. It was an experiment intended to increase the flow of information. In so doing, it would reduce the equity financing gap, by bringing together entrepreneurs and potential investors (mostly individual investors). Its concentration on information flow precluded it from any form of evaluation of entrepreneurs or investors, and from any role once the introductions had been made. Investors were seen as the best judges of investment opportunities, and entrepreneurs were advised to evaluate the suitability of potential investors. The clearly and narrowly defined mission enabled VCN to obtain "no action" letters from the Securities and Exchange Commission, enabling it to operate without registering under the Investment Advisors Act of 1940 or the Securities and Exchange Acts of 1933 and 1934.

To do its work, VCN needed a client base of entrepreneurs and investors. Initially, there are likely to be more entrepreneurial ventures seeking funds than individual investors seeking investment opportunities. Individual investors proved to be reluctant to enter the client base unless and until the network could demonstrate an adequate flow of venture opportunities and a high degree of confidentiality and professionalism. To attract investors, it had to be able to list enough ventures. To attract and maintain ventures, it had to be able to list enough investors.

VCN Operations and Financing

VCN established a confidential computerized data base of Investment Opportunity Profiles of entrepreneurs, and Investment Interest Profiles of investors. It submitted to investors those investment opportunities that met their screening criteria. At this juncture, the process was anonymous. If an investor expressed interest in further information about a venture, VCN introduced the entrepreneur to the investor.

To build the profiles, VCN asked clients to complete a registration form. Entrepreneur clients submitted an executive summary of their business plan. The form asked questions about industry category, financing stage, amount of capital needed, managerial and technical assistance needed, expected extent of investor involvement in the business, and whether the entrepreneur wished to have the details sent just to individual investors, or to venture capital funds, or both.

VCN asked investor clients to identify themselves as individual investors, institutional investors or venture capitalists. The registration form sought information about their financing criteria, geographic restrictions, the stages and amounts of financing in which they were most interested, preferred industry categories, and their willingness to participate with other investors in financing ventures. VCN asked investors to provide basic biographical data, to help VCN accumulate broad investor profiles.

As with any other start up venture, a network requires time --at least five years -- to build its organization and its client base to a viable level. During this period, the network must find financing to supplement client fees. Several public and private organizations provided significant funding to help launch VCN. The University of New Hampshire gave VCN considerable assistance by providing office space and all utilities except telephone charges. In the three years prior to VCN's move to M.I.T., the University also provided operating support. Client fees supplied about sixty per cent of VCN's operating budget during that period.

During the first fourteen months of operations, VCN permitted private investors to enroll for one year at no charge. Over three hundred investors enrolled during that period. Many were curious observers (or, perhaps, potential new entrants to the informal venture capital market) rather than serious investors. The number of investors dropped to about one hundred when VCN introduced enrollment fees. Despite the high attrition rate, open and free enrollment was an effective way of building an initial investor clientele. In addition, VCN experimented with paid advertising in the media, but it proved not to be cost-effective. VCN sought aggressively opportunities to speak about its mission and its services before professional and civic organizations of all kinds. Accountants, attorneys, bankers and venture capitalists were frequent sources of client referrals. The implied or explicit endorsement of VCN by a referral from these groups added a valuable element of credibility to VCN in the minds of investors and entrepreneurs.

At the time of its transfer to M.I.T. at the end of 1990, VCN was charging entrepreneurs $125 for a six month registration. It charged individual investors $250, institutional investors $500 and overseas investors $1,000, for a twelve month registration. At its peak, VCN's operating budget was about $130,000. This supported a staff of two full-time employees (Project Director and Operations Manager), two half-time employees (Assistant Operations Manager and

Secretary/Office Manager), and four work/study students, each working ten hours per week. VCN's president and principal external spokesperson served without pay while maintaining full-time faculty responsibilities at the Whittemore School of Business and Economics at the University of New Hampshire.

Discussions began with the M.I.T. Enterprise Forum, with which it had enjoyed a six-year history of collaboration on programs promoting the entrepreneurial cause, but which did not have a capital formation process of its own. VCN's reputation among entrepreneurs and individual investors, and the fact that over eighty per cent of the ventures that raised funds through VCN were technology-based, led to the relocation of VCN to M.I.T. as a not-for-profit affiliate of the Enterprise Forum of Cambridge. The move to M.I.T. was completed in December 1990. VCN was renamed Technology Capital Network, Inc., (TCN) in 1992.

VCN Investor Profiles, 1985-1992

VCN's entrepreneurs and investors expressed their strongest interest in manufacturing, especially high-technology manufacturing, service industries, and the medical and health care industry. They expressed some interest also in real estate, financial and high-technology related services, computer software, and the publishing and communications industry.

VCN enrolled 409 investor clients in the 1985-1992 period, of whom about three-quarters were individual investors and about one-fifth were venture capitalists. The characteristics of VCN's individual investors were similar to those found by other studies (see, for example, Krasner and Tymes, 1983; Aram, 1987 and 1989; Freear and Wetzel, 1989; Harr, Starr and Macmillan, 1988; Gaston and Bell, 1988; Postma and Sullivan, 1990). Sixty-one per cent lived in New England, and 70 per cent held a master's degree or doctorate. Investors reported professional backgrounds in executive positions, entrepreneurial ventures, venture capital, engineering, technology, marketing, finance or operations. They sought venture investments in New England and the Middle Atlantic states, with only 12 per cent expressing a willingness to invest outside the United States and Canada.

Individual investors looked for ventures with growth projections in the $1 million to $5 million range over five years. These expectations were lower than the $5 million to $40 million over five years of the

283

venture capitalists in VCN's data base. Individual investors expressed little interest in single investments of over $1 million, and venture capitalists showed no interest in investments of under $50,000. As individual investor interest declined at about $500,000, so venture capitalist interest began to pick up. This complementary relationship was identified by another study (Freear and Wetzel, 1990). Both individual investors and venture capital funds offered more than financing. They offered assistance in financial management and marketing, and to a lesser extent in production, personnel, and research and development.

Investors' growth expectations generally followed a declining pattern over the period as the recession set in. Investors' interest in the various financing stages indicated a willingness to consider all stages and remained stable over the 1985-1992 period. Over that period, the amounts investors were willing to invest remained somewhat stable, although the higher amounts of $500,000 and over declined in relation to amounts in the $100,000 to $250,000 range.

Most investors had made at least one investment over the preceding five years, and many had made several. Only 18 per cent had never made an entrepreneurial investment, and this percentage of "new" investors declined in the latter part of the period, 1989-1992. Nevertheless, the drawing in of new investors, attracted by the relative ease of access to investment opportunities through VCN, provides additional evidence of the existence of many potential "business angels" awaiting a chance to enter the informal venture capital market (see Freear, Sohl and Wetzel, 1994).

As other studies have found (Harr, Starr and Macmillan, 1988; Freear and Wetzel, 1989; Freear, Sohl and Wetzel, 1990), most of the investors were willing to participate with other investors in funding ventures in greater amounts than they were willing or able to invest individually. Investors offered non-financial assistance in the form of membership of the board of directors or informal consulting help. Less often, they worked part time, or even full time, for the venture. In only a few cases was the participation limited to the receipt of periodic reports and attendance at stockholder meetings. For the most part, though, individual investors prefer to invest in ventures that are located within about one hundred miles, probably so that they can more easily place their expertise at the disposal of the ventures in which they invest (Harr, Starr and MacMillan, 1988; Freear and Wetzel, 1989).

Measures of VCN's Effectiveness

VCN considered its geographical market to be the six New England states, with a population of about fifteen million. The total number of active individual investors in the region was estimated to be at least ten thousand. The total number of self-made, high net worth individuals, who might be regarded as potential individual investors, was estimated to be about eighty thousand.

Between 1984 and 1990, VCN served about 1,200 entrepreneur clients and 800 investor clients. Approximately 35,000 computer matches resulted in about 3,500 investor requests for introductions to entrepreneurs. About 25 per cent of VCN's entrepreneur clients received no introductions, principally because the submitted business plans were inadequately prepared or developed. Leaving aside the entrepreneurs who received no investor introductions, the typical entrepreneur met four or five potential investors. Once the introductions were made, VCN was precluded by its agreement with the SEC from playing any further role, and lost systematic contact with its clients at that point. Systematic contact ended also when an entrepreneur's registration expired. Thus, it has proved impossible to measure accurately the number of actual investments that occurred as a result of VCN introductions.

Nevertheless, it is known that VCN arranged more than 3,500 introductions for over 900 entrepreneurs from 30 states and over 300 investors from 33 states. Through follow-up telephone interviews and other sources, VCN learned that its entrepreneurial clients had raised some $12 million from about fifty investors, for thirty-one ventures. Approximately 80 per cent of those ventures were technology-based ventures, which may be a reflection of the nature of the New England economy and of the interests of its individual investors. Further, the interest in VCN has led to the formation, with VCN's active participation and encouragement, of at least six similar networks across the country and in Canada.

Conclusions

The informal venture capital market has been the least studied and is the least visible and understood of all capital markets. Its many participating investors have the potential to reduce substantially the equity financing gap between the needs of ventures seeking equity funds and the requirements of potential investors. Several studies have confirmed the size and potential of the market as well as the

285

complementary relationship (in terms of the amount and stage of financing) between the informal venture capital market and the professional venture capital market.

The informal venture capital market, however, tends to be in the form of self-contained local networks of investors, who obtain information about investment opportunities from a variety of mostly local sources. The evidence suggests that the most efficient sources of information are friends, business associates and "lead" investors. The localized nature of the markets stems from two important characteristics of angel investors. First, angel investors frequently bring expertise, knowledge and experience to the venture, all of which are more easily tapped by the venture if the investor lives nearby. Second, angel investors are sometimes swayed by local, non-financial considerations, such as the desire to create jobs in their own communities.

As individual investors seek a deal flow and entrepreneurs seek investors through informal, mostly local, networks and contacts, a more organized and formal network should improve information flows in the local "market." In addition, a network would allow access to informal markets over a wider geographical area. Venture Capital Network, Inc. (and its re-incarnation, Technology Venture Capital, Inc.) represents a case study of an attempt to increase the efficiency of information flows in the informal venture capital market. VCN's success has been limited by its own difficulties in finding adequate financial support, yet its success, and that of other networks based on its principles, are real and, to an extent, measurable.

Networks, however, will not solve all problems. There will be inefficiencies if the market for equity capital remains segmented. The existence of networks will not cause reluctant potential investors to enter the market, nor will it cause owners of "life style" firms to attempt to expand their businesses by using external equity capital. Networks organized along the lines of VCN offer no guarantees regarding the quality and attributes of either the investor or the entrepreneur clients, and bow out of the process as soon as the introductions are made. They have no role in quality control, nor in pricing, structuring or monitoring any deal, all of which are significant factors determining the ultimate success or failure of an enterprise.

Despite these limitations, networks such as VCN have a potentially important role in increasing market efficiency, and thus in reducing the equity financing gap. They provide a confidential means of drawing from a wider geographical area to bring entrepreneurs and investors together, and of offering investors a reasonable flow of investment opportunities. Further, they provide the means to expand the informal venture capital market by lowering barriers to the entry into the market of potential new individual investors.

References

Aram, J.D. 1987 Informal Risk Capital in the Eastern Great Lakes Region, Washington, D.C., Office of Advocacy, U.S. Small Business Administration.

Aram, J.D. 1989 Attitudes and Behaviors of Informal Investors Toward Early-Stage Investments, Technology-Based Ventures, and Co-investors, Journal of Business Venturing, 4 (5) pp 333-347.

Avery, R.B. and Elliehausen, G.E. 1986 Financial Characteristics of High Income Families, Federal Reserve Bulletin, 72 (3) pp 163-177.

Freear, J., and Wetzel, W.E, Jr 1989 Equity Capital for Entrepreneurs. In R. H. Brockhaus, et al., eds, Frontiers of Entrepreneurship Research, Wellesley, MA: Babson College.

Freear, J., and Wetzel, W.E., Jr. March, 1990 Who Bankrolls High-Tech Entrepreneurs?, Journal of Business Venturing, 5 (2): pp 77-89.

Freear, J., Sohl, J.E., and Wetzel, W.E., Jr. 1990 Raising venture capital: Entrepreneurs' views of the process. In N. Churchill, W. Bygrave, J. Hornaday, D. Muzyka, K. Vesper, and W. Wetzel, eds., Frontiers of Entrepreneurship Research, Wellesley, MA: Babson College.

Freear, J., Sohl, J.E., and Wetzel, W.E., Jr. 1994 Angels and Non-Angels: Are There Differences?, Journal of Business Venturing, 9: 109-123.

Gaston, R.J. 1989 Finding Private Venture Capital for Your Firm: A Complete Guide (New York: John Wiley and Sons).

Gaston, R.J., and Bell, S.E. 1988 The Informal Supply of Capital, Washington, D.C., Office of Economic Research, U.S. Small Business Administration.

Haar, N.E., Starr, J., and MacMillan, I.C. 1988 Informal Risk Capital Investors: Investment Patterns on the East Coast of the USA, Journal of Business Venturing, 3: 11-29.

Harrison, R., and Mason, C. May, 1993 Finance for the Growing Business: The Role of Informal Investment, National Westminster Quarterly Review, pp 17-29.

Krasner O.J., and Tymes, E.R. 1983 Informal Risk Capital. In Hornaday, et al., eds, Frontiers of Entrepreneurship Research, Wellesley, MA: Babson College.

Landstrom, H. 1992 The Relationship Between Private Investors and Small Firms: An Agency Theory Approach, Entrepreneurship and Regional Development, 4: pp 199-223.

Landstrom, H. 1993 Informal Risk Capital in Sweden and Some International Comparisons, Journal of Business Venturing, 8: pp 525-540.

Mason, C.M., and Harrison, R.T. 1992 The Supply of Equity Finance in the UK: A Strategy for Closing the Equity Gap, Entrepreneurship and Regional Development, 4: pp 357-380.

Obermayer, J.H., 1983 The Capital Crunch: Small High-Technology Companies and National Objectives During a Period of Severe Debt and Equity Shortages, Cambridge, MA: Research and Planning, Inc.

Ou, C., 1987 Holdings of Privately-Held Business Assets by American Families: Findings from the 1983 Consumer Finance Survey, Washington, D.C., unpublished manuscript, Office of Economic Research, U.S. Small Business Administration.

Postma, P.D., and Sullivan, M.K. 1990 Informal Risk Capital in the Knoxville Region, Unpublished report, The University of Tennessee.

Pratt's Guide to Venture Capital Sources, 1993 Morris, J., Isenstein, S., and Knowles, A., eds, SDC Publishing, Inc, New York, NY.

Riding, A., and Short, D. 1987 Some Investor and Entrepreneur Perspectives on the Informal Market for Risk Capital, Journal of Small Business and Entrepreneurship, 5: pp 19-30.

Rubenstein, A.H. 1958 Problems of Financing and Managing New Research-Based Enterprises in New England, Boston, MA, Federal Reserve Bank of Boston.

Seymour, C.R., and Wetzel, W.E., Jr 1981 Informal Risk Capital in New England, Washington, D.C., Office of Advocacy, U.S. Small Business Administration.

288

The Forbes Four Hundred, October 18, 1993.

Time, 1988.

U.S. News and World Report, January 13, 1986.

U.S. Department of Commerce, 1970 Financing New Technological Enterprise, Report on the Panel on Venture Capital, Washington, D.C., Commerce Technical Advisory Board.

Wetzel, W.E., Jr., Summer 1983 Angels and Informal Risk Capital, Sloan Management Review, 24: pp 23-34.

Wilson, I.G. 1984 Financing High Growth Companies in New Hampshire, Concord, N.H.: Department of Resources and Economic Development, State of New Hampshire.

Early Stage Venture Capital and SCOR: Needs, New Developments, and Concerns

Granger Macy and Chip Cooper

Mr. Macy is a member of the Department of Management, University of Missouri, and Mr. Cooper is executive director of the Missouri Innovation Center.

The entrepreneurial phase of a firm is often considered to include the time between the generation of the original business idea and the point at which the business offers publicly traded securities (Amit et al., 1993). This categorization has been utilized because issuing public securities has been such a difficult source of funding for early stage companies. The public sale of securities provides a clear cut indication that an early stage company has progressed to another level. Entrepreneurs have difficulty raising money for early stage growth companies because there is no organized market for early stage companies to sell there stocks. In large part, this problem is due to the difficulties imposed by registration restrictions.

This article will examine the market for early stage capital which includes the seed and startup stages. The Small Corporate Offering

Registration process will be discussed, as well as, recent developments in the market such as the SCOR Market Maker. Ultimately, these developments may lead to a broader and more efficient market, and a significant increase in early stage capital. The article concludes with some thoughts and cautions about the future of a viable early stage marketplace.

Limitations of Early Stage Venture Capital Funding

While there are a number of options for raising seed and start-up capital, many of the sources are difficult for most early stage ventures to reach. The use of debt capital, for example, is severely restricted to early stage companies due the lack of a stable financial history and the lack of appropriate collateral. Therefore, equity capital tends to be the primary funding vehicle for most early stage companies. Unfortunately, equity capital can also be very difficult for early stage companies to utilize.

The issuance of stock is an often mentioned option for venture capital; however, it is typically a much more limited option for either early stage or even smaller later stage companies than commonly assumed. Table 1 shows the requirements for listing on the various stock exchanges across the U.S. With minimum asset requirements of $ 2 million or more, it is clear that the exchanges are weighted towards the capital requirements of larger companies. This is a major limitation. A company with a stock listed on an exchange has many advantages when seeking capital such as a ready source of buyers, issuers and sellers, issuance support, increased liquidity, and access to analyst reports and recommendations.

The vast majority of small businesses that raise risk capital do it through non-registered, exempt private securities offerings directed towards 'friends, family, and associates". These offerings are far less expensive to execute than the traditional securities registration process, but are often of limited value in reaching an adequate number of investors. Typically no public advertising is allowed and a company can lose its exempt status should, for example, a news story appear discussing the company and its efforts to sell its securities. Registration processes and restrictions have been established by the state and federal government in an effort to protect "widows and orphans" and other vulnerable citizens from becoming the unwitting targets of unscrupulous promoters. Similar motives lie at the heart of most securities regulations.

While these motivations are undoubtedly noble and have made it more difficult for scam artists to operate openly, they have also had undesirable consequences as well. Most significant is the stifling effect that such regulation has on the free exchange of information in the market for small business securities. While there are millions of people who would be qualified to participate in such offerings very few ever learn of their existence. And most devastating to the development of an early stage marketplace is that very few people see enough transactions to develop a sense of fair market value for the offered securities. Consequently, potential investors either do not know about deals or they don't have any idea whether the deal they are looking at is reasonable or unreasonable. Human nature tends to avoid the unknown and this seems to be most often the case for the early stage marketplace.

Traditional Sources of Venture Capital

There are two primary sources of venture capital, venture capital funds and business angels. According to Pratt's Guide To Venture Capital Sources, there are about 500 venture capital funds managing assets of $35 billion. Business angels, on the other hand, are individuals with a high net worth who are more interested in holding potentially higher yielding yet risky investments in startups and early stage investments. They generally have substantial business or entrepreneurial experience and differing levels of ability to analyze potential new ventures. Presently there are perhaps 250,000 business angels investing in thirty thousand ventures annually. While venture capital funds are relatively easy to access through sources such as Pratt's Guide, the business angel market is much more difficult to identify and reach. For a number of reasons which will be discussed, both of these sources have been inadequate to meet venture capital funding requirements.

Venture capital needs in the U.S. exceed the sources of supply. While venture capital needs are very difficult to accurately estimate, a conservative estimate may be $50 billion annually (Freear and Wetzel, 1992). Although this is a relatively insignificant amount compared to the capital available in the regulated markets, it far exceeds the money available from venture capital funds. In fact, venture capital funds invest only about $3-4 billion annually. Although venture capital funds are often perceived as being a major source of venture development capital, business angels may invest as much as $30 billion annually (Gaston and Bell, 1988). Even this still leaves a major investment shortfall for potentially lucrative business development.

Business angels and venture capital funds appear to play complementary roles in the financing of new ventures. While venture capital firms may be easy to find, they are an increasingly more difficult resource for the early stage venture to access. Less than 4% of the companies contacting venture capital funds actually receive funding from them. Venture capital funds look for projects with very high growth potential, and very strong management in order to minimize their risk (Bygrave and Timmons, 1992). In addition, most funds also stay away from early stage investments because the amount of capital involved is often too small (Vachon, 1993). The median investment of venture capital firms is reported to be large, approximately $450,000 to $2,000,000. This compares to a median size of from $150,000 to $200,000 for angel financing rounds (Freear & Wetzel, 1990).

Business angels are more likely to invest in the smaller, crucial rounds of financing needed by early stage ventures. Business angels are also more likely to invest when anticipated growth rates rate are moderate, 10-20% per annum, which may not be attractive enough to professional investors such as venture capital firms. Business angels thus represent the critical source of early stage funding. A primary difficulty for a start up in this case, however, is locating and involving this informal and diverse group of investors. Because of the difficulty in locating these investors, they likely represent an under exploited source of venture start up capital. The lack of an adequate market in this sector is a crucial problem to the access of early stage funding. Most often such investors are found through the entrepreneur's informal network of contacts. Useful contacts to locate such individuals are often accountants, attorneys, bankers, and other entrepreneurs. By and large though this is a hit or miss process. There are likely to be many more individuals who could be better reached. If potential investors could be more effectively reached there may be a much greater potential for investment from this sector.

Information in the Venture Capital Market

The lack of adequate entrepreneurial funding may be a symptom of a larger informational problem in the venture capital market. There are several indications of the problem. One is the lack of widely available information about new ventures. As mentioned previously, securities regulations have severely limited the open exchange of information in the market for exempt securities. It is difficult to acquire consistent good quality information about new ventures. In addition, there is also a lack of available information on the performance of comparative companies due to the absence of an organized market which would provide access to such benchmarking information. These factors make deals difficult to locate, and difficult to value because of the lack of a an adequate information base of comparable opportunities. These limitations may be the key difficulty in the availability of adequate venture capital.

In addition, this information can be difficult to assess because of the high levels of uncertainty inherent in new ventures. Entrepreneurs identify and create new business opportunities and bring together the necessary resources to actualize the new business. Uncertainty is a key characteristic of new ventures. Uncertainty to the investor is intensified by the lack of available history for early stage companies which results in an inadequate basis for making sound estimates of return and management capability. This leads to the second problem with the venture capital market; the inherent difficulty in analytically assessing the potential of a new investment.

This uncertainty may be endemic to the nature of new ventures, but appears to inhibit formal investors such as venture capital funds from taking the risks. As a result of this uncertainty and the need to produce competitive returns, venture capital funds have been modifying their evaluation criteria in an effort to optimize the risk return ratio for their investors (Bygrave and Timmons, 1991). As information about the performance of venture capital funds improves through such sources as Venture Economics, Inc., the funds have begun to identify preferred investment criteria Thus venture capital funds have been growing increasingly more cautious and have emphasized later stage investments and demands for greater returns. Venture capitalists have been found to weigh the skill and track record of the founding entrepreneur or the management team very heavily (MacMillan et al., 1985). This is followed in importance by the assessment of competitive risks, implementation risks, and easy exit. Some of the personal ability of the entrepreneur may be difficult for him or her to communicate to the venture capital funds further limiting their ability to tap these funds. Amit et al. (1990a) have suggested that low ability entrepreneurs will more likely accept a venture capitalists price offer than high ability entrepreneurs. Presumably the value of the high capability entrepreneur is not adequately reflected in the price offer.

Overall, the true element of risk involved in early stage venture projects are difficult to know with reasonable certainty and the evaluation of this risk is likely to be highly subjective and vary extensively based on the preferences of the investor. Since the risks inherent in such new activities can not be analytically estimated with satisfaction, these endeavors are characterized by high levels of uncertainty. As venture capital funds change their objectives, they have become a relatively insignificant factor in the early stage marketplace. At present most of the informal investors participating in the early stage marketplace depend on personal networks of informed associates, and these investors will often attribute significant weight to the presence of a respected lead investor (Freear and Wetzel, 1989 and 1992).

In summary, uncertainty and a lack of consistent comparable information appear to be major limitations to the development of a viable early stage marketplace. Information about early stage deals need to be more widely available both as to initial offerings and with regard to historical performance. Only through an enhanced dissemination of relevant market information will potential investors feel less anxious about entering the uniquely structured deals found in the early stage marketplace. Improved information may significantly enhance the availability of needed funds, and possibly reduce the cost since the risk might be more adequately assessed.

The SCOR Marketplace

The preceding discussion has pointed to a number of problems in the early stage capital market. Capital from public stock offerings is generally not available to early stage companies. Venture capital funds and public stock offerings are appropriate to only large and later stage investments. Most offerings for early stage companies have been limited to "family, friends, and associates". This is a major limitation for venture capital funding since the organized markets provide many sources of support in the process.

Given the limitations of existing capital sources, it is clear that early stage ventures in the seed or startup phases suffer from major limitations in the existing capital markets. An early stage market, if it can even be said to exist, is underdeveloped due to previous SEC regulations. As a result the market for such stocks is very informal with associated information based problems. It appears that meeting the need for early stage investment must be met by improving the information characteristics of the venture capital market in order to reach informal investors. If information was more systematically distributed and the risks could be more readily assessed, a larger capital market for early stage investment might be developed. If the venture capital market can be opened to a wider audience, the possibility for funding good projects may improve. In this way new capital might be tapped for those projects which don't adequately match the criteria of venture capital funds or other large scale investors such as investment banks.

One of the recent improvements in the public funding of new ventures are changes in Securities and Exchange Commission's regulations concerning exempt offerings. The advent of the SCOR (Small Corporate Offering Registration) process is a regulator's attempt to better balance society's need for small business capital formation with their charge to protect the public from being defrauded. The SCOR process attempts to reduce the costs of public registration to be more similar to the costs of a private offering thus making public registration a far more viable option for many small businesses. And with the successful registration comes the freedom to sell securities to the general public and to use a variety of advertising and marketing techniques in doing so. Certainly this is good news for a variety of small businesses needing to raise capital, but the major impact of the SCOR movement will more likely be found in the opportunity to circulate relevant market information far more broadly.

There are restrictions imposed on SCOR securities. Regulation D which created the possibility for SCOR resulted from work between the SEC and state regulators to develop a uniform exemption from registration for small stock issues. Rules 504, 505 and 506 specify the conditions under which stock issues can be exempt. Rule 504 applies most directly to early stage companies. Rule 504 exempts companies that are not subject to SEC reporting to sell up to $1,000,000 over a twelve month period to any number of investors. Rules 505 and 506 offer larger issues but apply only to companies that are already subject to SEC reporting.

Many states allow for qualification under state law in coordination with Regulation D, and each has unique rules regarding the nature of the offering. In Missouri, for example, the Missouri Issuer Registration Procedure (15 CSR 30-52.271) regulates SCOR offerings. This procedure allows an issuer who has their primary place of business in Missouri to raise up to $1,000,000 through the sale of common stock and debt securities to residents with an annual gross income of at least $30,000 and with a net worth of $30,000 exclusive of home, furnishings, and automobiles. Alternatively, an individual with a net worth in excess of $75,000 can also invest. Insiders and investments under $500 are excluded from these requirements. The business may also test the water of investor interest without filing a full securities registration, and can presell up to $100,000 of securities pending final registration. The securities disclosure and registration requirements can be met through the use of the U-7 disclosure document.

The U-7 is the central feature of SCOR offerings. It is based on 50 questions which explain the nature of the business offering and the detailed characteristics of the securities. The form was developed be the North American Securities Administrators Association and its use is common in most state registrations.

Issues and Concerns in the SCOR Marketplace

In order to create a broadened early stage capital market, it is important to create a viable SCOR marketplace. This can only occur if potential entrepreneurs seek to undertake the SCOR process, and if potential investors can be found to participate in these offerings. This section will explore important concerns in developing these two elements of the SCOR marketplace.

Expanding the SCOR Company Market

Completing the U7 and undertaking completion of the SCOR process can be a daunting process. Education of the entrepreneur on the requirements and benefits of the SCOR process is the first essential step to expand this marketplace. There are numerous possible benefits from this process. First, registration can expose the entrepreneur to a much broader market and offer its investors greater liquidity. Completing a U7 may force a venture to more thoroughly examine its plans which may help reduce failures. Finally, the development of a large number of U7 filings will create a valuable, consistent source of information which will help to greatly improve the information characteristics for early stage offerings.

These benefits may be sufficient incentive to encourage SCOR registration and develop a more efficient market as long as state restrictions are not excessive. To encourage this process it would seem incumbent on state regulators to leave the process relatively open but place other market filters into operation. As a result, more offerings reaching investors might undergo review through the SCOR process and this would likely improve the quality of the offerings and provide investors greater safety. Such a process appears to be a desirable approach to mitigate potential problems of fraud and underinformed investors. Encouraging companies to use the SCOR registration will help develop this market which in the long term can make this a dynamic, viable and better screened market than the alternative market of privately placed securities.

Expanding the Investor Market

Simply reaching the existing early stage investors more effectively through public access to SCOR offerings would likely expand the venture capital market significantly. There is also the likelihood to reach an even broader market of informal investors. At this point the characteristics of this enlarged market can only be estimated. Several studies have previously attempted to determine the characteristics of individual investors (Gaston and Bell, 1988; Harr, Starr and MacMillan, 1988; Freear and Wetzel, 1989). Drawing a composite from these studies suggests that individual investors have a median age of 48 years and range from 30 to 80 years in age. The vast majority have a bachelor's degree and perhaps 50% could be expected to hold a master's degree or greater. Although the studies vary considerable, one might still conclude that approximately half of these investors have a net worth under $1 million and an annual income under $100,000. The median investment is typically reported to be $50,000 or less per investment. It would appear that there is a potentially larger market than has previously participated in early stage offerings, perhaps as large as 2 million investors, especially since much smaller investments can be practical in marketing SCOR offerings.

By their nature, small businesses, particularly very young, growing, privately-owned businesses, carry unique and substantial risk factors for investors. Because of the unique risks inherent in early stage offerings, greater education efforts are needed to serve the broadened market so that they may avail themselves of the enhanced information offered through the SCOR process. Education is also made more critical by a lack of professional investment support. Since investments are usually quite small at this stage and the transactions widely dispersed, there are not likely to be adequate incentives to attract competent professional service providers who can assist the casual investor wishing to invest relatively small amounts.

Although most business angels have substantial general business or entrepreneurial experience, the broadened pool of investors would likely have significant income but possibly less education or general business experience. Such investors are likely to be investing in the stock market or mutual funds, but have not had access to the venture capital market. This new type of investor reached by SCOR offerings are probably unaccustomed to the types of risks inherent in these investments. Informed investors will often want to review a business plan, meet the management team, perform background checks, or possibly examine a design or prototype for any new products to be developed. Investors who commonly invest in less risky investments may not be aware of the need for exercising due diligence in this type of an investment.

As new investors are attracted to the market, it is essential that a full disclosure be made of not just the risks of the market, but also the investment process itself. New investors must understand the full scope of the risks inherent in these investments and be offered the tools to help them evaluate these unique investment opportunities. Without such disclosures regulator concerns may be energized with the potential for more restrictive restrictions in the market. For the new SCOR market to satisfy regulators concerns, both education and effective screening must be viewed as essential components to help protect potential investors.

Recent Developments in the SCOR Marketplace

In some cities law firms and private placement firms have helped syndicate packages using Regulation D offerings. By and large, however, the problems of finding individuals to invest in such offering is still much of a hit or miss problem, similar to finding business angels interested in a given investment. Some recent developments, however, offer new possibilities for developing the greater access and information exchange needed for a viable SCOR marketplace.

Table 1 shows that the Pacific Stock Exchange will list SCOR offerings with a market value over $500,000. This is a three year pilot. While the size limitation will preclude many seed offerings, this is still a progressive attempt to develop a market for SCOR stock offerings. The success of this effort could help provide a much needed liquidity for early stage offerings. Listing will also provide the investor with the additional screening process of the Pacific Stock Exchange. At this point it is not clear if there will be enough activity or information to facilitate the broader evaluation and trading needed for an effective market. While likely providing a source of buyer and sellers, and possibly improved liquidity, it is doubtful whether analysts will participate in this market. Analysts could improve the information availability in the market and help less experienced investors, but it is unclear if the transaction volume and investment size will be sufficient to attract analysts into this market.

Another innovative effort is the SCOR Market Maker, developed at the Missouri Innovation Center (MIC). The MIC is a not for profit agency affiliated with the Missouri Division of Economic Development. This SCOR Market Maker is designed to seize the opportunity presented by the new regulations to build a skeletal marketplace infrastructure that would otherwise not be possible without the advent of the SCOR process. The program offers several features which deal with the problem of making buying, issuing and selling small stocks more convenient, and with the problem of training new investors to conduct there own analysis on these unique investments.

The SCOR Market Maker newsletter, published in newsprint and online, provides a forum for the public discussion of the unique circumstances surrounding investment in small, private companies and brings investment opportunities to the attention of the general public. Its goal is to broadly disseminate investment information throughout the state at no cost. The newsletter is inserted in business journals throughout Missouri and has a circulation of 100,000. The average net worth of investors reached through this method is over $1 million.

The newsletter approach has several advantages. First, by offering publication in the newsletter there is an incentive that makes it worthwhile for many small companies to subject their offerings to the review of state regulators through SCOR. Simultaneously, the presence of the Market Maker newsletter and its broad circulation to potential investors provides a vehicle for educating investors on not just the offerings but the criteria on which to evaluate these investments. The Market Maker can thus become a market where small companies can have their capital needs published, and where investors can find valuable investment advice.

To implement safeguards in this market, the SCOR process is the cornerstone of the efforts of the MIC. Publication in the SCOR Market Maker is used as an incentive to encourage small companies to subject their offerings through the SCOR process. The MIC also provides the technical assistance and training needed by those entrepreneurs who are willing to make the full disclosure required for SCOR offering. This is a particular help to very early stage seed and start up endeavors. This process encourages entrepreneurs to use the

SCOR process, and helps broaden the screening process to bring viable new offerings to the public. The center also actively develops and distributes educational materials for potential early stage investors helping then better understand unique risk factors and fair market value.

Conclusions and Recommendations

The screening process offered by SCOR registration is an important tool to help protect a broadened public market from potentially unscrupulous investors or poorly conceived business concepts. While it is literally impossible to eliminate the inevitable failures that litter the early stage marketplace it is possible and quite healthy to require issuers to go through the rigorous process of completing a registration document. Screening, however, is a two edged sword. While it provides some protection to investors, an excessively rigid screening process can deter profitable ventures from coming through the SCOR process and ultimately lead back to the old problems of limited capital access for early stage development.

While the SCOR registration process provides an important screening mechanism, it must also be supplemented by effective education. Listing on a stock exchange may help liquidity but it will not offset the increased educational needs of the broadened investor market. Making a full disclosure of the nature of the company and its associated risks to investors may be distasteful to the uninitiated and to the scam artists, but it promotes the flow of information into the public market, and helps ease the concerns of investors thus lowering barriers to entry, and will by definition result in a more active and efficient capital market over time.

There is good reason to be excited about the SCOR marketplace. If sustained it is highly likely that the effective public distribution of relevant market information will cause a marked increase in private capital available to fund the growth of small companies. However, we must be aware that the political backbone that birthed the SCOR movement in the regulation community may be short-lived in the face of future headlines telling of registered SCOR offerings that went bust in short order.

Let there be no mistake that regulators and the elected public officials responsible for their activities are nervous about doing anything to promote "blue sky" offerings. And well they should. These offerings, regardless of their importance to economic development, are

301

political time bombs waiting to go off. They reflect the raw risk involved in free enterprise at its most basic level. No amount of regulation can rid them of this inherent characteristic nor should it attempt to do so. Without continuing to shackle entrepreneurs and the U.S. economy the most reasonable goal of regulation must be to strongly encourage full disclosure to investors and to aggressively prosecute outright fraud; but not entrepreneur naiveté or stupidity. To sustain the SCOR movement, champions at all levels of government, the media, and the general public, must advocate for these goals and balance the short-sighted urge of some to criticize officials that register companies that simply fail.

In order to gain the benefit offered by the automobile we reluctantly accept casualties on our highways. To gain the benefit of the SCOR highway and the wealth of information it infuses into the early stage marketplace we must also accept casualties. But casualties can be reduced by proper education. We must not ignore this important component. The only other alternative is to seal off the entrance ramps and that would serve no one.

References

Amit, R., Glosten, L. and Muller, E. 1990. Entrepreneurial Ability, Venture Investments, and Risk Sharing. Management Science, 36, 10

Amit, R., Glosten, L. and Muller, E. 1993. Challenges to Theory Development in Entrepreneurship Research. Journal of Management Studies, 30, 5, 815-834

Bygrave, W. and Timmons, J. 1991. Venture and Risk Capital: Practice and Performance, Promises and Policy. Boston, MA: Harvard Business School

Bygrave, W. and Timmons, J. 1992. Venture Capital at the Crossroads. Boston: Harvard Business School

Freear, J. and Wetzel, W. 1990. "Who Bankrolls High-Tech Entrepreneurs?", Journal of Business Venturing, 5, 2, 77-89

Freear, J. and Wetzel, W. 1989. "Equity Capital for Entrepreneurs". in Frontiers of Entrepreneurship Research. eds. R.H. Brockhaus, Sr., N.C. Churchill, J.A. Katz, B.A. Kirchoff, K.H. Vesper, and W.E. Wetzel. Wellesley, Ma: Babson College, p 230-244

Gaston, R.J. and Bell, S.E. 1988. The Informal Supply of Capital. A report prepared for the Office of Economic Research, U.S. Small

Business Administration.

Harr, N.W., Starr, J., MacMillan, I.C. 1988. "Informal Risk Capital Investors: Investment Patterns on the East Coast of the U.S.A". Journal of Business Venturing, 3, 1, 11-29

MacMillan, I.C., Siegel, R., and Subba Narasimha, P.N. 1985. "Criteria Used by Venture Capitalists to Evaluate New Venture Proposals". Journal of Business Venturing, 1, 119-128

Vachon, M. 1993. "Venture Capital Reborn". Venture Capital Journal, January, 32

Table 1
Stock Exchange Asset Requirements

Stock Exchange	Net Tangible Assets
New York	18,000,000
American	3,000,000[1]
Chicago	2,000,000
Boston	3,000,000
Philadelphia	4,000,000
NASDAQ	4,000,000
Pacific	4,000,000
Pacific	500,000[2]

1 Market Value of Shares
2 SCOR Companies
Source: Freear and Wetzel, 1992

Stock offerings also appear to entail significant costs for the entrepreneur. Studies of initial public offerings have shown that, in general, new issues are often under priced approximately 15% (Smith, 1989). Going public thus entails significant costs. These costs are believed due to the asymmetry of information between the entrepreneur and the market. The acceptance of these costs is likely to be due to the need for capital, and perhaps the limited availability of other sources of capital. Prior to the IPO, venture capitalists or business angels may participate in the funding of the business.

Smith, C.w. 1989. "Investment Banking and the Capital Acquisition Process" Journal of Financial Economics, 15, 3-29

These risks are concentrated in the lack of a long history of successful operation and in the lack of substantial liquidity.

CHARACTERISTICS OF AN ENTREPRENEUR

JOHN L. HINES

The author, who was president of both Continental Illinois Venture Corporation and Continental Illinois Equity Corporation, is an extremely successful venture capital investor and was most helpful in the preparation of *Venture's Financing and Investing In Private Companies*.

It is difficult to enumerate in order of priority the most important characteristics of an entrepreneur. There are two reasons why this task is formidable. First, there are several characteristics which seem both inherent and essential to all successful entrepreneurs; a deficiency in any of these essentials usually portends failure. Second, most venture capitalists tend to be quite subjective when weighing other characteristics that may not be so universal or prominent. I believe that it is best to dispense quickly with the essential traits and then elaborate on the more subjective ones. These may be considerably more subtle and controversial. It is these more elusive qualities that seem to distinguish one entrepreneur from another, define individual style.

Essential Characteristics Defined

Every venture capitalist concurs that successful entrepreneurs must be honest, intelligent, skillful, and well educated in their chosen fields (not necessarily as a result of a formal education). There have been relatively few, if any, long-lived, successful venture companies led by people deficient in any one of these four essential qualities. Knowledgeable investors would decline participation opportunities in such ventures.

There are at least nine other characteristics which I value highly. Some of my priorities may be questioned by more experienced and knowledgeable venture capitalists. The values which I list are not meant to be all inclusive. I look for the following traits in all venture candidates in whom we have an interest (in no particular order of priority): energy level, ego, courage, enthusiasm, desire to make money, creativity, resourcefulness, tenacity, and leadership qualities. Unless an entrepreneur has an abundance of all these qualities, one might pause and be more careful when considering becoming his or her partner. The weighting of each of these characteristics must by necessity be purely subjective.

Energy Level: Staying Ahead of the Pack

Energy level is very important because all businesses, particularly new ones, need a person at the top to set a brisk pace. One who expects others to work and think more than eight hours a day must be able to consistently demonstrate an ability to stay ahead of the pack. If one's own energy wanes, one may excuse subordinates of the same pleasure.

Young businesses do not frequently possess the many and varied skills of larger and more successful enterprises. The entrepreneur, by necessity, must participate directly in a wide variety of challenging tasks. Raising venture capital is in itself an extremely demanding chore, especially if one is concurrently trying to expand sales and manufacturing capabilities and hire and train personnel.

Confidence in Ability to Excel

Ego is related to self-appraisal of one's own capabilities and pride in achieving. Unless entrepreneurs hold themselves in high esteem (are even a bit egocentric), it may be difficult to inspire confidence in others important to them--investors, creditors, and subordinates alike. Ego, if unmantled or uncontrolled, may be a glaring negative. It appears that many of the more successful entrepreneurs really believe that they possess most of the abilities necessary to succeed in their chosen fields. Generally, if they consider themselves lacking in particular skills, they tend to compensate by hiring and encouraging others who may posses them. Successful entrepreneurs tend to rate themselves at the top of their chosen fields. If they do not honestly believe this, they will be risking more than their financial backers--reputation, future, time, and capital.

Courage to Keep Forging Ahead

Courage is rate and elusive. It is extremely hard to appraise. Every growing business requires this quality of its leader, because they all encounter serious difficulties periodically. Among other qualities, it takes courage, and plenty of it, to cope with money woes, fuel shortages, labor difficulties, patent infringements, veiled threats of competitors and customers, regulatory agencies, and obsolescence of products and services. Most executives who are relatively secure in their jobs occasionally dream about owning and running their own "show"; few have the courage to start or buy a business. The best entrepreneurs are generally cognizant of many negatives inherent in their ventures but generally believe in their own solutions. These successful types possess the courage to keep forging ahead.

People Back and Follow a Winner

It is difficult to distinguish between enthusiasm and a positive spirit. Entrepreneurs who have these qualities generally have a better chance of engendering such spirits in their followers- money, people, customers, and employees. People like to back and follow a "winner."

If young entrepreneurs are truly enthusiastic about their product, the long-term business outlook for it, and the chance to build an enterprise to purvey it, they usually have a better chance for success. If they radiate optimism and enthusiasm, no matter how difficult times may be, they should have an easier time attracting those elements which may be necessary for their companies' success. It is difficult to sell any goods or services unless the sellers portray that they would be a buyer, and an enthusiastic one. One might interject the adjective "charismatic" here to help describe entrepreneurs who are able to affably reflect enthusiasm about their company and its prospects.

The Desire to Win Translates into Desire to Make Money

Many confuse the desire to make money with greed. I, on the other hand, confuse this money desire with the will to win, to be successful,

306

and to be able to demonstrate business accomplishments. Capitalism's score card seems to be money, return on invested capital. Unless the entrepreneur wants to win, respects the value of earning high returns on invested capital, and has a desire to acquire wealth, he may end up with just another start-up situation. Without this important quality, he will have little opportunity to earn returns on invested capital, much less make important social contributions. Either one of these ambitions should promote a desire to win or make money.

Creative Approach to Invention, Management, Finance, and Merchandising

Creativity is one of the most unique qualities. The ability to add a new "twist" to an existing product or service and merchandise, it is indeed unusual. McDonald's was a late starter in the hamburger business; Revlon in cosmetics; Polaroid in photography; H.R. Block in accounting; Intel in electronics; Syntex in drugs; and Hyatt in motels. Despite their tardy entries, the founders of these companies had one thing in common -- they were all creative. They all improved upon, invented, and delivered newly packaged products or services to consumers at attractive prices. Creativity for our purposes should not be confined to inventive genius. It should be coupled with management, financial, and merchandising skills. Creative entrepreneurs usually are able to adroitly package products and services and select growing market areas that they might penetrate.

Resourcefulness: Making Use of Talent, Defining Course of Action

Resourcefulness is a quality that entrepreneurs must possess if their companies are to be viable, much less be successful. Entrepreneur must be able to deal effectively with a multitude of problems quickly, to act and react with dispatch. Their actions do not have to be correct all of the time; however, they should be able to recognize their own mistakes and alter their positions frequently -- as would a field general.

Part of resourcefulness is making use of all the talent at hand; the ability to listen well is the key here. Resourceful entrepreneurs have the ability to assimilate conflicting views and varied inputs regarding complex problems and then to define skillfully their priorities and courses of action. Handling venture capitalists' negatives is a fine test of this quality, but only one small measure.

Tenacity Separates the Doer from the Quitter

Tenacity is also very difficult to judge, because it is often confused with stubbornness or inflexibility. It is important to place proper value on tenacity because most young, growing enterprises are plagued with problems that would cause average people to quit or compromise their ethics, standards, or objectives to the detriment of shareholders and others. I believe that tenacity for our purposes should include a toughness that causes an individual to hand on when circumstances are most difficult. Appraising tenacity is very much like appraising honesty; the task is difficult to perform unless the entrepreneur is tested under adverse circumstances.

Sensitivity to People's Needs

Leadership qualities embody all of the important characteristics already considered, and more. A key addition here is the ability of the entrepreneur to stimulate, relate to, and empathize with his employees, officers, directors, and shareholders. To lead effectively, one must be able to recognize and encourage the best qualities in one's people. This is one of the most difficult assignments, because the entrepreneur must be sensitive to people's needs, personal as well as economic.

The exercise of listing and actually making value judgements with reference to each one of these essential and/or subjective characteristics can be a most instructive exercise for any investment analyst, especially those dealing with venture situations. The fact that individual priorities will differ for each appraiser is of little consequence. The prime advantage to this exercise (formally listing one's priorities) is to sharpen one's own appraisal techniques and standards. The most important consideration in evaluating any venture company is the manager, founder, or entrepreneur. It is both necessary and natural to alter and refine one's standards and methods for making these value judgements.

DO'S AND DON'TS OF DEALING WITH BANKS

TEED WELCH

Teed Welch was, at the time of original publication of this article, President of Innovest, Inc., a Boston-based firm which specialized in preparing and guaranteeing loan packages for emerging growth companies. This article is based on a presentation made to a meeting of the Manhattan Area Venture Group.

These suggestions are designed to help entrepreneurs in their negotiations with commercial lenders. While some may seem basic, experience shows that many entrepreneurs overlook them nevertheless.

First, remember that bankers are not investors. They lend other people's savings. Therefore, they have a low tolerance for risk. A 1 percent loss rate is too high. To use a retail analogy, money is the banker's inventory. When analyzed on an incremental basis, bankers attempt to buy money (deposits) at less than the money market rate and sell it (loans) at more than the prime rate. There is usually about a 2 percent spread between the banker's cost and selling price for money or roughly a 20% to 25% gross profit. There are not too many other businesses that can survive on only a 20 percent gross margin and still afford "doubtful accounts." Therefore, as a purely stand-alone product, small business loans are seldom profitable. If a bank charged 1 percent over the prime rate, earning a 3 percent spread, using the figures above, a $250,000 loan would generate a gross profit of $7,500 over one year. That "gross" must cover all expenses related to the loan, including overhead, salaries, and reserves for losses. If the bank lost one loan of this size, it would erase the total gross profit on 33 other loans of the same size and rates.

Regarding your business account at the bank, remember that it is not important to the bank how much passes through the account. Much more important is how much money stays in the account. The fact that millions have been deposited and withdrawn is meaningless to the bank in terms of profit in most cases, except if there are fees associated with the transactions.

Remember that bankers earn raises and promotions by making loans, not by turning them down. Therefore, their incentive is to loan to sound customers.

As compared to venture capitalists, remember that venture capitalists tend to be more interested in the future while bankers are more interested in the past. For this reason, it may be a good idea to develop two business plans: a financing plan for the bank and an investment plan for the investors. The plan for the bank should specify the credit needed, how the proceeds will be employed, where the company is financially at present, and where it is going. Bankers tend to lend primarily against assets and less so against earning power. They normally consider that short-term loans will be repaid from conversion of assets to cash (for example, sale of inventory or collection of accounts receivable), and that long-term loans (for productive equipment or real estate) will be paid from cash flow.

Lastly for the do's, remember that financing packages are best approached on an "unbundled" basis. For example, if you are requesting $1,000,000 for "various" purposes, it is better to separate the need into its components. Each portion generally will have different terms and conditions and may even require different collateral. An unbundled loan package makes more sense and may be approved faster.

Bankers are individuals, and like the rest of us, they have their likes and dislikes. Here is a short list of the don'ts. Avoid these approaches, and you'll likely establish a better relationship with your account person.

Don't surprise your banker, especially with bad news. Keep him or her fully informed. Bankers often can be helpful in helping you to solve financing problems, if they know about them soon enough--and

310

if they know all the relevant details.

Don't overproject your growth. Bankers correctly are skeptical of companies that project huge growth rates--especially if your past results don't justify your present projections. It is better to be conservative and then surpass your projections.

Next, never tell a banker that your loan is risk-free. There always are risks, even with a loan made with cash collateral. For example, there are cases where a loan already repaid goes bad. How? In bankruptcy cases, the repayment may be classified as a preference payment, and may have to be refunded to the bankrupt party, for transfer to other creditors. Rather than denying the risk, tell the banker what the risks are and how you plan to minimize them.

Here is one of the most important don'ts: Don't be late with payments. Once a timetable is established, keep it.

And, bankers will love it if you heed this suggestion: Don't haggle over loan terms and conditions. It is much easier to change loan terms and conditions after the loan has been granted. Keep in mind your goal of getting the loan approved. If the company becomes successful and you still can't resolve an issue that is bothering you, remember you can always change banks. But, don't threaten the banker with that. This applies to loan documentation as well. Typically, loan officers have little authority to modify a preprinted form or document, so don't waste your time haggling over the form or having your attorney draw one. It is just not worth it.

Entrepreneurs need all the resources they can find. Remember these points and you may transform your banker from a stone face behind a desk into a business advisor.

FINDING YOUR ANGEL

WILLIAM BRYANT LOGAN

This article originally appeared in *Venture* and has been edited for this book.

Angels do walk the earth--at least in one New Hampshire neighborhood. Stephen Albano found one when he waved to Bob McCray, who was out for a spring walk through their neighborhood. Albano, thinking about starting his own company, wanted to toss around ideas with his tennis buddy. Six months after that front-lawn conversation, McCray grubstaked Albano with $30,000. "I like to get money around," muses McCray. "I like to help."

McCray is an angel, one of a host of private investors that so often puts up the first $20,000 to $200,000 to get a business off the ground. "I'd hazard a guess that at least 10,000 businesses get angel money each year," says William Wetzel, the University of New Hampshire business professor who authored the pioneer study in the field. Angels may, in fact, double the amount of money invested by venture capital firms, says Kirk Neiswander, director of entrepreneurial programs at Case Western Reserve University in Cleveland. "Let's say the venture capital community has put a couple of billion dollars into companies in the last few years," he estimates. "Private money at least equals that, if it's not two or three times greater," he speculates, based on his own research in northeastern Ohio.

Angels, a term Wetzel borrowed from Broadway and Hollywood, are playing an especially vital role for startups this year. Venture capital firms concentrate their investments in development and later stage companies as well as in follow-on investments in companies already in their portfolios. The share of the professional venture capital dollars going to seed and startup investments is tiny compared to the funds invested in later stage companies.

A not-very-efficient old-boys' network of lawyers, accountants, and business associates has been the traditional way of finding angels. Alternative channels in the form of enterprise forums and venture capital clubs promise to match up entrepreneurs with private investors, but sport a spotty record when it comes to actual deals. The formal angel network is an attempt to formalize the capital gathering process. The first one was Wetzel's Venture Capital Network Inc. (VNC). Similar systems, often modeled on the New Hampshire effort, are underway in a number of other regions and cities.

Look at Bob McCray to define the typical angel. McCray ran his own company, Worchester Controls Corp., for 26 years before selling out for $50 million. He's made four investments, each within fifty miles of his house. Like most angels, he invests anywhere from $10,000 to $100,000 in a deal, and usually brings other angels into the picture. In return, the average angel seeks 30 percent per annum return on any investment, fully aware that up to half the companies he backs will not produce the sought for return and may well devour all of the funds invested.

Unlike investors in syndicates or research and development partnerships, angels are often active investors, offering the companies they participate in their expertise, or interference, as well as their money. "He was our security blanket," says Albano of McCray. "He not only set us up, but I know that if we ever had tough times, he'd be there with more money and expertise." McCray introduced Albano to Ricoh, the Japanese copier company, and to investment banker Albert Bourgeois, who cut a deal that let Albano's company OFFTECH Inc., Malden, Mass., distribute Ricoh machines from day one. Five years after, that spring walk the company had $25 million in sales.

But there's also a dark side to the angelic soul. Because these private investors get so involved with their deals, they sometimes want to run "their" company. Possessive angels sometimes fight to keep new investors out of the company. Others simply assume that their investment objectives should replace whatever the entrepreneur wrote in the business plan. Equally, the entrepreneur can drive angels away by failing to reassure private investors that they're not simply being take for pigeons. Structuring the deal is just as important as finding the angel.

313

A few ventures find their angels the old fashioned way: by praying for them. Allen Michels began Convergent Technologies Inc. with $16.22. "About enough," he says, "to run it for three hours." William D. Rollnick had been one of Michels' best customers when Michels ran the microcomputer systems division at Intel Corp. "He was also my friend," notes Rollnick. "I could tell he was a friend, because we could fight and still like one another."

Rollnick had also just sold one of his computer rental companies. "I bought cheap and sold it for more than I paid," says Rollnick, "just like my daddy always told me."

"I asked him if he'd like to spend it (the money he's received from the sale)," says Michels. "To my astonishment he said yes." In 40 minutes they cut the deal for a $2 million investment from Rollnick and two of his friends; Michels gave up 64 percent of Convergent.

All three turned out to be important to the company, Michels remembers. One advised on contracts and potential liabilities. Another "was our consigliere. Early on, we were looking at a $40 million contract, bigger than we'd ever dreamed of. He helped us understand its subtleties," Michels adds. "Bill made people feel happy and secure about the situation," Michels says. "Every Saturday morning he'd show up with a huge box of donuts." The feast was of more than passing concern. "These were the world's best chocolate-covered donuts," Rollnick contends. "If I missed a Saturday, I got a lot of bitching all the following week."

Most beginning entrepreneurs are looking for much less money to start and expect much slower growth. For them, the path to angels is often more tangled. The traditional networks for finding private money operate through accountants, lawyers, and business acquaintances. William E. Conway, for example, a major owner of Best Sand Corp., a miner and maker of industrial sands in Chardon, Ohio, has invested through friends, through consultants, and even through a seminar held by Neiswander at Case Western. His investment in Clamco, a Cleveland industrial packaging company, came through his lawyer. Conway put a total of $40,000 into the firm in return for a 5 percent stake in Clamco and a subordinated debenture, payable over eight years. "The debenture promised current income," he notes, "and it helped the founder get a sizable capital infusion without giving away too big a stake in his company." The value of Conway's equity has increased over 40 percent over the last year alone, and Clamco has had sufficient income to pay off the debenture early.

314

Venture capital clubs and some business seminars try to formalize this networking. At the startup clinics run five times a year by the MIT Enterprise Forum in Cambridge, Mass., and other cities, one to three entrepreneurs each session get to present their business plans to a panel chosen to fit their companies. Later, the audience grills them again. "It's a board of directors meeting in public," says Paul E. Johnson, national director of the MIT Enterprise Forum. At the least, the entrepreneur comes away with an improved business plan and some fresh contacts. Or such is the theory.

And sometimes it works. Brooktrout Technology Inc. was almost out of funds after five months in business when its young founders--none of them over 30--appeared before the MIT Enterprise Forum, in Cambridge. Panelist James Geisman, a marketing consultant, liked their presentation and suggested to Joe Knowles, a MBA who had already made money in the stock market, that he look at the company. In return for 8 percent of the company and a seat on the board, Knowles guaranteed $200,000 in credit that kept Brooktrout swimming for six months.

But some of the more than 60 forums and venture capital clubs operating around the country never deliver. "Maybe 35 of them are real functioning clubs; the rest are just talking," says Steven Cohen, editor of *Venture's Capital Club Monthly* newsletter. "A country club's a better place to meet an angel than a venture capital club."

O. Jay Krasner, a professor of management at Pepperdine University who has studied angels on the West Coast, seconds that assessment. He has also been a principal in four firms, three of which did the club circuit and none of which got funding through it. "My impression is that they attract 80 percent 'con-ers' and only 20 percent 'con-ees,'" he says.

Vicki King and Bob Pnakovich presented their idea for a lap-computer screen light at the Los Angeles Venture Association (LAVA) one of the more active and better organized groups. "All kinds of people came up to us after the presentation and said 'that's a nice idea," but they weren't going to invest their own money," King recalls. Still, King doesn't regret the experience. "The people at the club were super. Time ran out on us, but next time we'll be ready."

Success at a venture club actually seems to have more to do with where the club is than the quality of the entrepreneur's business plan. "In Fargo, N.D., they may be meeting just because there's nothing else to do in town, and on Long Island they may be backing a pizza stand," says Cohen, "but in a place like Princeton, N.J., or Connecticut there are both money and brains to deal with." The Connecticut Venture Group (CVG), drawing on that state's Gold Coast population, is the oldest club in the country and one of the richest and largest.

Cyber Research Inc., a New Haven packager of systems for scientific and technical uses, needed angels from the Connecticut Venture Group, says founder Robert Molloy. The company was surviving on creative financing, buying on credit, and selling for cash to create cash flow. A venture capital deal had fallen through when the two firms that had agreed to invest--in return for 49 percent of the company and half the seats on the board--fell to bickering between themselves over the terms. Shortly after, Molloy and cofounder Matthew Kubitsky, attended a CVG luncheon where Kubitsky hit it off with the guy beside him at the table, Jim Mann, who had already made two other investments through the club. About six months later, Mann agreed to help, and within a few weeks Cyber Research had $50,000 to finance its first shipment and establish credit. "The people were reasonable, the management was well-rounded and experienced, and they knew where they were going," says Mann, who earned his wings as an attorney advising a London investment banking firm.

"Angels usually come in clusters," notes Molloy. "They're usually involved with others who trust their judgement and will invest with them." As chairman of the firm's finance committee, Mann brought in a second investor who contributed $10,000 cash and leased the company $15,000 worth of computers. He next got $50,000 more out of a group of friends in Zurich, Switzerland. In return, he and his co-investors received about 10 percent of the company. Mann, who invested in the form of 12 percent debenture convertible in one year, has seen his loan paid off and the value of his stock double. The co-investors have a straight equity deal, with the right to sell stock back to the firm in three years at double their investment.

Venture clubs aren't the latest word in matching entrepreneurs and investors. "It's a very random process," Wetzel comments, "and very inefficient." He and others have recently begun to develop more formal networks to smooth the path to seed money.

When it started two years ago, Wetzel's Venture Capital Network was unique in the country: a formal, non-profit system funded by university and government grants, for the purpose of matching entrepreneurs and angels. To protect potential investors' identities, Wetzel

316

set up a blind matching structure. Needy companies describe their aims and requirements; VCN compares those with a list of angels' goals and interests. The investor then receives a description of attractive firms; it is up to him or her to make further contact. When investors had a free ride on the system, Wetzel had up to 300 potential investors and 135 entrepreneurs listed. Enrollment dropped when he instituted a fee ranging from $100 to $250.

Of the 800 face-to-face meetings that have thus far come out of the VCN, at least four have resulted in deals. Douglas Renfield-Miller, a Stanford MBA, invested in two of those. A course given by Bill Brandt, author of *The Ten Commandments of Entrepreneuring*, first interested Renfield-Miller in helping small companies, especially when the business plan he wrote as part of the coursework succeeded in getting funds. "Writing it was very hard, but it made it far easier for me to evaluate other people's plans," he says.

Family money gave him the money to invest in two startups: $30,000 in General Clutch Corp., Stanford, Conn, and $16,000 in another company. Francis Mechner of General Clutch counts Renfield-Miller among 30 private investors. He prefers that arrangement to traditional venture capital. "Individuals are easier to deal with," he believes "because they are accountable only to themselves." Renfield-Miller put together a computerized financial model for his other company. "He's given me expertise I couldn't possibly afford to have on the payroll," says the second entrepreneur.

Not all angels do only good. Lucifer too had wings. Entrepreneurs do well to protect themselves against that angel from The Other Place, who can mortally wound a young company. Once a devil gets in, it may be too late, especially when he controls a majority stake in the company. One entrepreneur who saw a California high-tech company wrecked by a single majority shareholder believes the size of the holding itself may have contributed. "When you have more than 50 percent of a company, you think it's your baby. Someone who might otherwise have behaved very rationally can turn irrational, and his temperament and capriciousness play too large a role in determining the direction of the company."

One entrepreneur who's dealt with angels makes a practice of doing as much due diligence on potential investors as they do on him. He rejected two very substantial investors even though his company needed the cash. "The first told me about a lot of important men he knew," says the founder. "He didn't know I knew them too. When I called, they told me he'd been involved in taking people from firms in an unethical manner, and that he had a luxurious lifestyle that didn't match his sources of income. I had to reject him." The second was straightforward enough, but contacts told the entrepreneur that he tended to meddle in companies he invested in.

Bad angels can be either too meddlesome or too distant. One angel jumped in to save a failing company in Southern California. He did one thing right, bringing in a proven manager to lead the firm out of the red. The new president did what he promised, but when it came time to keep the computer systems maker going in the right direction, the angel balked, according to company insiders and other potential investors. Instead of preparing the company for an initial public offering, he began to use the company as a personal cash cow. As majority shareholder, he blocked the president's efforts to bring in top managers and installed a vice president to keep tabs on the president. Within a year, the president left, and the company resumed its downward spiral.

"Some angels are just making a cocktail party investment," says Harry D. Sedgwick, who has had 27 years of experience as both entrepreneur and investor. "They're too passive or too nervous, and you can't count on them when more money is needed or a crisis comes. Too often the angel is playing golf in Barbados when you really need him."

Friction between angel and entrepreneur occurs even under the best of circumstances. "Sometimes they have horns," reflects David Meyer, one of the founders of Micro-MRP Inc., Foster City, Calif., "but that's O.K." The software company met the first of its two angels at a cocktail party: One of the founders' girlfriends was the daughter of their investor's secretary. Within two days, they had $40,000 as a guarantee for a bank loan. They also had a new general manager, their second angel. "He was a short-term kind of manager, and I know that people in software are artistic, creative types. It made for some awkward times." Eventually, the principals compromised, replacing the bullish angel with a new president recruited from outside the company and its investor group. "We sacrificed our egos and held onto our wallets," Meyer notes.

But that wasn't the last of the awkward moments. The angels' feathers were further ruffled when a round of venture capital threatened to dilute their interest in MicroMRP to 10 percent from 40 percent. "In retrospect, it worked out fine," says Meyer. "They had 10 percent of a $7 million company just for putting their signature on a line." The company recently began a $100 million joint venture with IBM.

Almost every angel has been plucked at one time or another. Joe Knowles confesses that he would never again make the kind of investment he did at Brooktrout Technology. "You can't be an investor and operator at the same time," he concludes. "If you're the only person with money on the line, you're the only one with real risk."

Sometimes the entrepreneur thinks that the mere acquisition of money from the investor is the hallmark of success, says Rollnick, who has suffered at least one close call. "They get a palace with color-coordinated furniture. The really good managers have no time for that." In Rollnick's trip to financial purgatory, the board and the managers almost came to blows. "Fortunately, somebody finally blinked [in that game of chicken], and it didn't turn out to be a shoot-out."

More frequently disillusionment comes from a failure to examine the product thoroughly. Sumner A. Milender's one failure to date was with Air Designs, a company founded by a Buckminister Fuller protégé to manufacture chutes that could be used as fire escapes. The ex-tanner wisely counseled the founders that it could take a decade to get regulatory approval for a fire escape device; he suggested that they develop the product for materials handling instead. He had already found the company a test site when he discovered that Otis Elevator was producing a similar product. "Obviously, we hadn't checked into patents thoroughly enough," he sighs.

When Jim Mann invested in Right Products, he wasn't canny enough about the market. The Connecticut company packaged hardware products for supermarkets. The company showed promising figures, but it had done only one test for four months. Unfortunately, sales plunged after the fifth month. After two years the company folded. "At least it dropped dead on the spot," Mann reflects. "It's annoying when they die by inches."

Worst of all is the company that takes its angels for pigeons by pretending to have a product it does not. Private investors had already put up about $800,000 when Stephen P. Smith, the first director of marketing at Microsoft Corp., was brought in as part of a hand-picked management that acquired Metamorphic Systems. The founders had hoped to produce hardware to make the Apple compatible with the

IBM PC. "The money was there, the organization was there, but the product was late and too expensive," Smith says. According to one venture capitalist familiar with the deal, by the time the technical people had finished making all the product changes, the add-on cost almost as much as a new IBM. The angels ate their $1 million investment.

The lesson is simple, but hard to apply, Smith says. "It's wiser to have a completed product before you even seek funds," he concludes. "If you fund first, you just go along fooling yourself, the market, and the distribution channels"--and even your angels. But only for a while.

Finding a Perfect Match

It may be easier to get a camel through the eye of a needle than structure the perfect deal between entrepreneurs and angels. But even if perfection isn't attainable, a thoughtfully structured deal can diminish the conflict between investor and entrepreneur.

Clarity and simplicity. Get every issue on the table without sacrificing simplicity. "I advise against overcomplicating the structure of financing," says Grover Wickersham, a principal in Niesar & Wickersham, a San Francisco Bay area firm that specializes in entrepreneurial companies. "Aside from the unforseen consequences it could have, it may require so much explanation to new prospective investors that they may get scared off, making it hard for the company to raise additional funds."

"A major problem for investment bankers is simply disentangling the mess created by early-stage financing once the company has grown to the point where it needs us," says director of research, Joseph Arsenio of Birr, Wilson in San Francisco. "Implicit promises--of preemptive rights, for example--always create problems, especially when the founders don't want to honor them." From the very beginning, according to Arsenio, a company should keep in mind where it wants to be in five years.

Honest growth projections are indispensable to both sides. They help entrepreneurs determine their companies' capital needs, so they can discuss the possibility of additional rounds of financing with their investors. Projections also help investors determine how they will get their money out. A fast-growth company like Convergent Technologies Inc. looks from the start to go public or merge with a larger concern. But a less ambitious startup, like OFFTECH Inc.--

320

whose goal is to remain private at about $25 million in sales--must structure a means by which the angel can exit, typically a stock buy-back at a specified time, usually three to five years, and price.

Often, the investor will ask for a "put," permitting him to exercise his rights at a given time. "That could cause a cash drain on the company when it least needs one," says Dennis O'Connor, whose Lexington, Mass., law firm O'Connor, Broude & Snyder deals almost exclusively with emerging companies. "The entrepreneur might try to condition the put on certain levels of performance or even limit it to the original amount invested." Where the angel insists, a mutually protective clause could be written. "A staged put/call could be arranged," suggests Frank Macro of the Hartford law firm Shipman & Goodwin, "so the angel could put his investment in, say, four years, but if he did not, the entrepreneur could call it after four-and-a-half years." That way, the company could clean up its balance sheet and get the angel out before the investment became too valuable to buy back.

Angels frequently seek further protection. Noncompetition agreements prevent the entrepreneur from leaving to start another business in the same field. Buy/sell covenants bind the founder to sell stock back to the company if he or she should leave, preserving enough equity in the firm to attract another topflight management team.

Antidilution agreements bind the entrepreneur to preserve the angel's percentage stake in the company whenever future stock is sold. "The entrepreneur is better off without them," Macro says. "When he goes looking for more funds, the market may be bad or he may not quite have fulfilled his projections. It could be harder to sell new stock, if you have to then revalue the old." Giving the angel the right of first refusal on the next round of financing can have similar effects. "What new investor would want to go through a whole round of negotiations with a company, knowing that the company will pass the deal right back to the original investor?" wonders O'Connor.

Too much can be made of agreements set to paper. The best of the seraphic choir aren't too nervous about ironclad agreements. They know, as longtime angel Joseph Driscoll of Dallas puts it, "that the only real protection is the viability of the business."

Angel Chains

And he dreamed that there was a ladder set up on earth, and the top of it reached to heaven; and behold, the angels...were ascending and

321

descending on it. [Genesis 10:12]

The search for a better way to match entrepreneurs and private investors has produced several computerized screening systems, many modeled on the dating service run by Dr. Jeffrey Sohl, Associate Professor of Management Science & Director of the Center for Venture Research (William Wetzel's successor) Venture Capital Network Inc. (VCN) at the University of New Hampshire (603-862-3341). There are a number of venture capital networks operating around the country and Jeff Soh's office should be able to provide contact information.

HOW HAMBRO
SELECTS INVESTMENTS

Investors rely on the managers of a venture fund to exercise a rare combination of judgment, foresight, and prudence when selecting companies for their portfolio. To earn the return investors expect from a venture investment, the fund's managers must evaluate many factors - including the entrepreneur, the market, the product, production costs, and the risk. Some fund managers rely strictly on numbers; others add intuition to the formula. We asked Edwin Goodman, a general partner of the Hambro International Equity Partners - which, as of 1996, has over $180 million invested in young American companies - to describe how his fund selects companies for its portfolio, and we were pleasantly surprised by the candor with which he answered our questions. Perhaps Goodman's straightforward, no-nonsense approach helps explain the fund's success.

Q. We should start by making sure that the fund that we are about to profile for our readers is actively seeking investments in the United States - that the funds are available, and you are actively out there looking for deals.

GOODMAN: That is true.

Q. Approximately how many deals do you expect to close over the next six to twelve months?

GOODMAN: Anywhere between half a dozen and a dozen, depending on size.

Q. That is a great opportunity for twelve entrepreneurs. Does Hambro have an industry preference?

GOODMAN: No, we don't. We are by design quite eclectic. We have invested in most traditional areas as well as ones thought to be unusual for venture funds, such as magazines, distribution, broadcasting and such.

Q. I've noticed in the other venture funds that I have interviewed that they react to deals rather than seeking markets. In other words, if an entrepreneur comes in and says "Here is my deal, this is my market, I have to find the funds" that this is the way deals are closed. Does Hambro say "This is the market we want, let's go find an entrepreneur and then market him." Which approach does the Hambro Fund use?

GOODMAN: First of all, I think that every venture fund will tell you that they take the investing approach. But the fact is, in this business, people with capital have the luxury of being passive. We take both approaches. There are very good deals that come in "over the transom." Usually they come in through other venture capitalists or through intermediaries that we respect, so we have some confidence that it is a quality deal before we begin the process. Very few deals are done that come in absolutely cold from the entrepreneur with no introduction. We also go and identify markets we want and put our partners in a position so the deals can find them. For instance, if we want to be in the medical device of medical services field - which is a decision we made a couple of years ago--we said to one of our partners, "We want you to go to every conference and travel in circles such that you are going to see opportunities." This has worked well for us, so we do both.

Q. You mentioned going to conferences and talking to other venture capitalists. What else does Hambro do to increase its deal stream?

GOODMAN: One of the things that we do is talk to people like you who give us exposure to potential entrepreneurs. We try to get exposure in various publications. It is probably not terribly useful for venture capitalists to simply increase the volume of deal flow. It is probably more important for them to talk to people and maintain their relationships with key analysts on Wall Street, investment bankers, well-placed attorneys and accountants who are in the deal stream, and where again there is some kind of screening or professional assessment that takes place even before you see anyone, so you have some confidence that it deserves your time and attention. One of the big problems for venture capitalists is how they manage their time. We see about 1,000 proposals a year, so we are not interested in seeing 1,500. We would like to see 200 terrific ones to make our ten or twelve investments a year.

Q. Let's focus on the work "terrific." Could you give us a broad description of a hypothetical "terrific" deal?

GOODMAN: If I describe this to you, your readers may get discouraged, because this deal probably does not exist. First, what you would hope is that this is a very exciting market going for maybe fifty million at a hundred percent compound rate of growth, and no one else in the country has, for whatever reason, identified this market yet. That would be one. Two, there would be an entrepreneur who, if he had not excelled in this particular field, had started, built, managed and successfully sold a business in the past, and had relationships that he could call upon, so that he could assemble a full team with a chief financial officer, and a vice president of marketing, and a vice president of sales. Next, the entrepreneur would have a very enthusiastic view about his prospects and an also realistic view about valuation, so the venture capitalist could get a good piece of the business for their capital. These are all the things you would like to see, and you would like to be in very early, put your money in, and be able to play a role on the board and make a constructive contribution. You would like to see it reach critical mass of sales and profits within three years.

Q. Sounds terrific. I agree that no such deal exists. At least I have never heard of one.

GOODMAN: In fact, Apple was turned down by several astute investors because these guys (Gobs and Wozniak) were sort of scruffy, off-beat types who had not had any management experience. As a practical matter, you do not do too many of these deals. Basically, because when they have all of the ingredients, they tend to be chased by the venture capitalists. They tend to be seen and they tend to be competed for, and that drives the price up. So, where you really make money as in other investment businesses, is where you see value that other people don't see. The people that met Steve Jobs saw value and talent there that other people didn't see. He wasn't the central casting, management-oriented C.E.O., and to Arthur Rock's credit, he saw the potential.

Q. Let's say, though, that deal like that happens to come along. It meets your criteria for that perfect deal. How long would it take you to agree and write a check if all the pieces were there, and it was the most perfect deal you have seen? What is the turnaround time on that deal?

GOODMAN: I think you could do a deal like that very quickly. You could make the decision within a couple of business weeks, and have a handshake on the deal and the basic terms, and then you edge in to the period I call "lawyer logistics," and this would take another two or three weeks to get the documents to a closing. But, you can get capital to the entrepreneur in the right situation within a matter of ten business days. The loan then would be convertible into the final terms of the transaction worked out with the lawyers.

Q. And is that a technique you have used in the past?

GOODMAN: Yes, we have often done that.

Q. The conventional wisdom that I often hear is that the priorities that a venture capitalist looks for are: first, the characteristics of the entrepreneur, the right personality, the drive to succeed, the motivation. Second, the market size and market potential, and third, the product characteristics. Is that an accurate list of priorities here at Hambro?

GOODMAN: I do not think so. I do not think it is true of the business, but I will address whether it is true for us. There is a book called The New Venturers that I just read. It is very interesting reading about the venture business. It traces the successes of six or seven major firms, and the fascinating thing about it to me was there was not theme that was evident in the success of these various firms. One says that the technology is all important, one says it is only intuition about people that is important, and one says market size and growth is the crucial thing. In terms of the style of all these venture people, they are very, very different. Some are frenetic, some are philosophical and low key. They have all been enormously successful. So, I think one of the interesting things about the business is that it does not lend itself to formula analysis. I would say for us that we have to see characteristics in the entrepreneur and the entrepreneurial management to do a deal. And that has to do with tremendously high energy level, great dedication to succeed, resourcefulness, and what we think of as street smarts. If you have that, you can recover from mediocrity in other areas. If you do not have that, you probably cannot survive in the business. I think that is why, in a lot of venture-backed companies the entrepreneur that starts the process doesn't, in fact, end up managing the process.

326

Q. The venture capitalists call that "value added," the entrepreneur calls it being turned down. Can you give us an example of a deal you have done with an entrepreneur like that--their company has since gone public--where you have washed your hands of it, that readers might know?

GOODMAN: Well, one of our early successes, interestingly enough in the technology business, is a company called Ocillia Industries, which was in the mobile home business. We invested what looks, in retrospect now, a rather modest amount of capital in it. That money was repaid. It was a subordinated venture with warrants, and we had warrants for a position in the company. I think our basis was about $60,000, which came to be worth something in the range of 2.5 to 3 million dollars, which we have since sold and returned to our investors.

Q. It that the kind of return on invested capital that you normally look for?

GOODMAN: Well, again, that is very hard to answer because you cannot be that precise. I would say that if the mean return on a business is about 25 percent compounded (we hope to do at least that well), it means that we have to look for about 40 percent because we know that in certain situations we will strike out. We have to get a certain number of home runs to get the batting average up. Five times your money in five years is about 38 percent, so that is sort of a thumbnail rule. We know from experience you have got to do much better in a certain number of deals than that to offset the poor ones to get a portfolio return or something in the range of 35-45 percent compounded.

Q. Let's go back to the managing of time of the venture capitalist. Entrepreneurs often complain about how long it takes for the industry professionals to get back to them and turn it around. It takes three months to find out they finally got turned down. One of the things that we strive to do is to improve the interface between the venture capitalist and the entrepreneur and let them know what each is thinking, so that the whole process goes smoothly. could you give us a general picture of how many companies each of you professionals watches? Does each one have fifteen companies that they are concerned with? And how much time would they spend with each one?

GOODMAN: They watch seven to ten, somewhere in that range.

Q. And is that operating companies?

GOODMAN: Correct. And the obligation involved there with time varies tremendously. To elaborate on the analogy of that perfect deal, let's say it progresses in the perfect fashion, and you go to board meetings quarterly, and the entrepreneur beats plan, and you happily write occasional reports to your investors, and everything is fine. So that is an hour or two a quarter on such a company. Then you have the very troubled companies that require an enormous amount of time-- maybe 50 percent of a venture person's time--and then all the companies in between. It is very hard to conclude anything from saying that someone is watching seven or nine companies. one of the difficult things for people who are approaching venture firms probably is that they do not quite know what they are dealing with. They might come in on a great day, and have the undivided attention, and all the psychic energy of a partner, and then another day they might come in, and all hell might be breaking loose. They wonder why they have that twenty minute meeting and the six phone calls, and they feel they have been badly treated. It is also true, in fairness, to say that the assets of the venture business have climbed faster than the professional management, so that these time demands have increased on the general partners, which makes it tougher and tougher for people to get their attention.

Q. In addition to the seven to ten companies, how many proposals does each look at during the course of a year?

GOODMAN: Well, we get a thousand with five partners. You can figure it out. It is busy.

Q. When you described your perfect deal, you mentioned market size and growth and all those components, and yet now, you just talked about the reality of the deals you select, you mentioned personal excitement with the business idea. Besides what the market research and all the empirical data says, how big a role does that personal intuition play?

GOODMAN: It plays a tremendous role. The venture business is about making investment decisions with too little information and too little time. The gut that buys IBM stock is a lot closer to getting perfect information which is publicly available on large, identified markets, and having considerable time to make his investment decision. Then, of course, if he doesn't like it, he can bail out and get 90 percent of his money back. I think that there is a lot more intuition necessarily in our business. Particularly when it

328

comes to the chemistry that takes place of doesn't when you are trying to assess an individual that is going to be successful. I think that is what is the most fun in the business. After you do all your rational analysis, and you crunch the numbers as far as possible, you are really saying, I am going to be on this gut John Smith, I am going to marry him, I am going to be inextricably bound up in him in an economic entity for five or six years. Am I willing to do that? And he is going to make the same judgment about you, if he has any choices. If he has money offers from several people he is going to decide whose money he wants--who he wants to live with. I think it plays a big factor. What we try to do here to safeguard that not becoming disproportionate and misleading is to have the other partners listen to it, have them agree on it as well.

Q. The conventional wisdom of the industry now seems to be computer hardware and software, although software much less increasingly. Data communications, medical technology are the "hot" areas. I don't see much interest in retail markets, for example. Does Hambro concur? And the second part of that question is which markets do you see the greatest opportunity in the next five or so years?

GOODMAN: We basically do not concur. We think that venture business has defined itself too narrowly. We have not done that. The reason the venture business is now in some difficulty is because it was much too narrowly confined to electronics, computers and computer peripherals over the last five years. In over-financed companies in certain narrow markets, disk drive companies, for example. It is true that historically you are going to find the venture money flowing to areas with 50 percent greater compound growth, because you can make more mistakes. There is a greater margin for error in those kind of very high growth markets. It is also true that those markets attract a lot of competition and drive prices up, so the trick is to find a great market like that which no one has heard of yet.

We think it is wise to be opportunistic and open to various kinds of investments. We are becoming a service economy, yet the venture capitalists have avoided service companies, which is silly. There are some tremendous opportunities. We are reviewing one now, I don't know if we will do it, but I think it is kind of interesting, which is the rental of personal computers as a business--IBM and compact computers, which could be a very interesting business, I think. One of the areas we just got involved in is wholesale clubs, which is a new method of distribution, a new method of retailing. It is interesting--today it is quite fascinating if you look at Price Club, which is the prototype wholesale warehouse company started in 1977, and Apple Computer which started in 1977. They are both the same size, but not too many have heard of Price. It is $1.8 billion this year in sales. Apple is about $1.6 billion.

Q. I appreciate your time very much. One more question. Advice to the entrepreneur: When he approaches a fund, what is the most common failing? What can he do to get a better hearing?

GOODMAN: Well, first of all, a business plan and a business proposal will never make you successful, but it will screw you badly. If you do not care enough to correct a misspelling in your cover letter, and your business plan is done on a cheap printer, is not very legible, is not well organized, is not paginated, and you cannot find the things in a neat table of contents, why the hell should anyone take the trouble to read it carefully? In addition to a business plan, the business plan writer should be certain to include a summary. People are very busy. You ought to be able to send a summary to people, save a little money for yourself and save people's time, and give them a nice, crisp two-page summary of your business idea to get their attention. There is good marketing in back of that. It says to the investor: "I just do not send my business plan around to everybody. If you are interested, we will talk, and maybe I will hand deliver the plan." In the meantime, give the guy the executive summary.

The other thing is tenacity. People are busy. Don't get your nose out of joint if a guy does not return your call once or twice. Stay with it. You are excited, and you have an idea. Who ever sold anything by asking someone once quietly? I call guys who run pension plans thirty times over a four-month period to get an appointment.

The other thing is, when you get the appointment, be prepared. Try to make a realistic assessment. If you have twenty minutes, you can do one thing. If you have three hours, you can do another. If it is going to be lunch you can do one thing, and if you are going to be in a meeting room with all visual aids, you can do another thing. If it is going to be in front of eight people you can do one thing, and if it is going to be one on one, you can do another.

DON'T CALL
JUST ANY LAWYER

MICHELLE BEKEY

This article appeared in *Venture* and has been edited for this book.

Gordon Davidson, partner at Fenwick, Davis & West, Palo Alto, California, had seen his share of tough startup negotiations, but nothing like this.

Seven people--Davidson, the three entrepreneurs he represented, two venture capitalists, and their attorney--huddled in the startup's office back. It was around midnight. The group, which had been trying to cut a deal since eight o'clock that morning had hit a snag on the issue of patents. The venture capitalists wanted absolute assurance that the company's technology wouldn't infringe on any existing patents. Davidson's clients argued that they couldn't make such a promise--and that they had clearly stated as much weeks before. Tempers flared. Next, the investors insisted that the entrepreneurs' stock be parceled out over a five-year period. Davidson parried by demanding initial public offering rights favorable to the entrepreneurs. "What kind of a stunt is that?" demanded the venture capitalists' infuriated counsel. Somebody called a time-out.

Davidson took his disheartened clients out for a walk around the block, listening to them grumble about whether the money $650,000 worth of first-round financing was worth the aggravation. Davidson counseled them to shed their partisan feelings. "Just get the deal done," he said. Back in the conference room, cooler heads prevailed: Davidson withdrew the initial public offering request, the venture capitalist surrendered their patent stance, and both sides compromised on a stock payout schedule. Tension eased. Everyone agreed to make peace and order take-out pizza. By eight a.m.--a full twenty-four hours after the marathon session began--an agreement had been struck. Reflects Davidson: "I really don't think it would have happened if we hadn't all come to our senses."

Or, perhaps, if Davidson himself hadn't been present. Davidson is a member of a small, young, and highly influential fraternity: attorneys who specialize in venture capital transactions. A handful of firms attracts much of the work--and most of the recognition--in this burgeoning specialty because they operate in three cities where much of the startup and investing activity takes place. In Palo Alto, Fenwick Davis shares a lush office complex with Wilson, Sonsini, Goodrich & Rosati, a firm that helps finance an astonishing 40 percent of all Silicon Valley startups. Venture attorneys Cooley, Godward, Castro, Huddleson & Tatum also has offices in the same complex; Brobeck, Phleger & Harrison is a five-minute drive away. On the East Coast there's Testa, Hurwitz & Thibeault and Gaston Snow & Ely Bartlett in Boston, and in New York, O'Sullivan Graev & Karabell and Reavis & McGrath, which get a lot of business from Fred Adler, lawyer-turned-venture-capitalist. In most major law firms, attorneys sometimes are called on for this kind of work. And there are, of course, other active players in different parts of the country, Paul, Hastings, Janofsky & Walker in Los Angeles and Kirkland & Ellis in Chicago, for instance.

The fraternity's impact is unmistakable because the group has made itself indispensable to venture deals, no matter which side of the table it represents. Although most stock purchase agreements tend to be boilerplate and go off without a hitch, entrepreneurs have come to rely more and more on their lawyers. "I wouldn't put a deal together without outside counsel," avows an entrepreneur, himself an attorney. "Lawyers have a perception of today's market: They can put a note of reality on valuations."

More fundamentally, venture attorneys introduce entrepreneurs to receptive backers (and deal with venture capitalists - the lead investors), handle the negotiations, and draft the necessary documents, a process that can take three months or more. They can play a vital role even earlier on by helping entrepreneurs make fail-safe exists from their employers and assisting them with their business plans. And they can continue to advise young companies up to and beyond their IPOs.

When it comes to financing, lawyers can put startups on more or less equal footing with venture capitalists, who are intimately familiar with the ins and outs of agreements by virtue of doing a dozen or so deals each year. With entrepreneurs, who may go through the process once or twice in a lifetime, "You have a much greater educational role to perform," asserts Paul Jacobs, a partner at Reavis & McGrath. "Typically, when entrepreneurs shake hands, they're thinking about the $4 million they're getting for 50 percent of their companies. The first time they realize the complexity of the transaction is when the term sheet comes to them."

It's in contending with term sheets - the two-to-five page documents that "define who gets what" in a deal, according to Richard Testa, a partner at Testa Hurwitz - as well as with other contractual complexities, that lawyers can help entrepreneurs navigate a course to the completion of an agreement. The perils of deal making can include structuring various classes of stock and wrestling with a host of relatively new clauses designed to protect investors, including antidilution protection, forced buyouts, and demand registration rights. "Entrepreneurs are at an absolute disadvantage without someone competent to handle the negotiations," asserts Testa. Venture capitalists, too, have come to depend on such lawyers. Couldn't any qualified corporate attorney do the same? "Can it get done by other firms?" asks Bryan C. Cressey, general partner in Golder, Thoma, Cressey, Rauner, Inc. a Chicago venture capital firm. "The answer is, it can and it doe. But if I were doing a $1 million deal, would I? No."

A lawyer's expertise carries a high price tag. A senior partner typically earns $300,000 to $500,000 a year. "Most firms try for an hourly charge," says Jacobs of Reavis & McGrath. Senior partners command $250 to $300 an hour; partners get $175 to $200. Those fees don't include the occasional rewards firms may get by investing a tiny amount in startups they represent. Wilson Sonsini dropped between $1,000 and $15,000 into Rolm Corp. and LSI Logic Corp. and dozens of other startups early on.

Venture law firms have grown up right alongside the venture capital industry. A few players, like Cooley Godward and Brobeck Phleger, have venerable roots stretching back 60 years or more. But neither firm got around to opening a Palo Alto office until 1980. Most partnerships specializing in emerging company law are only about as old as the technology driven companies and venture capital firms they represent. Some firms have their origins in serving venture capitalists: Reavis & McGrath, for instance, has handled Adler & Co.'s legal load since the mid-1960s. Other attorneys have grown fat primarily by working for startups: Testa Hurwitz counts Digital Equipment Corp. among its clients; Fenwick Davis launched Apple Computer Inc. and has since worked with "well over thirty" former Apple managers, says Davidson. Cooley Godward ministers to both kinds of clients, representing myriad Silicon Valley startups and launching more than 50 venture funds over the last decade.

Venture lawyers have adopted a style that suits their intensity and youth. Many still don pinstripes, but frequently forego jackets. "You've got to be a stiff to wear a coat," cracks a lawyer. They're as likely as their entrepreneurial clients to grab take-out sandwiches for lunch. The Palo Alto brigade in particular projects a more casual image in offices where pale wood and glass walls predominate. "We don't want people feeling like they're going to see pompous asses who are going to look down on them," notes one partner at Cooley Godward. The downside: "People keep telling us that this place looks like a sushi bar."

As a rule, startups find venture attorneys through referrals from other entrepreneurs, lawyers, accountants, or venture capitalists. Because of their wide range of contacts, venture lawyers claim they can batch up an entrepreneurial team's concept and personality with the best financing prospect. "We run a dating service of sorts," says Joseph Bartlett, partner at Gaston Snow.

Firms rarely charge for their matchmaking services and frequently delay billing for legal fees until startups get funding. But they also try to limit the number of uncompensated hours. After entrepreneurs receive venture financing, they can expect to foot bills for their own and the venture capitalist's legal work: The total typically runs from $20,000 to $50,000 depending on the complexity of the deal and the time spent in negotiation, and may include such services as issuing stock, creating agreements for key stock purchasers, and employment contracts. The practice of an entrepreneur's picking up the entire tab is a carryover from investment banking, where the company raising money bears all the costs.

Their matchmaking roles occasionally force lawyers to become marriage counselors who must minimize conflict and try to instill a feeling of mutual trust based on common interest. "The trick is to be able to break down the defensiveness on both sides," observes Wilson Sonsini's Johnson. To reduce suspicion and establish a broader perspective, he tries to teach both venture capitalists and entrepreneurs to "take the other person's position against your own interest."

In one instance Johnson had to mediate a dispute between three contentious parties. Late in 1985 an entrepreneur and his colleagues decided to attempt a leveraged buyout of a communications division that represented the most promising technology within a failing startup. The trouble was that the team had to appease not only the parent company, which wanted to avoid Chapter XI, but also the parent's corporate backer, which wanted to salvage part of its original investment. The management buyout team itself was held together tenuously: Some had employment offers elsewhere, and the cash in the company's till was perilously low. "People were wondering how they would make their car payments," recalls the entrepreneur. But the venture investors were loath to put in funds until a deal had been struck.

It was just after Christmas when eight negotiators - the entrepreneur, parent company management, attorneys for the corporate investor, venture capitalists, and Johnson, who represented the buyout team - convened over several consecutive days as Wilson Sonsini. One evening around midnight, the issue of advances to fund salaries came up. The venture investors reluctantly agreed, but only if the parent company promised to repay the funds if the new venture failed. The parent company balked. Johnson persuaded the group that the magnitude of the deal - $4 million - didn't warrant getting hung up on an issue worth a few thousand dollars. The parent company relented and an agreement was signed. Johnson kept everyone focused on major issues, according to the entrepreneur: "Craig kept pointing out we all had an interest in seeing this company survive."

Ensuring survival is a significant part of the venture lawyer's work in drawing up the necessary documents in an agreement. Structuring deals, says Johnson, "is like launching rockets: If you're a tenth of a degree off to start, you can be 1,000 miles off course later on." And because they handle startup financing day after day, venture attorneys know which elements of a deal are standard and which ones aren't. They're also less likely to make the kinds of errors that can hamstring a startup's fund raising efforts or result in huge tax penalties to the founders later on.

Entrepreneurs often trip over stock-related issues. C. Bradford Jeffries, a partner in Cooley Godward and a principal in Sigma Partners, a San Jose, Calif., venture fund, recalls the case of a high technology startup whose lawyer made the mistake of issuing only a single class of stock. Founders bought their shares for five cents each; investors later bought in at two dollars. When it came time to attract new management with stock incentives, the shares were priced much too far out of reach. "Sometimes we have to blow up a company and start over," Jeffries says. Similarly, if founders hold on to too much stock, it can make it considerably more difficult to bring in fresh talent a few years down the road.

Venture lawyers usually counsel entrepreneurs to install a stock vesting schedule, under which the founders earn their shares on a steady payout basis - say, 1/48 of the total every month for four years. That frequently makes entrepreneurs uneasy because they may fear that venture capitalists will fire them before they've earned their due. But attorneys argue that vesting actually protects founders' interests: Without it, they say, entrepreneurs who leave a company early stand to reap the benefits of everyone else's hard work once the startup goes public.

Jeffries cites the example of a startup team that brought in a president after the company had sealed its funding. The team had only reluctantly agreed to accept vesting, but appreciated the decision after it kicked out its president who, at the time, owned a huge block of stock. The company was able to buy back some 80 percent of his holdings at five cents a share. A few years later, when the company went public, that block had a market value of $10 million.

The increasingly restrictive nature of venture capital deals - due, in some part, to venture lawyers who authored clauses to accommodate investors - can pose problems for startups. For example, ratchet clauses - which automatically grant new shares to existing investors if new funds must be raised at a lower price - can discourage later investors, who perceive the clauses as an undeserved windfall to original backers, and dilute the equity of founders. Equally vexatious are mandatory preferred stock redemption rights some investors insist on: These force entrepreneurs to buy out their backers if the company hasn't gone public in a few years. Multiply those clauses by several investment rounds, and startups can eventually face a $5 million to $10 million tab if they're not prepared to do an IPO within the allotted time.

336

Once they've worked out the intricacies of financing, venture lawyers can help entrepreneurs stay in business, often by remaining as their general counsel. With assistance from Gordon Davidson, Dan Glystra, the founder of VisiCorp - which was a San Jose, Calif., marketer of the VisiCalc spreadsheet program - survived a succession of legal battles with Software Arts, which developed VisiCalc. During that period of suits, Davidson saved Glystra from other recalcitrant software authors by refusing to give in to their shifting demands. En route to the final negotiations, Glystra says, Davidson cajoled a flight attendant into holding a plant until the balky authors could be coaxed aboard.

Glystra found himself on the opposite side of the bargaining table from Davidson when he left VisiCorp voluntarily in 1984 and negotiated a severance agreement. A year later, when he launched a new software startup, Glystra turned to a different venture lawyer to help with financing. Despite a close personal friendship with Davidson, Glystra thought the attorney's close ties to VisiCorp made hiring him problematic.

Lawyers are quick to downplay possible conflicts of interest, even though man y serve both venture capitalists and entrepreneurs. Most point out that they won't work both sides of the same financing deal, even though professional standards sometimes allow a dual role if both parties agree. What's more, attorneys swear that they reveal which venture funds they represent on an ongoing basis when startups approach them. They provide the same information to prospective venture capital clients. If either side feels uncomfortable, the would-be client is free to withdraw.

That's not to say that conflicts don't arise. Bartlett of Gaston Snow recently removed himself from negotiations when he felt he knew too much about the negotiation positions of both sides. "I don't want to find myself saying, `I know something and I can't tell you,'" he explains. Occasionally clients put pressure on lawyers to ignore conflicting loyalties. Attorney Testa says he has gotten calls for action from venture capitalists who know full well that he's representing one of their portfolio companies. "`Dick,' they say, `don't tell me there's a conflict: Go solve the problem.'"

Clause for Concern: Investors Tighten the Screws

Tighter money and concern over which way a company's valuation will travel between financing rounds have turned venture capitalists into tough negotiators. To protect their investments, they're packing more fail-safe clauses into purchase and sales agreements, some of them quite burdensome to entrepreneurs, including:

Participating Preferred Shares These entitle preferred shareholders (a/k/a venture capitalists) to be repaid first in case the startup is liquidated - or sold or merged - and also to receive a set percentage of remaining funds along with holders of common stock. The arrangement invariably leaves less to entrepreneurs.

Co-sale Provision If founders decide to sell their stock prior to an IPO, this grants investors the right to tender their shares as well. The provision can cause conflicts between first-round and later-stage investors, say it inhibits entrepreneurs' ability to cash out. "Very messy," says one lawyer.

Ratchet Antidilution Protection Investors automatically receive free additional stock, when converting their preferred shares, if the company's stock is ever sold at a price lower than what those backers originally paid. Sometimes this shifts the control of the startup to venture capitalists.

Weighted-average Formula A less drastic alternative to ratchet clauses, the provision can still reduce an entrepreneur's stake by issuing new common stock according to a formula based on the number and price of outstanding shares.

Piggyback Registration Rights This grants investors - but not necessarily founders - the right to register some of their shares in a public offering. Because investment bankers don't like a mass exodus of original backers and management in an IPO, entrepreneurs may be forced to delay cashing out. These rights aren't necessarily enforceable. Observes Joseph W. Bartlett, partner in Gaston Snow: "The underwriter controls the deal and can say, `You just sit down and shut up.'"

Demand Registration Rights With these powers, existing shareholders, even if they're a minority, can demand at least one public offering - not necessarily the IPO - within a specified time, say, three to five years. But given the amount of SEC-mandated preparation for an offering, these rights are tough to invoke. "If the company doesn't want to go public, it's very difficult to force a company to do so," says Lawrence Graev, partner in O'Sullivan Graev & Karabell.

Mandatory Redemption of Preferred Stock The clause requires a company to buy out investors at a predetermined price if an IPO doesn't occur within a particular period. A startup may not be able to afford the redemption if later investors get the same protection.

Forced Buyout Akin to mandatory redemption, the clause specifies that if management hasn't sold or taken its company public by a certain time, investors may find a buyer. This penalizes recalcitrant management by allowing investors to sell their stock to controlling shareholders or management for the full fair market price. "Draconian," admits one lawyer.

Key Man Insurance This is acceptable if proceeds are payable to the company. But if investors demand a policy where proceeds are payable to preferred stockholders, an entrepreneur may get the sense that someone's waiting for him to get hit by a truck.

Washout Financing This is a strategy of last resort that washes out all previously issued stock when existing preferred shareholders won't commit additional funds. All preferred and common stock is converted to a single class of common stock and new investors are issued a new series of preferred. This dilutes the holdings of all prior shareholders, including management.

Lawyers argue that these covenants serve chiefly as safeguards and that investors may bend on some clauses. Every deal has at least some form of antidilution protection, a vesting plan, and representation on the board, but the terms can be negotiable. If a company is failing, "god-damn words aren't going to save it anyway," insists Alan Mendelson, partner at Cooley Godward.

THE LEGAL PROCESS OF VENTURE CAPITAL INVESTMENT*

RICHARD J. TESTA

Richard J. Testa is a partner in the Boston law firm of Testa, Hurwitz & Thibeault. He and his firm serve as counsel for several professional venture capital companies, as well as for a large number of businesses financed by venture capital sources.

General Considerations Relating to Legal Documentation

Venture capital investing involves a long-term commitment of support for a company. As such, the parties involved in negotiating and implementing the investment transaction must bring to the process a sensitivity to the changing and differingobjectives and requirements (financial, legal, personal, etc.) of the business, and its principal participants.

A key element in the attainment of a successful relationship between a young business enterprise and its venture capital investors is the careful crafting of the legal structure of the investment transaction.

The legal documents must foresee the evolution of the enterprise from a development stage start-up to a publicly held company or viable acquisition candidate. Not only do the investment documents represent a charter of the legal rights of the parties spanning the growth cycle of the business, but they also set the tone of the relationship between the management/entrepreneurs and the financial backers of the enterprise, serving as a model for resolution of their often differing interests.

Despite standardization of much of the venture capital process, it remains fundamentally highly idiosyncratic, with each transaction reflecting the particular chemistry between entrepreneur and investor. Accordingly, there exists no such thing as the perfect model of legal documentation for the investment transaction. Each set of documents needs to be tailored to reflect the unique combination of styles and interests involved. Generally, however, each transaction will encompass the following common set of documents:

- The term sheet, or commitment letter, summarizing in broad strokes the principal financial and other terms of the investment.

- The investment agreement detailing the terms of purchase and provisions of the securities (equity or debt) being acquired.

- The stockholders agreement containing restrictions upon the transfer and voting of securities by management and (occasionally) investors.

- Employee stock purchase or stock option agreements governing the current and future allocation of equity in the business to key employees.

- Employee confidentiality and proprietary rights agreements assuring the retention by the business of its valuable trade secrets and business rights.

- Legal opinion of company counsel covering the legality of the securities, compliance with state and federal securities laws and related matters.

The Term Sheet

The handshake "agreement" between investor and entrepreneur is often set forth in a written term sheet or letter of intent. Some investors prefer to characterize this document as a commitment letter. Although the term sheet may take a variety of forms, from a cursory and informal letter to a more detailed and formal memorandum, it is intended to accomplish the following purposes:

- to reflect the agreed upon valuation of the business and to quantify the proposed allocation of that value between the entrepreneurs and investors;

- to summarize key financial and legal terms of the transaction which will serve as the basis for preparing definitive legal documents; and

- on occasion, to impose enforceable legal obligations upon the parties, such as requiring payment of expenses in the event the investment does not close or prohibiting negotiations with other parties pending the completion of the transaction.

Above all, the term sheet should be used by the venture capitalist to elicit those concerns of both parties which, if unaddressed and unresolved, might later develop into "deal killers". For example, if the venture capitalist intends to require that the entrepreneurs submit their stock ownership in the enterprise to buy-back or forfeiture restrictions in the event they end employment, such a condition should be covered in the term sheet, because it encroaches into an area in which the entrepreneur will be especially sensitive. Other sensitive topics include the composition of the board of directors and matters relating to the terms of employment of the entrepreneurs.

A term sheet is particularly valuable for the entrepreneur who has never seen venture terms before. The chief executive officer, who is relatively inexperienced in financing transactions, is being introduced to a large number of new concepts. By contrast, the venture capitalist is usually experienced and familiar with the terms of the venture financing, as well as possible variations. The term sheet is particularly useful in bridging these differences in background knowledge and experience.

The Investment Agreement

Principal Purposes and Legal Consequences

The long form investment agreement has four principal business objectives:

- Most importantly, it sets forth the detailed substantive terms of the investment.

- It serves as the basic disclosure document setting forth or referencing the relevant historical, business, financial, and legal data relating to the enterprise.

- It presents, through the use of conditions precedent to closing, a "stop action" photograph or image of the issuer that must exist at the time of closing. The level of detail of this photograph will vary depending upon the round of financing involved in the transaction and the simplicity or the complexity of the company's operations.

- It defines several business parameters within which the enterprise must operate in the future. The commandments to management range from relatively simple "thou shall not's" (negative covenants) to complex "thou shalt's" (affirmative covenants).

The legal effect of the investment agreement is similar to that of many commercial contracts, although the practical consequences may differ. The most common consequence of a breach of agreement in the capital investment context is the ability of the investor to refuse to close the transaction because of the company's failure to satisfy a condition precedent, or the existence of a significant misrepresentation by the company. Once the closing has occurred, remedies in the nature of rescission are rare. Moreover, while claims for damages do arise, they are uncommon in the high-risk venture area. Common remedies available for breach of covenant are specific performance and injunctive relief. As a practical matter, however, remedies that are self-executing, such as "ratchet-down" provisions in an antidilution formula or extraordinary voting rights granted to a class of preferred stock, are more formidable than remedies which frequently amount to waving a stick in the air, such as accelerated repayment of debt securities.

Description of the Transaction

The investment agreement memorializes the terms of the transaction. Consequently, the agreement should include a description of the securities being purchased, the purchase price, and assurances that the securities have been properly authorized.

If the investor acquires a note (whether or not convertible) or a stock purchase warrant, the form of the security should be attached as an exhibit to the investment agreement. If the investor acquires a class of stock other than conventional common stock, the terms of the class of stock as set forth in the corporate charter should be attached to the investment agreement as an exhibit.

If more than one investor participates in the financing, the several purchasers may be listed or referenced in an exhibit to the agreement.

343

In some cases, the company will execute separate but identical investment agreements with each investor. Conditions of each investor's obligation to purchase may be that identical investment agreements have been executed simultaneously with each investor, such agreements have not been amended and are in full force on the closing date, and a specified minimum number of dollars has been raised by the company.

In some transactions, the entire investment proceeds will not be made available to the company at a single closing. If the purchase is made in two or more installments over fixed periods of time, the major condition precedent to closing each successive installment is the absence of any material adverse changes affecting the company since the initial closing. In a "staged" investment, the purchase of additional securities at subsequent closings is conditioned upon the accomplishment of certain financial or operational goals, such as the attainment of specified revenue levels or completion of development work on a new product, as well as the absence of any material adverse changes. A staged investment serves as an incentive to management to proceed diligently with the development of its business, as outlined in its business plan, and enables venture capitalists to target their investments with a maximum impact on the development of the business., as well as maximizing the investor's internal rate of return on cash invested.

Representations and Warranties of the Company

It is a rare issuer company that is totally "clean"; that is, a company which has no stated exceptions to the several business, financial, and legal topics addressed by the representation and warranty section of the investment agreement. Only a new start-up company with neither employees nor sales is likely to fall into this category. Because the venture capitalist has already conducted a thorough factual review of the company's business prior to issuing his term sheet or letter of intent, the representations and warranties are not intended to screen the company for suitability as an investment (although the disclosure of significant adverse information not previously known to the investor may scuttle the investment), but rather to provide full disclosure of the fine details of the company's operations that may be relevant in advising management with regard to the future conduct of the business.

The following list of specific representations and warranties is common in most venture capital investment agreements. Each category is prefaced by an affirmative declaration of compliance, subject to stated expectations that are normally appended as an exhibit.

- *Organization and authority:* The company is properly organized, in good standing, and has legal authority to conduct its business.

- *Corporate action:* All necessary actions under state corporate law, and the company's corporate charter and bylaws, have been taken to authorize the transaction and to issue the securities.

- *Governmental approvals:* All consents and approvals of governmental agencies necessary to complete the transaction have been obtained. In particular, this covers compliance with state securities laws and environmental regulations.

- *Absence of litigation:* No litigation or other proceedings exist, or are threatened, which would adversely affect the company's business or the financing transaction.

- *Employment of key personnel:* No restrictions exist relating to employment of key personnel or use of business information, particularly as a result or prior employment of such personnel by another enterprise.

- *Compliance with other agreements:* No violations of the company's corporate charter, bylaws, or other valid agreements exist, or will exist as a result of the financing.

- *Ownership of properties and assets:* The company possesses sufficient ownership rights in its business assets, particularly its patent, copyright, trademark, and other intellectual property rights to conduct its business.

- *Financial information:* Audited, and internal unaudited, financial statements have been prepared in accordance with generally accepted accounting principles and fairly present the financial position and operating results of the company. Statements as to specific categories of items, such as inventory valuation and status of accounts receivable, may be included. No adverse changes have occurred since the date of the most recent financial statements furnished.

- *Transactions with insiders:* Disclosure is made of any direct or indirect transactions between the company and its directors, officers or stockholders.

- *Third-party guaranties or investments:* Absence of continuing financial involvements with third parties.

- *Compliance with federal securities laws:* Certification that the transaction complies with federal and state securities laws, including the possibility that the transaction may be integrated with other securities sales.

- *Registration rights:* Absence of rights to cause the company to file any registration statement under the federal securities laws or any right to participate in any such registration.

- *Disclosure:* The business plan used to seek financing is accurate and complete and all material disclosures have been made to investors either in the business plan or in legal documents relating to the transaction.

- *Brokerage:* Disclosure of any finder's or broker's fees or commissions payable in connection with the transaction.

- *Capitalization:* Description of the company's authorized capitalization and status of outstanding securities, including warrants, options and convertible securities. Any transfer restrictions, repurchase rights or preemptive rights are also described.

- *Insurance:* The company has insurance in such amounts and covering such risks as is customarily carried by companies of similar size engaged in similar businesses.

- *U.S. real property holding corporation:* Certification that the company has not now and has never been a "United States real property holding corporation" and that the company has filed with the Internal Revenue Service all statements, if any, with its federal income tax returns that are required under related regulations.

- *Small business concern:* If a member of the investment group is an SBIC, certification that the company, including its affiliates, is a "small business concern" and the information pertaining to the company set forth in any required Small Business Administration forms is accurate and complete.

Covenants and Undertakings of the Company

The covenants section of the investment agreement contains several affirmative and negative undertakings of the company relating to the future conduct of its affairs. Affirmative covenants are actions, positions, or results that the company promises to achieve or undertake. Negative covenants are actions, positions, or results that the company promises to avoid.

If, under the terms of the investment agreement, the board of directors is to be controlled by inside management, the covenants are frequently extensive. In an equity-oriented venture capital investment, however, where the investors will frequently control the board of directors, the covenants are often kept to a minimum. In such a situation the affirmative covenants might merely provide that the investor will receive periodic financial information and will be represented on the board. The negative covenants might limit only the company's ability to amend its corporate charter, or merge or sell its assets without the investor's consent. Investors with board control will generally rely upon this control to influence the management of a company and will not, as a rule, find it necessary to impose extensive contractual restrictions on the conduct of the business by insisting on strict affirmative and negative covenants.

Both affirmative and negative covenants may remain in effect as long as the investors hold any of the investment securities or, alternatively, may terminate upon the occurrence of certain events, such as the completion of an initial public offering, conversion of debt-oriented convertible securities into equity, or the mere passage of time.

Among the customary affirmative covenants that are found in venture capital investment agreements are the following:

- *Payment of taxes and claims:* The company will pay all lawful taxes, assessments, and levies upon it or its income or property before they become in default. This covenant sometimes provides that all trade debt, principal and interest on debt securities acquired by the investor will be paid when due.

- *Property and liability insurance:* The company will maintain insurance against hazards, risks and liability to persons and property to the extent customary for companies engaged in the same or similar businesses.

- *Maintenance of corporate existence:* The company will maintain its corporate existence and all rights, licenses, patents, copyrights, trademarks, etc., useful in its business and will engage only in the type of business described in the business plan.

- *Legal compliance:* The company will comply with all applicable laws and regulations in the conduct of its business.

- *Access to premises:* Investors or their representatives will generally be permitted to inspect the company's facilities, books, and records. To the extent that confidentiality of corporate business information may be compromised by such rights of access, investors generally agree to confidentiality restrictions or to limiting access to lead or major investors.

- *Accounts and reports:* The company may be asked by the investor to agree to maintain a standard system of accounting in accordance with generally accepted accounting principles consistently applied, and to keep full and complete financial records.

- *Repair and maintenance:* The company will keep all necessary equipment and property in good repair and condition, as required to permit the business to be properly conducted.

- *Approval of budgets:* The investor will frequently require management to produce comprehensive annual operating and capital budgets for approval by the investor or by the board of directors. Revisions of such budgets during the year may also require advance approval.

- *Protection of proprietary rights:* The company will agree to take all necessary steps to protect proprietary developments made in the future, including causing all key employees to sign confidentiality and proprietary rights agreements.

- *Compliance with key agreements:* The company will enforce its rights under key agreements, such as the stockholders agreement, and will cause future stockholders to join the agreement.

- *Life insurance:* The investor will often require the company to maintain insurance on the lives of key officers and employees. The face amount in some cases may be as much as the purchase price of the securities, and the insurance proceeds are often payable directly to the investor, particularly if the investor holds debt securities.

- *Board of directors:* Venture capital firms will generally seek assurances that they will be represented on the company's board of directors. The right to be represented on the board may be backed up by voting agreements with the principal stockholders. If investors are not to be represented on the board, the company may be required to notify investors of the time and place of board meetings, and to permit investors or their representatives to attend such meetings and receive written material disseminated to directors. Frequency of board meetings and financial arrangements may also be covered.

- *Financial and operating statements:* The company will invariably agree to provide the investor with detailed financial and operating information. The information to be provided may include annual, quarterly, and sometimes monthly reports of sales, production, shipments, profits, cash balances, receivables, payables, and back log; all statements filed with the Securities and Exchange Commission or other regulatory agencies; notification of significant lawsuits or other legal proceedings; and any other information that investors may need for their own voluntary or involuntary filing requirements. Particularly where investors are acquiring debt securities or preferred stock containing extensive financial and other covenants, financial statements are required to be accompanied by a certificate from the company's chief executive or financial officer and, in the case of audited financial statements, its auditors, to the effect that the company is in compliance with all provisions of the investment agreement. The right to receive financial information is often terminated when the company goes public in order to avoid dissemination of "inside" information. Although companies generally concede the legitimate interests of investors to receive business information, negotiation over the scope and form of this information may be considerable in view of the operational burden and potential liabilities it can impose upon management.

- *Current ratio, working capital, or net worth:* These covenants normally are included only in debt financings and are agreements to maintain the current ratios, working capital, or net worth, either at a minimum amount or as specified for various time periods. They may be keyed to projections made by the company; accordingly, care should be taken by the company in preparing the business plan to project financial results and conditions that management is comfortable in undertaking to attain on a contractual basis.

- *Use of proceeds:* Often the company will agree to apply the proceeds deriving from the financing to a specified use. The investor will sometimes require that the proceeds be applied within a narrow area of the business in connection with a specific financing plan, or may simply require that the funds be used for working capital.

In contrast to affirmative covenants (which generally exhort the company to undertake actions that it would ordinarily choose to take in the normal course), the negative covenants contained in the invest-

349

ment agreement have more teeth and serve to limit the company from actions it otherwise might be inclined to take unless the investors have consented in advance. Typically, these negative covenants relate to matters that would affect the fundamental nature of the business in which the investment has been made (e.g., mergers and acquisitions) or would alter the balance of control between the investors and entrepreneurs reached in the investment agreement (e.g., controls on stock issuances). Since the negative covenants limit the scope of managerial flexibility, they are often the subject of sharp negotiation. This is all the more so because the investor's remedy upon material breach of a negative covenant is often quite dramatic - such a breach by the company may result in the immediate acceleration of indebtedness in the case of debt securities and may sometimes trigger rescission rights in the case of equity securities. As suggested above, there is a tradeoff between the degree of investor influence over the voting power and board of directors and the strictness of the negative covenants imposed on the company. Many typical negative covenants are described below:

- *Mergers, consolidations, and sale or purchase of assets:* Mergers, consolidations, acquisitions, and so forth, with respect to the company or any of its subsidiaries, are generally prohibited without the investor's advance approval. Liquidation and dissolution of the company or any subsidiary and the sale, lease, pledge, or other disposition of substantial assets without consent may also be barred. Restrictions may also be placed on the company's purchase of capital assets.

- *Dealings with related parties:* The company will covenant that no transactions between the company and any officers, directors, or stockholders of the company shall be effected unless on an arm's length basis and on terms no less favorable to the company than could be obtained from nonrelated persons. Approval of all transactions with affiliates by either the board or the investors may be required.

- *Change in business:* The company will not change the nature of its business as described in its business plan.

- *Charter amendments:* The investor may prohibit the company from amending its corporate charter or bylaws without the consent of the investor. More narrowly drawn covenants might prohibit only certain specified actions (such as a change in the capital structure) without the investor's consent.

- *Distributions and redemption:* The company typically agrees not to make any dividend distributions to stockholders. Dividends may be prohibited until a given date or until the completion of a public offering of the company's stock, or may be limited to a fixed percentage of profits above a set amount. In addition, the company may covenant not to repurchase or redeem any of its securities except in accordance with the terms of the securities purchased by the investor (e.g., redeemable preferred stock), employee plans (e.g., forfeiture of stock upon termination of employment), or agreements with stockholders (e.g., right of first refusal).

- *Issuance of stock or convertible securities:* The investor may prohibit the company from issuing any securities that would result in dilution of the investor's position. This covenant includes restrictions on the issuance of securities of the type purchased by the investor and any securities convertible into such securities at a price less than that paid by the investor. Alternatively, a formula may be employed so that such an issuance will automatically trigger an improved conversion rate for the securities purchased by the investor. Frequently, these covenants are included in the terms of the securities themselves.

- *Liens and encumbrances:* The investment agreement (generally for debt-oriented securities, including redeemable preferred stock) may provide for restrictions on liens, pledges, and other encumbrances, with exceptions for such liabilities as real estate mortgages. Separate restrictions can be placed on leases of real property or equipment.

- *Indebtedness:* The company may agree to restrictions on future indebtedness. Unsecured bank debt is frequently permitted. Certain dollar limits on other debt is common. This provision is most typical of investments in debt-oriented securities.

- *Investments:* Restrictions against investing in other companies may be imposed by the investor. Exception are made for investments in wholly owned subsidiaries.

- *Employee compensation:* The company may agree to limit employment and other personal service contracts of management or key personnel to a maximum term and a maximum amount of annual compensation. In addition, the investment agreement may prohibit the acceleration or termination of vesting schedules applicable to stock held by officers, directors and employees.

351

- *Financial covenants:* Negative financial covenants are frequently imposed upon a company in a debt-oriented investment, such as prohibiting key ratios or financial conditions from exceeding certain limits, or limiting the company from incurring losses in excess of a certain amount. Semantics often determine whether a financial covenant is affirmative or negative in nature. Clear definition of financial and accounting terms is critical. Short of resulting in a default on securities, failure to comply with financial covenants may trigger adjustments in conversion ratios of securities, or give rise to preferential voting or other rights for the investor.

Registration Rights, Rights of Participation and Indemnification

In addition to the numerous affirmative and negative covenants described above, the venture capital investment agreement will customarily contain a number of more complex undertakings by the company that are generally set forth in the agreement. Two of the more typical of these covenants pertain to registration rights and rights to participate in future financings. Another such provision, indemnification of the investors for breach of the investment agreement, is also discussed briefly below.

Registration rights: The right to register securities for public sale under the Securities Act of 1933 and state securities laws represents the most advantageous vehicle for a venture capital investor to achieve liquidity and realize a return on his investment. The potential of an enterprise to achieve a size conducive to a public offering is an imperative to most venture capital investments; accordingly, the right of the investor to participate in the public market for the company's securities is an area in which the venture capitalist will concede few limitations on his ability of action. Registration rights are intricately bound up in the complexities of federal and state securities regulation and must be thoroughly understood by the investor and his counsel. The key elements of a registration rights provision in a venture capital investment generally include the following:

- *Securities available for registration:* Registrable securities will invariably be limited to common stock, including shares issuable on conversion of other securities. In addition, these rights often extend to common stock acquired by the investor in subsequent financings. If investors are participating in a second or third round financing, they must consider to what extent their registration rights will be coordinated or pooled with registration rights granted to investors in previous financings.

- *"Piggy-back" registration rights:* Investors will have the right to include shares in any registration which the company undertakes, either for its own benefit or for the account of the holders of securities. Exceptions are generally made for registrations involving employee stock plans or acquisitions. "Piggy-back" registrations will frequently be unlimited in number on the theory that no significant burden is imposed on the company by requiring it to include additional shares in a registration which it is otherwise undertaking. Except for the company's initial public offering, investors may be guaranteed a minimum participation in "piggy-back" registrations.

- *Demand registration rights:* Investors frequently obtain the right to require an issuer to register their shares upon demand and without regard to the registration of shares for the account of any other person. Demand rights assure the investor access to the public market. Theoretically, unrestricted demand registration rights enable an investor to force a company to go public; as a practical matter, demand rights are rarely, if ever used to this end, although their presence may influence the decision of a company to go public. Because of the expense involved, demand rights may be limited in number, unless registration is available on a short-form registration statement such as Form S-3. In addition, investors may agree to limit the exercise of demand rights to the holders of a minimum specified percentage of registrable securities to avoid unduly small registrations.

- *Marketing priorities:* "Piggy-back" registration rights generally contain provisions enabling the underwriters managing the public offering to cut back the number of shares to be registered by selling security holders on a pro rata basis if, in the underwriters' opinion, such a cutback is necessary or desirable to market the public offering effectively. If security holders other than the venture capital investors also hold registration rights, the relative priorities of the various groups, including management, in such a cutback scenario must be addressed.

- *Indemnification:* Each party will agree to indemnify the other against liabilities for which it is responsible arising out of a registration. Although the extensive indemnification provisions of an

353

underwriting agreement will frequently supersede the terms of the investment agreement, they are nevertheless important because underwriters will typically look to the company and any major selling shareholders for indemnification on a joint and several basis, and will leave those parties to their own devices to allocate any liabilities among themselves.

- *Procedural covenants:* Many registration right provisions contain undertakings to comply with certain procedural matters involved in a registration, such as participation in the preparation of a registration statement, qualification under state securities laws, and entitlement to legal opinions and accountants' comfort letters.

- *Availability of Rule 144:* The company will agree that once it has gone public, it will file all reports and take all other action necessary to enable the investors to sell shares (which they have not included in a company registration statement pursuant to registration rights) in the public market under the exemption from registration contained in Rule 144 under the Securities Act of 1933.

- *Expenses of registration:* Due to the cost involved in a registration of securities, investors will typically require the company to agree, at the time of the initial investment, to bear the expenses of registration, exclusive of underwriters' discounts or commissions applicable to the investors' included shares.

Rights to future financings: Venture capitalists often insist upon a right to participate in future financings by the company. On the upside, this offers the investor an opportunity to maintain or increase its interest in the success of the enterprise; on the downside, the investor receives some protection against dilution or loss of his initial investment in the event financing must be sought under distress situations. The right to participate may include:

- *Rights of first refusal* to assume the entire financing (each investor on a pro rata basis with other members of the investor group).

- *Preemptive rights* to participate in the financing to the extent that the investor's ownership percentage of the company's securities will be the same after the financing as before.

- *Rights of prior negotiation* to discuss and negotiate financing opportunities with the company prior to the company's making offers to others.

First refusal and preemptive rights typically contain oversubscription rights to permit an investor to absorb any portion of the securities not subscribed for by another investor or security holder.

Indemnification for breach of agreement: Particularly in the case of start-ups, venture capital investors may require founders and/or top management to share personal responsibility for the representations and warranties made by the company in the investment agreement and to indemnify the investors for any breaches thereof. From the investors' point of view, imposing the specter of personal liability on the insiders can be an effective means of assuring complete and accurate disclosure of all material business information. Indemnification by insiders also circumvents the anomaly of investors seeking indemnification from the company out of the capital which they themselves have invested in the business. On the other hand, personal liability for disclosure matters, which may be outside the reasonable knowledge of the entrepreneur, may be an unfair burden to place on him. For this reason, in cases where personal responsibility for representations and warranties is desired, care should be taken to focus that responsibility in areas of special knowledge of the entrepreneur (e.g., ownership of proprietary rights, compliance with prior employment arrangements, etc.) and to distinguish between the risks assumed by the company and those assumed by the individual (e.g., unqualified representations versus "best knowledge" representations). Termination of indemnification obligations often occurs after a stated period of time, usually not exceeding two years, or after the issuance of audited financial statements covering a one- or two-year period.

Conditions to Closing

The use of "conditions precedent to closing" in the investment agreement, provisions specifying conditions the company must satisfy at or prior to the closing, is a device used for two principal purposes. The most obvious is to guarantee that certain fundamentals relating to the securities and the particular transaction are in place, with receipt of favorable legal opinions being a classic example. In addition, conditions are used as negotiating tools to change or affect the affairs of the company. For example, a common closing condition may involve the contemporaneous execution of a bank loan agreement satisfactory to the investor or the consummation of a significant commercial transaction with a customer.

Many venture financings contemplate a simultaneous signing of the investment agreement and closing. Consequently, there is no technical need for a set of conditions designed to cover the time period between execution of the agreement and a closing. The use of express conditions serves to expedite the negotiations and to assist the closing process by serving as a checklist of actions to be taken in connection with the implementation of the transaction.

Closing conditions that are commonly seen in the capital formation process include: opinion of counsel for the company; execution of the several ancillary agreements including employment, noncompetition, and stock restriction agreements; elections and resignations of directors; and compliance certificates by senior management. Descriptions of certain of these ancillary agreements and documents are included below.

Terms of Investment Securities

General Considerations and Descriptions

Selection of the appropriate investment security for a specific transaction will depend upon the relative importance to the venture capitalist and the issuer of a number of factors including: the level of risk of the venture, investment objectives of the investors, capital requirements of the company, the relative interests and contributions of other security holders, the degree to which management control by the investors is desirable, liquidity of the securities, and so on. Among the securities which are commonly used in a venture capital financing are:

- Common stock
- Convertible preferred stock
- Convertible debt
- Non-convertible preferred stock or debt coupled with common stock or common stock purchase warrants.

Generally the venture capitalist will prefer to invest in a senior security which is convertible into, or carries rights to purchase, common equity. A convertible senior security affords the investor downside protection, in terms of the opportunity to recover the investment on a priority basis through redemption, repayment or liquidation preferences, with the upside potential of a liquid equity security traded at significantly appreciated values in the public market. Discussion of the relative merits and disadvantages of the various types of investment securities is beyond the scope of this article. Described in the following sections, however, are certain principal provisions of typical preferred stock and debt securities.

Principal Terms of Preferred Stock

Preferred stock is the investment security most frequently involved in traditional venture capital financings because of the flexibility it offers the company and the investor in tailoring the critical issues of the investment - principally management control and recovery/return on investment. Typically, the preferred stock utilized in a venture transaction is convertible into common stock and contains redemption provisions designed to enable the investor to recoup his investment if the enterprise fails to achieve its anticipated success. Convertible preferred stock provisions should address the following major issues:

Dividends: While the accrual of dividends may be specified in the prepared stock terms, "Plain vanilla" convertible preferred stock does not generally provide for the current payment of such dividends. Preferred will, however, participate with common to the extent dividends are declared. If dividends are desired, they may be on a cumulative or non-cumulative basis. Cash flow considerations will affect the ability of a start-up to pay dividends.

Liquidation: Holders of preferred stock will have a priority claim over the common stockholders to the assets of the corporation in a liquidation. The liquidation preference will typically equal the original purchase price of the security plus accrued dividends. Participating preferred may also share pari passu with common stock after the liquidation preference has been distributed. Convertible preferred stock provisions usually permit the investors to elect liquidation treatment in the event of a merger or acquisition in which the company is not the surviving entity.

Voting rights: Convertible preferred stock issued in venture capital transactions often votes with the common stock on all matters and is entitled to one vote for each share of common into which the preferred may be converted. In addition, the holders of convertible preferred stock, voting separately as a class, may have the right to veto certain corporate transactions affecting the convertible preferred stock (such as the issuance of senior securities, mergers, acquisitions and amendment of stock terms or charter provisions). Other preferential voting rights may include:

357

- Class vote for election of directors.

- Extraordinary voting rights to elect a majority of the board of directors upon a breach of the terms of the convertible preferred stock, such as a failure to pay dividends or make mandatory redemptions or default in the performance of financial or other covenants which may be contained in the convertible preferred stock provisions or underlying investment agreement.

Conversion: Holders of convertible preferred stock may convert their shares into common stock at their discretion (except as limited by automatic conversion obligations). Conversion provisions should address the following matters:

- Automatic conversion upon the occurrence of certain events, principally the completion of a public offering with specified price per share and gross proceeds thresholds or the attainment of specified financial goals.

- Mechanics of conversion.

- Conversion ratio, usually expressed by a formula based upon original purchase price, which initially yields a one-for-one conversion factor.

- Adjustment of conversion ratio to take into account stock splits, stock dividends, consolidations, etc. and "dilutive" common stock issuances, that is, sales of common stock at prices lower than those paid by the investors.

- Certification of adjusted conversion ratios by independent accountants.

The nature of the antidilution adjustments can have a dramatic effect on the number of common shares issuable upon conversion of the referred stock. "Rachet-down" antidilution provisions apply the lowest sale price for any shares of common stock (or equivalents) as the adjusted conversion value. "Formula" or "weighted average" antidilution provisions adjust the conversion value by application of a weighted average formula based upon both sale price and number of common shares sold. Antidilution provisions generally carve out a predetermined pool of shares which may be issued to employees or a de minimis amount that the company may issue without triggering an adjustment of the conversion ratio.

Redemption: Redemption offers both the investor a means of recovering his initial investment and the issuer an opportunity to eliminate the preferential rights held by the holders of the senior security. Topics to be addressed include:

- Optional or mandatory redemption.

- Stepped-up redemption price or redemption premium designed to provide investors a certain appreciated return on the investment (but it may be difficult to avoid a taxable constructive dividend under IRC §305).

- Desirability of a sinking fund.

- Redemption call by the company.

It should be noted that the prospect of mandatory redemption or redemption upon call by the issuer may force the holders of convertible preferred stock to exercise their conversion privilege lest they lose the upside potential of their investments.

Principal Terms of Debt Securities

The purchase of debt securities will enable venture capitalists to receive a current return on their investments through receipt of interest payments. In the case of a convertible debt instrument, the interest rate will be below market rates because of the equity feature coupled with it. Although the terms of convertible debt may be structured to resemble preferred stock in many aspects, significant differences between the two securities do exist.

First, debt securities do not carry the right to vote for the election of directors or on other stockholder matters. Accordingly, the investors' ability to influence management of the company directly is diminished, and they must resort to voting agreements and proxies in order to participate in the election of directors or, alternatively, rely on indirect means of influence such as the affirmative and negative covenants contained in the investment agreement. It should further be noted that the investors' status as a creditor of the company in any bankruptcy proceedings may be affected by principles of "equitable subordination" to the extent that equity-like control is actually exercised, with the result that the investors' debt security is subordinated in right of payment to the claims of other third-party creditors of the company who do not exercise control.

Second, the investors' rights to receive interest under a debt instrument are more secure than their rights to receive dividends on a preferred stock, inasmuch as payment of dividends may be restricted by state corporate laws relating to legally available funds and by the requirement that dividends must be declared by the board of directors.

359

Finally, although a debt security may rank prior to preferred stock in terms of a claim on corporate assets in liquidation, this advantage is at the cost of creating a weaker balance sheet which may have adverse effects in terms of trade and commercial bank credit, even where subordination provisions are present.

The following principal issues are generally addressed in the structuring of a venture capital investment in debt securities:

- *Interest rate:* Interest will be at a fixed rate, below market if debt is convertible or coupled with common stock or stock purchase warrants. Due to cash flow considerations of the issuer, interest payments may be deferred for a period of time.

- *Repayment:* Repayment of principal is often scheduled in quarterly, semi-annual or annual installments commencing four to six years into the term, or in a single "balloon" payment at maturity.

- *Optional prepayment:* The company may elect to prepay the debt, often at a premium. Since prepayment will have the effect of extinguishing any conversion rights, exercising the right to prepay generally will be deferred to such time as initial principal installments fall due. Issuance of stock purchase warrants in lieu of a conversion feature in the debt issuance will avoid this problem.

- *Conversion:* The debt instrument may be converted into common stock at a fixed price at any time. Conversion terms, including antidilution provisions, will be similar to those found in the terms of convertible preferred stock.

- *Subordination:* Debt is generally subordinated to bank and other institutional borrowings and may be thus viewed as equity by lenders. Complex subordination provisions are often required to regulate the relationships between senior lenders and subordinated noteholders in the event of defaults, insolvency, etc.

- *Affirmative and negative covenants.* Debt instruments are tied into extensive affirmative and negative undertakings by the company, which are usually contained in the purchase agreement. In addition to standard covenants used in a venture capital financing, these may include lengthy financial covenants of the variety typical in a commercial lending transaction.

- *Defaults:* Defaults include material breaches of representations and warranties; breach of covenants which are not remedied within a cure period; non-payment of principal and interest on debt instruments; acceleration (cross-default) of senior debt; and insolvency and bankruptcy.

• *Security:* Generally a debt instrument will be issued to a venture capitalist on an unsecured basis, although collateral is sometimes given in asset-based transactions such as leveraged buyouts.

Ancillary Agreements and Documents

Stockholders Agreement

The stockholders agreement is designed to control the transfer and voting of the equity securities of the company by key stockholders, so that stable ownership and management of the enterprise can be maintained for the term of the investment. This is accomplished through restrictions on the sale of stock by insiders, which have the effect of limiting the stockholder group to persons who are known quantities to the investors, and through voting agreements, which assure that the balanced composition of the board of directors will be perpetuated. The principal provisions contained in a typical stockholders agreement to achieve these results are:

• *Right of first refusal:* Key management stockholders will grant the company and/or the investors the right to purchase their shares on the same terms as those contained in a bona fide offer from a third party. Investors participate in the right of first refusal on a pro rata basis and have oversubscription rights to acquire any offered shares which are not picked up by another investor. Rights of first refusal are generally not extended to the company or insiders by the investors because the existence of such terms would tend to chill any sale of an entire block of shares by the investors to a third party. Transfers of shares by way of gift to members of an insider's family or as collateral in a bona fide loan transaction are permitted, provided the transferee or pledgee also agrees in writing to be bound by the agreement.

• *Buy-out provisions:* Some stockholder agreements provide that the company and/or the investors will have an option to purchase the shares of any insider at fair market value upon the occurrence of certain contingencies, such as death, personal bankruptcy or attachment of shares by legal process as in the divorce context. Detailed procedures, usually involving one or more appraisals by disinterested persons, are provided to assure a fair valuation of the stock.

361

- *Right to participate in insider sales:* Although philosophically at odds with a right of first refusal, a stockholder agreement may provide that the investors have a right to participate alongside management insiders in any sale to third parties. Although rarely exercised, this co-sale or "take-along" right limits the ability of management to bail out of the company leaving the investors at risk to recover their investment. Often this right of co-sale is triggered only by a sale which would have the effect of transferring actual or effective voting control to a third party.

- *Voting requirements:* All parties will generally agree to vote all shares for the election of directors in favor of specified nominees of the respective groups.

Restrictions under applicable state law need to be examined to determine the legality of stockholder agreements in any given jurisdiction, as well as to verify compliance with state procedural and substantive requirements. Stockholder agreements will generally terminate upon a public offering by the company or, required by state law, upon the earlier expiration of a stated period of time.

Employee Stock Purchase Agreements

Venture capital investors typically insist that appropriate equity incentives be implemented to attract, retain and motivate key employees. Both the entrepreneurs and investors are willing to suffer dilution of their respective equity interests (anywhere in a range from 5 to 15 percent of fully diluted equity) to achieve this end. The investment agreement will specify a pool of shares to be set aside for employee purchases and exempt the issuance of those shares from the various negative covenants, antidilution provisions and preemptive rights contained in the investment agreement, and the terms of the investment securities. Establishment of appropriate employee stock plans is frequently a condition of closing the investment. Incentive objectives and tax considerations play a significant role in determining the shape of an employee equity program. Among the typical employee equity incentives are the following:

- *Stock purchase plans*, providing for an outright sale to key employees, often at a bargain price, with the company retaining an option to repurchase the shares on a lapsing basis (generally over four or five years) if the employee terminates employment for any reason.

- *Incentive stock options*, enabling the employee to purchase shares with advantageous tax consequences at the fair market value on the date the option was granted.

- *Non-statutory stock options*, which may be granted in amounts which exceed the aggregate dollar limitations for incentive stock options under the Internal Revenue Code, and which may have exercise prices less than fair market value at the date of issuance and other terms not available under incentive stock options.

In all circumstances (other than incentive stock options) consideration must be given to the application of Section 83 of the Internal Revenue Code to issuances of stock to employees. Section 83 provides that employees are required to recognize income in respect of property (including corporate securities) transferred to them in connection with the performance of services, in an amount equal to the difference between the fair value of the property and the amount paid therefor. In the case of property subject to restrictions which lapse over time (such as forfeiture restrictions or repurchase options) the income is recognized at the time the restrictions lapse. Thus, an employee who acquires stock at a low purchase price in the early years of an enterprise and whose rights to those shares "vest" as forfeiture restrictions lapse over a period of years, will recognize income based on the appreciated value of those shares as each installment lapses. Section 83(b) of the Code ameliorates the harsh effect of this provision by permitting a taxpayer to elect to include the value of the transferred property in income in the year of receipt, by filing a special election.

Appendix J

WHY INVESTORS INVESTIGATE ENTREPRENEURS

As venture capital "winners" get harder to find, investors are looking beyond their traditional specialties for the return on investment that makes venture capital such an exciting and risky industry. When the capitalists consider new sources of deals, the term "due diligence" is being heard more often. With more entrepreneurs and deals being investigated than ever before, we visited the New York offices of Ms. Leslie Kaplan, director of due diligence, and Mr. Steven Vale, staff attorney, of Kroll Associates, a leading "corporate intelligence" firm. We discovered that Kroll is much different than a detective agency. Rather, it conducts full scale investigations, not of the economics of deals, but of the backgrounds and previous business dealings of the principals involved. For example, in one case, a commercial bank was approached by a businessman seeking to raise $50 million which he would secure with personal property. Kroll discovered that the property had been foreclosed or encumbered by liens. Based on the investigation by Kroll, the bank declined to finance the transaction. We wondered how common investigations had become, and how entrepreneurs should react to investigations of their backgrounds. The interview was conducted at Kroll's New York headquarters, where every office has its own access control code.

Q.   Leslie, in your experience at Kroll Associates, why have you found that investors investigate entrepreneurs?

L.K. Depending on the size of the deal that is being proposed, there are different reasons why an investor would investigate. In the bulk of the work that we do, which is larger deals for underwriters on Wall Street, we find that their fear is that they are going to underwrite an offering, either initial public offering or subsequent financings or in some cases even private placements, and find that a few months down the line, if in some cases even that long, they are confronted with a situation where, due to factors that they didn't know about, the company will have some financial problem, or that the individuals running the company were involved in some sort of activity which could be embarrassing to the company. So, the fear is twofold. First the reputation of the underwriter, and second the responsibility the underwriter has to the people who bought stock. We've been called after an investor and companies that have just filed an offering will fold--usually based on some activity that was not disclosed before.

S.V.   As I see it, the people involved in the deal want to do the deal. Somebody needs money, has got what he believes is a good idea, it's an opportunity, his life savings may have been involved in developing the product. The person providing the money, be it a large or a small investor, obviously hopes to make a dollar too, so everybody is focusing on getting the deal done, and they're not thinking of other underlying factors. They're looking at it in a positive manner because they're close to what is happening. We provide a dispassionate view.

Q.   You mentioned that private placements are investigated also. Can you mention the minimum size that people would bother to investigate?

L.K.   It really depends on the person. There are certain individuals, venture capitalists or underwriters who pick their own cut-offs depending on the size of their investment pool. For example, if they are working with a larger pool, they will say "well, the minimum that I would spend X amount of dollars to investigate is say, $5 million, $10 million, in some cases as high as $20 million." Depending on how much you have at stake and how large what you have at stake is relative to your other holdings, and also to the element of risk in the deal. If a deal could possibly double or triple your money in a short time and it would take a small amount of your investment pool, you'll say "well, maybe I won't do it" (investigate). If it takes a larger amount of your investment pool, you'll say "the risk is too great for me to go in without doing an investigation." Also, we look at smaller deals for smaller institutions and for smaller venture capital groups. The reason they are now being more concerned is that more and more people are going into markets that they weren't in traditionally. They're going into regional markets that they are not familiar with.

Q. When you say "they" you mean venture capitalists?

L.K. Venture capitalists, commercial banks, anyone who is in any way involved with putting up money for a smaller deal, and the focus is, that if I knew the individual, if it was in my market, if I could use my network, if I could tap resources, I would be able to do it myself, I wouldn't have to call in an outside investigative firm. However, if you're not familiar with the market, you're not familiar with the individual, it's easy to have the wool pulled over your eyes. We've had a case where an individual had a long background of taking people for a ride. He never looked for funds in his own area. He was in Texas, but he sapped money from people in California. In Hollywood he said "Well, listen, this actor has already invested with me," and went on and on, and everybody assumed that everything he said was true. In fact, the reason that this entrepreneur was misrepresenting himself was because he needed the money desperately at that time, and he knew that his credit and reputation in Texas were already marred. The only way to get funding was to go outside of his own area.

Q. So a local investor would have no resources of his own to be able to conduct an investigation out of state?

L.K. The resources available to a local investor are much smaller. You don't have a "cocktail network." You don't have banking contacts, access to litigation records, or a feel for what the person has done in the past. If someone is working in your own backyard, you have better access to that sort of information.

Due Diligence

Q. We often hear the term "due diligence" regarding these investigations. Is that a legal term?

S.V. It's a term of art, I think more than anything. It was originally applied by the Securities Exchange Commission in terms of an underwriter who is supposed to exercise "due diligence" in assuring the public that a deal is legitimate.

Q. Is there any standard that has to be met to prove "due diligence" on the part of the investor?

S.V. It's a "reasonable man's standard" more than anything.

Q. What a reasonable prudent man would do under similar circumstances?

S.V. Absolutely.

Q. And is that applied even to the smaller deals?

S.V. The use of the term just broadened and broadened as the capital markets themselves have expanded.

L.K. "Due diligence" is used at a number of levels to mean different things. For example, for the underwriter, due diligence is their responsibility to the people who buy the issue. To a commercial bank it is their requirement of the bank and the shareholders of the bank and the different individuals. At the venture capital level, there's the responsibility usually to your own pocket, and to the funds that you've raised. Due diligence can be anything ranging from e informal checks that a person will make to their friends in the business, and say, "well, gee, is there anyone that you know who knows this individual?" to an elaborate check done by firms such as ours. Because of the fact that people have been doing so well as entrepreneurs in recent years and the economy has gotten better, the approach has been, "well, if everyone and his brother is making money in this area, why can't I?" The level of care and the level of prudence in most entrepreneurs is not consistent. Although an entrepreneur can say, "well, my deals have always been very good, and my background and my track record has always been very good," there are others out there who haven't been as cautious with someone else's money. If anything, I think that the fact that venture capitalists and others are looking into deals means that those entrepreneurs that are honest and straightforward in their dealings will do that much better.

Q. In most cases will the entrepreneur know that he is being investigated?

L.K. It depends on the relationship with the venture capitalist. The difference is that sometimes you will have a couple of investment banks who want to do a deal, who want to take a company public, and there, if they go in and say that "you have to be investigated for us to do it, it is part of our procedure," they might back off, and say, "well, maybe I won't do that."

Q. If entrepreneurs discover they are being investigated, should that cause them great concern?

L.K. I would say not, particularly if they've got nothing to hide. The only instance that might be problematic is if the venture capitalists learns of something without the entrepreneur knowing the investigation was being conducted, which could be explained in some way.

Q. So, we're not talking about traffic tickets or a messy divorce.

L.K. No, and in fact the only place that a traffic ticket or a messy divorce would come into play is for example, if the divorce affected the business that the person was handling at the time.

Investigation a Positive Sign

S.V. If anything it's a positive sign that the entrepreneur is being investigated. It means somebody is considering his deal very seriously and is spending money to assure themselves that they can afford the deal.

L.K. It's not uncommon that entrepreneurs are being told that they are being investigated. In fact, more and more deals are coming through where that is standard policy for the venture capital group.

S.V. There are situations in which we will literally sit down with the entrepreneurs and interview them at the beginning for our own investigation, which simplifies the procedure a great deal.

Q. I'd imagine so. Could you give us an example of what you might ask an entrepreneur directly?

S.V. We work through a detailed list of questions. You don't just ask somebody whether he's been in jail; I don't know that's a relevant kind of question. You want to know what his other business interests are. At least you want to get negative answers from him that you can check. You want to know: Is he an officer for other corporations? Has he signed personal notes? It takes an hour, and you'll just have dotted the I's and crossed the T's through his business life.

Q. Is there any way that the entrepreneur should prepare for an investigation?

L.K. Generally, no. The only time that we've had people prepare for us is where they knew in advance that they had a problem and they wanted to have some documentation as to how they took care of it. For example, an individual for five years did not file and had other sorts of problems.

Q. Excuse me for interrupting, but someone who hadn't filed his income taxes...wouldn't that disqualify him right there?

L.K. More and more, that which seem to be problems turn out to be workable.

S.V. What the investigation can do is simply inform the investor what's out there. The deal itself may be sound, and you're going to go forward with a sound deal. It's just that you need that comfort in knowing what is out there so you can do your cost-benefit analysis of what's right for you--whether the risks are worthwhile for the return that you believe you will get in the deal.

Q. So even something like a failure to file for five years...

L.K. In that particular case, all it meant was that the group that was contemplating financing, restructured the deal in a way that they had more control. It was the entrepreneur's idea, and product. They thought that the product would do very well. The entrepreneur was familiar with his market, he was very successful. He had a personal problem which if they structured the deal a different way, they could deal with.

Q. So even if the investigation by your firm turns up negative information, it doesn't necessarily kill the deal.

L.K. Absolutely not. In fact, most often it leads to some level of compromise if the deal itself is sound.

S.V. By the way, most entrepreneurs have worked very hard, so they haven't had a lot of chances to get into trouble.

Q. Going back to the original question of why investors investigate in the first place, it's to protect their investment. What are the typical kinds of misbehavior on the part of the entrepreneur that would disqualify him?

S.V. This is a subjective view, and it's going to depend on who's doing the deal. There are people that I guess if he says he's graduated from Harvard and he hasn't, maybe that's enough. It's unlikely to be, though, if the deal is any good. It will usually be a series of factors, a pattern. An entrepreneur who has had three or four prior dealings and has left enormous debts that he has walked away from. That can be upsetting for an investor.

L.K. Other things might be associations with individuals who are less than savory. Even if the entrepreneur himself has kept his nose clean, there are associations which can be troubling to an investor. To what extent has this person been involved with individuals associated with organized crime? To what extent is he getting funding from sources that are not legitimate? To what extent is he paying more than he should for his money? Is there something that he is not disclosing that prevented him from going to legitimate sources for financing? Promissory notes, how you've dealt with banks is something that has killed a number of deals that we've worked on.

Q. Can an entrepreneur short circuit all of this by initiating an investigation of himself? In his business plan or cover letter, he could say "If you are considering this deal, why don't you call Kroll."

L.K. It's not very common, but it has been done. The element of impartiality, if you would, that it lends is reduced. However, if an individual goes to one source for financing, knowing that an investigation has been done, that a fee was paid, the report exists, and the deal did not go through for some other reason and then goes to someone else and they say "Listen, I want to do an investigation," you can then say "Well, I knew about this, they have a report on me, save yourself the X amount of dollars."

S.V. We also had one situation where a gentleman had been turned down for some proposed business deal and he didn't know why, and he paid for an investigation himself to find out what the problem might have been. Perhaps he understood the subject a lot better afterwards. In a situation like that for the entrepreneur, if he knew what his problem was at least he could go to the next investor and say "Look, there's this."

Q. I'd imagine that investors respect that attitude from the entrepreneur. It is like pointing out the risks in a business plan.

S.V. True. I don't think that you can stress enough to the entrepreneur that he's got to be honest. What the investor wants more than anything is information. You're bound to respect a person who's honest, particularly people that have a history of being aggressive in attempting to structure deals and have had problems with them. If you hide that, you're going to raise questions.

371

Q.   When you investigate an entrepreneur and he asks to see the report that you do on him verifying the information or refuting the information, is it common that you would share the report with him?

S.V. We wouldn't share the report with him.   The report belongs to the client and it may be the client's decision to share it, but we wouldn't make that decision.

Q.   Do you find that relatives investigate each other, that the brother goes to the brother-in-law and says, "Gee, let's make this a family business?"

S.V. We've had numerous occasions where that's happened.   I mean, how well do you know your cousin?   I know I have cousins that I see at family gatherings, but if money was on the line...

Q.   Is there some advice that could give to an entrepreneur who goes to a respectable venture capital firm which has a reputation of investigating?

L.K. To someone whose got a clean background, or even minor things in their background, there is nothing to be afraid of. There is increasingly a premium being placed on an entrepreneur being honest, not having surprises show up later. Even in instances where little things exist, it's more common that something can be worked out so that is not a problem. He's just got to be careful that the little inflations that slip into resumes don't over time become expanded--and again that probably isn't a problem in itself. Most deals that we look at go through. We find derogatory information maybe 20 percent of the cases. Of the cases in which we find derogatory information, may be 50 percent of those go through anyway.

S.V. It's certainly less than 10 percent of the deals that we look at that are negated by background information. We look at a large volume of deals and we also look at the deals where a question has been raised.

Q.   Is Kroll one of the larger firms doing this type of work?

L.K. I think we're unique in the sense that we draw on the backgrounds of investigators who have worked on this sort of thing for the state and for federal agencies. We have a number of lawyers on our staff who review a number of different aspects of the deals. We have people with advanced degrees in specialized areas so that when you're looking at a real estate deal, you'll have a different group of people looking at the entrepreneur than if you are looking at an oil and gas deal.

S.V. We may not be the largest in absolute volume, as some firms that do investigations are parts of larger public companies. We think we're the best.

Q. How often does it occur that you're asked to investigate a case after an investment has been made?

L.K. The increasingly has been happening as people who haven't done the due diligence in the first place find themselves in a situation where they have a judgment. In some cases, they are just looking to file a lawsuit against the people who have taken them for a ride and they find that a person has protected themselves pretty well from a judgment.

Be Up-Front with the Investor

S.V. The entrepreneur has to be up-front with the investor.

L.K. It affects the relationship that they will have long term and how well they will work together. If, for example, an entrepreneur has the sort of personality, as many entrepreneurs have, that they want a certain amount of independence, by being up-front in the first place and by gaining the investor's trust by being open and saying "go ahead and investigate me, there's nothing out there" and by an outside investigator proving that in fact is the case, the entrepreneur has gained something in the way of trust in the investor's eyes. It can be invaluable in the relationship.

Q. The deals that do get disqualified: is there something in common about them? It's basically withholding of information?

L.K. That's the most frequent problem.

Q. It may not necessarily be negative, it's the fact that is was withheld?

L.K. Both.

S.V. It's more than that. Usually when people omit information, there is a reason for it. If you want to say that I worked for 10 years for IBM, and I started my own company two years ago, and I've been working like a slave ever since, what have you got to hide? But, if you've been speculating with other people's money over a period of time, you may not wish to let that out.

373

VENTURE ANGELS OR AD"VENTURE"OUS OSTRICHES?

MICHAEL D. ALLISON

Mr. Allison is the president of International Business Research (U.S.A.) Inc., Princeton, NJ, a firm that specializes in "due diligence" background checks.

In the information age, pre-investment "due diligence" is now undertaken by a team of investors, lawyers, accountants, and investigators. The investor considers the whole transaction, the lawyer reviews key documentation, the accounant audits the books, and the investigator checks into the backgrounds and reputations of the borrower's management.

The role of the outside "corporate intelligence" company has grown enormously in recent years. The reason for this growth is primarily because such companies have have been able to provide timely and accurate reviews of the people in whom venture capityalists and others are about to invest. The value is obvious ... being the first to know, not the last to know! International Business Research (IBR) and other professional investigation agencies assisting investors utilize a combination of modern technology and time-honored, discreet background checking by phone, which ultimately enables their clients to be more well informed and thus able to maximize profit and minimize risk.

374

Many investors believe that they "know," or have gotten to "know," the personalities in whom they are about to invest. Many others only undertake rudimentary background checks, asking a few questions of friends or conducting a search of an online database, deceiving themselves with a false sense of security. AT IBR, however, we know that it is human nature to conceal failures and disgraces from even family members, much less from investors.

Professional investigation fees are usually considerably less that one percent of the capital at risk. Considering that most venture capitalists would regard a success rate of over 30 percent in all of their investments to be exemplary, the assistance provided by an investigator is a real bargain, adding real value by increasing the odds of success. Hiring an outside people auditor, early on, is probably the smartest thing any serious angel or venture capitalist can do, because the investigator will weed out the potential disasters and therefore raise the quality of the people and the transactions on which the angel concentrates time and resources.

After all, the ostrich, by burying its head in the sand, pretends that the worl in which it lives is full of friendly, decent, and honorable souls. Similarly, venture angels who choose not to examine the potential threat to theri investment through investigative research are, like the ostrich, potentially at risk.

ARTHUR LIPPER CORPORATION'S STATEMENT OF POLICY AND PROCEDURE FOR THOSE SEEKING FUNDING

We seek to earn an extraordinarily high return on our investments through intelligently assuming higher than normal risks. We are prepared to make our own judgments as to certain future events, including the likely reaction of other investors to predicted events. Our judgments are based, in part, upon both statements of fact and opinion as offered by those seeking funding. However, we require that the entrepreneur who hopes to benefit through our placing our financial resources at risk make a clear distinction between fact and opinion.

In order that there be no future misunderstandings, we will require those making statements of fact to so warrant and represent in the investment contract. Clearly, any statement made which is subsequently found to be other than factual will give rise to possible liability for the parties having made the statement.

Almost all investments involve the making of projections as to future events. We know that very few projections are ever achieved within the predicted time period. We also believe that those seeking funding for their business based upon the assumption of future events (as opposed to being based on current assets) are in a better position than ourselves to make such projections. As we will base our valuation of the business opportunity on projections provided by those expecting to receive the benefit of our funding and risk incurrence, we will hold the providers of the projections responsible. The form of penalty for nonachievement of projected results will be that of participation reduction. Similarly, we will usually permit entrepreneur/managers increased participation in the event projections are exceeded. Therefore, those preparing and submitting projections, which we, of course, require, are urged to provide only their "worst case" projections or those which the entrepreneur believes he or she is certain of achieving. If there is a projection shortfall, we expect to be insulated to the extent possible. Please be conservative. It will work out much better for you if you are.

You are in a position to be aware of the positive factors affecting your business project as well as possible adverse elements. If you are aware of adverse elements, we expect that you will advise us. In the investment agreement, you will be required to affirmatively state that you have advised us of any adverse factors known to you at the time which may negatively affect the investment under consideration.

Frequently, entrepreneurs and businessmen seek funding from more than one source at a time. We value our time and effort highly, and therefore require that we be informed of both the identity of those other funding sources already contacted and those with which there are negotiations currently in progress. It is possible that we will request either an exclusivity period, during which you agree not to have any contact with other sources of finance, or that you agree to compensate us for our time and out-of-pocket expenses in the event you reject a proposal we offer in good faith based upon the facts which you have presented.

We are professional providers of finance and, as such, probably have a level of experience and financial sophistication greater than your own. Therefore, we urge you to consult your attorney and other advisors prior to making or accepting any proposal. As it is not our intention to take unfair advantage of anyone, we do not wish to be in a position of doing so inadvertently.

Finally, we believe that entrepreneurs should "rent" money from financiers such as ourselves, rather than initially be given it in the form of equity. Therefore, our favorite medium of funding is through the provision of commercial bank guarantees. Such guarantees require the recipient of the loan to ultimately repay the loan as well as to pay interest on a current basis. Our inducement to provide guarantees frequently takes the form of revenue participation in the guaranteed entity. We may also require other forms of guarantee fee payment, all dependent upon our assessment of the individual situation. We are not inflexible as to format but do believe strongly that the investor's funds should, at least initially, enjoy a preference to the interests of those not at the same level of financial risk.

We try to be fair and to respect (and reward) the entrepreneur. We require, however, that our capital be respected. We have work long and hard to earn it.

Arthur Lipper III

President

REQUEST FOR PROSPECTUS USED BY A LEADING PROFESSIONAL PROVIDER OF VENTURE CAPITAL

JOHN L. HINES

The author, who was president of both Continental Illinois Venture Corporation and Continental Illinois Equity Corporation, is an extremely successful venture capital investor and was most helpful in the preparation of Venture's Financing and Investing In Private Companies.

For investment consideration please prepare a prospectus providing the following information.

- *The Company.* Name, nature of business, stage of development, history, mergers, acquisitions, divestitures, affiliates.
- *Funding History.* Details of prior financings, amount currently sought, proposed use of funds.
- *Product Lines.* Description, pricing, proprietary and patented features, lead times on competition, licenses.

- *Research, Development, Engineering and Design.* Development timetable, long-term product development strategy.

- *Manufacturing.* Production methods, operations cycle, capacity, level of integration, subcontractors, significant sources of supply, shipping, status of raw materials availability.

- *Service.*

- *Management, Directors, and Organization.* Resumes and compensation of key executives, organizational chart, union affiliations, training requirements, availability of labor, number of employees, incentives, stock ownership by executives.

- *The Market and Competition.* Segments, product substitutes, size and growth, seasonal or cyclical market, share of market, rate of technological change, lease to sale ratios.

- *Marketing Strategy.* Product literature, promotion, advertising, sales cycle (prospect to installation), pricing, credit, sales organization, leasing and rental options, dominant customers, sales and distribution of product.

- *Financial Summary and Projections.* Audited financial statements for last three years (if available), latest monthly financial statements, five-year projections of profit and loss, balance sheet and cash flow, together with all supporting assumptions pertaining to pricing, share of market, margins, volumes, inventory, receivable, and payable turnovers, capital expenditures.

- *Financial Information.* Capitalization, credit lines, leasing agreements, major stockholders, banking relationships, details of prior equity financings, purchase agreements from prior financing.

- *Legal Considerations.* Contingent liabilities, legal counsel retained, litigation pending.

STRUCTURING AND PRICING THE FINANCING FOR THE INVESTOR'S ADVANTAGE

My friend Stanley Golder originally gave me permission to edit his excellent article in Stanley Pratt's *Guide to Venture Capital Sources* from the standpoint of the investor, changing it from that of the entrepreneur/seeker of investment funds. Instead, I decided to reproduce his article as it was written and add my own observations--set off my brackets and italics -- to his text. Incidentally, *Guide to Venture Capital Sources*, in which this article and others appear, contains a listing of venture capital organizations that entrepreneurs may find helpful.

STRUCTURING AND PRICING THE FINANCING*
STANLEY C. GOLDER

Stanley C. Golder is a consultant in the firm of Golder, Thoma, Cressey, Rauner, Inc. in Chicago. Founded in 1980, the company currently manages $695 million in four venture capital funds. For the prior nine years, Mr. Golder was president of the Equity Group of First Chicago Corp., one of the

---

* Copyright © 1988 by Capital Publishing Corporation. Reprinted by permission from Stanley E. Pratt (ed.), Guide to Venture Capital Sources.

largest and most successful bank holding company business development investment affiliates. He is a past chairman of both the National Association of Small Business Investment Companies and the National Venture Capital Association. Golder, Thoma, Cressey, Rauner, Inc. is an active investor in consolidating fragmented industries.

Structuring

It is the experience of the author that the structure of the financing can have a material effect on the eventual result of an investment and, therefore, the structure is an important element in setting the price. *[I can propose a deal which will be satisfactory to me if the seeker of funding will provide just one element which will be satisfactory to him. If he sets price, I will set payment terms and performance crite-rion. If he sets maturity, I will set rate. If he sets maturity and rate (five-year loan and two over prime), I will set security requirements to make that an attractive arrangement. By attractive, I mean that which yields more than a comparable security having the same investor attractions. A good deal can be defined simply as one that you can sell immediately at a profit to an investor of equivalent sophistication to yourself. If the original investor cannot turn around on the day of the closing and remarket the securities purchased from the entrepreneur AT A PROFIT to another investor who shares the same acceptance of predicted future events on which the original investor premised the investment, then the deal was not well priced and/or structured. Packaging deals for investors is clearly a business in itself, and such activity is the essence of investment banking. However, I stipulated that the buyer be "of equivalent sophistication" to the seller, which is more difficult than selling securities to the pub-lic at a markup.]* At times, there are differences of opinion within the venture capital industry as to whether to purchase preference issues (such as convertible preferred stock, subordinated debentures, and notes with warrants) or to buy common stock. [There is never any doubt in my mind. The investor should have a preference in liquida-tion and dividends.] It is clear that new companies cannot afford to pay interest or dividends, and if venture capitalists structure an instru-ment that calls for their payment, they are merely taking back their own money. *[I do not necessarily agree. Money is a commodity to be rented. I believe it better to have a "return on investment" struc-*

tured into the deal, even if payment is deferred until profits reach a certain level, until the net worth of the company is at a particular level, or prior to any executive compensation changes. Money has to earn in order to multiply. The investor can always trade away the interest owed for something at a later date. That something can be an equity increment or another member on the board of directors or just a greater ability to influence and/or control the company. Interest due is an obligation, even if it is only interest which is contingently paid, and as such has value.] In addition, consideration should be given to the fact that the balance sheet will be more appealing to other creditors and suppliers if the investment is in the form of common stock rather than debt instruments. *[I agree, and a class A common for the investor can be used instead of a preferred, although I prefer to have the proper label on things.]*

Although these are truisms, they do not address themselves to several key questions, one of which is the possibility that a company might move sideways, rather than up or down. If a company does not go public or sell out to a large company, but remains on a modest plateau, it is difficult for the private investor to recover an investment held in straight common stock. *[Unless there is an agreement among the shareholders that the company or other shareholders will either purchase the shares of the investor or, better yet, agree to purchase on demand (a put) after a certain date. The price of the contracted sale, which can be conditional upon the achievement of agreed upon objectives, can be either a set amount or a function of earnings or revenues.]* Even if the company goes public, the market will not accept a large amount of stock unless the company makes major progress. The only way out for the venture capitalist would be the sale of the company. The company managers do not have the problem to the same extent for, after all, they can receive high salaries and fringe benefits. They may be strongly opposed to the sale of the company. *[Of course, if there is a buy/sell agreement in place, there need not be an impasse, since those who wish to maintain the status quo can acquire the shares of those who wish to exit or can themselves be bought out at the price they offered.]*

To avoid this kind of stalemate, it has been the preference of many not to make an outright purchase of stock in a case in which management has the controlling interest in the business or can block the sale or merger of the business with a larger company. Before taking a common equity position, there should be some waiting period to see if the company performs as expected and to see if management has objectives similar to those of the venture capitalists and, therefore, will protect their interests as a minority shareholder.

The question of ultimate liquidity for the investment is also very significant. To deal with both liquidity and capital protection, the best financial structure entails a limited amount of money invested in common stock, with the rest employed in debentures, notes, or preferred stock. These instruments will provide some income and protection in case the business starts to decline. By having fewer dollars invested in common stock, the pressure to liquidate is reduced, allowing venture capitalists time to find less painful ways to dispose of their holding.

The third major problem is that of control. Most businesspeople want to control their own businesses. The difficulty is that small-company management often consists of technical or salespeople, and there usually is not a well-rounded management team with depth of experience. The loan agreement or preferred stock indenture should give the management sufficient flexibility to run the business as long as things go reasonably well. On the other hand, such an instrument should give the investor an opportunity to exert pressures in case problems develop. Many people misunderstand the purpose of the terms of a loan agreement or preferred stock indenture. They presume that simply because a default exists, that could justify exercising the right to take control, the venture capitalist will immediately exercise such right. In fact, the record shows that this is rare.

There are major differences between investors. Not all money is the same in the venture industry, and nearly every group has different operating philosophies. While there may be a few waiting for a default in loan agreements so they can take over a company, decrease their equity costs, or increase their percentage of ownership, the majority of venture capitalists do not have this attitude. This does not mean, however, that any of us are "patsies" or that we will not use appropriate remedies when necessary to protect an investment.

It is important for entrepreneurs to understand the general philosophies under which most venture capitalists operate. Loan agreement covenants are not the key aspect of pricing, but they do bear on the issue. Reasonable loan and preferred stock covenants are nothing more than a reflection of a good business plan. They often act as a disciplinary measure for management. This discipline is particularly important for young, growing companies, in which management often has a tendency toward exuberance.

384

Venture Capitalists versus Entrepreneur

Naturally, there are some basic differences between the entrepreneur and the venture capitalist. Businesspeople are by nature optimistic and enthusiastic about their ability to succeed. While venture capitalists are not pessimistic (if they were, they would not be in this business), they can appropriately be described as skeptics.

Businesspeople feel their company is worth more than does the potential investor. Their projections show excellent growth over the next two-to-four years, and they believe that the investor should be willing to pay a high price to buy into this "bonanza." The venture capitalist, on the other hand, is skeptical because the young business simply has not proved whether its concepts and ideas will work. The business may be profitable, barely profitable, or, more likely, in a loss position at the time of investment. Competition can suddenly become much more disagreeable, or any number of other problems can arise to prevent a company from achieving its targets.

These major differences can raise major obstacles between entrepreneur and venture capitalist when they discuss structure and pricing, and the differences often prevent their getting together. Yet the problem can be resolved, and techniques for structuring the investment have been developed to help bridge this gap. The following examples have been developed to illustrate the use of structuring for three types of situations.

As will become apparent, these methods are somewhat complicated which in fact can have a negative impact both on the future prospects of the company and on the relationships between the entrepreneur and the investor. *It is better not to have such a formula* but rather to keep the arrangements as simple as possible. However, in certain circumstances the techniques described below can be very helpful and the examples serve to outline approaches.

Resolving the Differences

Example 1 is a new company, so both entrepreneur and venture capitalist had a free rein in structuring the financing from the inception of the deal. After the entrepreneur's projections were modified by our analysis, it was decided that the company would need $1 million. The projections indicated that profits would be generated within the first year, an unusual expectation for a startup investment. Management, although capable and experienced, had nominal funds that could be invested; thus the venture capitalists initially would

385

have voting control. *[Investors should decide whether or not it is in their best interests to require the entrepreneur to "invest" through the incurring of an obligation when the entrepreneur does not have funds available for investment. I think it better to have entrepreneurs put at risk, because then they have something to lose if decisions do not work out as anticipated. The investor should not be in a position of having all the downside risk, while the entrepreneur has only upside potential.]*

As the investors did have control, we were willing to invest in common stock. However, even if the projections were realized and a public market developed rather quickly, it would be impossible for the investors to sell all of their shares except over a long period of time. *[I do not understand the reason for being concerned because of an inability to sell all of a holding right away in a company which is doing well. The whole point of investing--when not reflecting the special needs of the venture capital general partner (which are different from the needs of the individual investor) to register a gain for profit calculation and profit sharing purposes--is to hold shares of companies which are doing well. There seems almost to be an unspoken statement that the name of the game is to invest only in companies before they go public and to sell out as soon as possible once they do go public. In my view, this approach is not necessarily in the investor's best longer-term interest. My own practice is to borrow on the shares of companies in which I have invested that have gone public and to use these borrowed funds to invest in new private situations. In doing this, of course, an investor has to be careful not to become too highly leveraged.]*

This arrangement, by which the management can receive a maximum equity position through reaching its projections, is called an earn-out. Critical aspects of this transaction were the considerations under which the earn-out numbers were determined. Originally, the proposal was that the earn-out be based on an earnings formula for the first three years of operation, but this approach created problems for us as the venturers. Although there was no disagreement with the principal, and although the formula was considered fair in practice even if the company could meet its projections for three years, we would not have a value to show on the books or a gain that could be realized. In addition, it was important to focus the company management's attention on providing the investors with ultimate liquidity.

For these reasons, it was decided to use a market value formula to avoid an argument about the value of the company. The higher the

386

earnings multiple placed on the shares by the market, the easier it would be for management to get its maximum percentage under the formula. While none of us wanted to create a premature public offering, it was generally agreed that sometime in the three-year period, market conditions would be such that the company could go public. A three-year period was chosen to give management flexibility in deciding when to go public.

If a public market has not been created at the end of that period (because of inadequate earnings growth or some other management-related problem), we considered that a multiple of five times net after tax earnings was appropriate for pricing the shares purchased. *[I prefer to use a relative price/earnings ratio to setting an absolute one. After all, in certain markets five times after-tax earnings may or may not be attractive. Is it not easier to establish that the multiple will be a percentage of the multiple of the Standard & Poors 500 or some stock which is in an industry comparable to that of the company or an index of stocks in the same industry?]* You will note that the valuation formula included a 30 percent discount from the public market price of the shares. This represented an estimate of the average discount appropriate for the nonregistered stock. Since the investors would own about 50 percent of the company, the shares could not be easily sold in the public market without a long holding period or considerable registration expense. The discount was considered appropriate to take these problems into account. (Actually, if such shares were sold in a private transaction, the discount could range from 25 percent-to-50 percent of the price in the public market.)

Management's projections seemed reasonable to us, and in turn the managers agreed to a formula for pricing the equity that wou'd be tied to the future profit performance of the business. In many cases this suggestion results in a severe downward revision of projections of profits by the entrepreneur.

A preferred stock issue backed by a sinking fund was created to provide liquidity for the investment. Because of the early expectation of profits, it was felt that this company could afford the sinking fund payments in years four through six without jeopardizing its equity position. If things worked out badly, we could have 82 percent of the equity. On the other hand, if projections are met, and the company were to go public within three years at a multiple of 10 times earnings or better, the investors would be cut down to 51 percent and management would receive 49 percent of the equity with only a nominal investment. We wanted management to have every possible incentive to bring the company to an optimum growth rate. However, the longer it takes the company to go public, the lower will be management's equity. *[Note the concept of the "rental" cost of money for the period of illiquidity and assumption that the investor automatically sells out to the public.]* We reasoned, too, that this move would protect our interests until the "earn-out" arrangement becomes effective.

The above situation was made somewhat easier because we were dealing with a brand new company without a previous capital structure. But imaginative structuring and pricing is also possible with existing businesses.

Beginning capital structure	
6 percent sinking fund preferred	$900,000
(sinking fund reduction in years 4-6)	
Class A common	102,500
Class B common	22,500
Total capital	$1,025,000

Class A shares initially represent 82 percent of the company ownership and can be diluted down to 51.25 percent if the earn-out formula is achieved. Class A shares are owned by the investor group. *[In this case, the assumption is that the shares are given to entrepreneurs. It is also possible to have entrepreneurs purchase their shareholdings through the issuance of notes. The notes can be for a variable amount, depending on the achievement of earnings. In other words, the shares could be "given" through the variable amount being very low in the event that the earnings objectives were achieved or exceeded; conversely, if earnings were disappointing, the variable amount could be at least that of the per-share cost to the investor.]*

Class B shares initially represent 18 percent of the company ownership, which votes on a share-for-share basis with Class A ownership and is subordinate to Class A in liquidation. Class B shares are convertible into Class A shares at the resolution of earn-out and are owned by management.

Earn-Out Arrangement

The earn-out is based on the first public market price of the company, provided a public market is established in the third to fifth years. *[A public market is defined as either (1) an offering in which at least 20 percent of the company is sold to the public, or (2) a merger in which control is sold to a listed company.]* Management will receive no more than 18 percent of the company until the value of the original Class A position meets the following values.

Time of First Public Offering	Class A Value
Year 3	$5,000,000
Year 4	6,000,000
Year 5	7,000,000

If a public market is not established by the end of the fifth year, then for earn-out purposes an "internal" value will be calculated which is five times the lower of (1) average earnings in the third to fifth years, or (2) fifth-year earnings.

Because of the restricted nature of the original Class A position, a 30 percent discount will be applied to the public market value for calculating the company value used for the earn-out formula. Assuming a public market is established in the third year, placing a value on the company of $12 million (or $8.4 million), and the management group would increase its position from 18 percent to 40.5 percent through conversion of Class B into Class A stock.

The company's projected after-tax earnings for the third through fifth years are as follows:

Year	Net profit
3	$1,525,000
4	1,892,000
5	2,303,000

Assuming the company went public in year four, the following chart shows the net profit that would be required in year four to enable management to earn its full 48.8 percent ownership participation at different price-earnings multiples:

Multiple	Net Profit Required ($000)
8 times	$2,091
9	1,858
10	1,672
12	1,394
15	1,115

Under this arrangement, management would receive its full percentage earn-out if it achieved its fourth-year projections and the

stock sold at an 8.8 multiple. Looking at the earn-out a little differently, if the company's stock sold at a multiple of 12 times earnings in
the fourth year, management would have to earn approximately 74
percent of its projections to earn the full percentage.

Example 2 involves a company that was in existence, had a capital
structure, was already publicly-held, but was not profitable when the
investment was completed. Its prospects appeared good, though. A
reasonable deal was worked out, but not until a number of problems
had been resolved.

The market price of the stock was about eight dollars at the time of
negotiations. The problems were whether or not the company would
make the profits it projected over the next two years, and whether or
not the marketplace would recognize these profits in terms of a
healthy price-earnings multiple. The company wanted to convert
subordinated debt into common stock as soon as possible to improve
the balance sheet. The solutions were evolved through the use of a
sliding scale in the exercise price of warrants. At the same time,
though, investors gained the protection of a market price provision
that must be met if the sliding scale prices are to be effective. This
was further modified by establishing minimum earnings levels
between those anticipated by management and those anticipated by
the investors.

While this situation required a simpler capital structure than the
case in Example 1, the needs of both management and venturer had
been resolved satisfactorily.

1. *Investment.*
   $3,700,000 (8 _ percent subordinated note payable in years four
   through seven).

2. *Warrant.*
   To purchase 518,260 shares of the company's common stock; the
   warrant exercise price per share is calculated as follows:

   a. Basic exercise price.
      1) Years 1-3. $6.50 per share.
      2) Years 4-5. $7.75 per share.
      3) Years 6-7. $9.00 per share.

   b. Effectiveness of basic exercise price.

      1) Years 4-5: common stock must be valued at least at $15.50
         per share at the end of the third year, otherwise, the exercise
         price is $6.50 per share.

    2) Years 6-7: common stock must be valued at least at $18.00 per share at the end of the fifth year, otherwise, the exercise price is $7.75 per share.

  c. Exercise price modification for earnings.

    1) If earnings are less than $.20 per share for the first year, the exercise price shall be $4.00 per share.

    2) If earnings are less than $.40 per share for the second year, the exercise price shall be $4.00 per share.

    3) If earnings are less than $.20 per share for the first year but more than $.40 per share for the second year, the exercise price shall be $5.25 per share.

Example 3 created particular problems for the venture capitalist. This situation represents third-round financing for a profitable company that needed significant money for additional expansion, beyond amounts that would be available from senior sources. A majority of this company's equity is controlled by one individual. The entrepreneur thought he might want to go public, and he was willing to give up some shares of the business to develop a partner-like relationship with the venture capitalist in order to obtain the needed funds. However, he could have changed his mind for any number of reasons.

Since the company is controlled by the entrepreneur, our firm did not want to be a common stockholder under any circumstances short of holding liquid, nonrestricted securities. The structure adopted was a subordinated loan with warrants to purchase a convertible preferred stock. The loan was fully subordinated and carried an eight percent interest rate.

We agreed that the investment called for a 10 percent equity participation. We also agreed that if the company went public in the next five years, our warrant would be exercisable only into common stock. *[Note that even though the warrant conversion was into a convertible preferred, the conversion was to be into common if the shares were publicly traded within five years. I might have tried to scale the conversion privilege to provide an incentive to the entrepreneur to go public sooner, and have the 10 percent equity be the low figure in the early years. I also assume that the agreement called for the shares either to be registered or to have full registration rights, not just piggyback-registration rights.]* However, if the company had not provided a public market at the end of five years, we could convert the balance of the subordinated note into preferred stock, which carries a high dividend rate (10 percent in nondeductible expense). Even though 10 percent is a high rate for a nondeductible expense, the actual $20,000 in dividends was small in relation to the anticipated profits. There was a specific reason for setting the dividend rate high: If the company had not provided the expected public market it was felt that the investor was entitled to a high current return to compensate for the long holding period of the investment and the risks incurred. In this example the investor was a corporation, which meant that dividends were subject to the 85 percent dividend received credit (100 percent credit for a Small Business Investment Company).

1. *Investment.*
   $400,000 (eight percent subordinated note payable in years four through seven).

2. *Warrant.*
   To buy a 10 percent cumulative, convertible preferred stock:
   a. Exercise price: $200,000
   b. Not exercisable into convertible preferred stock before the end of the fifth year.
   c. If a public market is established prior to the warrant's being exercised into preferred stock, the warrant is exercisable only into common stock.
   d. Expiration date: 10 years. *[I prefer warrant expiration dates to be for a number of years after the repayment of debt rather than for a fixed number of years; in this case, it would be for three years after full repayment of debt, including accrued interest. From the standpoint of entrepreneurs, it will make no difference if they do what they have promised to do.]*

3. *Terms of convertible preferred.*
   a. Convertible at par at any time, into 10 percent of the company's common stock.
   b. The holder is required to convert into common stock if a public market is established. *[I might have established a premise that the initial public offering price had to be at a minimum price of either a fixed dollar amount per share or a percentage over the exercise price of the warrant. Also, there should be a definition of "public." How many shares trade in an average trading day? What percentage of the company shares are in the hands of nonaffiliated public investors? Clearly, investors do not want entrepreneurs to be able to acquit their responsibilities by buying a "shell" company, such as an old mining company for a couple*

thousand dollars, and merging in the company for which the investor had an obligation to convert into common shares.]

c. Put: the holder can put the convertible preferred to the company any time after the seventh year at a price of $400,000, as long as net worth is at least four times the put price just before the exercise of the put.

d. Call: the company can call the convertible preferred on 30 days' notice after the seventh year at the following prices:

Year	Call price
8	$1,000,000
9	900,000
10	800,000
11	700,000
12	600,000
13 and thereafter	500,000

[One of America's most successful investors advised his son always to get and not to give options. I agree. Why should the investor give away the right to maintain a position except to improve the position? The entrepreneur has had the investor's money to work with all these years at only a very low rate of rent. Call provisions only work against the investor. Entrepreneurs and investors can at any time negotiate a transaction. Investors should retain and acquire options and not grant them, without adequate compensation or inducement.]

Liquidity

This still leaves the liquidity question: How do we get our money out of the situation if management changes its plan? A put-and-call arrangement was the solution. If the company built net worth of $1.6 million, the stock could be put to the company for $400,000 (cost basis was $200,000). At the same time, the investors provide management with a call at a high price in the eighth to thirteenth years of business. This protects us, the venture capitalists, from being bought out just before a public offering, in the event the company is successful. The call price declines with each passing year.

You might note that we were willing to accept a lower rate of return on the investment (smaller percentage of equity for a given amount invested) in Example 3, as compared to Examples 1 and 2. Our assessment indicated that the downside risk is less in this case than it is in new ventures or in companies running in the red.

Each situation in these three examples has its own peculiarities, each carries different assessment of risks and rewards, and there are any number of structuring pricing possibilities that can be applied to take these differences into consideration. The needs of both the entrepreneur and the investor must be coordinated if a successful financing arrangement is to be negotiated. Generally, there is always some reasonable way to meet the needs of both in an attractive project. *[While this is true, investors must remember that they do not "have to do" any deal, and that the deal must be to their advantage for it to be a good deal. Investors lose control after the documents are executed unless they have structured in their protections. Investors can always be a "nice person" and modify or amend terms once into the deal. But they should be able to do so from a position of strength. Therefore, they have to have strong deal points originally. Unlike the case for the venture capital partnership general partner or Small Business Investment Company manager, the money being invested here is the investors' own and, thus, (1) they are not under pressure to invest since this is not what they are being paid to do, and (2) money lost (or not made) will have to be made up by their own hard work and the incurring of risk not otherwise necessary. No. Is a complete sentence and "no" is also the single most important word in the Angel's vocabulary.]*

Pricing

Pricing refers to the total return expected to be received over the life of the investment and includes both current income (interest and dividends) and the capital gains. The common denominator used is the valuation of the business -- a $500,000 investment that receives 25 percent of the equity of the business values the company at $2 million (25 percent X $2 million = $500,000).

Arriving at a price for any investment is a matter of negotiation between the parties. This section will examine some of the considerations involved in setting a price, and methods for reducing some of the subjectivity of pricing from the perspective of the venture capitalist.

How Venture Capitalists Think about Pricing

The variable ingredients that go into price determinations are covered in the following questions.

1. How much money is the entrepreneur putting up relative to the total funds initially required? *[This raises the question of whether*

the entrepreneur's money has a greater value than that of the investors. I am not sure it does. Perhaps the entrepreneur should invest on the same terms as the investors and be paid bonus shares for performance.]

2. What is the total in equity financing needed to launch the business? Or, conversely, how much additional dilution over the years will be necessary to keep the business moving forward at the desired pace? *[This is a most difficult question to answer, and the one which most often causes problems because of the investors' inability to understand that, in most cases, the entrepreneur will, intentionally or otherwise, understate the ultimate capital requirement of the business.]*

3. How attractive will the company and industry be in the stock market, and what kind of price-earnings multiple will it be able to command in the marketplace now and in the years when the investors become interested in liquidating? *[The concept that the investors will be interested only in liquidating their positions when the company goes public is overstated by many venture capitalists. This is a function of their situation as managers of a money pool which is, they usually hope, ever-increasing. The investor should focus on additional profit possibilities, such as negotiating an additional tranche of warrants to be issued at the public issue price at the time of the offering. Most entrepreneurs will not fight this suggestion, and it can be a very important source of future profit for the investor.]*

4. What is the upside potential of the investment; that is, how much in profits can be generated and in what period of time? What are the odds that the earnings and time projections can be met? *[Certainly, the evaluation must be made. However, the shortfall between achieved and projected results should be paid for by those making the projections.]*

5. What is the downside potential; that is, what percentage of the total investment is likely to be lost if the project does not progress as anticipated? what are the odds that a loss will occur? *[To whatever extent possible, the investor should structure the deal in such a way as to benefit personally through the sue of the losses. This can be done most readily through the use of partnerships and S corporations. However, the individual investor can also provide (pay for) services to the entrepreneur and, if not reimbursed, may be able to claim a deduction against taxes. Marketing tax shel-*

ters, as opposed to research and development tax shelters, some-times can be used by investors. In this case, the investor pays for, say, advertising for the company in return for a royalty on sales. Such a royalty can be structured in conjunction with other ele-ments of the investment and favor the investor.]

These considerations are directly related to many of the key issues discussed in other parts of this text concerning the cash flow of the business; how much lead time is needed before new products are accepted by the marketplace or by key customers; what it takes to educate a new market; how much as to be invested to carry losses while the operation is building up; what equity investments will be required to carry receivables, inventories, build new plants, and so forth; and how much the business can expect to borrow from conven-tional lenders and whether such financing will entail equity rights. *[And remember that Murphy's law is fully operative. It is almost axiomatic that revenue production items take longer and production costs are higher than was anticipated.]*

Profit Targets Set by Venture Firms

It is also important to keep in mind that venture capitalists have dif-ferent profit targets. In fact, different investors could and do have dif-ferent ideas of the appropriate expected rate of return for the same investment. For example, if venture capitalists want a return of four times their money in four years, the compound annual rate of return would be 41 percent. To illustrate rates of return, the following table has been prepared.

Profit Targets of Venture Capitalist	Compounded Annual Rates of Return (pre-tax)
Triple their money in three years	44 percent
Triple their money in five years	25
Four times their money in four years	41
Five times their money in three years	71
Five times their money in five years	38
Seven times their money in three years	91
Seven times their money in five years	48
Ten times their money in three years	115
Ten times their money in five years	58

These are internal rates of return. As a general rule, if venture capi-talists are financing startups or first-stage projects, they are looking for expected returns at the high end of the scale. Thus, these investors would be looking for 40 percent, 50 percent, or more compounded return on their investment. On the other hand, investors in second-stage financings tend to be looking for a 30 percent-to-40 percent return per year and those making third-stage deals generally seek 25 percent-to-30 percent per year. *[All of these calculations are on a cash-on-cash basis. In other words, the implicit assumption is that all of the cash was invested on day one. This does not have to be the case, and the rate of return calculations would be different for a staged investment (and so would the risk assumption if there achievement requirements which had to be met prior to the funding commitment becoming effective). Further, the return on investment tables assume a cash investment rather than a leveraged one. It is frequently better either (1) to invest in a more secure venture on a leveraged basis, rather than in one having higher potential but greater risk on a cash basis, or (2) to structure a senior (and possibly secured) instrument, with a lesser equity-related play, using borrowed funds in part. I reject the idea that the act of borrowing funds for private company investment is by definition more speculative than investing all cash. It depends on how the money, borrowed or otherwise obtained, is put to use.]*

In reviewing venture capitalists' pricing attitudes, it is important also to keep in mind certain other things that have been repeated often throughout this text.

1. Nothing progresses along the originally projected pathway. (Murphy's Law stated another way: if things can go wrong, they will.) This is one of the world's more unpredictable activities, thus venture capitalists leave a great deal of room for such errors in arriving at valuations.

2. It is likely to take more money to accomplish objectives than indicated in projections by both management and venture analysts. Thus, venture capitalists like to leave room in the pricing for more dilution than might otherwise be expected. *[The two preceding paragraphs of this excellent article are worth committing to memory.]*

3. It is difficult to realize profits on venture investments. Shares received are not readily tradable as marketable securities. Instead, they must be sold under special rules established by SEC (Rule 144 stock sales), or they must be sold pursuant to the expensive and somewhat unpredictable action of obtaining a registration

statement. *[Or, shares must be sold by prior arrangement to the company or its other shareholders. A buy/sell agreement would be very applicable here. Also, the pension and profit-sharing plans of the company can, and perhaps should, own either pre-ferred or common shares of the company.]* The complications and obstacles involved in both of these alternatives are described by others in this text. The third alternative is to sell the entire busi-ness to a large listed company. This is also a complicated proce-dure and requires cooperation by all parties involved.

Obviously, it is erroneous to assume that venture capitalists can use yardsticks like those used by regular securities analysts in arriving at a fair valuation for their investment in a company.

Calculations Used by Venture Firms in Setting Price. On the other hand, some of the security analyst's tools are used in setting guide-lines for valuation. The venture capitalist is likely to make a list of the various companies that are in the same industry as the firm requesting financing. Such a list will include industry leaders, medi-um-sized companies, and small firms. Key operating statistics for each company are likely to be compared; these include sales, operat-ing costs, profits and margins, overhead administrative expenses, and net profit and its ratio to sales. *[This comparative analysis should be prepared and presented by entrepreneurs in their business plans. First, if the entrepreneur does not do this work and use the experience of others engaged in the same areas, his projections, upon which the business and to a degree the structure of the deal are premised, will be weakened. Second, if the entrepreneur does not know well the industry operating statistics, and particularly those of the direct com-petition (certainly, if publicly available), then the investor should be skeptical of the entrepreneur's having sufficient sophistication for the running of a business.]* Net worth and return on equity will also be calculated, together with long-term debt and current ratios. Price-earnings ratios in the current market are likely to be compared with an average worked out for the different classes of companies. If stocks of the leading firms are selling at 25 times earnings, medium companies at 15 times, and small companies eight times, there will certainly be a hesitancy to consider a price-earnings ratio of more than 10-to-12 in estimating what the venture equity could be worth at the time of sale. *[Ratio analysis is of much greater utility in compar-ing publicly traded securities than in valuing private companies. The focus should be on those elements of information regarding other companies which can be used to validate projected operating results. Using market-place ratios as a means of determining private company values is, I believe, overly simplistic and possibly misleading. Certainly, the investor must have an awareness of current market valuations and also, perhaps more importantly, of current valuations being placed upon initial public offerings and subsequent market performance. However, the major focus must be on that which is being projected by and for the company in which investment is being considered. No one can predict with certainty the stock market for any length of time, and certainly not for the three to five years a private company investment is likely to be illiquid.*

I believe that in the present market and economic environment, the ranges of return suggested in this article, as being expected by venture capitalists, are fair and realistic for the individual investor also. Therefore, investors should select their target expectations (hopefully, the natural greed of investors will not prod them to heights of expectation that are unnatural and, therefore, exceedingly dangerous) and structure the deal so that the earnings yield of the company providers the desired returns over the period of the investment. An earnings yield is the reciprocal of a price-earnings ratio. It is calculated the same way a dividend yield is calculated. Stated another way, the cumulative projected earnings yield (investor's pro rata share of a company's earnings divided by the cost of the investment) should be substantially greater than that of publicly traded shares of companies having similar prospects. Private company investors would, I believe, make better investment decisions if they forgot about price/earnings ratios and assumed that the companies in which they are involved will not go public. The lure of a public offering (which is frequently an act of taking advantage of those who are less sophisticated) often confuses the investor's decision-making process.]

To further illustrate this thinking, let's assume that the financing situation will be as follows. A company makes a medical instrument that has major potential for treatment of a serious disease. An analysis shows that the stocks of leading medical instrument companies are selling at 30 times earnings, medium firms at 20 times earnings, and small companies at 12 times earnings. Assume that the company seeking financing has current sales of $750,000 and is losing money, but evaluated projections by a venture capitalist indicate that in five years sales will be 7.5 million and earnings $600,000 after taxes. (The entrepreneur's projections might have been $12 million in sales and $1 million in after-tax earnings.) Key questions about management, marketing, finance, etc., have been satisfactorily answered. *[It is important in this process also to have an idea as to the earnings increases being projected for the publicly traded companies being used in the comparative analysis. The figure charts on pages 144 and 146 display the discount ranges necessary to equalize the accumulated earnings yield of companies if one accepts the basic premise that the acceptance of illiquidity entitles the owner of the money to a premium return of: 5-10 times for seed capital financings, 3-6 times for startups, 2-4 times for developing stage, and 1..5-3 times for investment in an already profitable company.]*

Venture capitalists might assume that in five years they will be able to liquidate their holdings on the basis of the company's being valued in the marketplace at $7.8 million (13 times earnings). They feel that this investment should produce a 44 percent compounded return on capital. Analysis indicates that it will take an initial investment of $500,000 to accomplish the five-year plan of the company. (Venture capitalists might also have to calculate a dilution factor if additional capital will be required.) Calculating the present value of the $500,000 investment for the five years using a 44 percent annual compounded growth rate factor, the $500,000 investment must have a value of $3,205,500 at the end of the fifth year. Assuming that the company will have a value of $7.8 million by that date (earnings of $600,000 times a multiple of 13), they would then require an initial 41.09 percent equity interest for their investments.

There are many variables. Will venture capitalists really use a price-earnings multiple of 13 to calculate their value at the end of five years? *[I prefer the approach of thinking in terms of a percentage of the multiple of the Dow Jones Industrial Average or an industry index that relates to the business of the company rather than in absolutes. A multiple of 13 can be either high or low depending on the timing of market cycles.]* This factor often depends on the state of the stock market. In good times, venture capitalists might well use such a calculation, but during down markets, a price-earnings multiple of 10 or less is more likely. The difference has a major bearing on the equity percentage they will want for their $500,000. How accurate will the projections be? Will the company really be able to get by with only $500,000 in equity, despite the fact that it will grow from $750,000 to $7.8 million in five years, an average growth per year of 58 percent compounded?

These are only a few of the questions that venture capitalists would ask themselves in pondering the return they want on their investment and the price to pay for the equity position.

The Pricing of Startups

In the case of startups, the pricing question becomes considerably more obscure. While the venture capitalist may go through a similar calculation, the returns expected are likely to be much higher than they are in the above illustration; thus, the investment will require a greater percentage of equity. Naturally the factors of unpredictability are much greater.

As a rough rule of thumb, if the venture capitalists are putting up all of the capital in a startup venture, they will probably want voting control of the venture. *[As should the individual investor in some form, in case the venture should fail to achieve projected results.]* As described above, they might also include an earn-out program in the investment so that if certain prescribed targets are met, the entrepreneurs will be able to "earn" increasing amounts of equity. On the other hand, over the years some notable investments have been made where venture capitalists receive only 33 percent of 45 percent of the equity after putting up all the capital. However, such transactions were generally worked out during strong stock markets with companies whose management represented some of the nation's leading executives in a "hot" industry.

Naturally, the greater the amount that the entrepreneur can invest, the less equity will be requested by the venture capitalist. For example, if the entrepreneur is putting up 30 percent of the capital, the venture firm might require only a 40 percent equity interest. Obviously these questions relate directly to key factors such as potential, quality, and risk. It should be noted that venture capitalists generally want entrepreneurs and their team to retain sufficient equity interests to ensure that they will be properly motivated. At the same time, if initial members of the management team are found to be inadequate or if they decide to leave, many venture capitalists will want to provide for a practical way to retire a portion of their initial stock interests. *[The issue here is the price at which the entrepreneur or members of the management team invest. I suggest it be on the same terms as the other investors. The entrepreneur and members of the management group can and should be given options and bonus shares in some form. They have to be motivated, but rewards and capital risk assumption are different considerations and should be treated differently.]*

How the Stock Market Affects Pricing

There is a direct relationship between venture pricing and the overall condition of the securities market. When the stock market is high and speculative stocks are quite popular, pricing will be quite different than it is during a down period when venture capital is more difficult to obtain and prices of small, speculative securities are quite low. While such conditions don't affect the pricing of startups as much as ongoing businesses, obviously the best time to raise money is when the stock market is strong and speculative fever is high.

The most astute entrepreneurs and managers will attempt to time their money-raising forays during these periods and then use debt during the down periods to implement the cash flow of the business, but these are highly unpredictable periods, and luck is as important as brains in raising capital during such periods.

During good times, venture capitalists generally feel that public offerings are the best way out of their investments. They are more generous with assumptions about price-earnings multiples than they are during periods like the 1973 and 1987 liquidity crises in the over-the-counter (OTC) market, when it was virtually impossible to float a new issue and prices of small OTC stocks were exceedingly depressed.

Double-Check Values with the Venture Firms

There are ways to double-check pricing and valuation questions. Because most entrepreneurs will talk to various capital sources, they should compare the investors' suggestions on reasonable valuation. If three or four venture firms tend to agree on the equity percentage for a given investment, the entrepreneur should have more than adequate proof. Counsel with intermediaries such as accountants, lawyers, special consultants, investment bankers, and others can also help entrepreneurs decide what is the reasonable value of their companies. *[A large part of the investors' "valuation" of a project is going to depend upon their instinctive reaction to the entrepreneur. In my case, it is almost instantaneous. I either like and want to do a deal with the individuals or not. "Like" is perhaps not the best word -- "respect of their ability and presumed integrity" is a better description of the feeling. The drive and need to succeed of the individual is also a key factor in the initial instinctive reaction.]*

To transfer some of the qualitative assumptions about an investment into quantitative terms, the following model was developed while the author was at First Chicago Corporation. It can be a useful tool, but it is only a tool. None of the methods discussed is necessarily right or wrong generally or in a given situation.

XYZ Corporation is placing $300,000 in seven percent convertible debentures. The company has been in existence for several years. The current year's operations will result in breaking even at $1,800,000 in sales. The product involves a high degree of technology. four-year projections of sales and earnings are as follows (Figures are in thousands).

Year	1	2	3	4
Sales	$2,800	$4,300	$6,300	$9,200
Net earnings				
Before tax	420	890	1,300	1,900
After tax	210	445	650	950

The problem is to determine what percent of equity would be fair compensation for investing $300,000 in XYZ Corporation. *["Fair" is a matter of perspective and perception. Frequently, the investor is more financially sophisticated than the entrepreneur. The investor may propose a deal -- I think it better for the entrepreneur to propose the deal and the investor to make counter proposals -- that is truly fair, yet the entrepreneur is not sophisticated enough to realize it. After all, to gauge fairness one has to have a reasonably good idea of current marketplace values for comparable properties.]* It should be pointed out that there are three pricing methods compared in this illustration, described as traditional method, fundamental method, and The First Chicago Model.

Traditional Pricing Approach

Assumptions:

1. Basic profit criterion is five times invested funds in four years, for example, 50 percent compounded return on investment.

2. No explicit adjustment for risk.

3. Price earnings ratio of 15 in Year 4. *[A price-earnings ratio (P/E) of 15 is very conservative for a company which has enjoyed a 50 percent annual average compound growth in earnings. The P/E multiple and profit criterion are not the same, but clearly , save for a "greater fool" theory, there is a correlation between the earnings growth and investment gain.]*

Calculation:

1. Year 4 net after-tax earnings are $950,000; therefore, total value of XYZ Corporation in Year 4 is $950,000 X 15 = $14,250,000.

2. Desired value of investor's position in Year 4 is $300,000 X 5 = $1,500,000 + $300,000 = $1,800,000.

3. Percentage of equity required is $1,800,000 / $14,250,000 = 12.6 percent. *[This is a perfectly standard approach to pricing a deal. However, it fails to take into consideration market cycles and presumes that a fifteen P/E is valid. Would it not be better to use the average or mean P/E of a group of preselected stocks as the basis for equity participation calculation? I am assuming that the investor has accepted some of the views reflected in this book and is initially holding an instrument which will ultimately relate to equity but, in the initial instances, is senior thereto. Why should the investor be the only party to have a risk of general market in determining his ultimate profit or participation? The matter can also be addressed on a dollar amount basis where the investor at X point in time and under Y conditions has the right to the greater of agreed upon percentages of the then outstanding shares or an amount of shares which have a minimum market value of an agreed upon amount.]*

Fundamental Pricing Method

The basic premise is that a venture investor ought to receive 20 percent or more, compounded annually, on all invested funds; [I prefer the concept of relativity to long-term fixed-income rates or the performance of an index to a fixed-percentage return figure. Today, a 20 percent compound return, from speculative investments is not that attractive, and certainly was much less so in 1982 when the interest rates were hovering around that level.] therefore, the percentage of the company's equity accruing to the venture investor should equal the sum of the compounded earnings on the new investment divided by the total pre-tax projected earnings for the company over an equivalent period to time.

The earnings on $300,000 at various compounded rates over four years are as follows (figures are in thousands).

Rate	Year 1	2	3	4	Total
20%	60	72	86	104	322
30	90	117	152	198	557
40	120	168	235	329	852

Dividing each of the totals (less interest received) by XYZ corporation's four-year cumulative pre-tax projected profits of $4,510,000 produces the following percentages of equity required.

$$(322 - 81) / 4,510 = 5.3 \text{ percent}$$
$$(557 - 81) / 4,510 = 10.6 \text{ percent}$$
$$(852 - 81) / 4,510 = 17.1 \text{ percent}$$

[All of this assumes that the investor can sell the equity for something close to the then current quotation to realize a profit. This is most often not the case and should, therefore, be factored into the basis for establishing the means of profit potential. It is not unfair for the investor to say to the entrepreneur: "To justify the investment you want me to make, I have to earn a minimum of three times the yield which I would receive from a money market fund, and, therefore, such a return, paid in stock of the company, is the least I will consider. Now, let's work together to see if we can structure an arrangement which will insure that result."]

First Chicago Pricing Model

There are three basic directions a venture situation can take:

1. Successful: profitable to the point of being a solid public company. *[Or, it should just continue to provide returns to the owners. The individual investor has the advantage of being able to profit in ways the professional venture capital investment manager cannot. The individual can draw income in fees. He can enter into joint ventures with the company. He can borrow money from the company or have the company buy preferred stock in, or lend money to, other companies in which he may have or can create an interest. All this assumes, of course, that the other owners of the business agree. The point being made here is that going public is not the only answer, nor in some cases even the best answer, to the issue of how to profit from the success of a venture.]*

2. Sideways: marginally profitable with limited growth--not a viable public company but able to service debt over a period of years.

3. Failure: bankruptcy or reorganization.

Cash Flow for the Successful Investment. The cash flow to the investor if the company is quite successful might look like this (assume capital gains are realized in Year 4; figures are in thousands).

	Year						
Rate	1	2	3	4	5	6	7
Principal	0	0	0	0	0	0	0
Interest	21	21	21	18	0	0	0
Capital gain	0	0	0	X	0	0	0

Cash Flow for the Sideways Investment. The cash flow to the investor would be different, however, if the company became a limited growth situation (figures are in thousands).

Year	1	2	3	4	5	6	7
Principal	0	0	0	75	75	75	75
Interest	21	21	21	18	13	8	3
Capital gain	0	0	0	0	0	0	0

Cash Flow for the Failure Investment. If, unfortunately, the investment turned out to be a disaster, the cash flow might follow this pattern (assume a 10 percent recovery in Year 2; figures are in the thousands).

Year 1	2	3	4	5	6	7	
Principal	0	30	0	0	0	0	0
Interest	21	0	0	0	0	0	0
Capital gain	0	0	0	0	0	0	0

Compared Cash Flows. Comparing the cash flows for each of the three directions a venture investment might take produces the following (figures are in thousands).

Year 1	2	3	4	5	6	7	
Successful	21	21	21	18+X	0	0	0
Sideways	21	21	21	93	88	83	78
Failure	21	30	0	0	0	0	0

Probability Selection. The next step in this method involves assigning probabilities (P) to each of the three possible directions. The sum of these probabilities must, of course, equal 1.0. For the purposes of this example, we have chosen the following probabilities, but each type of project might well receive different weightings for probabilities of success and failure.

$$P\uparrow = .3 \text{ (3 chances in 10)}$$
$$P\rightarrow = .5 \text{ (5 chances in 10)}$$
$$P\downarrow = .2 \text{ (2 chances in 10)}$$
$$\overline{1.0}$$

Total Pricing Layout. After having selected an appropriate discount factor (for the entire portfolio), the overall layout is as follows (we have assumed an annual twenty percent compounded target portfolio return; figures are thousands).

Discounted

value of dollar	*.83*	*.69*	*.58*	*.48*	*.40*	*.33*	*.28*
Year	1	2	3	4	5	6	7
P↑ .3	21	21	21	18+X	0	0	0
P→ .5	21	21	21	93	88	83	78
P→ .5	21	30	0	0	0	0	0

Reduction to Present Value Equivalents. The next step is to reduce these numbers to their present value equivalents by multiplying them by the discount factor at the head of the column.

Year	*1*	*2*	*3*	*4*	*5*	*6*	*7*
P↑ .3	17	15	12	9+.48X	0	0	0
P→ .5	17	15	12	45	35	27	22
P→ .5	17	21	0	0	0	0	0

Pricing Equation. We now total each row and then construct the basic equation that will provide the desired output.

Probability	Raw Total
P↑ .3	53 + .48X
P → .5	173
P → .5	38

Using the probabilities shown above,

$$300 = (.3)(53 + .48X) + (.5)(173) + (.2)(38)$$

Design Matrix

				Percentage of Firm Needed at		
P1	P2	P3	X	P/E10	P/E15	P/E30
0.8	0.0	0.2	648.0	6.8	4.5	2.3
0.7	0.1	0.2	704.7	7.4	4.9	2.5
0.6	0.2	0.2	780.3	8.2	5.5	2.7
0.5	0.3	0.2	886.1	9.3	6.2	3.1
0.4	0.4	0.2	1,044.9	11.0	7.3	3.7
→0.3	0.5	0.2 ←	1,309.5	13.8	9.2	4.6
0.2	0.6	0.2	1,838.7	19.4	12.9	6.5
0.1	0.7	0.2	3,426.2	36.1	24.0	12.0

The row set in bold type shows the present value of $300,000 if a 20 percent compound growth rate is to be achieved, based on different probability assumptions shown on each line. The line marked → ← shows the assumptions given in this problem about success, failure, or sideways movement of the investment.

Thus, if a price-earnings multiple of 15 is to be used to calculate the value of the company, a 9.2 percent equity will be required to achieve the compound growth rate of 20 percent, given the probability requirements in the example. The columns headed P/E 10 and P/E 30 show the percentage of equity needed under those price-earnings multiples.

Comparison of Three Pricing Methods. The percentage of equity required under the three pricing methods is as follows: traditional, 12.9 percent; fundamental, 5.3 percent; First Chicago, 9.2 percent.

Effect of Varying the Interest Rate. What happens if the interest rate on the debenture is doubled, from 7 percent to 14 percent, for example?

				Percentage of Firm Needed at		
P1	*P2*	*P3*	*X*	*P/E10*	*P/E15*	*P/E30*
0.8	0.0	0.2	529.2	5.6	3.7	1.9
0.7	0.1	0.2	566.3	6.0	4.0	2.0
0.6	0.2	0.2	615.9	6.5	4.3	2.2
0.5	0.3	0.2	685.2	7.2	4.8	2.4
0.4	0.4	0.2	789.2	8.3	5.5	2.8
0.3	**0.5**	**0.2**	**982.5**	**10.1**	**6.8**	**3.4**
0.2	0.6	0.2	1,369.1	13.8	9.2	4.6
0.1	0.7	0.2	2,348.9	24.7	16.5	8.2

This table shows that the equity percentage required on the investment will drop from 9.2 percent to 6.8 percent and still produce the same return to First Chicago if the interest rate on the debenture doubles, from 7 percent to 14 percent.

Effect of Varying the Time Horizon. What is the effect of pushing out the realization of capital gains to Year 7?

				Percentage of Firm Needed at		
P1	*P2*	*P3*	*X*	*P/E10*	*P/E15*	*P/E30*
0.8	0.0	0.2	1,119.7	11.8	7.9	3.9
0.7	0.1	0.2	1,217.7	12.8	8.5	4.3
0.6	0.2	0.2	1,348.4	14.2	9.5	4.7
0.5	0.3	0.2	1,531.2	16.1	10.7	5.4
0.4	0.4	0.2	1,805.6	19.0	12.7	6.3
0.3	**0.5**	**0.2**	**2,262.8**	**23.8**	**15.9**	**7.9**
0.2	0.6	0.2	3,177.2	33.4	22.3	11.1
0.1	0.7	0.2	5,920.5	62.3	41.5	20.8

This table shows the effects of moving the realization of capital gains from the fourth to the seventh year, keeping all other assumptions the same. The investment now will require a 15.9 percent equity interest rather than 9.2 percent.

My friend Dr. Robert Lawrence Kuhn, author, educator and CEO of The Geneva Companies has that which is perhaps the best definition of a good deal. Robert says simply that "a good deal is one which brings a smile to my face on remembering it."

WHAT'S IT WORTH?

ANDREW FEINBERG

Valuations are crucial in the sale and for the negotiations leading to the sale. So how do you get the best? This article appeared in *Venture* and has been edited for this book.

"Sellers have some strange ideas about their companies," says Jeff Jones, president of Certified Business Brokers of Houston Inc. "A guy who owned an office supply operation with about $100,000 in sales thought General Motors would want to buy him, because he heard the company was diversifying."

Obviously, sellers don't always know what buyers want - and they certainly don't know what their companies are worth. "Everyone knows that sellers often overvalue their companies," says John E. Bakken, president of Business Appraisal Associates in Denver. Just as often the seller will miss on the low side. "Quite often an entrepreneur doesn't realize how far he has come, and so he undervalues his company considerably," says John Hempstead, president of Hempstead & Co., a business appraisal firm located in Haddonfield, NJ.

Business appraisers - experts in valuing a business - can take some of the mystery out of a valuation, tell you what to expect, and, perhaps most significantly, let you know how to boost the value of your company once you consider selling.

Unfortunately, choosing an appraiser isn't simply a matter of randomly picking a name out of a phone book. Appraisers come in all shapes and sizes, from investment banking firms, to nationwide appraisal specialists, to local boutiques, to public accounting firms, to franchised business brokers. To make things worse, anyone can hang out a shingle as an appraiser, since there are no licensing requirements. As you would expect from this situation, appraisers tend to compete by bad-mouthing the work done by their competition.

Investment bankers or business brokers have a built-in conflict of interest, say accountants, since their fees are partly or wholly contingent on a sale. A sale at a distress price is far better than no sale at all, at least for the banker counting on a fee. CPAs, the brokers and bankers argue, don't necessarily know anything about what a company is worth, just what it should pay to Uncle Sam each year in taxes. Firms that specialize in business appraisals say good things about their ""reputable" brethren - and in the next breath suggest that few of their colleagues are reputable.

Welcome to the wonderful world of business valuation.

Most sellers deal with an appraiser whose office is relatively nearby, but there are some valuation specialists with national reputations and a nationwide clientele. Arguably, the two best-known experts are Shannon P. Pratt, president of Williamette Management Associates Inc. in Portland, OR, and Irving L. Blackman, a partner in the Chicago accounting firm of Blackman Kallick Bartelstein. Not coincidentally, each has written comprehensive books on the subject.

Having a big-name valuation expert on your side, says Blackman, is only important when a dispute, usually a court case, arises. The best way to find someone who is well qualified is to ask professionals who deal with valuations on a regular basis - your accountant, your banker, and your lawyer. Sometimes a fellow entrepreneur can be helpful. Many appraisers belong to one of two professional associations: the American Society of Appraisers, Washington, and the Institute of Business Appraisers Inc., Boynton Beach, FL. Membership does supply some reassurance to the business owner. The American Society of Appraisers, for example, requires that its members pass an examination and have at least two years of experience.

In some cases valuation experts will ask for money up front. All, however, should be able to give you a pretty good estimate of the cost before they begin the job.

A valuation should take from one to two months if's not complicated, although rush jobs are possible if a deal is actually on the table.

Experts say a valuation can cost anywhere from $5,000 to $100,000 depending on the complexity of the company, e.g., the number of offices and plants, financial covenants, ownership structure, etc. Most businesses worth between $2 million and $20 million can count on paying $7,500 to $20,000 for a valuation. That will represent about 100 hours of billed time at a rate of $75 to $200 an hour.

Theoretically, appraisers use many different valuation methods - tangible book value, discounted future earnings, liquidation value or replacement value, or a multiple of earnings or cash flow - but in practice almost all valuations are based on some multiple of earnings or cash flow, usually an earnings projection discounted to the present. Book value, however, does play a more important role for companies with a great portion of their value in inventory or real estate.

Valuing a fast-growing company presents its own set of problems. There may be no earnings record and not much of a sales record. Projecting revenues and then discounting them to the present helps, but how fast will revenues really grow? "In such instances," says Pratt, "you have to study very carefully the growth prospects for the industry. We would talk to trade associations, securities analysts, and read the trade publications in the field. Then we would go to potential or actual customers and ask their opinion of the new product that is being offered." After that the valuation expert makes growth projections and then discounts if all back to the present.

A new valuation model, developed by Margeaux Cvar, is designed to address some of the problems involved in pricing a young, fast-growing company. "The basic flaw with standard valuation techniques," says Cvar, "is that they look at the current bottom line to estimate the future bottom line. I think you should estimate earnings by analyzing a company's negotiating leverage in the marketplace. What kind of leverage does if have over the competition, its suppliers, its customers, and potential new entrants."

Cvar's method relies on a growing data base and an interesting twist to "comparables," a common method for figuring the value of a company by comparing if with some similar, easily valued public company. Future earnings are the key to a company's value, Cvar agrees, but she believes many investment bankers and business appraisers miscalculate the future value of a company because they look for comparable companies only within one particular industry. Her valuation approach seeks comparables across industries by looking at growth rate, market share, industry rank, comparative cost of production, and dominance in a segment.

413

Most entrepreneurs don't approach the valuation process with any-thing like that sophistication. Often sellers find themselves at logger-heads with their own valuation experts because the valuation doesn't conform to some rule of thumb the entrepreneur may have learned.

Almost every industry has a rule of thumb. Cable TV franchises are supposedly valued at 11 times cash flow; ad agencies at 75% of gross income; day care centers at $500 to $1,000 for each child enrolled; motels at $12,300 to $14,600 per room; and garbage pickup routes at two and a half times gross income.

"If you rely on these rules too much, you can be led astray," says Hempstead. "The rules don't take into account whether you are in a growth market or a declining one, or if the major employer in your city is thinking of closing a big plant."

All rules come with a heavy dose of wishful thinking, says Pratt. "On average, businesses sell for one-third less than the accepted industry rule of thumb," he adds, stating what some might contend is yet another rule of thumb. "Sometimes this discount is hard to per-ceive because if comes in the payment terms, not in the dollar price itself."

Sellers may have unconscious rules of thumb. "People sometimes overvalue their companies because the sum will provide them with enough interest income to maintain their life-style," says Hempstead. "Or occasionally people think their business is worth $1.0 million times however many partners there are."

Most common, though, is to use the market value of a comparable publicly traded company as a rule of thumb. Here, too, there can be so many mitigating factors as to make the comparison almost point-less. While in theory a private company will usually be sold at a dis-count of 24 percent to 40 percent to the price/earnings multiple (or, for companies without earnings, price to sales ratio) of a similar pub-lic company, such comparisons have almost no validity unless the pri-vate company is at least one-tenth the size of the public company.

"Even then," says Christian Bendixen, manager of financial valua-tions at a major accounting firm in San Francisco, "if is absolutely crucial to factor in things like management depth, market niche, patent protection, and other considerations."

Although for all these reasons valuations may not have bedrock credibility with buyers, they are nonetheless crucial for the sale - and for the negotiations leading up to the sale. Generally, a buyer will get

414

his own valuation of your company, so the valuation you get from your appraiser is more for negotiation purposes than for closing the deal. "We look very carefully at the other guy's valuation," says Blackman. "When you both want to see the deal done, you're really friendly adversaries. If I'm representing a buyer, we may actually pay the seller every penny of his valuation - although in cases like that we'll usually do some pretty heavy negotiating on the payment terms."

Recognize, however, that the valuation you tender delineates where the negotiating will start. As in most deals, in buying and selling a company, the parties tend to begin at extreme positions and work their way toward a compromise.

There are ways to make a valuation more believable, appraisers say, thus boosting the price you get for your company. Remember that the buyer will be suspicious of everything. "If there is any uncertainty involved," says Hempstead, "the buyer will assume the worst." A history of audits, for example, is wonderful, but not essential if you have a lot of records to back up your claims.

One of the diciest issues in the sale of any private company, of course, is the question of "real" earnings. "Entrepreneurs don't want to optimize their earnings," says Ken MacKenzie, assistant executive director at the Institute of Business Appraisers. "They want to optimize their life-style." With that goal in mind, private company books often show expenses - for multiple company cars, for instance - that wouldn't pass muster at a public company. The entrepreneur still has the use of the cars, he may pay no income tax on the cost of the cars, and the company gets an expense to use against its taxes.

If you're going to be selling your business in the near future, MacKenzie and others say, try to establish a history of at least two years of real earnings - without excessive perks and personal spending disguised as business expenses. But no need to go overboard. If you took a legitimate trip to a convention and brought along your family, clear records will show a potential buyer which portion of the outlay was a necessary business expense and which part was personal. If an offer arrives suddenly, and there is no time to establish a two-year record, you should have an appraiser restate earnings for the last five years, says Pratt.

If your records are bad - or fudged for tax purposes - you'll profit from being totally candid with the person doing the valuation. "Don't worry about the IRS getting involved," says Blackman. "The thing to do is create a pro forma statement indicating what the business would have earned if, say, there hadn't been any skimming off the top. Normally, the buyer will discount this somewhat, but not always. I just helped sell a large retail business in which the family had been skimming for years. They told the buyer exactly what they had done, and that income wasn't discounted at all, mostly because the family had such a fine reputation."

Planning a couple of years ahead for a sale can let you take some steps to increase the value of your company, experts say.

Spin off or sell a losing unit or division. If you run a company with several distinct lines of business, sell the parts separately. You'll get a better price.

Make annual business projections so that you can show a buyer a history of making your numbers. This can increase any buyer's comfort level.

Take physical inventories every year. The buyer will know you haven't managed earnings by "adjusting" inventory levels.

If you are about to sell and have excess cash on the balance sheet, pay yourself a special dividend. A buyer will probably not pay you dollar for dollar for that cash if is part of the package.

Time the sale of your company the way you would time the sale of a stock. Listen to what the experts say is the trend in the public markets for companies like yours. They will probably be wrong, but they might be interesting.

And remember, you have a great deal more control over boosting the value of your company than you do over the stock market.

BUYING STOCK...
OR ASSETS

MICHAEL A. KAHN

There's more than one way to buy a company, but a buyer should protect his investment with certain contractual safeguards. The author is a partner in the New York law firm of Golleb & Golleb. This article was published in *Venture*.

You've decided to buy XYZ Corp. Your army of experts has meticulously examined the company's financial structure, operations, labor, plant and equipment, markets, rights and obligations. After arduous negotiations you've agree on a purchase price. The only remaining question is whether to buy XYZ's stock or its assets. What's the difference? Plenty!

Your tax specialists will highlight the differing tax treatment of a stock purchase and an asset purchase. For example, the buyer of assets of a manufacturing facility, including its physical plant and equipment, can increase the value reflected on the seller's books to a figure taking into account the purchase price. He can then depreciate these assets without regard to any depreciation previously taken by the seller. If, on the other hand, stock of XYZ is bought, no new depreciation is allowed.

Which Way Is Best?

The question of whether to buy a company's stock or its assets

417

depends upon circumstances. While there is no clear-cut answer, each type of purchase offers different benefits (see table).

However, there are legal implications as well when acquiring a business. For example, although XYZ may be willing to turn over a lease or contract it holds to a purchaser of its assets, not all leases or contracts may be assigned. If the buyer acquires the shares, there is generally no need for approval by the other party to lease or contract.

Advantages of Buying

Assets	Stock
1. Certain assets can be depreciated regardless of prior depreciation claimed by the previous owner.	1. In most cases, contracts and leases come with the purchase
2. The company is not burdened with unwanted minority shareholders.	2. If minority shareholders exist, control can be gained by acquiring less than 100 percent of the stock, thus reducing the amount of investment.
3. Unwanted obligations, such as union contracts, are not acquired.	3. Sales tax is avoided.

Of course, the seller may be burdened with unfavorable contractual obligations, such as expensive employee benefits. If this is the case, the buyer might benefit by purchasing assets instead of stock.

Minority shareholders may present problems in either case. If you buy a majority block of stock, you'll be marrying partners who have voting rights that may thwart your plans. On the other hand, by acquiring only a portion of a company, your capital investment may be less.

To avoid partners, you may choose to purchase assets. By law, a sale of assets may require the affirmative vote of a stated proportion of the company's shareholders. Even if the required number of shareholders agree, dissenters may be entitled to have their shares appraised and purchased by the selling corporation.

A purchase of assets could also involve sales tax, while stock sales are immune.

Generally, the buyer of assets is not responsible for a seller's liabilities. However, "Bulk Sales" acts provide for prior notice of the impending sale to the seller's creditors. If sufficient notice is not given, the seller's creditors may have a right to the acquired assets. Since the obligations of the business generally are unaffected by a sale of the corporation's stock, the purchaser of shares may be buying potential litigation as well.

Whether the acquisition is a purchase of shares or assets, the contract should contain seller representations in order to disclose any condition that might affect the acquired firm or its assets, and to provide the buyer a remedy (by way of litigation against the seller, if necessary) for any false statements. Typically, such representations provide that the selling corporation was validly organized and exists under the laws of the state where it is located; that the agent who will sign the purchase agreement is authorized to do so by the bylaws; that any required consent to the transaction by shareholders will be obtained; and, that no legal impediments to the sale are known to the seller.

Other representations should state that the seller has good "marketable" title to the assets (whether sold outright or acquired through a stock purchase) and that there are no liens or encumbrances against them; that no legal actions are pending against the seller and that it is not a party in any bankruptcy proceeding. Additional representations that the buyer may ask the seller to make may relate to financial statements, tax liabilities, and employment contracts.

One of the more important safeguards in the purchase contract is the indemnity, a kind of insurance policy that protects the buyer against liability or loss. For example, an indemnity may cover claims of patent infringement. If a court later holds that a piece of acquired equipment violates patent rights of a third part, the seller is responsible for any damages the buyer sustains in litigation. Indemnities should also protect the buyer against the seller's misrepresentations, product liability claims or suits, and tax arrears.

To better ensure that the seller's representations are true, the contract should require an opinion of the seller's counsel confirming that the seller validly exists, that the person signing the agreement is authorized by the bylaws, that there are no legal impediments to the transaction, and that no claims or litigation are pending against the seller. These are some basics to consider, but every acquisition is different. So, have your attorney look at any contract before you sign it.

THE DANGERS OF OVERCAPITALIZATION IN THE STARTUP STAGE

RICHARD H. BUSKIRK

This article is from *Frontiers of Entrepreneurship Research*, Proceedings of the 1982 Conference on Entrepreneurship, Karl H. Vesper (ed.), at Babson, College Center for Entrepreneurial Studies, Wellesley, Mass. The thirteen footnotes and the commentary at the end are by Arthur Lipper III and did not appear in the original publication of this article.

Abstract

A startup venture is faced with a crisis four years after its inception when its technical product is not quite ready for production, no customer exists, and its 1.5 million dollar equity investment is dissipated.[1] Investors hire consultants to evaluate the situation to determine if the enterprise should be folded or new capital be infused. Serious questions arise as to the wisdom of management's use of the original $1.5 million.[2] There is evidence that several parties billed the new firm more on the basis of how much money was in the till than on the basis of the market value of their services.[3]

---

[1] Why was the investment made as equity? It would have been better as debt or in some form giving the investors control in the event of nonachievement of objectives.

[2] Was the disposition as promised in the business plan and was it authorized by the board of directors? If not, is there redress possible from those committing certain acts which may be contrary to the plan which was used to induce investment by the investors?

[3] Are any of these billings recapturable by negotiation? Die they overcharge to the extent of a possible legal recovery action being pursued?

Video Learning Systems, Inc.

On February 1, 1982, the six person board of directors of Video Learning Systems, Inc. of Newport Beach, California assembled in the offices of one of its large, non-director investors, Dr. Brady, an anesthesiologist, to hear the report of two consultants who had been retained a month previously by Dr. O'Malley, director and largest investor ($600,000), to evaluate the company's situation and prospects for the future.[4] The consultants had proposed to conduct their study in three stages. The first stage, which was to be completed within the first month, was to answer three questions:

1. Does the company have a workable, marketable product? Does it do what it is supposed to do?
2. Is there a market for the product? If so, what is it?
3. What competitive threats are on the horizon?

The second stage, if approved by the board, was to answer the questions:

4. What organizational structure is needed?
5. How much more money will be needed and from where will the funds come?
6. What marketing plan should be adopted?

The final stage of the project was to be a detailed business plan for the enterprise.

The company had been founded in 1978 by Dr. O'Malley, a family physician of national note, who had been distressed by the poor quality of continuing educational material used by physicians in their efforts to keep abreast of their practices. As national president of his professional association, Dr. O'Malley undertook a comprehensive investigation of alternatives to the existing educational media. He was impressed by some of the work done in video educational media and was told by some of the industry's leaders that the future was to be found in what was called "video interactive systems." In such systems, the student could interact with the program at any point; questions could be asked to determine if the student comprehended the material being presented. For each answer, the program could branch into other material if it were so desired. For example, should a wrong answer be given, the program could present additional material to

---

[4]Unless "observation" rights had been contracted for by Dr. Brady, I see no reason why he should receive special information not available to other investors. The directors have a responsibility which is special, but all investors have the same inherent rights.

clarify the point and then test on that new material. Thus, remedial material could be provided where needed. It was this branching capability, in contrast to the existing looping techniques, that gave promise of great things for video interactive learning systems. Such systems consisted of microprocessors that drove either video tape or video disc machines. Thus, the programs were on either tape or discs. The front end costs of discs combined with their inflexibility for program modification led the consultants to conclude that for the time being the Video Learning System unit should incorporate a video tape unit in it. A Panasonic tape drive was used in the prototypes. Several inputs could be used:

1. A small hand held console was most popular for most programs.
2. A standard computer keyboard could be used.
3. A light wand to respond to screen stimuli was used in several medical programs, i.e., to point to the gallbladder.
4. A wide variety of special sensors could be used for special applications, i.e., manikin used for a CPR program was wired with 100 sensors that informed the computer if the student were doing the CPR properly.

Dr. O'Malley then retained some local experts in video-computer systems and financed initial research for the project. The initial results were encouraging, so he formed Video Learning Systems and sold some stock to fellow physicians who had become interested in his project.[5] Dr. O'Malley had a good reputation among the local medical fraternity for some of his previous ventures which had proven profitable. Obtaining the needed funds was easy; the profit sharing pension funds of the physicians were overflowing with venture capital ready for work.[6] Over the next four years, $1.5 million was invested by 26 different investors.[7] It was the opinion of the company's legal counsel that the firm was in complete compliance with all laws pertaining to security sales.[8]

---

[5]What representations did he make? Is he liable for the investments of the others?

[6]Is there liability to others in the plans?

[7]What representations were made to the investors at different times, and did all the investors and shareholders have the same information available to them?

[8]It would be good for the investors if that legal opinion was in writing and could be looked to in the event the counsel was found to be incorrect.

In December 1981, the company's capital had been depleted. The firm could not pay its bills except by raising new money. Each point (1 percent) of the company was being sold for $60,000.[9] The company's overhead in the late months of 1981 was running about $40,000 per month. (See Exhibit 1.)

Exhibit 1	Monthly Overhead Costs[10]
President's salary	$12,000
Technician's salary	2,000
Occupancy	1,000
Office expenses	1,000
Travel and entertainment	4,000
Legal and accounting	5,000
Consulting fees	15,000
Total	$40,000

In 1979, Mr. McDonald, the former president of a large pharmaceutical supplier, was given a three-year contract to be president of the new concern at a salary of $60,000 a year plus expenses. Much distress among investors developed a year later over Mr. McDonald's performance. One investor said, "We are dead in the water. Nothing is happening. We keep pouring money into that company but nothing comes out."

Then two consultants were hired by Dr. O'Malley without the knowledge of Mr. McDonald. One of their assignments was to be an evaluation of Mr. McDonald and the other people involved with the enterprise. The other full-time employee was David McDavid, an electronic technician in charge of developing the prototype. Dr. Connor, the consultant in charge of the project, after talking at length with both employees had concluded that McDonald was out of his element, he was a corporate type, not an entrepreneur. He just did not know what to do to make things happen. On the other hand, Connor was pleasantly surprised with McDavid and planned to continue his employment.

One of the consultant's first tasks was to find out what happened to the money. A source and application of funds statement (Exhibit 2)

---

[9]Was this another round of equity? To what extent did it dilute the holdings of the existing shareholders?

[10]Both the president's salary and consulting fees seem way out of line for a startup situation.

was developed. The consultants were dismayed at how little of the funds actually went into research and productive activities.

The board of directors was composed of:

Dr. Goldberg, M.D., plastic surgeon   (2 percent of stock)
Dr. O'Malley, M.D., family practice   (10 percent of stock)

Exhibit 2   Source and Applications of Funds - 1978 to 1982

Source of funds:	
Sale of 25 percent of authorized stock	$1,500,000
Application of funds:	
Management salaries	$ 210,000
Consultant fees	415,000
Legal fees	230,000
Accounting fees	160,000
Occupancy costs	65,000
Research expenses	285,000
Prototype costs	55,000
Office operations	45,000
Marketing costs	15,000
Working capital	20,000
	$1,500,000

Dr. Mahan, M.D., retired pathologist   (2 percent of stock)
Mr. Harris, investor·   (2 percent of stock)
Mr. Coman, stock broker   (2 percent of stock)
Dr. O'Brien, M.D., family practice   (2 percent of stock)[11]

The board meeting convened at 10 am. After 10 minutes of routine business, Mr. Harris asked in brusque tones by what right Dr. O'Malley had hired the two consultants. The two consultants were then asked to leave the room while the board loudly argued for the next 90 minutes. The consultants were then asked to rejoin the group to give their report. The consultants' retention was approved by a vote of five to one.

---

[11]The whole situation is "amateur night." The way it was set up ensured it would be a loser. No businessperson with entrepreneurial experience was involved. The money went in as equity. No controls seem to have been imposed by the investors. Salaries and fees are silly. The directors hold too little stock and are inexperienced at building businesses.

The consultants gave a three-hour report of their findings and recommendations. The essence of the report was:

1. The company had a good product that was a definite improvement on the state of the art. But, it was not quite ready for production. The competition did not have similar capability, particularly the grading and recording cartridge by which each student's performance could be permanently recorded.

2. There was a huge market for such a training system, particularly in corporate programs. It was strongly recommended that the company focus on intercepting existing corporate training dollars as its initial marketing target. The consultants recommended discontinuing existing thrusts into the medical training markets because of marketing difficulties.

After the report, the directors spoke on various matters and asked questions. One pertaining to money caused Dr. Connor to recommend that the firm should terminate not only the contract of the existing president, but the consulting contracts of two of its board members. To this, Dr. Mahan took strong exception by saying "I am owed $55,000 a year by the company for consulting, and I expect to be paid in full soon."

The consultant who was running the meeting asked him, "Exactly what did you do for the $55,000?"

"I made myself available. It's not my fault that no one asked me to work," was his reply. Dr. Mahan had some experience in making video training films and had been hired as a consultant for that expertise. Dr. O'Malley also stated he expected to be paid but only after the firm was profitable. He had done considerable work for the firm and was acting as de facto president. He had raised all of the money. Mr. Harris then erupted into a tirade against Dr. O'Malley at which point Mr. Coman, who had been silent until then, stood up and threatened to punch Mr. Harris in the face. Dr. Mahan broke in to demand his money, at which point Mr. Connor tried to say something. Dr. Mahan pointed a finger at him and said, "Shut up, you. I am talking to my partners, and it's none of your business." Dr. O'Brien asked the two consultants to leave the room once again. The ensuing verbal fight lasted 45 minutes. When Dr. Palmer, the other consultant, suggested to Dr. Connor that perhaps they should keep walking right out of town, he was told, "No, there's too much at stake here. This can be big, very big."

After the consultants had been asked to rejoin the board, they were told that Mr. Harris had offered his stock for sale for his cost ($129,000).[12] Mr. Harris was not happy and was most subdued for the rest of the meeting. The consultants then outlined what work was to be done for the next meeting, March 13, 1982.

That night, the board of directors, without Harris, joined several other investors at the home of Dr. Brady for an evening of Irish cuisine. Several potential investors were at the party and were eager to know more about the firm's future. Great care was taken not to "hype" the stock. "Cautious confidence" was the adopted slogan after Dr. Palmer had cautioned several board members about some of their statements.

The next day the consultants delivered their message to a special meeting of the company's stockholders held at the Marriott hotel. All went well. Mr. Harris did not attend.

In planning their activities for the next month, the consultants reviewed where the firm now stood. It had a product, but one that was not quite ready to go into production. About $50,000 was needed to make some needed modifications. Previous management had neglected three simple, but critical, technical factors. Dr. Palmer, who had ten years experience in electronic production, had quickly detected that the units needed:

1. Ventilation. The heat buildup inside the unit would eventually damage the video tapes. No provision had been made for ventilation. It was a simple matter but had been overlooked.
2. No shielding had been provided to keep radiation from affecting the operations of some of the computer circuitry--again, a simple matter.
3. No provision had been made for quality-control check points in the unit so that the production units could be quickly checked by instruments to detect deviations from specifications. The firm had spent $55,000 for ten prototypes to be made by a large electronics company, but the work had been farmed out to some uninterested unit that was only able to make three units, none of which worked consistently well.

---

[12]The position of Mr. Harris is typical of the disgruntled investor. He feels that he should be able to get his money back, just because he is disenchanted and wants out. I would guess there is not much chance of this happening.

426

Pursuit of the first customer was at the top of the list. To date, despite all efforts of previous management and the promises of great things, no customer has been developed. The consultants had targeted five potential customers who had indicated great interest in the system.

In his final statement to the stockholders, Dr. Palmer had urged them to give serious thought about what they would want to do in May when the final report was submitted. It was suggested that about $3,000,000 would be needed to take the company to its breakeven point. The stockholders would have to decide if they wanted to provide the additional money or whether they wanted to go outside for it, thus, diluting their position.[13]

Comments by Arthur Lipper III

The author of this article, Richard H. Buskirk of the University of Southern California, provides a service by bringing this situation to the attention of investors and entrepreneurs, because it contains so many of the usual mistakes made in private company investing. The basic problem in this case was that apparently no sufficient challenge of the business plan was made, if in fact a real business plan was ever developed. The investors simply relied on the reputation (as a doctor, not as a businessman) of Dr. O'Malley and on their general acceptance of the idea for the business. (As it happens, I know something of the business the company originally intended to enter, as well as the reorientation suggested by the consultants. I agree with the consultants, yet I understand Dr. O'Malley's premise concerning medical education. Here, we have a very appealing idea being developed by amateur businesspeople, with the result that time and money were wasted.)

There is no mention of patent protection, and there seems to be no awareness of the fact that the real business investment will be in the software and not in the hardware. The software is the key to the success of the business. All too often investors fail to understand where their company is situated in the development-

production-distribution-servicing-utilization cycle. In this case, in a field dominated by giant equipment manufacturers, to try to be sim-

---

[13]One of the key points the investor should note is that the original money went in all at once and without any achievement requirements for subsequent investment. If there had been a staged investment, not nearly so much money would have been wasted before calling in the consultants.

ply a manufacturer of equipment is unrealistic. Even if the company was successful in developing a product, a bigger company with greater resources would benefit from their experience and market a rival product. Products have to be sold and serviced, and small companies are at a great disadvantage in the product manufacture and distribution areas.

In any case, if the company's directors do decide to seek an additional $3 million, in all probability the new investors will be senior to the investors of the original $1.5 million, and it will be a long time before the original investors see a profit on their investment, as derived from the buildup of retained earnings. This undoubtedly is another case of investors being less concerned with the growth of retained earnings, as they are with the likelihood of selling their interest to new investors willing to pay highly for projected future earnings.

TERM SHEET USED BY WHITEHEAD ASSOCIATES

Jack Whitehead of Whitehead Associates (WAI), one of the most sophisticated and successful venture capital firms, was also the founder of Technicon (the very successful medical technology company that was acquired by Revlon). Thus, he had the experience of both running an important company and managing successfully his own very substantial portfolio. This term sheet is being used with his permission. The addition of my comments is not intended to be critical in any way of the Whitehead form.

Name of Company

Summary of Principal Terms of Whitehead Associates, Inc. Investment

A. *Equity Interest*

_____ percent (_____%) of fully diluted common stock outstanding calculated based on common shares outstanding, options outstanding, and share issuable upon exercise of warrants or convertible securities represented by (convertible preferred stock), (convertible debentures), (common stock), (Debt and _____)

B. *Type and Terms of Security*

C. *Price to be Paid by WAI*

D. *Registration Rights*

_____ after closing, one mandatory at the expense of _____, two additional mandatory registrations, the cost of which shall be shared by WAI and _____. Unlimited S-16 registration at company expense. Piggyback subject to underwriters approval.

E. *Voting Rights*

Equal to percentage ownership of fully diluted common stock.

F. *Right of Co-Sale*

If a management stockholder receives a solicitation to sell all or any portion of his equity in _____, such an offer will not be accepted unless a similar offer on the same terms is made pro rata for the same proportion of securities held by WAI. If WAI chooses not to sell on these terms, WAI may, at its option, purchase from management stockholder group those securities proposed for sale.

G. *Pre-emptive Rights*

WAI will have the right of first refusal for its pro rata share of any sale of securities by _____ prior to the first public offering.

H. *Covenants*

a. Annual financial statements certified by Certified Public Accountants.

b. Monthly financial statements, budgets, and business plan, as provided internally.

c. Noncompete agreements.

d. Standard contractual covenants and representations.

e. The Company shall not be merged or sold or sell substantially all of its assets without WAI's approval.

I. *Board Seat*

Same representation as ownership percentage, but in any event at least one board seat for WAI.

J. *Expenses*

Legal expenses to be paid by _____.

430

Comments by Arthur Lipper III

A. I would add a provision for revenue participation certificates.

B. I assume that elements of the guarantees which may be required of the entrepreneur, as well as a description of the assets being acquired or used as collateral, would be listed in this section.

C. The staging of the investments would be included in this section, as well as the criterion established for any follow-on investments.

D. Registration rights can be seen as a two-part issue: (1) the require-ment of the company's cooperation, since without such coopera-tion it is almost impossible to effect the filing of a registration statement by the selling shareholders; and, (2) the cost of the fil-ing to the selling shareholder. I have never required more than piggyback rights (allowing my inclusion at such time as others were filing a registration statement to sell stock), believing that my overall controlling features have always been such that it has been unnecessary for me to do otherwise or believing that the con-trolling shareholders wanted to go public as soon as possible. The registration rights required by WAI are reasonable, and they are but one of the many things I have learned in the preparation of this book. I will insist on similar rights in my own deals in the future.

E. Voting rights at shareholder meetings on which matters? Note that the WAI form refers to a "fully diluted" basis, which I assume means that they vote the shares underlying convertible securities or shares into which warrants are exercisable. Do all shares vote equally on a merger? Do all shares vote equally on a change in capitalization? What about the appointment of auditors? Or the election of directors? Is an acquisition a matter the investor wish-es entrepreneurs to control (should they have the major block of voting common stock)? Consideration should be given to embed-ding, in the bylaws of the company, shareholder percentage voting requirements for certain corporate acts which will permit investors to veto what is not in their best interests. The whole problem may also be solved by the issuance of different classes of stock, with the classes having different voting rights on different issues. Investors should not lose sight of the importance of having the company bylaws reflect the desires of the investors.

F. This is a highly effective clause that I will use in my own future deals. However, the buy/sell option, described elsewhere in this book, could have the same effect for an investor who wishes to buy the interest of the management group. Yet, the concept of having a right to receive the same offer as management is excellent. A problem exists--one which has arisen in two of my companies--how does the investor value increases in the manager's salary, additional pension benefits, unlimited expense account, country club dues, automobiles, stock options in the acquiring company, and other perks offered "management" by the acquiring company? These perks have a value and can cause the management to urge the acceptance of the offer. The investor has to be aware that managers typically look to their own interests in times of pending enrichment, and their loyalty and prior obligations tend to evaporate with concern for personal gain.

G. This is an interesting requirement, and one which investors would do well to use.

H. I agree with all these covenants, except possibly the requirement for certification, because the added expense is at times not worth the added protection. Also, I would require an attestation by the CEO and entrepreneur as to all financial statements, including monthly reports. If they present them, they should say they are true and complete.

I. The investor should realize that there can be bylaw requirements concerning the number of director votes needed to take or propose shareholder actions, etc. Perhaps division of the board into committees should be part of the shareholders' agreement, for example, investors or their appointee could be chairman of the finance committee.

J. I am not certain that expense reimbursement should be limited to legal expenses when a technical analysis or survey is required. This is negotiable and should not be thought of as a profit center by the investor. However, the investor must remember that seriously researching deals is an expensive affair, and that the better job done the better will be the result. Yet, as Karl Vesper often reminds me, it is possible to have a bad result from a good decision. Such is the case with deals that are passed over by one investor and done by others to their benefit. Looking backward in the private company investment business is profitable only if one learns from mistakes made, and that is not always a function of how much money might have been made or lost in deals passed over. Buyers' remorse and sellers' remorse are common afflictions, to which need not be added "passers'" remorse.

ANTIDILUTION PROTECTION, A STANDARD TERM*

SETH L. PIERREPONT

The author was, at the time of original publication, a vice president of Continental Illinois Venture Corporation and Continental Illinois Equity Corporation. He is currently managing Sage Venture Management, Inc. In Lake Forrest, Illinois.

Unlike other terms negotiated prior to closing a financing, antidilution clauses can change both the price of the stock sold to an investor or the investor's percentage ownership of the company after the deal is signed and sealed; it is this potentially retroactive effect that should lead us to negotiate these clauses carefully. While potentially the most treacherous term in an entire agreement, antidilution clauses can help both the entrepreneur and the venture capitalist achieve their common goal of greater wealth. Too often, however, entrepreneurs and their attorneys encounter the concept of antidilution protection too late in negotiations to argue effectively for one form of antidilution protection over another.

This article discusses the following eight aspects of antidilution protection: splits, weighted average protection, the price ratchet, the percentage ratchet, participating protection, expiring protection, the management carve-out, and rights of first refusal.

Splits Protection

This clause protects the investor from dilution caused by stock splits, reverse splits or certain stock dividends. It keeps the percentage interest of all stockholders exactly the same. The concept is simple and is illustrated by the following example: Suppose a venture capital investor buys 100 shares of X Co. for $1.00 per share, and there are 1,000 shares outstanding following the financing. Then, in order to reduce the price per share of stock, management decides to split its stock ten for one. As a result, there are now 10,000 shares outstanding worth $.10 per share each. In this case, splits protection allows investors to receive an additional 900 shares of stock for free to prevent the dilution of their ten percent ownership as a result of the split. All other shareholders would also receive free stock, so that everyone is treated equally. The effective cost of all the shares of stock is simply reduced from $1.00 to $.10 per share.

	Original Capitalization	New Capitalization
Total Shares	1,000	10,000
Price Per Share	$ 1.00	$ .10
Venture Capitalist's Share	100	1,000
Venture Capitalist's Percentage	10%	10%

While this simple form of splits protection is generally harmless, there are some subtleties.

What is X Co. creates such a large split or reverse-split that the stock becomes unmarketable? For example if X Co. reverse-splits its stock one for 200, the investor is now holding .05 shares of stock worth $200.00 each. There may be no market for partial shares at any price. The investor may be able to gain liquidity only through negotiating the sale of his stock back to the company. He has suffered a material loss of liquidity. Sophisticated investors may include a specific prohibition in their financial agreements to prevent this type of result. Some form of splits protection is contained in almost all agreements.

Other forms of antidilution protection may produce far more problematic results. The next three forms discussed are almost always found in agreements which utilize convertible securities, or when the investor buys a different form of equity security from that owned by

434

management, especially if the investor pays a higher price than management paid for their stock. For example, suppose a venture capital investor pays $1.00 per share for one million shares, or 10 percent, of *Y Co.* There are 10 million shares outstanding after the financing. Now suppose that the company has trouble meeting its projections and needs to raise an additional $2 million quickly. Initially, no one wants to invest; finally, a new investor agrees to lead a turn-around financing for $2 million, but only at a new price of $.10 per share. The original investor is now facing severe dilution. The mathematics of the proposed financing look like this:

	Original Capitalization	Proposed Capitalization
Original Investor Shares	1,000,000	1,000,000
New Shares		20,000,000
Total Shares	10,000,000	30,000,000
Ownership Percentage	10%	3.3%

Percent Dilution = 67%

If the original investor's one million shares are protected by one of the following antidilution clauses, the investor would feel much better about the proposed financing.

The Weighted Average or Standard Institutional Formula

This is the most common form of antidilution protection. It is used in most deals proposed by financial intermediaries. It is considered a compromise between two extreme views of antidilution that are explained below.

One view, typically that of the entrepreneur, is that investors should not have the benefit of any antidilution protection other than for splits. The entrepreneur argues that the investor has had complete access to all of the *Y Co.'s* files during the due diligence process, is sophisticated and well informed at the time of investment, and has agreed to buy stock in *Y Co.* at $1.00 per share. Furthermore, if the investors participate in the management of the company as directors or as advisors, they may be contributing to the very difficulties from which they are demanding protection. Thus, if the price of the stock falls dramatically in subsequent financings, that is only indicative of the investors' poor judgment, poor advice, inactivity, or ill luck .

The opposite extreme view, typically held by investors, is that they do not have and cannot have access to all of the entrepreneur's knowledge. They believe that entrepreneurs are optimistic by nature, are in a potential conflict of interest position during the due diligence process, and may mislead potential investors. Therefore, if the company does poorly and stock must be sold at a price below that at which they originally purchased stock, then in retrospect they paid too much. They want their original purchase price adjusted. Furthermore, investors believe that the threat of this type of protection encourages entrepreneurs to tell all of the truth during the due diligence process, to be very conservative in their projections, and to work extra hard to increase the value of the company.

Conceptually, the standard institutional formula protects old investors from decreases in company valuation to a limited extent, based upon their percentage ownership of the company prior to the financing. Those investors who have provided a large amount of financial support to the company in the past, and thereby have acquired a large percentage of the company, should receive *proportionately* more protection than other shareholders.

Standard (Weighted Average) Institutional Formula

Let X = total number of common shares (on a fully diluted basis) immediately preceding dilution
Let OP = old price per share
Let Y = total number of new dilutive shares being issued
Let NP = new price per share of dilutive shares

$$\frac{(X \times OP) + (Y \times NP)}{X + Y} = \text{new price or conversion price per share}$$

For example, in the *Y Co.* example, had the original investors been protected by a weighted average antidilution clause, they would have suffered only 21 percent dilution, far less than the 67 percent dilution that would have occurred without the operation of this clause.

Y Co.

$$\frac{(10,000 \times \$1.00 + (20,000 \times \$.10)}{10,000 + 20,000} = \$.40$$

436

The investor's conversion price falls from $1.00 to $.40 per share. The original investment of $1 million h=ow buys 2,500,000 shares rather than 1 million shares. While originally owning 10 percent of *Y Co.*, he now is diluted down to 7.9 percent of *Y Co.* However, without the operation of this clause, he would only have owned 3.3 percent of *Y Co.*

The Price Ratchet

This clause simply states that the price per share of the original investment will ratchet down to the same price as the new shares issued. It sounds innocent, but this clause is the most powerful of the antidilution provisions and can be the most onerous to entrepreneurs. Nevertheless, it has been quite common over the last ten years. Applying the operation of this clause to the example of *Y Co.*, an additional 9,000,000 new shares would be issued to the old investors.

Price Ratchet

Original Dollars Invested ÷ New Price Per Share	Less	Original Dollars Invested ÷ Old Price Per Share	=	Number of Additional Shares Issued to Old Investors

Y Co.

$$\frac{1,000,000}{.10} - \frac{1,000,000}{1.00} = 9,000,000$$

The investor in *Y Co.* now owns a total of 10 million shares out of 39 million shares, or 26 of *Y Co.* Again, without this clause, the investors would have only owned 3.3 percent of *Y Co.* However, even more startling, they owned only 10 percent of *Y Co.* before the "dilutive" financing! How is this result justified? The answer is that in real life, the clause rarely works or is permitted to work as described in the above example.

The price ratchet has a geometric effect relative to the difference between the new and the old price. If the new price per share is not dramatically lower than the old, the effect is more reasonable. If, for example, the new price per share for *Y Co.* had been $.90 instead of $.10, only 111,111 additional shares would be issued to the original investors; they would still suffer 10 percent dilution (going from 10.0

437

percent ownership to 9.0 percent ownership). It is important to note that even in mild cases of dilution (such as the preceding example of a $.90 share price), price ratchet antidilution is still stronger than weighted average antidilution.*

If an extreme price ratchet is projected, the new investors may demand that the original investors waive some or all antidilution protection. The new investors may also require the original investors to co-invest as part of the new investment group reducing the "free-ride" aspect of antidilution protection. The power of this type of clause may also be limited contractually.

Unfortunately, the work ratchet (possibly derived from an instrument of torture such as the rack) may connote too negative an impression. The price ratchet is a useful clause in certain circumstances. The primary argument in favor of the clause is that the original investors need proportionately stronger protection as the risk of the company increases. It is most appropriate where the entrepreneur has . denied the investor full access to customer information, or other circumstances raise serious concerns about the entrepreneur's projections. In such cases, this type of clause can enable a deal that might otherwise fall apart to be negotiated.

The Percentage Ratchet

This clause states that the conversion price of the original investment will change so that the old investor owns the same percentage after the dilutive financing as before. The percentage ratchet is more powerful than the price ratchet in cases of small price differences, but far less powerful in cases of large price decreases. It is used most frequently in cases where seed or bridge capital has been invested in a company, and where there is great uncertainty about either the appropriateness of the pricing or the timing of the next round of financing.

In sum, the first four forms of antidilution discussed result in a broad range of effects as shown below:

---

*The standard institutional formula method would yield an 8.2 percent ownership instead of the 9.0 percent ownership resulting from the price ratchet method.

Y Co. Example

(Original Investor: $1.00 Per Share, 10.0 Percent of Company)
(New Investors: $2.0 million at $.10 Per Share)

Form	Per Share	Adjusted Price Ownership	Adjusted Comment
Splits Only	$1.00	3.3%	Offers no protection
Institutional Formula	.44	7.9%	Compromise
Price Ratchet	.10	25.6%	High Risk
Percentage Ratchet	.33	10.0%	Early Stage

I would emphasize that all of these methods have advantages depending on perspective, the potential occurrence of a highly dilutive financing, and numerous other factors. The next four types of antidilution concepts to be discussed (participating protection, expiring protection, management carve-out and rights of first refusal) are not antidilution methods themselves, but they are used in conjunction with the prior four methods to change their effectiveness. For example, while price ratchet antidilution may appear very onerous to the entrepreneur, if it is also participating (i.e., available only to investors who continue to support the company), it may be very beneficial to the company.

Participation Protection

This feature denies antidilution protection to any investor who does not support the company by participating to the full extent of his pro rata share in each successive financing. As such, it provides a strong incentive to all members of an investment syndicate to stay together. It protects the lead investor of the syndicate and those with "deep pockets" from having to give small or weak investors a "free ride" on antidilution benefits. It helps the entrepreneur raise additional financing when times are tough. On the negative side, it may force investors to invest good money after bad and deny them the protection or price adjustment that they really deserve because they have been misled.

Expiring Protection

This feature simply means that the degree of antidilution protection will be reduced or will expire after a certain amount of time has

439

elapsed. The concept is based on the theory that antidilution protection is primarily a protection against a misjudgment by the investor at the time of the original investment. After two or three years, most original problems will have surfaced and possibly have been solved, and by that time the investor may be in control or at least partially responsible for any of the problems. Arguably, the investor should not receive any special protection (relative to management) from ongoing systematic risks and it may be reasonable to reduce or eliminate antidilution protection over time.

The Management Carve-Out

Frequently, antidilution provisions are drafted to exclude a certain number of shares for issuance at a low price to key employees. Without a specific carve-out, the sale of gift of such stock might trigger antidilution protection. The carve-out is justified on the basis that the investor is a member of the board and probably a member of the compensation committee who controls such stock sales. If an investor is not well represented on the board, the carve-out is normally limited contractually to a small number of shares (one or two percent of the company) at a time. A small carve-out forces management to approach the investor whenever more shares are needed for compensation purposes.

Rights of First Refusal

It is also quite common that investors demand the right to maintain their original pro rata ownership in a company by obtaining the right to purchase a portion of any future issuances of any equity-type securities. While this is a form of antidilution protection, it differs from the main theme of discussion here in that the investor must buy additional shares rather than receiving them for free.

An extreme form of rights of first refusal requires the company to give its old investors the option of buying all of any equity being sold in the future, rather than just an antidilutive portion. This right can cause all sorts of problems and should be avoided at all costs. For example, a right of first refusal on all of any equity being sold can prevent the company from receiving a fair market price for its equity. The onerous operant may be quite subtle. For example, a clause that requires the company to allow existing investors to match any bonafide offer for a 30 day period may appear innocent. However, sophisticated venture financiers know that 30 days is a very long time to keep a bonafide offer outstanding. In fact, such a clause may prevent any serious offers from ever being made by outsiders. In effect, the management and the original investors may not be able to attract new investors, because the new investors will not want to risk their time studying the company if original investors can legally exclude them. Such clauses, if used, should be limited to a small percentage of any financing (i.e., 20 percent of the equity to be sold) or for a shorter period (10 days)).

Rights of first refusal can also be useful in preventing dissident shareholders (or management) from selling stock to potentially adverse parties, but that is a different subject.

A few common forms of antidilution protection have been summarized herein, but antidilution protection is a subject that should be discussed in depth with experienced legal counsel prior to beginning negotiations. Antidilution protection is obviously both a complex and important part of investors rights. Management and prior investors should recognize the potentially serious effects of these clauses.

TAX TREATMENT OF S CORPORATION SHAREHOLDERS

CLEBURNE E. GREGORY III, JAMES T.
RAUSCHENBERGER, AND CLINTON RICHARDSON

Mr. Gregory is the head of the tax department of the major Atlanta, Georgia law firm of Arnall Golden & Gregory. Mr. Rauschenberger is a partner in that tax department. Mr. Richardson is a partner in the firm's corporate department and author of The Growth Company Guide (Pfeiffer & Co., 1993).

An S corporation represents one form of taxable entity which may be utilized in organizing and operating a business. The rules governing the tax treatment of S corporations permit the flow-through of tax consequences to the shareholders so that there is generally only a single tax on the corporation's earnings, and distributions can generally be made to shareholders without (subject to certain exceptions) incurring a separate shareholder-level tax. However, the restrictions and requirements for S corporation treatment mean that use of the S corporation will not be an attractive option in all situations. In evaluating the desirability of using an S corporation for a venture capital activity, the following advantages and disadvantages of S corporation status should be considered.

Advantages

1. *Avoidance of corporate-level taxes.* Subject to certain exceptions regarding S corporations that were C corporations, there is no tax imposed on an S corporation. As a result, both the general corporate tax, as well as special corporate taxes such as the alternative minimum tax and the tax on excess accumulated earnings, can be avoided by S corporations.

2. *Limited Liability.* Use of the corporate structure better ensures the limited liability of investors. While the same protection can be obtained for investors through a limited partnership, there are significant restrictions on the activities which limited partners can engage in without sacrificing their limited liability protection.

3. *Tax-free exchange.* An S corporation can be a participant in a tax-free reorganization, so that an acquisition of an S corporation can be effectively tax-free through the receipt of stock of the acquiring corporation.

4. *Pass-through of losses.* As with partnerships, the S corporation permits the pass through of losses to shareholders for use against their other income. However, changes made by the 1986 Tax Act prohibit shareholders who do not materially participate in the activities of an S corporation from currently using any losses from the S corporation to offset wages, interest and dividend income, and any other income other than that attributable to other activities in which they do not materially participate. These passive loss limitations significantly reduce the benefits of the pass through of losses to S corporation investors.

5. *Corporate law.* Rules regarding corporate law are relatively well established and provide a greater degree of certainty than limited partnership law.

Disadvantages.

1. *Limitation on types of shareholders.* As only certain types of shareholders are permitted, the use of S corporation prevents use of some sources of equity financing such as venture capital corporations and partnerships.

2. *One class of stock requirement.* This requirement restricts the ability to tailor equity investments to suit the needs of particular investors.

3. *Taxation of shareholders.* Flow through of income tax liability to

the shareholders is a double-edged sword. While taxed at lower individual rates, the income, nonetheless, requires payment of tax by the shareholders. A startup company with significant cash needs may not have sufficient cash available to distribute to shareholders to permit them to pay their taxes arising from the S corporation. In such a situation, it is important that shareholders have the wherewithal to pay their taxes attributable to the S corporation even if no distributions are made by the corporation.

4. *Subsidiaries not possible.* Because an S corporation may not have 80 percent controlled subsidiaries, future acquisitions by an S corporation may be significantly restricted.

5. *Tax Rate Differential.* The maximum individual marginal tax rate was, for 1995, 39.6% for taxable income in excess of $250,000. The maximum marginal tax rate for corporations was 34% for taxable income of more than $75,000 and less than $10,000,000, and 35% for taxable income in excess of $10,000,000. As a result, electing S corporation status results in a net increase in income taxes if the corporation typically retains all of its earnings in excess of income taxes. If the corporation distributes additional amounts to shareholders, of course, S corporation status overcomes this disadvantage because the distributions by a S corporation will not typically result in the dividend income associated with distributions by a C corporation.

6. *Ineligibility for the Exclusion of up to 50% of the Gain from the Sale of Stock of Certain Qualified Small Business Corporations.* Section 1202 of the Code, as enacted in 1993, permits noncorporate taxpayers to exclude up to 50% of the gain realized from the disposition of stock of a "qualified small business corporation" which has been held for more than 5 years and was acquired after August 10, 1993 (the date of enactment of Section 1202). A "qualified small business corporation" is a corporation which satisfies various requirements, including requirements concerning its capitalization (generally, less than $50 million) and business activities. While a detailed examination of all of these requirements is beyond the scope of this discussion, one of the requirements is that the corporation be a C corporation. The inability to exclude 50% of the gain from a stock sale must be taken into consideration before electing S corporation status. This disadvantage is difficult to quantify, of course, since the ultimate disposition of the business may be years into the future and may, ultimately, involve an asset sale rather than a stock sale.

Tax Treatment of S Corporation Shareholders

Similar to partnerships, S corporation income or loss flows through to shareholders, who include their pro rata share of the corporation's income or loss in computing their income tax liability for the year.

Computation of income/loss. In determining a shareholder's share of an S corporation's income or loss, the corporation's items of income (including any tax-exempt income), gain, loss, deduction, or credit whose tax treatment could be affected by the tax situation of each shareholder are separately stated and not included in the overall computation of S corporation income or loss. Accordingly, items such as capital gains and losses, section 1231 gains or losses, charitable contributions, and tax-exempt interest must be separately stated. Separately stating such items simply means that the ultimate tax treatment of the item is determined at the shareholder rather than the corporate level. An S corporation's nonseparately computed income or loss is then determined by excluding all separately computed items and netting the remaining items of income, gain, loss or deduction. Elections concerning the tax treatment of items derived from S corporation operations are generally made by the S corporation and not by the shareholders.

Shareholders' pro rata share. S corporation shareholders compute their taxable income by including their pro rata share of the S corporation's separately and nonseparately computed items. If an S corporation's shareholdings do not change during a taxable year, the shareholder's pro rata share of S corporation items (both separately and nonseparately computed) is simply based on their proportionate holdings. However, if shareholdings change during a taxable year, a shareholder's pro rata share of S corporation items is generally determined on a "per-share, per-day" basis. This means that each S corporation items is allocated equally to each day of the taxable year, and the portion allocated to a day is then split pro rata among the shares outstanding on that day. A shareholder's pro rata share of each item is then determined by totaling the amount allocated to the shareholder's shares for each day of the taxable year. If a shareholder's interest in an S corporation terminates (whether through transfer or redemption), the pro rata shares of S corporation items for all shareholders can be determined in accordance with an actual closing of the corporation's books as of the date of the termination of the shareholder's interest. However, the "actual income" allocation is available only if all shareholders during the taxable year consent to use of that method.

445

Losses limited to basis. While other limitations on the deductibility of losses (for example, the passive loss limitations of the 1986 Tax Act and rules limiting deductions from an activity to the amount at risk in the activity) can affect an S corporation shareholder's ability to deduct losses, limitation is also imposed by Subchapter S on the deductibility of losses from an S corporation: The aggregate amount of losses currently deductible by a shareholder cannot exceed the sum of the shareholder's adjusted basis in his stock and any amounts loaned by the shareholder to the S corporation. Losses are applied first against available basis in the shareholder's stock, and only after the basis in the stock is reduced to zero are losses applied to reduce the shareholder's basis in any indebtedness of the corporation to the shareholder. Any losses which exceed a shareholder's adjusted basis in both the shareholder's stock and amounts loaned to the corporation are indefinitely suspended until there is available basis.

A shareholder's beginning basis in his or her S corporation stock is equal to the amount contributed to the capital of the corporation (if the stock is acquired by contribution), or its cost (if the stock is purchased from a third party), and is increased for any subsequent capital contributions. The basis is further increased for all items of S corporation income and gain (whether separately computed or not) and is decreased by (1) items of loss or deduction (whether separately computed or not); (2) distributions by the corporation which, as discussed below, are not includible in the shareholder's income; and (3) nondeductible expenditures that are not capital expenditures. As discussed above, a shareholder's basis in his or her stock cannot be reduced below zero. Furthermore, to the extent a shareholder's basis in debt of the corporation to the shareholder is decreased, subsequent net increases in basis (other than from capital contributions) are first applied to restore offset basis in the debt before being applied to increase the basis of the stock.

Distributions. The tax treatment of distributions from an S corporation depends upon whether or not the corporation has accumulated earnings and profits attributable to a period prior to its status as an S corporation.

For S corporations which have been an S corporation for their entire existence or which have no accumulated earnings and profits for periods prior to their first year as an S corporation, corporate distributions are not taxable to the extent they do not exceed the shareholder's adjusted basis in his or her stock. Distributions in excess of the shareholder's basis are generally treated as capital gain, which is long-term or short-term, depending upon the shareholder's holding period for the stock.

With regard to S corporations that have accumulated earnings and profits, distributions are not taxable to the extent they do not exceed the "accumulated adjustments account" (the "AAA"). Distributions in excess of the AAA are treated as dividends to the extent of the corporation's accumulated earnings and profits, and are treated as gain from the sale of a capital asset to the extent they also exceed the corporation's accumulated earnings and profits.

The AAA of an S corporation is its income and gain (whether separately computed or not), less its losses and deductions (whether separately computed or not), and less any and all previous distributions. In other words, the AAA is an S corporation's accumulated, but undistributed, S corporation net income. However, unlike a shareholder's basis in his or her stock, a shareholder's AAA can be reduced below zero so that subsequent income or gain will not permit tax-free distributions until they exceed the negative AAA. However, losses nd deductions that are suspended under the basis rules do not decrease the AAA. Finally, while tax-exempt income (and expenses attributable thereto) does affect a shareholder's basis in his or her S corporation stock, it does not increase the AAA, and distributions attributable to tax-exempt income can therefore generate taxable income for shareholders.

Tax Treatment of S Corporations

Generally, an S corporation is not subject to federal income tax. However, for S corporations that were C corporations prior to their election of Subchapter S treatment, there are two situations where a corporate-level tax may apply.

Tax on passive income. Only S corporations which have accumulated earnings and profits attributable to a period prior to the S election are subject to the tax on passive income. The tax applies if, during any taxable year, such an S corporation's "passive investment income" exceeds 25 percent of its gross receipts. For these purposes, passive investment income includes royalties, rents, dividends, interest (other than interest attributable to inventory sales), and annuities.

The tax on passive income is imposed at the highest corporate rate (which is 34 percent for taxable years beginning after July 1, 1987) on an S corporation's "excess net passive income." Net passive income is the corporation's passive investment income less deductions directly connected with that income. Excess net passive income is the portion of the corporation's net passive income that bears the same ratio to total net passive investment income, as the excess of the corporation's passive investment income over 25 percent of its gross receipts for the taxable year bears to the corporation's passive investment income for the year. If an S corporation's passive investment income does not exceed 25 percent of its gross receipts, the corporation has no excess net passive income, and the tax on passive investment income is therefore not imposed. In the event the tax is imposed, the amount of tax imposed reduces the shareholder's flow through income of the S corporation in a like amount.

Tax on built-in capital gains. S corporations that were C corporations will be taxed on gain subsequently recognized by the S corporation that is attributable to a disposition of assets, where the fair market value, as of the first day of the corporation's first S corporation taxable year, of any assets disposed of exceeded the adjusted tax basis of the asset at that time. Such excess of fair market value over basis on an S corporation's first day of its first taxable year as an S corporation is referred to as the "built-in gain." The tax applies only to S corporations which were C corporations and only to dispositions of assets during the first 10 taxable years of the corporation's S election. The tax is equal to the highest corporate tax rate (34 percent applied to the lesser of the built-in gain for the year, or the amount which would be the taxable income of the corporation if it were not an S corporation. However, as with the tax on passive income, the pass through income of the S corporation is reduced by the amount of any tax imposed on the corporation's built-in capital gain.

At the time of writing this discussion (March, 1995), the Clinton administration had submitted a proposal which would have revised the tax on built-in gains for certain C corporations electing S status. The proposal would treat any C corporation that elects to be a S corporation and has a value of more than $5 million as having sold its assets in a taxable transaction solely by virtue of electing S corporation status. The built-in gain would effectively be realized immediately. If enacted the proposal would become a significant deterrent against any C corporation electing S corporation status, and could easily become a trap for the unwary.

Eligibility for S Corporation

S corporation treatment is only available with respect to a corporation that is a "small business corporation." A small business corporation is a corporation that has 35 or fewer shareholders, has only eligible shareholders, has only one class of stock, and is not an ineligible corporation.

Number and type of shareholders. A small business corporation may have no more than 35 shareholders. This corresponds with the private placement exemption allowed under federal securities law. For purposes of applying this numerical limitation, a husband and wife are counted as one shareholder.

Shareholders a small business corporation may have include individuals, an individual's estate, trusts such as grantor trusts whose property is treated for tax purposes as owned by another (a "deemed owner trust"), and voting trusts. However, neither nonresident aliens nor foreign trusts may be a shareholder of an S corporation. A trust created under the terms of a will may also be a shareholder, but only for the 60-day period beginning on the date the stock is transferred to the trust. A grantor trust may continue to be an eligible shareholder following the death of the grantor, but only for a 60-day period following the grantor's death. (The 60-day period will be two years if all of the trust is includible in the grantor's estate.) Finally, a trust which has (1) a single current income beneficiary who is a United States citizen or resident alien and to whom all of the trust income is distributed at least annually, and (2) satisfies certain other requirements, may be an eligible shareholder (such a trust is hereinafter referred to as a "Qualified Subchapter S Trust"). However, unlike other eligible S corporation shareholders, a Qualified Subchapter S Trust will be an eligible shareholder only if the current income beneficiary files an election is made independent of the shareholder's consent to the S corporation election discussed below.

For purposes of applying the 35 shareholder limitation, the estate is treated as the shareholder of a trust created under a will, the deemed owner of a "deemed owner trust" is treated as the shareholder, and each beneficiary of a voting trust or a Qualified Subchapter S trust is counted as a shareholder. The trusts themselves are not counted as a shareholder.

One class of stock. A small business corporation may only have one class of stock. Accordingly, corporations that have both common and preferred stock will generally not be eligible to be an S corporation unless the preferred stock is removed in some manner from the corporation's capital structure. The one class of stock requirement is not completely inflexible. First, differences in voting rights are not considered to create two classes of stock. Accordingly, a small business corporation may have both voting and nonvoting common stock. Second, notwithstanding that under a "thin capitalization" approach a corporation's debt might be treated as equity and, therefore, a second class of stock, debt will not be treated as a second class of stock if: (1) the debt is evidenced by a written unconditional promise to pay a definite sum on demand or by a specified date; (2) interest is not contingent on profits, the borrower's discretion or similar factors; (3) the debt is not convertible into stock; and (4) the lender is an eligible S corporation shareholder (for instance, the lender cannot be a corporation). Failure of debt to qualify for this "safe harbor" will not itself result in the debt being treated as a second class of stock -- rather, it simply means that the debt is not protected from being recharacterized as equity and a second class of stock.

Ineligible corporations. Certain corporations, even if they only have eligible shareholders, may not be a small business corporation. These ineligible corporations are: (1) foreign corporations, (2) members of an "affiliated group" of corporations -- for example, the corporation may not own 80 percent or more of another corporation, (3) banks, (4) insurance companies, (5) corporations electing to claim the Puerto Rican and possession tax credit, and (6) domestic international sales corporations ("DISCs") or former DISCs.

Election

A small business corporation will not be treated as an S corporation for federal income tax purposes unless it properly elects to be treated as an S corporation. The election to be treated as an S corporation is made by filing a Form 2553 with the Internal Revenue Service (IRS). To be effective, all persons who are shareholders on the date of the election must consent to the election. The consent of shareholders may be obtained by their signature on Form 2553 or through a separate consent filed with Form 2553.

An election for S corporation treatment must be timely made. The election is timely made if it is filed with the IRS before the beginning of the taxable year for which the election is to be effective. The election is also effective for a taxable year if it is made by the 15th day of the third month of the beginning of the taxable year. However, a corporation must satisfy all of the requirements for a small business corporation for every day of a taxable year, notwithstanding that the election is made after the beginning of the taxable year. If the corporation does not satisfy the requirements for the period of the taxable year before the election is filed, the election will not be effective until the next taxable year. Furthermore, all shareholders during the first taxable year must consent to the election notwithstanding that they have sold their stock by the time the election is made. Such former shareholders' consent is required because the election will result in a flow through of the corporation's income or loss to them for the portion of the year that they were a shareholder. Once made, an election is effective until revoked and requires no additional consents from new shareholders.

For purposes of applying the requirement that the election be made by the 15th day of the third month of the taxable year, the taxable year of a new corporation begins on the earliest of (1) the date the corporation first has shareholders, (2) the date the corporation first has assets, or (3) the date the corporation begins doing business. Mere incorporation should not start running the period for making the election. For new corporations whose taxable year may begin in mid month, the end of the two-month and 15-day period is determined by counting two months and 15 days for the date on which the taxable year begins. For example, if a corporation begins its first taxable year on January 5, an election will be effective for the first taxable year it made on or before March 20.

Termination of S Election

S corporation treatment will end if a corporation's shareholders affirmatively elect to revoke the election, or if the election is terminated.

Revocation. The shareholders of an S corporation can revoke the election only if shareholders holding more than one-half of the outstanding shares of the corporation consent to the revocation. Generally, a revocation will be effective for the first day of a taxable year if it is made before the beginning of the taxable year or by the 15th day of the third month of the taxable year. However, the shareholders may specify a prospective date during a taxable year when the revocation is to take effect.

Disqualification. Failure to satisfy the requirements for a small business corporation will result in termination of the election, as of the date that the requirements cease to be met. For example, the sale of S corporation stock to a corporation will terminate the election as of the date of the sale.

The IRS has discretionary authority to waive the disqualification of an election provided that the disqualification was inadvertent, steps are taken to correct the disqualification within a reasonable period of time following discovery, and the corporation and its shareholders agree to adjustments which are consistent with S corporation treatment that are required by the IRS. However, because the IRS' authority to waive a disqualification is discretionary, care should be taken to ensure that corporation and shareholder transactions do not inadvertently terminate the election.

S corporations that have accumulated earnings and profits from periods prior to their election for S corporation treatment will have their S corporation status terminated if, for three consecutive years, 25 percent of their gross receipts are "passive investment income" (computed in the same manner as for purposes of applying the disqualification rule for passive investment income discussed above). Disqualification by virtue of such passive income is effective as of the beginning of the fourth taxable year.

Effect of termination. If the S election is terminated, the corporation will be treated as a C corporation beginning on the day the election terminates. If a termination occurs in the middle of a taxable year, the corporation will have two short taxable years: the final year for the S election, and the first year for C corporation status. Any corporation that has its election terminated is barred from re-electing S corporation treatment for a five-year period.

Other Provisions Affecting S Corporations

The following identifies some of the other provisions which can affect S corporation.

Taxable year. As S corporation must use as its taxable year either (1) a calendar year, or (2) a fiscal year from which it establishes to the satisfaction of the IRS a business purpose. Prior to the 1986 Tax Act, the IRS ruled that S corporations could use a taxable year that resulted in a deferral of income to shareholders of three months or less. Under this rule, S corporations could elect a September 30 taxable year without any showing that such year corresponded to the corporation's normal business year. However, the 1986 Tax Act revoked this three-month deferral rule for both existing and future S corporations. As a result, an S corporation desiring to use a taxable year other than a calendar year must generally establish to the satisfaction of the IRS that the desired fiscal year corresponds with the normal business year of the corporation. The IRS has provided that S corporations that recognized 25 percent or more of their gross receipts during the last two months of a desired fiscal year the three-year period immediately preceding the corporation's first S taxable year may use that fiscal year as their S corporation taxable year. In addition, an S corporation is also permitted to use a fiscal year that corresponds with a fiscal year of shareholder(s) owning more than 50 percent of the outstanding stock of the S corporation.

As a result of the requirement that, absent a business purpose, a calendar taxable year must be used for an S corporation, existing corporations that have a non-calendar taxable year will have a short taxable year for the first year for which the S election is effective. For example, a corporation with a March 31 fiscal year will have a short taxable year beginning April 1 and ending December 31 for its first year as an S corporation.

Fringe benefits. In applying the provision of the code dealing with fringe benefits, the S corporation is treated as a partnership and any shareholders owning more than 2 percent of the corporation's stock are treated as partners. Special rules also apply to any qualified pension plans maintained by an S corporation.

Expenses owed to shareholders. When an S corporation uses the accrual method of accounting and owes amounts that are deductible expenses to shareholders or certain other related entities using the cash method of accounting, the Code contains provisions which, in effect, require the S corporation to be on the cash basis with regard to deducting such expenses. As a result, the corporation may not deduct the expenses until the shareholder or other entity receives payment.

STANDARDS OF VALUE*

SHANNON PRATT

Dr. Shannon P. Pratt is a managing director and one of the founders of Willamette Management Associates. Founded in the 1960s, Willamette Management Associates is one of the oldest and largest independent valuation consulting, economic analysis, and financial advisory firms in the country. It has regional offices in Atlanta, GA, McLean, VA, Chicago, IL, and Portland, OR.

Willamette Management Associates is well known for its extensive research library, with a constantly updated collection of books, articles, transaction data sources, and court cases involving business valuation issues.

Dr. Pratt is the author of *Valuing Small Businesses and Professional Practices*, *Valuing a Business: The Analysis and Appraisal of Closely Held Companies,* and is the co-author of *Guide to Business Valuations.*

Dr. Pratt is also Editor in Chief of *Shannon Pratt's Business Valuation Update*, a monthly newsletter presenting timely news, views, and resources regarding business valuations.

---

* Excerpted from Valuing a Business, 3rd ed., by Shannon Pratt, Robert F Reilly, and Robert P. Schweihs. (Burr Ridge, IL: Irwin Professional Publishing, 1996), Used by special permission. All rights reserved.

(Note: I advise all of thoses considering making investments in private companies to become familiar with the above books and newsletter as the essence of private company investing is one of valuation. Arthur Lipper III)

The word *value* means different things to different people. Even to the same person, value means different things in different contexts, as we discussed in the previous section.

Without carefully defining the term value the conclusions reached in the valuation report have no meaning.

Is the objective of the appraisal to estimate fair market value, market value, fair value, true value, investment value, intrinsic value, fundamental value, insurance value, book value, use value, collateral value, ad valorem value, or some other value?

Clients rarely give it much thought. Many don't have enough technical background in business valuation to raise the right questions. One of the professional appraiser's most important tasks is to work carefully and thoroughly with the client and/or attorney to arrive at a definition of value that is appropriate to the specific purpose of the valuation engagement.

In this book, a standard of value is a definition of the type of value being sought. A premise of value is an assumption as to the set of actual or hypothetical transactional circumstances applicable to the subject valuation.

For many situations, the standard of value is legally mandated, whether by law or by binding legal documents or contracts. In other cases, it is a function of the wishes of the parties involved. The standard of value usually reflects an assumption as to who will be the buyer and who will be the seller in the hypothetical or actual sales transaction regarding the subject assets, properties, or business interests. It defines or specifies the parties to the actual or hypothetical transaction. In other words, the standard of value addresses the question: "value to whom?" The standard of value, either directly by statute or (more often) as interpreted in the case law, often addresses what valuation methods are appropriate and what factors should or should not be considered.

Fair Market Value

In the United States, the most widely recognized and accepted standard of value related to business valuations is fair market value. With

455

regard to business valuations, it is the standard that applies to virtually all federal and state tax matters, such as estate taxes, gift taxes, inheritance taxes, income taxes. and ad valorem taxes. It is also the legal standard of value in many other -- though not all -- valuation situations.

Fair market value is defined by the ASA as "the amount at which property would change hands between a willing seller and a willing buyer when neither is acting under compulsion and when both have reasonable knowledge of the relevant facts."[1] This definition comports to that found in the U.S. Tax Code and in Revenue Ruling 59-60.

In most interpretations of fair market value, the willing buyer and willing seller are hypothetical persons dealing at arm's length, rather than any particular buyer or seller. In other words, a price would not be considered representative of fair market value if influenced by special motivations not characteristic of a typical buyer or seller.

There is also general agreement that the definition implies the parties have the ability as well as the willingness to buy or to sell. The market in this definition can be thought of as all the potential buyers and sellers of like businesses or practices.

The concept of fair market value also assumes prevalent economic and market conditions at the date of the particular valuation. You have probably heard someone say, "I couldn't get anywhere near the value of my house if I put it on the market today," or, " The value of XYZ Company stock is really much more (or less) than the price it's selling for on the New York Stock Exchange today." The standard of value that such a person has in mind is some standard other than fair market value, since the concept of fair market value means the price at which a transaction could be expected to take place under conditions existing at the valuation date.

The terms market value and cash value are sometimes used interchangeably with the term fair market value. The use of these essentially synonymous standard of value terms is often influenced by the type of asset, property, or business interest subject to appraisal.

In the United States, the most widely recognized and accepted standard of value related to real estate appraisals is market value. The

---

[1] American Society of Appraisers, Business Valuation Standards -- Definitions.

Appraisal Foundation defines market value as follows:

MARKET VALUE: Market value is the major focus of most real property appraisal assignments. Both economic and legal definitions of market value have been developed and defined. A current economic definition agreed upon by agencies that regulate federal financial institutions in the United States of America is:

The most probably price which a property should bring in a competitive and open market under all conditions requisite to a fair sail, the buyer and seller each acting prudently and knowledgeably, and assuming the price is not affected by undue stimulus. Implicit in this definition is the consummation of a sale as of a specified date and the passing of title from seller to buyer under conditions whereby:

1. buyer and seller are typically motivated;

2. both parties are well informed or well advised, and acting in what they consider their best interests;

3. a reasonable time is allowed for exposure in the open market;

4. payment is made in terms of cash in United States dollars or in terms of financial arrangements comparable thereto; and

5. the price represents the normal consideration for the property sold unaffected by special or creative financing or sales consequences granted by anyone associated with the sale.

Substitution of another currency for United States dollars in the fourth condition is appropriate in other countries or in reports addressed to clients from other countries. Persons performing appraisal services that may be subject to litigation are cautioned to seek the exact legal definition of market value in the jurisdiction in which the services are being performed. [2]

The most salient change in the above definition of market value compared to definitions widely accepted a few years ago is the phrase "the most probable price" in substitution for "the highest price."

Business appraisers should be cognizant of the subtle, but important, differences between fair market value standard (as defined by the ASA, for example) and the market value standard (as defined by the Appraisal Institute, for example).

---

[2] Uniform Standards of Professional Appraisal Practice (Washington, D.C. The Appraisal Foundation, 1995).

Investment Value

In real estate terminology, investment value is defined as "value to a particular investor based on individual investment requirements, as distinguished from the concept of market value, which is impersonal and detached."[3] Fortunately, business appraisal terminology embraces the same distinction in most contexts.

One of the leading real estate appraisal texts makes the following comments regarding the distinction between market value and investment value:[4]

Market value can be called "the value of the marketplace"; investment value is the specific value of goods or services to a particular investor (or class of investors) based on individual investment requirements. Market value and investment value are different concepts; the values estimated for each may or may not be numerically equal depending on the circumstances. Moreover, market value estimates are commonly made without reference to investment value, but investment value estimates are frequently accompanied by a market value estimate to facilitate decision making.

Market value estimates assume no specific buyer or seller. Rather, the appraiser considers a hypothetical transaction in which both the buyer and the seller have the understanding, perceptions, and motivations that are typical of the market for the property or interests being valued. Appraisers must distinguish between their own knowledge, perceptions, and attitudes and those of the market or markets for the property in question. The special requirements of a given client are irrelevant to a market value estimate.

The distinctions noted in the above quote can be carried over to business appraisal. There can be many valid reasons for the investment value to one particular owner or prospective owner to differ from the fair market value. Among these reasons are:

1. Differences in estimates of future earning power.

2. Differences in perception of the degree of risk.

3. Differences in tax status.

4. Synergies with other operations owned or controlled.

---

[3] The Dictionary of Real Estate Appraisal, 3rd ed. (Chicago Appraisal Institute, 1993).

[4] The Appraisal of Real Estate, 10th ed. (Chicago Appraisal Institute, 1992) p. 586.

The discounted economic income valuation method can easily be oriented toward developing an investment value. Whether or not the value thus developed also represents fair market value depends on whether the valuation projections used would be accepted by a consensus of market participants.

If sound analysis leads to a valid conclusion that the investment value to a particular owner exceeded market value at a given time, the rational economic decision for that owner would be not to sell at that time unless a particular buyer could be found to whom investment value would be higher than the consensus of value among a broader group of typical buyers.

Of course, the concept of investment value as described above is not completely divorced from the concept of fair market value, since it is the actions of many specific investors, acting in the manner just described, that eventually lead to a balancing of supply and demand through the establishment of an equilibrium market price that represents the consensus value of the collective investors.

Finally, the term investment value often has a different meaning when used in the context of dissenting stockholder suits. In this context, it often means a value based on earning power, as described above, except that the appropriate discount or capitalization rate is usually considered to be a consensus rate rather than a rate peculiar to any specific investor.

Intrinsic or Fundamental Value

Intrinsic value (sometimes called fundamental value) differs from investment value in that it represents an analytical judgement of value based on perceived characteristics inherent in the investment, not tempered by characteristics peculiar to any one investor, but rather tempered by how these perceived characteristics are interpreted by one analyst versus another.

In the analysis of stocks, intrinsic value is generally considered the appropriate price for a stock according to a security analyst who has completed a fundamental analysis of the company's assets, earning power, and other factors.

Intrinsic value. The amount that an investor considers, on the basis of an evaluation of available facts, to be the "true" or "real" worth of an item, usually an equity security. The value that will become the market value when other investors reach the same conclusions. The various approaches to determining intrinsic value of the finance literature are based on expectations and discounted cash flows. See expected value; fundamental analysis; discounted cash flow method. [5]

Fundamental analysis. An approach in security analysis which assumes that a security has an "intrinsic value" that can be determined through a rigorous evaluation of relevant variables. Expected earnings is usually the most important variable in this analysis, but many other variables, such as dividends, capital structure, management quality, and so on, may also be studied. An analyst estimates the "intrinsic value" of a security on the basis of those fundamental variables and compares this value with the current market price of this security to arrive at an investment decision. [6]

The purpose of security analysis is to detect differences between the value of a security as determined by the market and a security's "intrinsic value" -- that is, the value that the security ought to have and will have when other investors have the same insight and knowledge as the analyst. [7]

If the market value is below what the analyst concludes is the intrinsic value, then the analyst considers the stock a "buy." If the market value is above the assumed intrinsic value, then the analysis suggests selling the stock. (Some analysts also factor market expectations into their fundamental analysis.)

It is important to note that the concept of intrinsic value cannot be entirely divorced from the concept of fair market value, since the actions of buyers and sellers based on their specific perceptions of intrinsic value eventually lead to the general consensus market value and the constant and dynamic changes in market value over time.

Case law often refers to the term intrinsic value. However, almost universally such references do not define the term other than by reference to the language in the context in which it appears. Such references to intrinsic value can be found both in cases where there is no statutory standard of value and in cases where the statutory standard of value is specified as fair value or even fair market value. When references to intrinsic value appear in the relevant case law, the ana-

---

[5] W.W. Cooper et al., eds., Kohler's Dictionary for Accountants, 6th ed. (Englewood Cliffs, N.J; Prentice Hall, 1983). p. 285.

[6] Ibid., p. 228

[7] James H. Lorie and Mary T. Hamilton. The Stock Market: Theories and Evidence (Burr Ridge, Il. Richard D. Irwin, 1973), p. 114.

lyst should heed the notions ascribed to that term as discussed in this section.

Fair Value

To understand what the expression fair value means, you have to know the context of its use. In business appraisal, the term fair value is a legally created standard of value that applies to certain specific transactions.

In most states, fair value is the statutory standard of value applicable in cases of dissenting stockholders' appraisal rights. In these states, if a corporation merges, sells out, or takes certain other major actions, and the owner of a minority interest believes that he is being forced to receive less than adequate consideration for his stock, he has the right to have his shares appraised and to receive fair value in cash. In states that have adopted the Uniform Business Corporation Act, the definition of fair value is as follows:

"Fair value," with respect to a dissenter's shares, means the value of the shares immediately before the effectuation of the corporate action to which the dissenter objects, excluding any appreciation or depreciation in anticipation of the corporate action unless exclusions would be inequitable.[8]

Even in states that have adopted this definition, there is no clearly recognized consensus about the interpretation of fair value in this context, but published precedents established in various state courts certainly have not equated it to fair market value. When a situation arises of actual or potential stockholder dissent, it is necessary to research carefully the legal precedents applicable to each case. The appraiser should solicit the view of counsel as to the interpretation of fair value and, in most cases, cannot assume that there is a definition that is clear and concise.

The term fair value is also found in the dissolution statutes of those few states in which minority stockholders can trigger a corporate dissolution under certain circumstances (e.g., California Code Section 2000). Even within the same state, however, a study of case law precedents does not necessarily lead one to the same definition of fair value under a dissolution statute as under that state's dissenting stockholder statute.

---

[8] Oregon Revised Statutes, Section 60.551.

Several countries undergoing privatization have adopted the term fair value to apply to certain transactions, often involving specific classes of buyers, such as employees. Such statutes vary widely in their definitions of fair value.

Exhibit 1 gives some examples of matching certain valuation purposes with applicable standards of value.

Exhibit 1

Examples of Matching the Valuation Purpose with Standard of Value

Valuation Purpose Application Standard of Value

Gift and estate taxes and charitable contributions Fair market value (governed by federal statute and case law; very large and reasonably consistent body of case law precedent)

Inheritance taxes Fair market value (governed by state law, but usually follows federal)

Ad valorem taxes Fair market value or market value (governed by state law, and some important statutory and/or regulatory differences are found from state to state; It is important to note whether the appraisal subject is a bundle of assets or a bundle of securities)

Employee Stock Ownership Plans (ESOPs) Fair market value (governed by both federal tax law and ERISA)

Buy-sell agreements Anything the parties choose to agree on

Financial acquisition* Fair market value

Strategic acquisition* Investment value (buyers, of course, do the best they can to avoid paying for the synergistic value)

Going private Fair value in most states (governed by state statutes; even where statutory language is consistent among several states, case law interpretation often varies considerably)

Corporate or partnership dissolutions under minority oppression statutes Fair value (only California, New York, and Rhode Island have such statutes at press time; case law interpretations in those states tend to be different from case law interpretations of fair value in dissenting stockholder actions in the same states)

Marital dissolution No standard of value specified in most state statutes. Case law inconsistent , often within the same state. Case law also tends to be confusing, e.g., even if "fair market value" specified in decision, actual valuation practices used frequently differs

462

markedly from strict interpretation of fair market value as found in tax case law.

Antitrust cases Damages based on federal case law precedent, with variations from circuit to circuit.

Other damage cases (e.g., breach of contract, lost profits, lost business opportunity, condemnation, insurance claims, wrongful franchise termination) Mostly governed by state statute and case law precedent; vary by type and from state to state

* Note that most acquisitions can trigger minority stockholder dissenters' rights, requiring dissenters to be paid the value of their shares according to state statutes, which is "fair value" in most states.

Going-Concern versus Liquidation Premise of Value

Virtually all businesses or interests in businesses may be appraised under each of these following four alternative premises of value:

1. Value as a going concern -- Value in continued use, as a mass assemblage of income producing assets, and as a going-concern business enterprise.

2. Value as an assemblage of assets -- Value in place, as part of a mass assemblage of assets, but not in current use in the production of income, and not as a going-concern business enterprise.

3. Value as an orderly disposition -- Value in exchange, on a piece-meal basis (not part of a mass assemblage of assets), as part of an orderly disposition; this premise contemplates that all of the assets of the business enterprise will be sold individually, and that they will enjoy normal exposure to their appropriate secondary market.

4. Value as a forced liquidation -- Value in exchange, on a piecemeal basis (not part of a mass assemblage of assets), as part of a forced liquidation; this premise contemplates that the assets of the business enterprise will be sold individually and that they will experience less than normal exposure to their appropriate secondary market.

While virtually any business enterprise may be appraised under each of these four alternative fundamental premises, the value conclusions reached under each premise, for the same business, may be dramatically different.

Each of these alternative premises of value may apply under the same standard, or definition, of value. For example, the fair market

463

value standard calls for a "willing buyer" and a "willing seller." Yet, these willing buyers and sellers have to make an informed economic decision as to how they will transact with each other with regard to the subject business. In other words, is the subject business worth more to the buyer and the seller as a going concern that will continue to operate as such, or as a collection of individual assets to be put to separate uses? In either case, the buyer and seller are still "willing." And, in both cases, they have concluded a set of transactional circumstances that will maximize the value of the collective assets of the subject business enterprise.

The selection of the appropriate premise of value is an important step in defining the appraisal assignment. Typically, in controlling interest valuation, the selection of the appropriate premise of value is a function of the highest and best use of the collective assets of the subject business enterprise. The decision regarding the appropriate premise of value is usually made by the appraiser, based upon experience, judgement, and analysis.

Sometimes, however, the decision regarding the appropriate premise of value is made "for" the appraiser. This occurs when the appraiser knows -- or is told -- that the subject business enterprise will, in fact, be continued as a going concern of will be sold in a certain set of transactional circumstances. For example, if the business assets are, in fact, going to be sold on a value in exchange basis, it is not relevant for the appraiser to consider the value in continued use -- or going-concern -- premise of value. Of course, if appraising a minority interest, one would normally adopt the premise of business as usual unless given reason to do otherwise.

In some circumstances, it may be relevant -- and, in fact, critical -- to appraise the subject business enterprise under several alternative premises of value. For example, it may be extremely important to conclude the value of the same business enterprise under several alternative premises of value in appraisals performed for bankruptcy and reorganization or for financing securitization and collateralization purposes.

Sources of Guidance as to Applicable Standards and Premises of Value

The experience and expertise of the professional appraiser include the skill to seek out and interpret guidance as to the standard and premises of value that are relevant to the assignment at hand. Some of the most important sources of guidance as to the applicable standard and premise of value for the given situation are the following:

- Statutory law (state and federal).
- Case law (cases decided under the controlling statutory or common law).
- Administrative regulations (e.g., IRS Revenue Rulings).[9]
- Company documents (e.g., articles of incorporation or partnership, bylaws, meeting minutes, agreements).
- Contracts between the parties (e.g., buy-sell agreements, arbitration agreements).
- Precedent established by prior transactions.
- Directives issued by the court (in some litigated cases where the standards or premises are not clear, the appraiser may take the initiative to seek direction from the court regarding definition of value).
- Discussions with an attorney involved in the valuation matter or experience in similar matters.
- Legal case documents (e.g., complaint, response, and so forth).
- The appraiser's experience and judgement.

Form of the Work Product

In many cases, the purpose of the report will largely determine the form of the report. The appraiser's report to the client can be oral, written, or a combination.

An oral report can be anything from a quick phone call to lengthy meetings with the principals, attorneys, brokers, and/or other parties involved. The form and extent of a written report can range from a single-page letter report to a detailed, hundred-page-plus volume.

---

[9] Note that the administrative rulings do not have the force of law, but represent the position of the agency administering the law as to their interpretation of the law and rules for applying it.

LIMITED LIABILITY COMPANIES (LLCs)

SHANNON PRATT

Dr. Shannon P. Pratt is a managing director and one of the founders of Willamette Management Associates. Founded in the 1960s, Willamette Management Associates is one of the oldest and largest independent valuation consulting, economic analysis, and financial advisory firms in the country. It has regional offices in Atlanta, GA, McLean, VA, Chicago, IL, and Portland, OR.

To be an LLC, the business must have at least two owners or "members." Thus, an S corporation is the only entity through which a sole proprietor can enjoy both a single level of tax and limited liability.

Pass-through tax treatment for many LLCs will depend on the absence of continuity of life and the absence of free transferability of interests because, for a variety of nontax reasons, an LLC may desire centralized management and, of course, limited liability. On the other hand, some organizations may specifically desire to lack centralized management -- either because of business reasons or because they are unable to comply strictly with the ruling guidelines to lack continuity of life or free transferability of interests.

---

* Excerpted from Valuing a Business, 3rd ed., by Shannon Pratt, Robert F Reilly, and Robert P. Schweihs. (Burr Ridge, IL: Irwin Professional Publishing, 1996), Used by special permission. All rights reserved.

LLCs are not subject to the ownership restrictions applicable to S corporations and, thus, offer increased flexibility. An unlimited number of persons or entities (including partnerships, corporations, and nonresident aliens) may own interests in an LLC, and an LLC may be used in multi-tiered structures. LLCs may issue more than one class of equity, giving them the flexibility to use special allocations and to offer equity interests designed to meet the needs of different investors.

A large number of owners, however, may not be feasible from a practical standpoint, because the unanimous consent of all the remaining "members" may be required to prevent dissolution on the withdrawal of a single member. Obtaining unanimous consent to continue an LLC's business on the event of dissolution (e.g., death or bankruptcy of a member) may be extremely burdensome, especially for large organizations and fragile family arrangements.

A possible approach that could be considered for a large group of investors would be to have several limited partnerships (which do not dissolve on the withdrawal of an owner) form an LLC, provided that both the limited partnerships and the LLC can be classified as partnerships for income tax purposes.

Obviously, the structure and flow of the rights and privileges of the subject ownership position need to be understood by the analyst before its value can be determined.

LLCs as an Estate Planning Device

It may be easier to transfer gifts of interest in property, such as real estate or stocks and bonds, with an LLC. For example, if an individual owns real estate, an gift of a fractional interest in a deed is cumbersome and potentially expensive with respect to filing fees and legal costs. On the other hand, the transfer of real estate to an LLC will allow the owners to then make annual gifts of "membership units" without needing to file fractional deeds. The transfer of real estate or other property either to an LLC or to a partnership will generally be income tax free, but this is not necessarily true for the transfer of property to a C corporation or to an S corporation.

Another advantage of an LLC (or of a partnership) over a corporation is that the liquidation or distribution of assets to members or partners can be tax free (per Section 731). However, the liquidation of a C corporation or an S corporation -- or the distribution of an appreciated asset in an S corporation -- will result in taxable income (per Section 336).

If business or nonbusiness assets are hale in an LLC, the owners can make annual gifts of LLC units up to $10,000 in value ($20,000 if the taxpayer is married) to children and grandchildren, free of gift tax. Although the same annual gifting mechanism can be implemented with a corporation or partnership, an S corporation has several limitations that complicate estate planning. Unlike an LLC, only certain types of trusts can hold S corporation stock -- that is, a Section 136(d) QSST Trust. These trusts must be carefully drafted or the S corporation can lose its S taxpayer status. Since trusts are often used in many estate plans, this limitation is significant.

Also, a QSST must always have only one income beneficiary, and income must be distributed annually. There is no similar problem with an LLC (or a partnership), since there are no restrictions as to who can own an LLC membership.

If the transferor dies during the process of transferring his or her interests to children or grandchildren, the use of an LLC is preferable to a corporation. This is because of the ability to elect to step up the basis of assets inside the LLC (per Section 754). This step-up in basis will allow greater depreciation deductions for inherited assets and a deferral of any gain on the sale of assets by the LLC.

An LLC can be used just like a limited partnership to hold a variety of assets (e.g., real estate, cash, securities, etc.). Such flexibility in asset ownership allows a business owner to transfer ownership to second- and third-generation family members while still keeping control of the assets in the parent generation.

Membership interests, just like limited partnership interests or shares in a corporation, can be limited as to voting power and transferability rights. Consequently, if assets are transferred into an LLC, the estate or gift valuation of the individual membership units transferred may be substantially discounted -- perhaps by 30 to 40 percent for each lack of marketability and lack of control discount. (The same argument can be used for a corporation or a limited partnership.)

Caveats Regarding the Valuation of Transferred LLC Interests

It is unclear whether an LLC is preferable to a limited partnership for holding business or other assets for purposes of the marketability and minority discounts in a family transfer situation. Section 270(b) provides that restrictions by agreement on liquidation rights should be ignored for gift and estate tax valuation purposes if: (1) family members control the entity before the transfer and (2) after the transfer, the family members could remove the restriction on liquidation.

For gift and estate tax purposes, Section 270(b) may require that -- for purposes of valuing membership units -- any language in the LLC operating agreement limiting liquidation rights be ignored. Therefore, the value of a member's interest would be closer to the pro rata portion of what the entire asset could be sold for, without consideration of any lack of control or lack of marketability discounts. Until further guidance is issued by the IRS, it is unclear how Section 270(b) impacts the valuation of an LLC. For this reason, a term of years structure is often utilized for LLCs in the manner as it is for limited partnerships.

Some observers believe the above valuation problem will not apply to limited partnership interests because of the difference in the rights of limited partners on a dissolution of a limited partnership. Nevertheless, caution may require consideration of the use of a limited partnership rather than an LLC -- for family transfer purposes -- when lack of control and lack of marketability valuation discounts are desired.

Another way to address this Section 270(b) concern, if the use of an LLC is desired, is to give someone other than a family member the right to limit the dissolution of the LLC. Because a non-family member is involved in determining dissolution, the LLC membership units should qualify for the lack of control and lack of marketability discounts.

Recapitalization of the Family-Owned Business

A C corporation recapitalization is still possible under Sections 2701-2704, but it is expensive due to the double taxation of dividends. An LLC can be drafted in such a way as to create an interest similar to preferred stock. However, since an LLC is not a taxable entity, there would be no double taxation of the dividends.

Use of an LLC Instead of a Trust

An LLC can function in many ways just like a trust, but without the adverse estate and income tax consequences. If a trust accumulates income, it will be subject to the 39.6 percent marginal tax bracket once it has $7,500 of taxable income. An LLC will pass through all of its income to the members, who may be in a lower income tax bracket. Also, the donor can retain interests in the LLC without causing all the assets in the LLC to be included in his or her estate, per the Section 2036 retained interest rules. Finally, an LLC may be changed to real-locate interests, while a trust would be irrevocable.

The use of an LLC may be a valuable new tool for estate planners and other advisors to closely held business owners. However, as with any new estate tax planning device, it must be used carefully. Both the potential tax benefits -- and the potential tax costs -- should be evaluated when considering the use of an LLC in an estate plan.

Comparing the LLC to the S Corporation

An S corporation may continue in perpetuity and is not subject to the fixed termination date imposed on LLCs in many states;. The possibility of an inopportune termination may be of significance to a family-owned entity that may plan to continue through multiple generations.

From a nontaxation stand point, S corporation shareholders unquestionably enjoy limited liability in all states; however, there are serious concerns about the limited liability protection that will be afforded LLCs doing business in states without LLC statutes (rapidly approaching approval in all 50 states, as of this writing).

An S corporation clearly may use the cash method of accounting, while an LLC with nonmanager members may be required to use the accrual method of accounting.

S corporations have flexibility concerning restrictions on the transferability of their stock, and there is no risk of dissolution on the occurrence of the death, disability, bankruptcy, retirement, or resignation of a shareholder. Many LLCs must restrict the transferability of their interests and provide for dissolution upon the occurrence of certain events. The consequent requirements to transfer interests and to continue the business upon the occurrence of an event of dissolution may not be feasible.

The taxation of S corporations may be simpler in many situations than the taxation of LLCs. Because an S corporation may have only one class of stock, its items of income, loss and gain, and deductions are shared pro rata. Thus, the complexities associated with special allocations, available to an LLC, are avoided with an S corporation.

THE "MINI-SOCIETY" PROVES EXPERIENCE IS THE BEST TEACHER*

COLIN J. GIBSON

For more information about the Kourilsky Economic Education Programs, write to Dr. Marilyn Kourlisky, Vice President, Center for Entrepreneurial Leadership, 4900 Oak Street, Kansas City, MO 64112-2776, (816) 932 1000.

When are children ready to grasp the fundamentals they will need to become "economically literate" citizens? "Kindergarten is not too soon!" says Dr. Marilyn Kourilsky of the University of California at Los Angeles. And surprisingly, students from kindergarten through the second grade who participated in an economic education program she designed scored better on a test of economic literacy than a key sample of American adults.

Before receiving special training, teachers are no more economically literate than the rest of the adult population, says Kourilsky. On tests covering such economic basics as scarcity, costs, profits, supply, demand, and competition, they score an average of 68.5 points, she finds. After the "Kinder-Economy" program, children between the ages of five and seven score an average of 72.5!

471

Research also shows that children in Kourilsky's programs increase their self-esteem and assertiveness, acquire a greater sense of control over their lives and have a more positive attitude toward entrepreneurship and risk-taking. Before the program, children asked to draw pictures of successful businessmen usually depict them as corpulent bald men with cigars, sweating profusely. After the program "they draw self-images," says Kourilsky.

She attributes these impressive results to the "experience-based character" of her program. "Reforms in the teaching of economics have usually been presented as units of study similar in design and approach to the traditional curriculum," she says. In the Mini-Society, "students actually experience and then resolve economic and social problems through the creation and development of their own classroom society."

Teachers in Mini-Society classrooms do not teach in the ordinary sense. Instead, they create learning situations and "debrief" students after each session.

The Mini-Society starts, as all economies do, with a scarcity situation. For example, the teacher brings a number of felt-tip pens to class, deliberately fewer than the number of students. Because all the students want pens, they are motivated to resolve the dilemma. Should the pens be allocated on a "first come, first served" basis? Should there be a lottery or a free-for-all? Autocracy? Violence?

Students discover that they can use a price mechanism to allocate scarce resources, provided there is some sort of currency and a distribution of income. The class agrees, for example, that students receive ten "quiblings" for punctuality, five for completing work and two for not disturbing others. Those willing to pay the market price in "quiblings" get the pens.

The incentive system exists primarily to introduce money into the Mini-Society, but it also teaches a lesson about the natural result of incentives--an unequal distribution of income and wealth. Once they agree on the rules, the children discover that wealth "naturally" accumulates in the hands of the most punctual, studious and courteous in the class.

Students also learn that they can't increase the wealth of their Mini-Society simply by "printing" more money. If they try, the price of pens rises, but the number of pens does not increase.

Wealth is created in the next stage. With the money they earn, children buy and sell goods and services, such as pencils, erasers, and

472

their time. Some start businesses, such as tutorial and cleaning companies, banks, wallet factories, and food concessions.

The list is limited only by the children's imagination. Mini-Societies differ from each other--unlike ordinary simulation exercises--because the number and type of businesses depend exclusively on student entrepreneurship.

Teachers offer their services as paid consultants and perform the executive functions of government. The students, meeting in a discussion group, enact laws. To pay for government services, such as cleaning the cage of a class pet rabbit, taxes are levied. Once the money supply is in circulation, children often decide to put an end to "government payments" for attendance, etc., and to reduce taxes.

Some of the best Mini-Society teachers are selected to train other teachers. Edna Graff, an elementary teacher from Cincinnati, Ohio, was so impressed with the program that she moved to Los Angeles to work with Kourilsky. She is now a PhD candidate in UCLA's Graduate School of Education, concentrating in economic education.

Graff says using the Mini-Society system requires different skills, but is not necessarily more demanding than teaching economics in traditional ways.

"You debrief only what students have lived," she says. "Once they have experienced an economic dilemma, you can explain it in any terms you want--and you might as well use the correct ones so they don't have to unlearn it later."

Kourilsky stresses that Mini-Society "clarifies, but does not simplify" economic concepts. Simplification is unnecessary, she says, because the study of economics is fundamentally "common sense made difficult."

Children in Mini-Society classes often surprise teachers with their economic sophistication and knowledge of the real world, Graff says. In one of her classes, the public treasury ran out of money, and the students suggested printing more. "That would lead to inflation," said Graff. "Why not do it anyway?" asked one girl. "We'll have to get used to inflation by the time we grow up."

SOME TALKS AND ARTICLES BY ARTHUR LIPPER III

WHAT I'VE LEARNED FROM THE MISTAKES I'VE MADE
ABOUT INVESTING IN PRIVATE COMPANIES

As presented to the 10th Anniversary meeting of
the Los Angeles Venture Association ("LAVA") -
December 13, 1994

(Also presented at George Washington University
in Washington, D.C. on February 21, 1995)

I've learned a great deal during the past 40 years regarding what to
do and, more importantly what not to do, within the private company
investment process - if earning an extraordinary risk related return is
the investor's primary objective. Although I frequently make the same
mistakes over again I also have an ability to find and make new mistakes to add to the list. The title of this talk suggested to my wife and
some of my other friends that the length of the presentation could
well be much longer than intended by the LAVA Program Committee
Chairperson and you would clearly have stopped listening before I
stopped talking. Also a fuller cataloging of the mistakes made would;
1) deter most of you from ever investing in a private company, which
is not my intention and 2) lessen my inventory of horrors which I use
when charging client companies a consulting fee.

Investing in private companies is enormously important for the country as a whole and for every community therein. Private company investment is an activity which should be favored, rather than penalized, by all governments in terms of tax relief and other legislation. Unfortunately it isn't. Elected politicians seem to yield more frequently to the voice of the electorate which, by definition, has neither the asset base permitting investment nor the entrepreneurial mind-set of employers, who are in a position, if financed, to make a positive difference to others.

In part, this is due to the lack of tangible recognition on the part of government as to the importance of fostering entrepreneurial activity which requires private company investors to demand a higher level of return from the entrepreneur than would otherwise be the case. It is almost as if the government is saying "we won't help you profit, even recognizing the risk which is being undertaken, and even though in success we, the government, win both directly in taxes paid, and only a bit less directly in the employment and general business activity created by the development of a successful enterprise". I believe we'd have a better functioning government if it were required that at least one-third of all elected representatives have been business founding employers (law firms being excluded) otherwise known as entrepreneurs. Incidentally, the exclusion of law firms is not on, as you might suspect, grounds of morality. Rather it is due to my perception of the result of the professional training of attorneys, which is to seek comfort only in finding precedent, rather than being the more right-brain dominant, innovative problem solvers, required to off-set those bureaucrats who are intellectually and emotionally captives of the past and fearful of change.

Mistakes made and lesson learned:

Not understanding my own motivation - for being involved in a relationship without really knowing why. Why was I considering making an investment in a private company, any private company? Was it because I am an incurable opportunity and excitement junkie? Probably so.

Could it be because I really wished to help whoever was pitching me the opportunity? Possibly so. In any case, whatever my motivation I damn well should understand what is driving me to become involved, as it is difficult for all and impossible for me to passively invest in private companies and therefore the investment should be expected to be more than just money. This is, of course, especially true as the recapture of the funds invested is usually dependant on the business succeeding. In the book *Venture's Financing and Investing In Private Companies* I list some of the reasons why people invest in private companies, other than to make a high return. It is surprising to me how few angels, those who spread their wings and open their wallets to entrepreneurs, are really only profit driven. Most have other than only profit on their agendas. Angels are frequently quite wonderful and interesting people and must be protected as were they to become extinct, due to more frequently than not, being the recipients of capital punishment, their losses become our losses, if their losses prompt them to abandon the exercise and leave the game.

Non-defining of success in considering an investment - For any of us to succeed we have to define success and to define success we have to have a clear vision of that which we are trying to achieve.

Do we crave power or a feeling of power and/or do we have a hope for recognition? Do we want to be a father-figure for an entrepreneur or his employees? Do we want to have an activity into which we can throw ourselves? Do we want to be in a position of the entrepreneur and others becoming dependant upon us? What do we want and how much of this want is responsible for our being willing to lose money?

I don't wish to suggest what anyone's motivation should be, I have just learned that we all would do a better job of investing to achieve an objective if we understood precisely the objective we were trying to achieve.

Not treating my money as if it weren't my money - Lots of times I have made the mistake of forgetting or failing to articulate what my objective was and have just gotten swept up in the challenge of making the deal - rather than continuing the decision making process, up until the time of closing, if I should do the deal. That's when I've been investing my own money. I have not made the same mistake when I have been acting as a fiduciary. Therefore I urge all investors to pretend they are responsible for acting on behalf of others when making investments, especially in private companies. I promise you that a much better quality decision will be made if you think of yourself as a fiduciary.

Fear - and allowing my fears to unreasonably determine the deals that I will and won't do and how they are structured. What am I most fearful of in making investments in private companies? Losing the money invested? No. I am prepared to lose that which I invest and I recognize that losing all of the money invested in any single private company, especially those which have the greatest early stage potential, is a reasonable possibility. That which frightens me most is that I may become liable for more than has been invested by virtue of investing more money in the deal to save or protect the money originally invested and probably more accurately "already lost". I describe such follow-on investments as "investment hostage" or ransom payment investing, being the practice of investing new money to recapture or resuscitate already lost, dead, capital. I have seen but a very few instances where follow-on investments, prompted by disappointing results, have yielded a satisfactory result or return. Usually they just increase the ultimate loss of the investor. I am also concerned with the possibility of becoming so involved in trying to assist the company in which I've invested that I end-up putting myself in a position where it can be asserted that I have incurred personal liability. For instance, no one wants to have a director's liability in a company having or causing environmental problems or employee and/or customer harm.

Fear of loss in investing is probably a good thing to have as long as the fear is not at such a level as to immobilize the investor. A key lesson taught and learned at Paris Island, the Marine Corp's primary boot camp, San Diego not withstanding, was "move, don't freeze, when receiving fire". Investing successfully in private companies has some of the same elements as combat and the investor has to be prepared to be in motion, and not just stay in a fox hole of inactivity, waiting for it all to pass or for the "one he never hears." I've learned not to be afraid to take affirmative action to protect the invested assets for which I am responsible.

In structuring transactions I've learned to first determine my investor candidate's priorities. If I am structuring an investment opportunity for truly affluent investors, not just those purportedly qualifying as "accredited", I focus on risk analysis and abatement as rich people do not want to be embarrassed by losses as they recognize they have no monetary motivation to expose themselves to risk. If I am attempting to appeal to a broader range of investors then I focus more on the possible magnitude of gain and favorable risk/reward relationship. After all greed is but a fear of not profiting to a maximum level, much as being obsessed with physical fitness reflects a fear of being sick and frail.

Being greedy - resulting in my embracing the entrepreneur's vision of success and future profits. We all want to win, however we define

477

the win and, as I've noted previously, it is vital that we do define for ourselves the definition of the win.

Why have I accepted sales and earnings projections which require the acceptance of the entrepreneur's product or service without the company having made the level of marketing investment similar to that of other comparable and competitive companies? Why have I not required the entrepreneur to respond to a series of "what if" questions such as what if; you die or become an alcoholic, are faced with a patent infringement action, lose your key engineers or salespeople, the primary vendors on whom you are depending for components go out of business, the primary sales prospect decides not to buy, the bank doesn't do that which you expect them to do and finally, it takes twice as long to develop the product and/or make the sales envisioned? Why? Because I wanted to make the investment, gain a participation in the project and get rich as a result.

Being lazy - too lazy to thoroughly check the background of the entrepreneur, even though I had the opportunity to do so. Few of us really enjoy the process of prying into the lives of others. However, as once money has been committed to private company investment it become a captive of the process. Therefore, it is vital that we really know who it is we are, all too frequently, "giving" our money to. Many of us know what to do and simply fail to do it when it comes to researching an investment opportunity.

Being cheap - as in being unwilling to recognize that making investment decisions requires the expenditure of funds. A professional background check on an entrepreneur will cost in the area of $1,500 if more than a litigation and credit check is involved. It is money well spent.

In one case recently an associate of mine and myself paid $7,500 for the preparation and distribution of a newspaper insert marketing effort on behalf of a company whose product interested us. Copies of the insert for San Diego Photo Restoration Services are in the room. If the insert drew as few as 150 responses in a 22,500 business journal distribution then we'd get our $7,500 back and know that we would make money by rolling out the service nationally. If we didn't recapture the marketing money then we'd have learned something which would save us a lot more than the $7,500. By the time I present this talk we will have known if we'd made or saved money.

In another case, I recently advised and arranged for a client to have a background check run on a charismatic individual having proposed a joint venture. The background of the individual it was learned included several jail terms and lots of litigation. Needless to say, the relationship did not occur as had been originally contemplated, though there may be a different form and level of relationship.

In some cases, professional investors seek to recapture from a funding (and sometimes even without a funding occurring) their legitimate due diligence expenses through the imposition of an investigation fee or reimbursement agreement. My approach has been to require the entrepreneur to pay the entire cost of our due diligence if we uncover significant factual data which is in opposition to that which the entrepreneur presented to us or which is relevant and negative and should have been disclosed. It is going to cost, one way or another, at least $5,000 to $10,000 to professionally reach a decision of whether or not to invest in a private company assuming the proposition is not rejected out of hand. Private company investors must either be willing to spend the money or trust to their intuition, experience-based judgment and/or luck. Again, were you investing as a fiduciary you'd probably spend the money - and obtain a better overall portfolio result.

My friend and associate, Don Campbell, an active and experienced smaller enterprise consultant, who assists companies in organizing themselves, prepare a business plan and obtain financing, reminds me that one of the aspects of both being cheap and of denying the ever presence and efficacy of Murphy's Law is being under insured. Don also points out that too few entrepreneurs are pressed by those investing in them to set aside, beyond their control, amounts sufficient to assure the expense of remaining in "good legal standing" for subsequent years after the investment is made. Don is right in that if the company fails to maintain its legal standing then it can loose its right to litigate or even effectively contract. Strange and murky things happen when companies get into trouble and some of them can be guarded against by experienced investors overriding the entrepreneurs super abundance of confidence that all will be well because that's the way it has to be (in his eyes).

Becoming dependant - upon the entrepreneur as an individual. Investing in private companies is a people assessment exercise as much as a financial analysis. I and most other private company investors usually know within a very short period of time, minutes or perhaps even seconds, if the entrepreneur is a person with whom a business relationship is wanted. However, I have paid the price of losing money by not requiring that there be more than one individual worthy of my admiration in a company being financed. Aside from the fact that entrepreneurs, though many would dispute the fact, are mortal, there should be in place a team of credible people on whom the investor can rely. If the entrepreneur being financed only attracts and recruits people of lesser quality and ability than he or she then there is a problem. Successful entrepreneurs frequently say the secret to their success was in hiring or attracting people who were smarter and better qualified than themselves. One of the distinctions between those having an entrepreneurial mind-set and those who think of themselves as inventors is that of the inventor being typically reluctant to share in the development of the intellectual property whereas the entrepreneur wishes to capture the resources and efforts of as many people as possible for his benefit.

Being non-diversified - in the creation and management of a portfolio of private company investments. None of us are so smart and experienced as to be able to predict which of the truly promising opportunities we are exposed to, and with which we become involved, will be winners. We know that most will fail to achieve the initial objectives of the entrepreneur and some will actually fail. Therefore we should put ourselves in a position of "sprinkling money amongst talent" rather than restricting our investment to one or two private company investments, if we wish to be serious in the effort of making money. However, I and I hope you, recognize that, again - it all goes back to the investor's motivation.

Being unrealistic - as to the absence of competition for the product or service being financed. Entrepreneurs all too frequently are either uninformed as to competitive factors or so very sure of themselves and secure in their vision that they minimize or discount the threat of competition. The result of such disregard of margin shrinking or revenue reducing competition is typically one of under estimation of the amount of funding required. Entrepreneurs typically under estimate both the amount of time, and therefore money, required in reaching a point of being cash flow positive.

Being too tough - in the structuring of transactions. The essence of structuring a transaction is the shifting disproportionate amounts of reward to the stronger party and risk to the weaker party. The reality is that the stronger party, the one with the resource needed by the entrepreneur, has to be fair and make certain the entrepreneur understands why the deal is fair. In cases where the entrepreneur perceives that he is being taken advantage of a destructive and investment threatening attitude can develop. The investors should protect himself on the downside and be prepared to be generous with the entrepreneur on the upside. For this reason I prefer to provide risk capital in forms of other than equity.

Falling in love - with an investment. Frequently there are opportunities for the investor to recapture his investment while still retaining an interest in the enterprise. In most cases when I have had such opportunities my greed and need for vindication of initial judgment has prevented my taking advantage of the opportunity. Structuring transactions with an exit strategy is important and the difference between a professionally negotiated deal and one made by and with amateurs is the presence or absence of an exit. A frank and open discussion with the entrepreneur, prior to the making of the investment, is desirable in order the entrepreneur understand the investor's need to recapture and recirculate capital. The investor in private companies should not confuse his role with that of the entrepreneur. We all have to know who we are in any given situation.

I hope the foregoing, perhaps all too revealing, disclosure of some of the mistakes I've made will allow you to avoid making the same mistakes. As noted at the beginning of this talk, I seem to have a wonderful ability of not only making some of the mistakes repetitively but of also finding new mistakes to make in investing in private companies. Perhaps on the 20th anniversary of LAVA you will allow me to return in order that I might share with you a listing of the new mistakes I've discovered and made.

I've enjoyed each of my five LAVA presentations and hope that LAVA members have gained some benefit from my effort.

Best wishes to you all and congratulations to those having made LAVA so successful over the last 10 years.

Structuring The Deal

It usually turns out that most deals are neither made in heaven, nor the capital providers, as the recipients of capital frequently come to believe, made in, or should be going to, hell. An understanding of relative realities of both the owners and consumers of capital will be useful in structuring arrangements meeting the natural needs of both of these co-dependent parties in that which promises a mutuality of profit.

Karl Marx was a fair observer in noting "the essence of capitalism is the exploitation of labor". However, labor is only one asset which may be available to a business owner or manager and which may be subject to exploitation. Of course, we should understand that to exploit means "to make the most of", which is certainly an objective we all seek to achieve in most of our activities.

Also it should be understood that the essence of any commercial transaction is the utilization of assets to earn profit. In the case of labor the exploitation can be fair or unfair to those who perform the labor, depending on the perspective of the observer and there can be a wide variance as to conclusion.

Capital, in the form of money, is another asset which is available for exploitation. A businessperson to succeed must earn more on the capital acquired than the cost of acquisition and use of the money. Capital and labor are essentially the same in that a return, attractive to the available alternatives, has to be earned to justify the application of either.

Job functions which entail greater risk usually are compensated more highly than those which are safer and more secure. One of the justifications for seemingly outrageous levels of compensation of high profile athletes and other entertainers is that their careers are subject to risk in that their popularity or ability to perform is likely to be less than the 30 year work span normally associated with those employed in less visible and perhaps demanding activities. The steel worker functioning on a beam 50 floors up gets, and is probably entitled to, greater pay than someone performing a similar job at ground level. The pay differential is a function of both reality and perception. The skywalker may not believe that his job is inherently riskier than those who work at ground level and he may even prefer the height and excitement of his environment and therefore his personal reality is different from those observing and paying him.

I remember all too well, while serving as a Marine Corps platoon Sergeant in Korea, of senior USMC reserve officers who would be flown in to "observe" for one or two days, never being positioned to be in real danger. The deal was that any time spent in a combat zone entitled the officer to "combat pay" for that month. I do not know if the, mostly social, visits were scheduled to occur at a month's end if so if the officer could then claim an entitlement to combat pay for both months. This is a fair analogy of a "worker of the system" receiving a premium for the appearance of risk, without his believing the risk was ever at a level of justifying the premium. One of the realities is that entrepreneurs almost never perceive the same level of risk as those observing them do. Of course, the reality of statistics may well show a greater incidence of injury to those receiving the premium compensation than they believed would be the case - but such is the "risk of justice" being applied by a greater force.

Obviously, the best of both worlds, from the perspective of the provider of presumed higher risk level service, would be one of receiving the risk related premium and yet taking precautions to assure that the risk was the same or perhaps even less than that of the less well compensated service provider. In other words, it could become an arbitrage of locking in the wage differential by equalizing the risk - or receiving venture capital returns for taking less than all or nothing risks.

I believe artful deal making, from the perspective of the capital provider, to be the same exercise, namely receiving a return associated with the acceptance of a higher risk while finding a means of lessening the risk.

For example, is there a significant risk associated with investing in an early stage technology development company? You say "yes" and I say "it depends on how the investment is structured".

Is the risk still present if there is a third party willing to guarantee the capital provider against loss? You say "no, there isn't" and I say "of course there is, unless the third party has collateralized the undertaking in such a manner as to permit the capital provider to withdraw, without recourse, all of the capital originally provided".

Would such an arrangement be a good deal for the capital provider? "Yes, you say" while I believe "it would only be a good deal if there had been an adequate return received for having entered the transaction and/or after being relieved of all risk there was still a sufficient level of residual interest or profit potential".

[I am currently considering, as The Guide for Venture Investing Angels is being written, the creation of a for-profit guarantor of private company investments on the basis of the angel being able, for a twenty percent premium to purchase a two year put at seventy-five percent of cost.]

The real essence of professional deal making is not to take advantage of the need of the other party but rather to construct a deal which is more predictable in result for the party having less control over the outcome of the business activity utilizing the capital. In other words, the user of the money should have greater upside than the owner of the money but in return the owner of the money should have a greater ability to know the result of the transaction.

The simple buying of stock in a company, especially a non-publicly traded stock, only subjects the investor, under the very best of circumstances, to the same level of risk and reward as that of those controlling the business, and usually to a greater risk and lesser reward potential, due to the fact the investor is not normally in a control position.

I prefer renting money to "giving" money (through the purchase of non-marketable equity) to entrepreneurs. I use the term "renting" to imply an obligation on the part of the user of the money, to return the money and a lack of intention, on the part of the money's owner, to give up ownership of the money. Money is a fungible commodity and should be thought of as a hard and finite asset, not as something which is amorphous, vague and always replenishable. In several books I've written I've used the analogy of money being like "green slaves" in that the more of it you have the less work you have to do yourself. I define work as that which one does for the primary benefit of others versus that which one does to satisfy one's own needs.

One further observation before discussing my favorite basis for structuring transactions between those with and those seeking capital.

Successful business development and management is a function of causing revenues, hopefully in increasing amount, to be generated while assuring the cost of producing and delivering the product or service is at a level sufficiently less than that of the selling price to earn a profit. However, there is more. The profit earned has to be of a magnitude which is relatively attractive to available alternatives requiring the same level of capital, effort, skill and risk acceptance. If the profit isn't as great as can be earned in other available application then the capital should be re-directed, if asset maximization is the objective of the money's owner. In many cases, an entrepreneur will prefer to own his own business, with all of the good and bad which that activity implies, in preference to realizing the capital employed in his business and investing it in someone else's business even with the capital earning a higher level of return, but placing the entrepreneur in a passive or, at least, non-controlling position. In such a case, the entrepreneur is really saying either "I place a premium on being an owner/manager of a business which has to be added to the actual return received on the capital in the business which could be extracted on the liquidation of the business before calculating my ROI" or "I know the profits earned by my business are going to increase in the future". Unfortunately, the "knowings" of entrepreneurs are frequently their undoing. It would be far better for them and those they involve in their enterprises if their statements of faith were constructively challenged.

Fact follows - "it is easier for anyone, regardless of their level of knowledgeability about a business, to accurately predict revenues than cash flow or profits".

Fact follows - "those responsible for the outcome of an enterprise truly believe in their ability to cause predicted events to occur".

Fact follows - "if those willing to accept risks inherent in assisting entrepreneurs continue to suffer disappointment they will cease the activity and thus be lost as a possible resource for other entrepreneurs".

Fact follows - "most new businesses and young businesses are financed by non-professional, individual, investors, usually the family and friends of the entrepreneur, and thus are not in a position of negotiating an advantageous, let alone sound or even fair commercial arrangement with the entrepreneur".

There are essentially only two means of compensating an investor for providing capital and accepting risk. One is through the payment of interest or a fixed fee and the other is through providing an interest in the activity being financed, which it is generally assumed will grow.

The fixed interest which a business, especially a young enterprise, can afford to pay is not usually sufficient risk-related compensation to attract capital. Businesses which become burdened with high interest payments are very fragile and are therefore inherently dangerous to the providers of the capital.

There are two primary means of participating in a business activity. One is through an ownership of shares or partnership interest, which in either case could be described as an ownership of profit points and the other through the ownership of revenue points, otherwise known as a royalty or as I describe it as a Revenue Participation.

After more than 30 years of involvement in the financing of privately owned companies I have concluded that Revenue Participation, as reflected in negotiable Revenue Participation Certificates

485

("RPCs"), is the best approach for both the capital provider and for the entrepreneur - with one critical reservation. The reservation and caveat is simply that in agreeing to pay based upon revenue the business owner must be accurate in his or her cash flow and profit projections as achieving predicted revenue levels without the concomitant profit margins can result in a disaster for the business owner.

However, as a provider of funds for ventures (not a venture capitalist, as usually the funds invested have either been mine or those for which I have a replacement responsibility) I urge entrepreneurs to never show me other than their very worst case profit projections - as if there is any shortfall in the actual results achieved the difference between the generated and expected profit is going to come from their share of company's ownership. It's very simple, if I am responsible for investing money based upon a projection then I am doing so on a calculated future price earnings ratio which is compared to known and available alternative use for the same capital. I did not make the projections upon which the investment was premised - I just accepted them. The party making the projections has the ability to present conservative, worst case projections, or hopes. I do not want to invest in hopes or wishes (in other people's businesses as I reserve that folly for investing in my own businesses).

Specifically, my favorite transaction is one where I provide a bank loan guarantee, limited to several years and collateralized by only a Letter of Credit ("LC") for a fixed amount. In my ideal transaction my risk exposure can never be more than the amount of the LC. As compensation for the risk acceptance inherent in becoming a guarantor I seek a RPC.

Elements of the RPC which must be negotiated include:

Initial and subsequent levels of Revenue Participation.

RPCs can:

scale up or down, be "capped" as to total periodic return,

have a minimum, guaranteed, periodic return,

be secured or unsecured,

be convertible into securities of the issuing company at the holder's option,

be convertible into securities of the issuing company at the issuer's option upon the meeting of threshold requirements and

be denominated in designated currencies and paid as directed by the holder.

Maturity of the RPC.

Possible third party endorsements and guarantees of either/or the return of the capital and/or the performance of the party being guaranteed.

Negotiability and assignability of the RPC.

Termination (of the RPC arrangement) agreement.

In making any guarantee, I always assume the guarantee will be called and that I will therefore, reluctantly but inevitably, become a direct lender to what will then be a troubled company.

As the terms of the bank's loan agreement with the borrower will inure to my benefit, through rights of subrogation, after the original lender takes my money to satisfy their loan, I insist the terms of the loan which I am guaranteeing, be highly protective of the lender's capital.

I have yet to be exposed to a company, regardless of the stage of development, in which I would not rather have a 3% of revenue interest as opposed to a 49% equity interest. Also I have yet to encounter the business owner seeking capital who I have not been able to persuade to trade capital use for revenue points. The caveat, as noted previously, is one of the business owner having to be able to accurately predict minimum cash flows and earnings, as otherwise a RPC arrangement will create a real problem for the issuer of the RPC.

It should be noted, however, that the having of rights does not mean that it is always in the best interest of the holder of the rights to exercise them. There are certainly instances where the RPC holder is well advised to exchange or modify their entitlement in light of subsequent events. However, for sure, the RPC holder is in a much better position in such a circumstance than they would have been had they owned equity in the same company as finds it necessary or desirable to renegotiate the RPC.

How do I arrive at a FAIR level of revenue sharing? I start on the basis of assuming that I am negotiating a convertible note with the business owner and then extrapolate the worst case projections of earnings to revenues. If the projections are for $10.0 million in revenues and $1.0 in pre-tax profits then an entitlement to 5% of revenues would be approximately the same as ownership of 50% of the business, were combined tax rates 50%.

The real issue is the period of time for which the RPC is operative. Should it be "between perpetuity and forever" as I jokingly suggest or should it only be for the period of time in which there is risk associated with the guarantee, as the entrepreneur is likely to suggest. The answer is obviously somewhere in between.

The actual determination as to maturity of the RPC contract is a function of the type of business, the risk incurred at the time of risk acceptance, the alternative yields available to the capital provider, the quantity and quality of continuing relationship or involvement between the owner and user of the capital and what is FAIR in terms of market place alternatives.

In order to reduce the risk and therefore the justification for higher rates of return the capital provider may seek: security in addition to that required by the funding institution loaning the borrower money against the capital provider's guarantee. The capital provider may also seek third party endorsements either or both as to the repayment of the loan and/or the performance of the company in terms of its obligation re the RPC.

Finally, I believe that it only fair to the entrepreneur to negotiate a RPC termination agreement as if one does not exist and the company wishes to go public or to sell or merge the existence of the RPC will be a detriment, in which event the RPC holder would be in a position to block the deal unless accommodated. In determining a fair basis it is important to understand that the capital provider is accepting maximum risk at the time of initial risk acceptance and should therefore receive a very substantial premium, even if the loan is repaid the week after the deal is done.

One of the reasons for individual investors having less than satisfactory experiences in providing capital for entrepreneurs is that they usually are non-diversified, by being involved in but a single investment, whereas the professional investor tends to have a portfolio of risk. Therefore, my advice to individuals is to "sprinkle money amongst talent" and to be involved in a number of relatively small transactions rather than only one larger investment.

The other major reason for unsatisfactory private company investment performance by non-professional investors is an unwillingness or inability to monitor investments once made and to take corrective measures as the opportunity permits. Generally, the sooner the investor's involvement in a situation producing sub-expected results is terminated the better for the investor. Also I have seen very few follow-on investments in companies having produced disappointing results which in the end do more than increase the size of ultimate loss.

In closing, I urge all who can afford the financial loss and psychological stress to financially and otherwise support entrepreneurs in their quest for: power and control, recognition, satisfaction, freedom, wealth - and corporate profit. We, as a society, depend upon successful entrepreneurs for positive change and without the support of people such as yourselves many ventures, which might become successful, will never be launched. I also ask you to invest intelligently as if you do not have a successful investing experience you may not be there when I need you to help me with my next venture.

LESSONS TO BE LEARNED FROM SECURITIES ANALYSTS
For: *San Diego Business Journal* column

I once created a sign which hung on my wall which read "Capital Punishment Is The Result of Inadequate Investment Research". The Financial Analysts Society of San Diego used "Innovation: The Ripple That Starts the Wave" as the title for the conference the Society co-hosted with the Association for Investment Management and Research which was attended by more than 900 investment professionals when held at the Hotel del Coronado earlier this week.

Being a part of the professional investor scene and Wall Street community for 40 years I was interested to learn how the thinking and actions of these analysts, who influence the investments of millions of investors and many billions of dollars, have changed and relate to the interests and needs of business owners and entrepreneurs. The answer was "a lot and not much".

This was not a gathering of venture capitalists or entrepreneurs who focus on the future. Nor was this a meeting of lawyers who only are trained to be precedent aware and therefore only focus on the past. It was a meeting of responsible individuals who are charged with the responsibility of making predictions relating to the future price of securities and who must therefore be both aware of the past and be able to use that knowledge in assessing the future.

Dale M. Hanson, the Manager of the well managed, powerful and constructively activist California Public Employees Retirement System told the first day luncheon attendees that some progressively managed and shareholder conscious major companies are being business, as well as financially, audited so that the Board of Directors of the company can have an independent view of how well or otherwise the company is being managed. It makes sense to me that all business owners should want to have a similar audit prepared regarding their own businesses and I can envision a whole new range of really helpful services which professional auditing and counseling firms might offer entrepreneurs and, at least as importantly, those who finance them.

I found an increasing interest in various approaches to quantitative analysis and in the use of computer programs to augment the experience and skill of the professional. This is not surprising as there are more issues to cover, more complexity of regulation and financial structure within companies while at the same time the pressure on the analysts is ever greater to provide ever more quickly information-based opinions.

I also found the analysts attending the conference were better professionally educated than in prior decades and more aware of technology generally. Nevertheless, they were by nature and calling a conservative lot, of course, with exceptions. Being more of a futurist than an archeologist I sought to identify the exceptions - the risk takers who might be willing to constructively make the trade off between buying a bit of the unknown at the sacrifice of the basing all judgments on the known. I found a few and they will probably either become rich or unemployed.

The lessons to be learned for the private company business owner from attending the sessions and meeting the serious and hard working analysts include the analysts respect for consistency of results. The consistency and therefore predictability and therefore "quality" is of greater importance than the sheer magnitude of potential future earnings.

The analysts stock in trade is being right in the predictions made and the career penalties for being wrong are greater than the career credits for being right. Therefore, the analyst is usually going to opt for the security and comfort of predictability of consistency.

Therefore, those entrepreneurs and business owners seeking to gain the approval of securities analysts should both manage their businesses and present their case focussing on predictability of performance. Part of predictability of performance is understanding the macro environment and part is in micro-managing. Surprise is usually the enemy of both the business owner and the analyst which is to be defended against as most surprises are disappointments.

The analysts I met were truly interested in the innovative and entrepreneurial type of companies which abound in San Diego. They were however leery of surprise and concerned with the level of valuation which in many cases presumed the achievement of optimistic predictions, without recognition of the possibility of disappointment. After all these analysts spend their professional lives assessing the hopes and predictions of managers of large companies, which frequently are incorrect, and know therefore how very much more difficult it is for smaller enterprises to predict their future.

It is important for business owners to be aware that securities analysts interact within their firms and the investment community with investment bankers and that the securities analyst may be an appropriate and effective means of the business owner accessing those directly in a position to be of assistance in the financing of the business.

THE IMPORTANCE OF ENTREPRENEURSHIP IN GLOBAL FINANCE

"Great Decisions" Lecture talk text - February 21, 1995 at the University of North Carolina, Chapel Hill, NC

Let's start with a mission statement for this talk and some definitions.

My objective is to convey to you facts and opinions regarding entrepreneurship in a rapidly changing world which will both increase your understanding and prompt you to consider the relative importance of entrepreneurs to all societies and perhaps to encourage those of you having entrepreneurial tendencies to create businesses of your own. One of the changes I ask you to bear in mind is the increasing, absolute and relative, number of "have-nots" who are being thrust upon us. Dealing with an under-employed and unemployable populations, in some cases nations will be one of challenges of our time.

I define "global finance" as being a phrase describing the interdependance of economies. I see the world as being a machine or computer software program with a vast number of working parts or elements, each part having a function. The machine or program can

491

operate with less than the full number of parts or elements performing their assigned tasks, but not with the critical parts being non-functioning. Of course, the machine or program will function best with all of the parts functioning. What is the ideal or desired function of the inter-dependant global finance machine or program? What's the best that a well functioning world economy can do?

All people want pretty much the same for themselves, their families and for those for whom they feel a responsibility. Basically they want good health, relative wealth, power and a sense of security. Stated negatively, but perhaps more effectively, people fear; sickness, poverty, being powerless and having an absence of control over their own lives.

Question. What is the best form of government for the greatest number of people in a society? Question. What is or should be the objective and justification for government as opposed to an anarchy?

Would you accept the fact that democracy, which I assume most of you would vote for as the best form of government tends to become more totalitarian, certainly more centralized, during periods of economic stress? Can you think of a democracy which has withstood the test of economic disaster? If you can't do you accept the thought that democracy is a luxury which flourishes during periods of economic expansion, such as we, in this country, have been fortunate enough to enjoy since our nation's founding, with only relatively brief periods of fear engendering depression? Do we agree that during the Great Depression of the 1930's the people were content for the Washington-based federal government to grant unto itself vast new powers, never to release them back to the people or to the smaller geopolitical entities? Is it possible therefore that during periods of economic expansion and prosperity that it really doesn't make too much difference what the form of government, be it a monarchy or a dictatorship? Can we agree that during periods of fear the people want, or are willing to have, the government have the power to do something to relieve the pain?

Ayn Rand, the philosopher and author, believed the appropriate function of government should be restricted to the protection of national borders and maintenance of order. She believed that people should have the ability to provide for their own welfare given an economic ability to do so. I hope that each of you, who have not already done so, will invest the time and energy to read some of her writings - with an open mind. We, in this country particularly have come to

492

believe that "government" has far greater responsibilities and powers than did Ayn Rand and it could be interesting for you to consider the alternative to the present parent/child relationship between those having the right to vote and those elected and appointed.

My definition of the appropriate and best objective for those believing they influence the course of economies is one of providing an environment wherein those who are the most productive will reap the greatest personal benefit. It's that simple. Those who have been prepared to make the greatest contribution to the system by creating the most wealth should be in a position of being able to reap the greatest personal benefit. All of you here tonight, by virtue of the education available to you, are privileged to be in the process of wealth preparation if so motivated. I only hope for you that you will find yourself governed by those believing in the benefit of wealth creation rather than wealth re-distribution.

One of the realities of political power is that the less educated the population the greater will be the centralization of power with lessened personal freedom as a result. Therefore, the furthering of other than trade school education is a risk for those governing.

Recently in Australia I agreed to become involved in the development of a commercial, for profit, university to be located in a developing Southeast Asian country. The university will be "on-line", via satellite, with Australian universities and will grant degrees which will be acceptable in Australia as being the equivalent to Australian located university degrees. Another group tried to obtain construction permits for a university in the same area but were not able to obtain them due to their site selection being difficult for the army to isolate should it ever be thought necessary. The lesson to be learned is that governments want education for their youth educated but also fear the educated youth as being impatient for change.

It is the prospect of uncontrolled change which is that which those in power fear the most.

Now we come to the definition of entrepreneurship. Entrepreneurship is a word which most people have trouble spelling and with which many have fallen in love with and use to describe a broad range of people and characteristics. Jack Kemp used to run around to meetings of businesspeople and campuses noting cutely that the original French term meant undertaker, one who undertakes, not a mortician - forgetting that many undertakers are, indeed, entrepreneurs. Using the undertaker definition almost anyone who gets up in the morning could be described as an entrepreneur. One even sometimes hears about those in government, academia or some other bureaucracy, described as being entrepreneurs. There are even those who describe employed senior executives of major publicly traded companies as entrepreneurs.

For the purpose of this talk, I will use the term entrepreneur to identify an individual who has an active involvement in the creation and possibly management of a commercial enterprise. In other words, one who starts with an idea and who somehow gathers the resources, including capital, necessary to start a business which employs people.

There are those of us who believe there are but three kinds of people in the whole world, regardless of location, nationality, sex or religion. These three types of people are; those who are unemployed, those who are employed and those who employ. It is the employers, many of whom are entrepreneurs or "business-founding-employers", who are in a position of wielding the greatest power and making the greatest societal contributions and being able to be the greatest force for change of the three types of people.

It is these business-founding employers who are both revered and feared by the people and those governing. The more successful the entrepreneurs become the greater the reverence and fear generated.

What are the characteristics of successful entrepreneurs? Note that I stipulated successful entrepreneurs as it is only successful entrepreneurs one can study and survey as unsuccessful entrepreneurs are or become; unemployed, employed, consultants or self-proclaimed experts on the subject of entrepreneurial characteristics.

First of all, successful entrepreneurs are almost always people who enjoy excellent health and who also have a higher energy level than their chronological peer group. Boone Pickens, the entrepreneurial CEO of Mesa Petroleum, who once, when the share price of his Mesa was higher than is now the case, did a lot of campus lecturing, advised university students who wanted to own their own businesses "don't smoke", which though in this state may be a bit of heresy, is probably good advice for those who will be putting their minds and bodies under greater than normal future stress.

Successful entrepreneurs are usually driven to prove something. The something can be that they are able to do that which they have been told can't be done. They want to prove something to their father if they are female and to their mother if they are male and/or to a previous boss or group of associates. Strive and quest are good terms to use in describing the actions of entrepreneurs.

Successful entrepreneurs are not money driven. They are achievement driven. They know, or at least believe, that wealth will result from the achievement of their objectives.

Frequently successful entrepreneurs are those who, as children, thought of themselves as being different. By different I mean, smaller, fatter, uglier, smarter, something which made them believe they were different from their contemporaries. In school the successful entrepreneur was more likely to have engaged in field and track, swimming, tennis. skiing, wrestling - all individual sports where the player was in control to a greater extent than in team sports. In the cases of team sports the successful entrepreneur was frequently the team a manager.

I believe that those having entrepreneurial tendencies are identifiable at an early age and that through profit-oriented education relevant experience and necessary skills can be conveyed. Most successful entrepreneurs had obs before they were 12 years old and a recent study conducted by the U.S. Trust indicated that 46% of entrepreneurs having created companies earning more than $6.0 million annually did not complete college.

As one who earned his high school diploma by giving a graduation address, the same way I earned my MBA and who also earned a college equivalency ranking in the Marine Corps testing and training process, I understand the problems of those who have difficulty as young people in finding education relevant to their needs. It took me 40 years before I reached the understanding that education is and was the key to easier and faster achievement. There really isn't a need to re-invent the wheel or make the same mistakes as have wasted the time and other resources of those treading a similar path.

Educating those having entrepreneurial tendencies is particularly challenging as one of the characteristics present in entrepreneurs in a distrust bordering on contempt for conventional authority figures. The challenge for the educators is how to make that which they are selling obviously relevant to the needs and desires of future entrepreneurs.

UNC students are fortunate in that Professor Rollie Tillman, professor of marketing and the Chairman of the Kenan Institute of Private Enterprise, knows as much about successful entrepreneurs as anyone in the country. The Kenan Institute, the beneficiary of Frank Kenan's vision and generosity, Frank himself being a remarkably successful entrepreneur, is the home of the Entrepreneur of the Year Award Hall of Fame. Rollie and the Kenan Institute have been involved in the Entrepreneur of the Year Award program since the program's inception.

Thus far I've touched upon the justification for government and something about those courageous, creative, resourceful benefactors of society known as entrepreneurs but have not linked the verbiage to The Importance Of Entrepreneurship In Global Finance, the assigned title of this talk.

Why are successful entrepreneurs operating in one country important to those of us living in other countries? Because we have, due to the world of instantaneous communications in which we find ourselves aware of the success and failure of companies and countries. Because it is the presence and effective functioning of entrepreneurs which create commercial activity permitting the expansion of trade. Because it is impossible for there to be a successful entrepreneur without the business created by the entrepreneur benefitting others in the community. The benefit takes the form of employment, purchases, fee and tax payments and the creation and transfer of skills.

Ted Turner's CNN is perhaps the world's most important information provider and opinion influencer. CNN and other international information providers, especially television, create economic wants, as does the world's most watched program source - MTV. These economic wants are likely to result in frustration for most of the viewers. In the days when I was financing the first television station in the Arabian Gulf, in Bahrain, Hawaii Five-O was the world's most watched tv show, probably because it was fast paced, simplistic, multi-racial and very American lifestyle focussed.

Incidentally, it was much easier for the South African government to maintain a status quo before the introduction of television. Once those living in Soweto were able to see for themselves how much better the lifestyle was in areas unburdened by apartheid change was inevitable.

Entrepreneurs cause change and change is frightening to many of those in a position of being the "haves".

Entrepreneurs are encouraged by the knowledge of other entrepreneurs succeeding.

Entrepreneurs get ideas for businesses through an awareness of that

496

which is being tried and is working elsewhere. Communication makes it all happen faster and perhaps more predictably.

Change is the result of pressure. Change is the cause of progress. From destruction comes progress. Think of the wonder city which Kobe will become 3 years after the terribly destructive earthquake and the amounts of money which are going to be earned in the rebuilding of the city.

THE ENTREPRENEUR'S NEED TO BE TOUGH

For presentation to the Young Entrepreneur Organization in conjunction with the Association of Collegiate Entrepreneurs 10th annual conference.

We all like to be liked. We all prefer to be respected than feared. We all wish to be thought of fondly by those for whom we have assumed responsibility - whether or not they understand our assumption of responsibility for, at least, a part of their lives and well being.

Who are those for whom employers are responsible other than their employees? And as many of you already know, I believe there are only 3 types of people in all of the world - employers, employees and unemployed. Well, they include a lot of people such as; the owners and employees of vendors, customers, lenders, investors and family members.

Now, please understand this is not a presentation of stakeholder versus stockholder in terms of the obligations of the entrepreneur or the Directors. I firmly believe that company Directors have but a single master and that master be the owners of the business. This is not to say that the best interest of the owners of a business are always or perhaps even ever in conflict with other affected by the business. Indeed, much as it is beneficial to be honest and/or (the ever present cynic in me again emerges) have the reputation for honesty, it is usually good business to be a "good business" in social terms. The distinction I draw is simply one of motivation, not result. The obligation of the business owner is to succeed.

Let me say that again - The obligation of the business owner is to succeed - it is an obligation as the failure of a business is so disruptive and harmful to so many people other than the business owner.

It's very much the same as it being impossible for an entrepreneur to succeed and become wealthy in the process without benefiting the immediate community and frequently an extended community.

The problem I wish to explore with you today is the conflict between being nice or thought of as being nice and being effective in terms of the primary obligation to succeed.

Very quickly, in a logical extension of the dilemma, one reaches similar issues as those relating to euthanasia. Is Dr. Kervorkian and those who will follow him nice, effective or both. Putting the burden of religion inspired thinking aside, the patients despatched prematurely certainly think the good doctor is nice and their painless and sought for departure is testament to his efficacy.

Please understand that I understand the pain of having to cause pain. Not one of us would not go to almost any length not to have to break someone's rice bowl by depriving them of a living. There is little in running a business less pleasant than having to terminate an employee, especially in an environment where the employer knows the difficulty which will be experienced by the employee as a result of the termination.

No one is so tough or insensitive as to be unaffected by having to close a plant or office, abandon a project, or take an action which forces the irrefutable and non-recovery recognition of a loss. One's ego is damaged and one's purse is perceived to be lighter. Of course, actually the loss occurred a long time before being recognized and could have been minimized had the actions been taken when the loss was first knowable.

Triage is the only means of allocating resources which is societally positive as it awards that which is necessary for survival to those who are capable of surviving. One of the reasons why our education system is other than that which we'd all wish for is the fact that the major portion of resources are allocated to the students least capable of making a social contribution at the expense of those most capable of helping us all. In designing curriculum to meet the needs of the student of less than average ability we are constantly reducing the expectation level and therefore performance level of the class. Only in competitive athletics does one find a true meritocracy and effective triage being practiced in that those who are most likely to assist in the win are accorded the greatest allocation and those least likely to be useful are dispensed with. Un-nice? Sure. Tough and effective? Yes.

I have started, owned and managed some fair sized businesses. I do not currently own or manage a substantial business. Today I assist by consulting to and with owners and managers of both privately owned and publicly traded companies. I find that whereas I was myself but a fair manager, and there are those who would question that laudatory a description, I am a great consultant. Why because I've seen the mistakes made in so many other companies and have made so many of them myself. However, as a consultant, unburdened with the ego of creation or assignment to implement, I have no emotional or psychological reasons not to become immediately aware of those same problems and opportunities in a client's company. I am so very experienced in terms of the mistakes I've made that I changed the name of Arthur Lipper Corporation in 1989, after having to sell Venture magazine, to DAIS-NAID which is an acronym for Do As I Say- Not As I Did.

I promise you it is much easier for you as it is for me to walk through someone else's business and know immediately where the problems are or will be and also know what has to be done than it is to do the same thing in your own business. It is this advantage of experience and detachment which, in part is responsible for the success of The Executive Committee or TEC Group operation.

One of my problems in running businesses was that I wasn't tough enough. I talked tough. I gave every outward sign of being tough. But, in the end, I delegated the tough jobs and delayed taking corrective action because it was easier and I wanted to be liked and thought of as nice. T'was a mistake.

Who and how to be tough with is the question business owners must ask and answer.

To start, and perhaps end, with one must be tough with one's self. One must force one's self to address the hardest of issues first as well as last. My wife and partner for more than 30 years is very good at making me address the issues I'd rather postpone and delay addressing. Much as in my consulting role where I can force attention and demand focus she does the same thing. My response is to growl at her and then to do as she suggests. I believe that we all can use a trusted consultant, one who shares our objectives but who is able to step back and be objective in the prioritization process. No one says it's easy to face difficult, embarrassing or other situations where the entrepreneur cannot predict or control the outcome. We all know that as entrepreneurs we have a need to be in control and the situations which tend to be put aside are those which relate to matters over which we have the least amount of control.

We also have an obligation to be tough with our employees and associates. It is simply unfair, let alone unproductive, for us not to insist that the least effective employees either increase in productivity or be replaced. Who is it unfair to? It is unfair to our best and most effective employees as well as to the individual in need of improving their performance. Being demanding as an employer is part of the job of being an employer as if the company fails or even fails to become as important as it could have become then you are short changing all involved and to whom you have a responsibility.

Business owners, especially those who start businesses are burdened with responsibility to a broad constituency including employees, customers, suppliers, lenders and the community at large. Responsibility is a bore - but it goes with the territory.

Business owners must be tough with suppliers as a vendor's failure to perform jeopardizes the performance of the business owner and therefore everyone else involved in the food chain - to segue a plug for my last book Thriving Up and Down The Free Market Food Chain - The Unrestrained Observations and Advice of a Business Darwinist. Incidentally, the title was conceived by HarperBusiness. All I did was supply 90,000 words to match the title. Suppliers must be made to understand and acknowledge that they have a responsibility and that they will be held accountable. They also must be allowed to earn a profit sufficient to provide an incentive. It does no good to drive the price paid down to a level where the supplier really isn't on your team.

Entrepreneurs also have to be tough with their customers. This toughness can take the form of making the customer understand that the entrepreneur is dependant upon the customer's integrity and growth. Goods and services must be paid for as agreed. That is not to say that terms of payment must be cash on or before delivery. It is to say that customers must know the cause and effect of their not adhering to that which had been agreed. Whether it be in the form of charging a high level of interest or in factoring the accounts receivable or taking some other previously discussed and agreed action in the event of non-payment the customer must know in advance that something is going to happen automatically, without further discussion, in the event of their non-performance. If the entrepreneur is to provide the best value possible to the customer then the entrepreneur must rely on a specific result in calculating the charge and basis for service. The unreliable customer is simply creating a situation where he or she must be charged more to factor into the equation the lack of reliability.

500

Similarly, business owners should be tough with the professionals serving them, especially the lawyers and accountants. I am currently involved with a company which audits legal fee invoices and which will, I trust, evolve into a business which establishes legal fee limits, especially for the property and casualty insurance company industry. Again, especially due to the natural closeness of relationship existing between client and professional, the services of a third party, not directly involved in the process can be helpful in guiding the entrepreneur as to fairness of billing, necessity of work and effectiveness of service of the professionals. It is my experience that simply in asking for a hourly breakdown of fees that a 15% to 25% adjustment results.

And now comes the toughest decision for an entrepreneur of all - when and how to sell the business. I say when and how because most of us who have started and owned businesses are not going to go public and we do reach a point where we decide that it really isn't a lot of fun anymore or that we don't want to have the business taken over by our kids or their spouses. But, of course, the threshold issue is do we really WANT to sell? Sure, if the business has been successful, we'll end up with a lot of money. But will the money be as satisfying as the power and control and other satisfactions and fulfillments which come form owning and running a business? Assuming that we've reached a decision to sell then what to do and how best to do it? One of two ways are normal directly and personally or through an agent. If through an agent then the same toughness as is necessary to use effectively any other professional is required. If the entrepreneur makes, what I believe to be a mistake, and tries to market the business himself then a toughness or resolve to carry through the process is necessary. Once it becomes known that a business is for sale, even only, the owner will believe - at first - to a close knit group, the business will suffer. There is a far greater likelihood of it becoming known that the business is for sale if the owner attempts to handle the matter personally as opposed to using an agent. I believe that entrepreneurs make a mistake in not selling their businesses sooner than they do. I know that I made that mistake. The entrepreneur's greatest skill is frequently in causing change and therefore something to happen, not necessarily in managing a process. The greatest return in terms of time effort and exposure to risk is frequently earned by selling a business before it become mature and when potential buyers have reason to believe they can do a better job of exploiting the earlier efforts of the entrepreneur then can the entrepreneur.

In the end, and we are at the end of the talk, I urge entrepreneurs to accept that fact that they have an obligation to themselves and those who depend upon them to forsake the human and natural desire to be liked and to be tough. Being tough doesn't have to mean being nasty or brutal. The Christs, Gandhis and Mother Teresas of the world were and are tough. You can be too and all will benefit.

THE YOUNG ENTREPRENEUR'S ATTRACTION TO INTERNATIONAL BUSINESS

For presentation to the: Association of Collegiate Entrepreneurs 10th annual conference - New York City United Nations Delegates Dining Room

"Go abroad young person" is the current, politically correct, advice offered replacing the traditional American "Go West Young Man" recommendation of Horace Greenly in the 1800's. My advice to you, as one who prides himself on the economical use of the language, is simply to "GO WEST - But don't Stop at the water". Actually the title for this talk could have been Oceans Are Only Hours.

There are lots of reasons why many of us have found international business attractive.

For starters, we are instant experts once in a foreign land or, for that matter, when we are more than 50 miles from our home or more simply away from those who know more than we do or who know us. Being thought of as an expert is useful in business, especially a service business as one who is an expert can charge more than one who is dealing in a commodity, which are usually subject to more intense price competition.

Also it is fun to be able to have the respect resulting from the perception of expertise and such respect can be used advantageously. Therefore, the entrepreneur should present and package himself authoritatively. Your job is not to become a friend with those with whom you are dealing. Your job is to create business with those who will pay their bills or meet their delivery commitments and who may become friends.

Networking, which you are all already pretty good at, is the key to success in foreign lands. Getting to know targeted contacts quickly is not difficult for a well spoken foreigner. If you are well introduced it is even easier to get to know people. Introductions not only speed the process of creating transactions but also permit more advantageous

502

pricing, whether buying or selling. The reason it is better to make contact quickly is just being away from your business is expensive and has risks associated with the absence.

When I first established myself as a stock broker with European institutions I did so based upon a letter of introduction from a satisfied and supportive client, the Vice President in charge of securities research at the Morgan Guaranty bank. You too can obtain, simply by asking, letters of introduction from your bank to the bank's foreign correspondent banks if your bank has a relationship with you. The letter does not have to say that you are wealthy or successful. All it has to indicate is that you are responsible as far as the experience you have had with the bank. Similarly, the commercial attache at the country's embassy in Washington or the country's consul in many large cities will also provide introductions both to government offices as well as to individuals and companies. The point is to have introductions on landing so that you hit the ground running. Even better would be to have had communication with those you'd like to meet prior to your leaving America. Also, and perhaps this is most important, you should never leave a meeting with someone you have not met before without gaining at least one name and possibly an introduction to another person in the country who might be of assistance to you.

Ok. Now you know a few people. They like you (it appears to you) and they may buy whatever it is that you are selling. Incidentally, you may be buying in which case the leverage is much more on your side and you do not need to have the same concerns - though you will have others and some of the principles are the same. The next step is to close - you are not there as a tourist - you are there to do business. For many years, I used to go to Europe every Sunday night, 30 plus weeks a year - and most frequently never saw more than the airport, the city from the window of a car, my hotel or apartment, my office, clients offices, a few restaurants and then, the city from a car window, an airport, etc. You are there to do business.

It's fine to be a tourist but do it when you can afford the luxury of time to do it right. What about "smelling the roses"? Well, I just do not know any truly successful "well balanced" entrepreneurs. I am not suggesting to you that you make a decision to become anal compulsive. You either are or you are not. I, obviously am. I am saying that the only truly successful entrepreneurs I know or have known of have a level of passion for their business which overrides other considerations in their lives. It may be good or it may be bad - but it is the case. Being a business founding employer isn't for everyone. Indeed, the game of life and business obviously is structured so that there are fewer employers than employees.

Closing a transaction is easy. Closing a transaction which will predictably produce a profit is more challenging.

Remember, you are not dealing in a country where the laws and business customs are familiar to you. You are dealing in a country where there are many disadvantages to your doing business.

The laws and practice of commercial dispute resolution, if there are any, almost always favor the local party. When a television station I had financed in Bahrain in the early 1970's was expropriated by the government I found that I could sue, but only after posting 7% of the amount claimed - and that was in a case against the government. I am still trying to collect money in Indonesia, after almost 20 years, as my partner there decided that on his investing more money in the business we both had financed there that he immediately had the right to all the shares of the business. I participated, as the General Partner, of an oil drilling partnership which found a vast amount of oil in the Sinai, in 4 years of arbitration and litigation with the Government of Israel, eventually having to settle a $300 million claim for $10 million as the limited partners lost their taste for paying legal fees, which were more than $3.0 million.

And now the really hard question. Incidentally, I have posed this question to my entrepreneurship academic and YEO friends here seeking help in answering the question - and have received none. The question is "how should an American entrepreneur react to the vastly different cultural and ethical issues which arise in doing business in jurisdictions other than America?".

Yes, I am focusing on bribery as relating to government officials, purchasing agents, company executives, etc. Yes, I am stating that bribery is a way of life and business in many countries, especially those new to free enterprise. I suggest to you there isn't an oil or mineral producing country where government allocations are required where "deals" are not made. I suggest to you that it requires a suitcase full of cash to expedite the unloading of cargo from a ship in Shanghai. I suggest to you that "business agents and representatives" are used by most American companies in doing business abroad as the companies are preclude by the Foreign Corrupt Practices Act from doing that which is necessary to do the business - and they want to do the business.

I posed this dilemma to my friend, partner and wife of more than 30 years, the lovely Anni - who is also, as I noted in a talk to the YEO group yesterday, my in house consultant. Anni suggested that perhaps this generation of young American entrepreneurs could be the first to do business honestly in these areas. I think not as the harsh reality is that they won't do the business if they insist on imposing their American Judeo-Christian values on people and situations having different backgrounds and values.

I do not believe that it constructive that we be judgmental and do not believe that we should preach or try to change other societies. It is all well and good to be antipathetic to apartheid and especially easy for Americans to favor its abolishment - but what about the economic consequence for all South Africans which will inevitably result from the imposition of one man, one vote democracy? I do believe that we can be true to our own ideals and beliefs and elect not to do business in a manner which if later disclosed would be embarrassing. For the record, I have been able to do business in a lot of strange and wonderfully interesting areas without ever paying or authorizing the payment of a bribe. I've just done a lot less business in those areas and businesses than competitors investing the same energy and talent in also being there have done. this is not to say that I am a better person than anyone else. It is to say that I've been fortunate enough never to have had to business so badly as to have to do business on other than my terms.

Each of you will have to reach you own decision as to what is right for you. All I am doing is alerting you to the prospect of having to reach a decision and therefore to perhaps be better prepared to make the decision you will be happy with for a longer period of time than might otherwise be the case.

Thanks to overnight couriers services, the facsimile and a general improvement in communications doing business internationally is much easier now than ever before. I'll bet that not one of the students here have ever used a telex machine or Petersen Code book or had to wait 36 or even 12 hours for a voice circuit. Now with improved communications and communications is the key, doing business in most countries is not too different from doing business in Mississippi - and frequently more satisfactory in many respects.

Language is the most basis form of communication and the American educational system is woefully deficient in language instruction - along with its other deficiencies. If you are interested in doing business abroad make the investment in learning the language of the people you are dealing with. Sure, you can force them to deal in English but you will never achieve the level of trust, comfort and intimacy you desire unless you speak their language. Make the investment of effort necessary as if you do not feel the investment worthwhile in terms of the potential profit you expect from the area then you probably should invest the energy elsewhere.

Entrepreneurs are the agents of change. Entrepreneurs operating internationally have an opportunity to help those they are dealing with expand their horizons and achieve mutual enrichment.

I wish each of you well in your quest for profit, however defined, and hope that you will find it good business, as I have, to help others earn profit through your efforts. And please remember that even more so in doing business internationally than domestically, preparation is the key to success. Prepare intelligently and you will succeed.

INVESTING IN SMALL CAP STOCKS

Investing in companies having a smaller capitalization is sufficiently similar to investing in private companies as to provide me with an authority I might not otherwise be perceived to possess and thus this presentation.

The first issue in addressing the subject is one of defining small cap. I am currently involved in a neural network artificial intelligence computer project in which a computer program ranks for year ahead, total return, future performance of some 2,000 stocks. In that project we define small cap as being stocks with an equity base of $200 million or less.

I suspect that stocks having a $200 million market value are still considerably larger companies than most of you are interested in and that you are really most interested in companies much closer to the tips of the branches of the food chain tree - in other words you want to sniff, taste, nibble on and perhaps devour and become enriched by identifying the pre-leaf buds.

Let's remember that capital is similar to the necessary sunlight in the photosynthesis process as far as the high potential buds are concerned as they cannot and will not develop without the availability of capital.

506

In private company investing the investor has the ability to negotiate and therefore create value directly with the entrepreneur. In investing in companies which are already publicly traded the market or more probably those "making the market" have established the current value and the investor is only left with a binary, yes or no, decision to make.

The question we are faced with then in regard to a small cap stock we are considering is simply one of is this a stock I should buy or sell. If you do not already own the stock (and the stock is borrowable) there is the added possibility of selling the little beast short. Shorting stocks, the inverse of buying stocks, is or can be a highly speculative activity, but one which can be most rewarding in the case of stocks selling at levels which are disproportionate to the likely potential for achieving significant earnings in the foreseeable future. I am not one who believes that shorting stocks is un-American and am one who believes that most of life can be described in terms of it being an arbitrage or series of trade-offs.

There are a great many disadvantages facing the investor attracted to small cap stocks. These disadvantages are a function of the market for the stock being naturally thin as there isn't that much stock existing. Being thin, as the market makers in the stock do not usually have the luxury of having a meaningful size bid and offer to trade off of, means that the spread between the bid and the offer, in percentage terms, especially in lower priced issues, can be significant. The market for a stock being thin also means that one can't expect to do a serious amount of business at the same price unless the investor is taking actions contra to the way the market makers see the trend. In other words, the investor will only be able to buy a substantial amount of stock when the market makers predict the market will decline. Similarly the ability to sell a substantial amount of stock on the quoted bid is dependent upon the market maker believing the stock will increase in price after investors stops selling. It is, however, the breadth of the spread which adversely impacts the investment performance of the active investor in small cap stocks.

Clearly, the spread and thinness of the market are not nearly as important a consideration for the investor making a long term commitment as they are for short term speculators.

SCOPE is the first consideration in deciding to invest in either a private company or small cap stock. Will the appreciation be really dramatic if most, or even all, of the good things predicted by either the broker or the company's management come to pass? I cannot envision a sophisticated investor accepting the relative illiquidity of a serious sized position in a small cap stock unless the investor believed the stock would at least double in a three year period - without an expansion in price/earnings ratio. The win has to be big enough to justify the position. In Venture's Financing and Investing In Private Companies I recommend to readers that they only invest in private companies that if as successful as anticipated by the entrepreneur that the benefits of the investment to the investor will be such as to enable the investor to change his life style. It is really a matter if one is hoping to hit singles or home runs. The incidence of home runs is far smaller than that of singles - and I believe that for most equity investors - as opposed to venture lenders, only the possibility of hitting home runs justifies the permitting of someone else's enterprise taking control of the investor's capital.

The decision re scope has to do with not only projected earnings growth but the probability of the earnings growth being maintained. The investor must have a view as to the probable profit margins the company will enjoy two to three years out as if the profit margins are shrinking, even if the absolute earnings are increasing, there is likely to be a reduction in the price earnings ratio the market applies to the higher earnings and thus there may not be much, if any, profit for the investor even though the company is earning more money.

I believe that profit margin analysis is a very important part of determining the relative attraction of all stocks. There is absolutely no reason for investors to invest in companies for which a commodity-type of product or service pricing is likely to become necessary. The only reason to invest in technology-based businesses, regardless of capitalization, is the fact that intellectual property ownership allows non-commodity or competitive pricing of products. Intelligent investors must have a view as to the profit margin maintenance characteristics of the companies in which they are invested.

In smaller companies, much as in privately owned companies, the investor is really betting on the management of the company. If the management of a small cap company falters there is less likelihood of a new management or savior coming in to salvage. Those who typically come into troubled smaller companies are more likely to be vulture capitalists in one form or another than in the larger enterprises. Therefore, the investor really has to make a personal assessment of the intelligence, experience, motivation and integrity of the managers of the enterprise. If the investor is not willing to make the effort of attending shareholder meetings or visiting the company then I believe he or she is better advised to invest in small cap stocks through the ever increasing number of mutual funds specializing in such investments.

One rule I have found generally useful, though the few exceptions are like sirens luring those succumbing to their disaster, is NEVER to average down, relative to the market generally or to the specific market segment, or to make follow on investments in small cap or private companies to justify or to protect the original investment. My observation is that it is almost always better to pay more per share in reflection of success of the company than to pay less in the hope that things will get better (or become in the future as good as was originally predicted). For the most part averaging down in smaller cap and privately owned companies simply increases the size of the ultimate loss.

One other thought which is worth considering in terms of investing in small cap companies, though not necessarily in private companies, is that of investing in several companies which will benefit from the same macro factors. The investor must have a view as to the prospects for the industry in which the specific company functions. Therefore, it is possible for the investor to also invest in other, perhaps directly competing companies, in the same industry if a part of the premise for the investment is the growth of the industry as it is frequently most difficult to predict the specific or exclusive winners.

VALUE as a requirement for investment can prevent the investing in stocks which prove to be great investments. However, being value conscious the investor is likely to have a better success rate than will be the case otherwise. Value can be measured in many ways but always, in the end, must relate to earnings. Therefore, one can always, through assuming a predicted level of future earnings present value them back so as to make a comparative investment analysis possible. Also simply using a chart or calculator the earnings growth rate or future level of earnings assumed by a price earnings ratio is determinable on either an absolute or relative (to the market as measured by an index) basis.

Lastly, I urge individual investors to spread the risk and take advantage of diversification as it is unlikely that they will be knowledgeable enough to successfully follow a portfolio management policy of concentration. I believe the individual investor should have about 20 positions as a 5% holding, at cost, seems about right to me. Again in many of my writings I advise those investing in private companies to "sprinkle money amongst talent" and in terms of small cap publicly traded companies that advice also seems to make sense.

Some of small capitalization stocks will provide investors with outstanding returns and some will be disasters. I once created a sign that I hung over my desk which read "Capital Punishment Is A Result of Inadequate Research" - which it is and is therefore frequently avoidable.

SPLITTING UP - WHO GETS THE BUSINESS?
San Diego Business Journal

Query: My husband and I own a small business together, and we are getting a divorce. Can I force him to sell or buy me out if he doesn't want to?

Response: The question indicates a lack of planning on the part of both parties, not only in terms of divorce but also regarding estate planning.

In direct response to the question - you're stuck. An owner of a business cannot force another owner of the business to do anything unless there is a shareholder agreement or a court so orders.

Sure you can be obstinate and make a nuisance of yourself in the hope that your husband will buy you out - but at what price and on what terms?. You can offer to buy him out - but at what price and on what terms. First of all, you do not want to pay a "fair" price as you really wish to pay less than a fair price as what is the advantage to you to pay the same fair price that a non-involved, but equally well informed, independent buyer would pay?

There are lots of questions which have to be answered prior to rendering valid advice. Whose business was it really? Who had the passion for the business - you or your husband? Why might you want the business? Is it spite or profit? Who made the greatest contribution to the business? Who is more likely to make the business a success without the other? Do you really want the business to become your life, probably to the exclusion of attracting and accommodating another husband? How capital intensive is the business? Will you be able to finance it alone? Will customers and suppliers deal with you as readily, or perhaps more so, than with your husband?

Assuming the business is owned equally by you and your husband, and there should have been a buy/sell agreement in place as there should be in an any partnership relationship, you can propose to your husband that you and he enter into a buy/sell agreement. In such an agreement either of you may, at anytime, including immediately after the agreement is entered into, unless otherwise agreed, inform the other of the price and terms of payment which the party proposing the transaction is either willing to pay or accept. For instance, you could state that you are willing to pay $300,000 in cash for his half of the business and that you are also willing to sell your half for the same amount. By virtue of the terms of the buy/sell agreement the party receiving the proposal has a stipulated period of time in which to respond - but respond, either way, he must.

I have always liked the open buy/sell approach between parties who have an ability to be equally knowledgeable as opposed to trying to fix a formula relating to revenues or profits or book value. Businesses can be worth more than formulas to certain people at certain times and why create formulas which are artificial or subject to question as to their applicability?

My feeling is that the business should go to the person most likely to make it successful and that party should be willing to pay a premium to gain full ownership. Incidentally, you could also propose paying $30,000 initially and either a fixed amount periodically or a percentage of revenues, say 10%, for a set period of time or until $300,000 was paid. There are lots of approaches to buying a business which can be applied but just remember that in making the bid you can never be sure that your husband will not say "ok, I'll buy your shares on the same basis as you are bidding for mine" and that is why the approach is fair and keeps each of the parties honest.

Now what happens if he doesn't agree and you are stuck in the position of owning a part of a business which he is running and has no obligation to buy you out. This, incidentally, is the dumb position a lot of people who invest is privately owned companies find themselves in. Much will depend upon the state of incorporation and that state's laws as well as the language of the charter and by-laws of the business itself in terms of what rights you have. As this is such a normal situation your lawyer, and his, will be experienced and able to advise you.

The problem is that businesses are fragile, workers side-taking and both customers and suppliers requiring stability and reliability. Your causing the sort of problems you believe you are capable or doing may not be in your best interest - and could subject you to personal liability.

Perhaps it is the male chauvinist in me, but in most cases I believe it better for the husband to carry on the business - unless the woman is the more capable and motivated. If the husband does carry on the business then it should be possible to structure a pay-out or exchange of common shares for preferred shares which can be or must be redeemed as agreed. The exchanging of shares for a revenue interest, which itself can be bought out in the future, is that which makes the most sense to me. After all, the spouse continuing the business doesn't want to share decision making though they may be willing to share revenues. The worst thing for you to do is to make an agreement which contemplates the sharing of profit as profit, especially in a privately owned business, is always subject to definition and "management" by management.

I am sorry that your personal relationship hasn't been successful and hope that one disappointment does not cause the destruction of a successful business as successful businesses are important to more than just the owners.

PLANNING - THAT WHICH MANY ENTREPRENEURS DO LEAST WELL - AND FREQUENTLY NEED THE MOST.
San Diego Business Journal

Query: As a business owner, I always seem to be putting out fires instead of planning for the future. Is this a common problem, or am I just poorly organized?

Response: Two of the descriptions re entrepreneurial planning, itself possibly an oxymoron, are that: 1) an entrepreneur's planning consists of determining where to go for lunch and who's going to pick up the check and 2) Ready, Fire, Aim.

Entrepreneurs, especially those who have founded businesses as opposed to buying them, are notoriously poor planners. In part this is because the entrepreneur is, and knows that he or she is, highly intuitive. Also the entrepreneur "knows" (as opposed to believes) that he or she can solve problems as they arise.

Entrepreneurs hate doing business plans. I believe this is because the committing to paper of a plan is felt to be restricting and somehow limits the entrepreneur's freedom to wing it.

One of the reasons why there are so many successful partnerships is that typically the entrepreneur having the marketing and creation skills is allowed to be successful by having a partner whose skills are in administration and planning. This phenomena is reflected in the "Larry and Barry" characters I used for years in my Venture magazine Chairman's Comment column. Larry was the outside partner, the one who "made the rain" and brought in the business. Barry was the Chief Operating Officer who made it all work. Larry borrowed the money and Barry figured out how to pay it back. Larry made the promises to the customers and Barry made sure Larry's promises were kept - if keep-able.

I do not know many truly successful and yet well balanced entrepreneurs. Most successful entrepreneurs are compulsive in the extreme. Many successful entrepreneurs need to have people on whom they can rely and who they trust to keep them organized.

The benefits of planning can be bought externally from consultants or be provided by those on staff. There may also be better planners available to you than you represent yourself. My suggestion to you, the entrepreneur, is to find such a person, rather than trying to change your habit patterns. Get a partner, promote an employee to be responsible for organizing you, use a computer organizer program. Recognize that you are a talent and need managing much as you are like a missile which needs guidance. Do that which you do best. Don't try to be what you are not.

Entrepreneurs can buy the skills and effort of assistants, administrators and planners pretty cost effectively. However, it doesn't work in reverse, as some of America's largest companies have learned - opportunity conceivers, natural leaders and dedicated doers, otherwise known as entrepreneurs - are not as readily or inexpensively available.

THE STRENGTH OF AMERICA IS THE SIZE OF AMERICA
San Diego Business Journal

Not until one drives across the country, as my wife and I did in moving to California, does one really appreciate the magnitude of the landmass and the potential represented.

The vastness of the country and the ability to support millions of future immigrants is an asset of inestimable importance. In no other developed country does such an asset exist in such abundance.

Having spent much time in southeast Asia and therefore being aware of the availability, importance and potential represented by the Asian human resource pool, I have begun to contemplate the possible means of profiting from what could be a mass migration.

Our country has been built by immigrants and most of us living here have benefitted. Traditionally the immigrant groups have been constructive and have contributed more than they taken once established. Non-constructive immigration occurs when the new arrivals absorb more of the public's capital than they create. That which makes the difference is education and cultural attitude.

It is possible for the country to control the level of immigrant education by edict - and there is a great potential business for a number of companies in providing the required education to prospective immigrants. It is practical, skill or vocational trade related education, which is required. Ideally, the immigrant should arrive in the United States speaking, reading and writing English and having a job skill which is in current demand.

Of course, there would be howls of objections from those claiming to represent those already here who are neither literate nor possessing of skills from which income can legally be derived. The answer could be to offer vocational education to those here who were literate and possibly even those who are illiterate. In our current and predictable society the correlation between literacy and productivity is inescapable and only the productive can prosper. So there are, I believe, a number of great business opportunities present in the offering of education at all levels.

What would be wrong with our government mandating the acceptance of immigrants by job skill classification? Also what would be wrong with only the qualified being admitted? Also why not require the new immigrant to have been here for a proscribed period of time and to have proven his ability to earn a living before admitting his family members? Finally, what would be wrong with permitting immigration on the provision of the immigrant establishing a working residence in areas other than major metropolitan areas? Yes, I am proposing for discussion and consideration, restricting the privilege of immigration to individuals, not families, having the skills and ability to make a contribution and requiring that, for a period of time, they live and work in areas which are not already joking on population and in which there is demand exceeding the supply of social services.

I believe that were our government to truly want to stem the flow of illegal immigrants from Mexico and the Caribbean that we possess the military manpower and equipment necessary to do so. It is the resolve we lack, not the ability.

The prosect of our attracting many millions of desirable immigrants is one of the few positive trends I can see as being likely in the coming years. I can envision whole new cities being developed on parts of the one-third of the nation's land mass currently owned by governmental bodies. America can again be enriched and rejuvenated by foreign born people who choose to live and work her. We can all profit from their success. All we have to do is recruit the right new Americans.

MAKING MONEY IN BED OR IF YOU ARE NOT MAKING MONEY WHILE YOU ARE SLEEPING YOU ARE NOT MAKING SERIOUS MONEY
San Diego Business Journal

The essence of wealth creation is leverage and timing. It is not necessarily the leverage of borrowing money. It is the leverage which comes from having people, money or equipment producing profit for you all of the time, while you are awake and sleeping.

In Venture's Financing and Investing In Private Companies and again in Thriving Up and Down the Free Market Food Chain - The Unrestrained Observations (and Advice) of a Business Darwinist I present the same thought through describing dollars as "green slaves". I observe that the more green slaves you have the less work you have to do yourself. In other words, dollars working - perhaps by producing interest if loaned to a bank in the form of deposits or in the form of dividends if invested in a commercial enterprise, produce a return which permits you to do less work yourself.

Most of us who think that we have businesses or who aspire to be in the position of business ownership, especially service businesses, really do not have businesses at all. Rather we have or wish to have "practices".

The difference between a practice, requiring our personal effort, and a business is that the business can go on longer than we do. If your "business" is not likely to survive your demise then you have a practice - and perhaps would be well advised to consider turning it into a business.

515

The transition of practice to business is a function of lessening the traditional personality reliance on the business founding owner or entrepreneur. To accomplish this feat in a service business requires the delegation of authority which is the single greatest challenge for most entrepreneurs. In a service business the course of action producing the greatest possible return to the creator of the service business is one word. "Franchising" is the word. The key to franchising success is simplicity and discipline of operation. Doing something useful for the ultimate customer, the same way all of the time, is the ideal situation. If there is a great variance in profitability between franchisees in terms of the number of customers served then it's probably not a great franchise idea as there is too much personality (of the franchisee) dependance. The best franchise operations are those where it is not possible to distinguish one franchisee's unit or quality of service from that of another franchisee. For this to be the case the franchise concept has to be both simple and simple to implement. For more information re franchising read The Franchise Advantage, for which I was pleased to provide the Foreword.

Remember, you are only really making money if you have arranged your life and assets in such a manner as you've got something working for you when you're not working.

ON THE SIDE OF THE ANGELS
CAPITAL RIGHTS - INVESTING VERSUS AWARDING

For presentation to the Greater Austin, Texas Chamber of Commerce in association with the SCOR Task Force Conference on Buying and Selling Stock In Small Business Through Small Corporate Offering Registrations
March 29, 1996 - Four Seasons Hotel, Austin, Texas

Four letter words are frequently dramatic and even shocking. Some four letter words follow; love, hate, hope, sell, loss, lose, gain, cash, flow, free, give, take, soon, jobs and SCOR are applicable to the focus of this meeting. In deal-making, however, there is another four letter word which is defining as to that which should be the essence of the relationship between capital provider and capital consumer and that word is FAIR. FAIR could also be an acronym for "For Angel Investors Respect or Reasonableness".

It is my observation, and I have the scars to support the contention, that investing in private companies is highly rewarding in many ways, but not necessarily in achieving the highest financial return consistent with accepting the least risk - and that is really what serious investing is all about.

In terms of investor protection, I do belief that "disclosure cures all". If each of the parties to a transaction have the same knowledge as to relevant facts they can legitimately share or have different conclusions as to future events. This is the basis for securities regulation - creating a level playing field and should not be sacrificed in the cause of financing new enterprises. Being fair to the angel includes providing the angel with the negative information regarding the entrepreneur and the likelihood of the project generating sufficient profits to reasonably create a valuation or other basis of return for the angel commensurate with the capital risk being accepted.

The issue in regard to securities offerings made by smaller companies and, perhaps by definition, therefore involving less sophisticated issuers and buyers of securities, is one of prediction. There is both an angel's need for prediction to provide a rationale for accepting risk, probably disproportionate to the quantum of likely reward, and a capital seeking issuer's issuer's liability-based fear of prediction. I really like the Vancouver Stock Exchange approach to promoter projections, that of escrowing a significant part of the entrepreneur's promotional or founder's stock pending achievement of the projections used to entice investors.

I also believe that entrepreneurs typically deal themselves too generous a slice of the pie. What's wrong with my saying to you "I have a great idea for a business. You put up the money and pay me a fair salary and also pay me 20% of the profits."? By the way, I have a number of really exciting business opportunities which I would share with you on just such a basis. You don't have to let me have any of the stock of the company. You, the angel, can keep all of the shares. Just let me have a wage and 20% of the profit.

Also what's wrong with the entrepreneur making predictions as to future earnings and then being compensated relative to the earnings actually generated? The entrepreneur would receive a premium for exceeding the prediction and a penalty for underachievement - and the investor would have been able to make a more intelligent judgment as to the price earnings or price sales ratio which was present versus alternative competitive opportunities for capital employment which are ever present.

517

There are certain aspects of investing in initial public offerings of broker/dealer underwritten small cap companies which should be considered by those involved in SCOR offering process. These include:

Creating liquidity for the investor by requiring the company issuing the shares to re-purchase them on an agreed basis, probably a ratio to per share book value or per share earnings or revenues, at an agreed time in the future.

Substituting an investor ombudsman-type representative to replace the normal underwriter functions for protecting the interests of purchasers through pricing and requiring investor protection and corporate governance and controls. In self-underwritten offerings some of these investor rights are absent and the investment is more like a gift to the entrepreneur promoting the company. There is nothing wrong with supporting entrepreneurs with gifts but the donor should know that he or she is making a gift and not an investment.

The greatest risk to the investor, other than the company not being successful is one of the company being successful and requiring additional funds - which are provided by more sophisticated investors and therefore on a basis causing the SCOR investor significant dilution. The SCOR investor should have an understood anti-dilution protection.

The provision of corporate information to investors has a purpose of other than allowing investors to have a view as to when to buy or sell the stock of the company providing the information. The other purpose is to allow investors in the company to have a view as to if and when the management of the company should be changed or augmented. Of course, there has to be an effective mechanism in place for change to occur if a sufficient percentage of the owners of a company are dissatisfied with the performance of the managers of an investor financed enterprise. One useful mechanism for investors to negotiate is a procedure where with the failure of the managers of a business to perform as promised the voice, in the form of vote, of the investors increase relative to that of management.

The ever present consciousness of the value of a company can be achieved by an investors as simple as by only thinking of the company in terms of its enterprise valuation (as opposed to share price) as determined by multiplying the number of shares outstanding by the price of the stock plus all debt. To have a basis for value investing the investor should have a current awareness of the same enterprise valuation for competing companies and/or for alternative investing opportunities.

SCOR offering investors should balance their investment portfolio with other investments in larger companies. I cannot see the rationale for an investor only investing in SCOR offered companies. Diversification is the only real protection an individual investor has as the likelihood of the investor zeroing in on winning investments would be counter to the experience of most investors.

The historical record of the broker/dealer underwriter in terms of their value recognition and presentation is absent in the case of SCOR offerings. Perhaps some level or form of investment industry professional ranking or vetting might be developed for the benefit of investors.

What's the upside of investing in SCOR offerings? For whom is the correct response.

The entrepreneur may become financed so that he is in a position to go forward to, predictably, a point of requiring more funds. There is a possible entrepreneurial enrichment as a result of the closing of an offering.

The professionals, lawyers and accountants, will be able to sell some time and service.

The investor may be able to feel good about his having helped in the creation or early stage development of an enterprise - and that is indeed a good feeling.

The community will be enriched as the entrepreneur will be able to hire people and do all of the positive things which commercial activity requires.

The making use of electronic distribution through Internet and other means of investment related information is a logical development and good thing. The sacrifice of investor protection is not a good thing. It isn't necessary for investor rights to be sacrificed by virtue of the means of communications utilized to deliver data.

Those of us involved in assisting smaller enterprises can make a contribution by prompting realistic profit projections and basing finance structures on results which do not require that everything goes according to plan. We have to continually hope for the best and plan for the worst.

I used to keep a sign on my wall which read "Capital Punishment Is A result of Inadequate Research". I also had a sign which read "No. Is a complete sentence."

Although I support all procedures which result in investors being positioned to benefit from the informed and intelligent acceptance of risk, especially in risk which furthers entrepreneurial activity, I know that programs which, on balance, in the aggregate, produce more loss than gain for the investor should not survive or succeed.

Of course, it is easy to demonstrate that customer losing propositions can and do succeed witness the predictability of continuing prosperity of Las Vegas, Atlantic City, race tracks, Internet gaming and other forums where P. T. Barnum's observation of "there being a sucker born every minute" is repeatedly proven. Perhaps the $20.00 I am prepared to, and do, lose in the slot machines when I change planes in Las Vegas is similar to placing bets on appealing entrepreneurs in their efforts to launch fledgling enterprises. There are some winners. The bell does go off every now and then announcing a slot machine has paid off big. Someone has to win. Why can't it be me? Is allowing "the wish to become the parent of the thought" really so bad - as long as one can afford the loss?

All I am really trying to impart is a hope that investors, without having the benefit of the assistance of professional advisors and liability bearing financial intermediaries, will read and consider carefully self underwriting issuer SCOR offering documents - recognizing that Murphy's Law of "what can go wrong, will go wrong" is alive and well.

Also you should all know that some years ago I thought it only fair to rename Arthur Lipper Corporation DAIS-NAID, Inc. This decision was reached after my disastrous financial, but otherwise wonderfully fulfilling and rewarding, tuitional experience of owning Venture Magazine. DAIS-NAID Inc. is an acronym for Do As I Say - Not As I Did. I really do know what investors should do. However, being human and subject to all of the same emotional pressures and psychological needs as others fortunate enough to have the ability to invest, I tend to make many of the mistakes about which I warn readers and audiences. I just hope that enough angels will have a sufficiently positive experience to keep them in the game as we, as a nation, depend upon entrepreneurs for our innovation and growth - and therefore ultimate financial stability and security.

ANGEL CAPITAL - THE NECESSARY INGREDIENT

Draft article for the: *St. Louis Small Business Monthly*, February 21, 1996

The creation of an enterprise requires the identification, collection and application of many assets, including monetary capital. The assets which are necessary, in addition to money, are: the energy, inspiration and dedication of one or more entrepreneurs, the individual or collective skill and experience of those assuming the responsibility of managing the business and a well conceived plan for creating revenue which will generate positive cash flow and profit before the initial capital is depleted.

In the case of most new businesses the amount of money necessary to achieve a level of sustained profit is more than those conceiving of the business can provide from their own resources, including that which they can obtain from sources not having the earning of extraordinary, risk related, returns as their primary objective, namely; family and friends.

It is the angels of America, those; wonderful, terrible, brave, gullible, ever hopeful, enterprise assisting and enterprise meddling, honest and altruistic, grasping and greedy, clever and dumb individuals who non-professionally and frequently non-successfully, provide capital permitting entrepreneurs to strive, quest, learn and earn.

Having been involved in the financing of businesses for the past 40 years I've made a sufficient number of mistakes to become aware of most of the pitfalls awaiting unguided angels. I also know of the rewards, monetary and psychological, which angels can experience when the ventures in which they have invested succeed. On balance, I advise those able to accept the risk of all of the funds invested in private companies to become angels - but to do so intelligently and, to the extent possible, with their egos under control.

Predicting any future event with accuracy is difficult. Surprise is the enemy of managers. Even the world's largest and most sophisticated companies frequently fail in predicting their earnings during a specific period of time. All prediction is difficult. The precise prediction of earnings, especially for; smaller, privately owned and newer enterprises, is almost impossible. Therefore I am always concerned and a bit amused when the financing of newer businesses are predicated, in terms of the angel's incentive for risk acceptance, on the achievement of specific levels of future earnings.

How does an angel structure an investment in a newer enterprise without focussing on future earnings? What other measure of success can be used to calculate the return on the amount of money the angel has exposed to risk? How might it be possible for the entrepreneur to retain the maximum amount of equity in his or her business? What is easier for a manager to predict than future earnings? The answer to all of the above is revenues.

I believe that angels structuring their financing of private companies on receiving a share of revenues, rather than on a share of profits will enjoy greater success.

The risk to the entrepreneur and it can be a significant risk, is one of not being able to adequately predict profit margins and therefore earnings. The entrepreneur with increased revenues and a less than anticipated margin of profit is going to be in an unhappy position. Revenue participation based financings work well with companies having high profit margins and should not be used with companies having commodity-type business margins.

The issue being addressed is one of who should bear the responsibility for predictions which are used to attract the use of angel capital, the maker of the prediction or the provider of the capital? I believe it is those making the predictions.

My favorite investment approach is to guarantee loans for companies in return for guarantee fees based upon the revenues of the company. In The Guide for Venture Investing Angels - Financing and Investing In Private Companies (Missouri Innovation Center) a number of investment approaches are described, including the use of Revenue Participation Certificates.

The ability of entrepreneurs to have continuing access to angel capital is important as an almost uniquely American natural resource and national asset. It is not the professional investors, fiduciaries and venture capitalists who make up the short fall between the entrepreneur's capital and that which is required. Its the angels who bear the burden of capital risk - for the benefit of all of us. Angels are entitled to earn extraordinary returns when companies they finance succeed - as they will most likely lose most of the capital invested when they fail.

INDEX

Banks
  bankers and, 310-11
  commercial, 29
  loan terms, 310-11
  low tolerance for risk, 309
Bartlett, Joseph, 334, 337-38
Bendixen, Christian, 414
Bergman, James, 20, 81, 88, 143
Berkley, William R., 21, 42, 98, 110,
  151
Berkley, W.R., Corporation, 21
Best Sand Corporation, 314
Bids, 84
Bigler, Harold 183
Bigler Investment Management
  Company, 183
Birr, Wilson, 320
Blackman, Irving L., 412
Blackman Kallick Bartelstein, 412
Board of directors
  compensation for, 114-15
  composition of, 115-16
  director liability, 113-14
  experience of appointees, 112-13
  fully independent, 119
  hired management, 113
  investor interests, 112
  number of appointees, 111-12
  quality of, 111
  selection of, 116-18
  terms of, 114-15
Borrowing
  assets and, 238
  borrower profitability related loans,
    237
  defined, 236
  interest rates, 239-43
  lender alternatives, 238
  leveraged buyouts (LBOs), 243-46
  profit and, 237
  success on-pass (SOP) loans, 243-45

Brandt, Bill, 317
Brobeck, Phleger and Harrison, 332
Brooktrout Technology Inc., 315, 319
Business Appraisal Associates, 411
Business appraisers, 411-16
Business discontinuance, 107-8
Business valuation
  buyers and, 414-15
  choosing an appraiser, 411-12
  comparables, 413
  credibility of, 414-15
  methods of, 413
  physical inventories, 416
  real earnings, 415
  rules of thumb, 414
  tax records, 415-16
  time spent on, 411-12
Business value, 454-65
Buskirk, Richard H. 427
Buy/sell option, 170

C . . . .

Capital, 6
Capital stock, 83
Capitalism, 223
Cash flow projections, 177-78, 224
Certified Business Brokers of Houston
  Inc., 411
Clamco, 314
Cohen, Steven, 315
Collateralized guarantees, 130-31
Community Guarantee Corporation
  (CGC), 45-46
Compound interest rates, 241-43
Confidentiality, 91-92
Conflict of interest, 84
Connecticut Venture Group (CVG),
  316
Consultants, 119-20
  as overseers, 203-4

Financial intermediary, 21-22
  exclusivity of relationship, 34
  expenses, 34
  fee arrangements, 33-34
  role of, 34-35
  services, 32-33
Financial reporting of revenue partici-
    pation certificates (RPCs), 133
Financial statements, 82
Financing
  financial statements, 82
Finders, 84; *see* also Financial
    Intermediary
  negotiation fees, 187-88
First Chicago pricing model, 405
Floating rate of interest, 241
Food operations, 38-39
Forbes, 71
Forced buyout, 339
Fortune, 71
Franchisability test, 39-41
Franchise/franchisor relationships, 38-
    39
Franchises, 36-37
*Frontiers of Entrepreneurship
    Research* (Vesper, ed), 420

G . . . .

Gaston Snow and Ely Bartlett, 332,
    334, 337
Geisman, James, 315
General Clutch Corporation, 317
Gifted children. 10, 226-29
Gifted Children Monthly, 10
Glystra, Dan, 337
Godward, Cooley, 333, 334
Golder, Thoma, Cressey, Rauner, 333,
    381
Golleb and Golleb, 417
Goodman, Edwin, 323-30
Graev, Lawrence, 338
Greenberg, Maurice R., 203

Guarantees, 128-33
  collateralization of, 130-31
  conditional or contingent, 129-30
  entrepreneurial, 143-47
  fees, 131-32
  subrogation, 131
  terms of, 131
Guide to Venture Capital Sources
    (Pratt), 381

H . . . .

Hambro International Equity Partners,
    323
  selecting investments, 323-30
Heidrick and Struggles, 115
Hempstead and Co., 411
Hempstead, John, 411
*How to Lose $100,000,000 and Other
    Valuable Advice* (Little), xviii
Howell, Robert A., 117

I . . . .

IBM, 328
Illiquidity, price of, 161
Income, 6-7
Indemnifications, 128-29
Independent businesspeople, delega-
    tions of, 253-55
Industrial Fabricating Company, 117
Industries overseas, 25-26
Informal investors
  attracting participants, 110-11
Initial public offering (IPO), 338
  business of company, 248
  deal structure, 249
  defined, 246-47
  management, 248-49
  other investors, 249
  pricing, 249-50
  supporting players, 249
  underwriter, 247-48